SELECTED ESSAYS

SELECTED ESSAYS

Michael Slote

UNIVERSITY PRESS
2010

OXFORD
UNIVERSITY PRESS

Oxford University Press, Inc., publishes works that further
Oxford University's objective of excellence
in research, scholarship, and education.

Oxford New York
Auckland Cape Town Dar es Salaam Hong Kong Karachi
Kuala Lumpur Madrid Melbourne Mexico City Nairobi
New Delhi Shanghai Taipei Toronto

With offices in
Argentina Austria Brazil Chile Czech Republic France Greece
Guatemala Hungary Italy Japan Poland Portugal Singapore
South Korea Switzerland Thailand Turkey Ukraine Vietnam

Copyright © 2010 by Oxford University Press, Inc.

Published by Oxford University Press, Inc.
198 Madison Avenue, New York, New York 10016

www.oup.com

Oxford is a registered trademark of Oxford University Press

All rights reserved. No part of this publication may be reproduced,
stored in a retrieval system, or transmitted, in any form or by any means,
electronic, mechanical, photocopying, recording, or otherwise,
without the prior permission of Oxford University Press.

Library of Congress Cataloging-in-Publication Data
Slote, Michael A.
[Essays. Selections]
Selected essays / Michael Slote.
    p. cm.
ISBN 978-0-19-539143-5
1. Ethics.   2. Philosophy.   I. Title.
BJ354.S58 2009a
191—dc22   2009002809

9 8 7 6 5 4 3 2 1

Printed in the United States of America
on acid-free paper

For
Daniel, Joshua, Rachael, Stefan,
and their wonderful children

ACKNOWLEDGMENTS

Most of the chapters in this volume have been published previously. I would like to thank the *Journal of Philosophy* for permission to reprint "The Theory of Important Criteria" (1966); "Value Judgments and the Theory of Important Criteria" (1968); "The Rationality of Aesthetic Value Judgments" (1971); "Morality and Ignorance" (1977); "Understanding Free Will" (1980); "Selective Necessity and the Free-Will Problem" (1982); and my review of Alvin Plantinga's *God and Other Minds* (1985).

Thanks also to *Philosophical Studies* and Springer Science and Business Media for permission to reprint "Inapplicable Concepts" (1975). Thanks to the *Philosophical Review* and Duke University Press for permission to reprint "Time in Counterfactuals" (1978); and to *Analysis* for permission to reprint "Is Virtue Possible?" (1982). I want to thank the *American Philosophical Quarterly* for permission to use "Morality Not a System of Imperatives" (1982) and "Utilitarianism, Moral Dilemmas, and Moral Cost" (1985).

Thanks also to the *Pacific Philosophical Quarterly* and to Blackwell publications for permission to reprint "Object Utilitarianism" (1985); and to *Philosophical Topics* and the University of Arkansas Press for allowing me to use "Rational Dilemmas and Rational Supererogation" (1986).

"Moderation, Rationality, and Virtue" was given as a Tanner Lecture on Human Values at Stanford University, April 17 and 22, 1985, and appeared in Volume VII of *The Tanner Lectures on Human Values*, published by the University of Utah Press. They have given permission to publish this two-part lecture in the present volume, and I want to thank them for that permission.

I am reprinting "Utilitarian Virtue" (1989) with the kind permission of *Midwest Studies in Philosophy*; and "Ethics Naturalized" (1992) with the kind permission of *Philosophical Perspectives* and Blackwell publications. I am also indebted to *International Studies in Philosophy* for permission to reprint "Nietzsche and Virtue Ethics" (1998). "Caring versus the Philosophers," which appeared in the anthology *Philosophy of Education* (1999), is being reprinted by permission of the editor, Randall Curren; and "Some Thoughts for the Future" was originally published in *Normative Ethics: 5 Questions* and is reprinted here by permission of the editors of that collection, J. Ryberg and T. Petersen. I am grateful to these editors for their permission to do the present reprintings.

Finally, I want to thank Peter Ohlin of Oxford University Press for all his help with the present book project.

CONTENTS

Introduction	3
1. The Theory of Important Criteria	13
2. Value Judgments and the Theory of Important Criteria	23
3. The Rationality of Aesthetic Value Judgments	39
4. Inapplicable Concepts	53
5. Morality and Ignorance	58
6. Time in Counterfactuals	76
7. Assertion and Belief	94
8. Understanding Free Will	103
9. Selective Necessity and the Free-Will Problem	115
10. Is Virtue Possible?	131
11. Morality Not a System of Imperatives	138
12. Review of Alvin Plantinga's *God and Other Minds*	150
13. Utilitarianism, Moral Dilemmas, and Moral Cost	156

14. Object Utilitarianism — 167
15. Utilitarian Virtue — 180
16. Moderation, Rationality, and Virtue — 194
17. Rational Dilemmas and Rational Supererogation — 222
18. Ethics Naturalized — 236
19. Nietzsche and Virtue Ethics — 255
20. Caring versus the Philosophers — 260
21. Global Caring, Global Justice — 271
22. Empathy and Objectivity — 287
23. In Place of Moral Reasoning — 303
24. Some Thoughts for the Future — 317
Index — 325

SELECTED ESSAYS

Introduction

The present volume contains a selection from among papers and reviews that I have published and papers that I haven't previously published. The principle of selection has been my sense of the interest papers might hold for contemporary discussion. Some of these papers were published around forty years ago, and others that I have chosen *not* to reprint were also published (at least) that long ago, so I have had to be choosy in my selection—at least I hope that I have been. I would like here to introduce the papers that appear in this book. In some cases I shall compare them with other people's ideas/publications; in others I shall indicate how I think they might be further developed in contemporary terms; in still others I make what I hope are useful comparisons *among* the essays that appear in this volume. Again, my choice of what to say in this Introduction has been determined by my sense of what might be useful to contemporary philosophy or philosophers. And let me just mention before I begin that the order in which the papers appear in this book and are discussed in this Introduction is (roughly) chronological.

The first paper in this volume is "The Theory of Important Criteria" (from the *Journal of Philosophy*), not the first thing I ever published, but something that did come from my doctoral dissertation on *Certainty and Language* (Harvard University, 1965). This article and the dissertation it comes from reflect the preoccupation with Wittgenstein that animated philosophical discussion during the early 1960's. Such work may appear, at least from a typical American standpoint, to be somewhat dated, but I have included it here because I believe it has something to say today. Wittgenstein had a theory about "cluster concepts," concepts that have a variety of criteria for their application, that was widely accepted at the time. That theory, the theory of family resemblance, held that cluster terms like "game," "religion," and "democracy" each possess various different criteria of application no single one of which is necessary to the correct application of the term. "The Theory of Important Criteria" argues that this is mistaken by offering a positive view of what happens when people dispute, say, about whether Hinayana Buddhism, which lacks belief in a deity or deities, counts as a religion. In a nutshell, the idea is that they disagree, not about the meaning of "religion," but in their value judgments about what makes an important difference—philosophically and sociologically—to institutional systems. The paper says that there can be common criteria for the application of terms like "religion" and even "game," but that that doesn't rule out the possibility of deep and seemingly intractable disputes about *which* are the common or necessary criteria of application.

"Value Judgments and the Theory of Important Criteria" (from the *Journal of Philosophy*) applies what I in the earlier paper called "the theory of important criteria" to evaluative phenomena. The theory of important criteria says that a cluster term applies just when its most important criteria apply, and the later paper applies that idea to common value judgments like "this is a good knife." More interestingly, I think, for contemporary purposes, the second paper also offers a theory of what emotive or evaluative meaning amounts to in the case of such ordinary value judgments. It treats evaluative meaning as a cancellable and detachable Gricean implication of value judgments, an implication to the effect that one likes or has a positive attitude toward what one calls good; and I think that this idea might be useful to present-day philosophers. On the other hand, I am inclined to think that *moral* judgments have an *empathy-based motivating force* that goes beyond any cancellable Gricean implication, and I discuss the motivating force of morality at some length in an article called "Hume on Approval" that is part of a volume called *Essays on the History of Ethics* that I am currently publishing with OUP. A comparison between the kind of evaluative meaning "this is a good knife" has and the more strongly motivating emotional implications/content of "this is morally wrong" would be worth making.

"The Rationality of Aesthetic Value Judgments" (from the *Journal of Philosophy*) has an odd, but interesting history. It anticipates most of the themes that later were sounded by the "Cornell School" of moral realism, but did so in application only to judgments of aesthetic value. That may explain why, when the Cornell realists defended the realism-friendly explanatory uses of moral judgments, my earlier article wasn't used in support of their views. (Nicholas Sturgeon has told me that at the time he was writing, he didn't know of my earlier, similar ideas.) In any event, given the contemporary importance of the Cornell School, I think it might be useful to call the present generation's attention to the parallels that can be drawn with aesthetic value judgments, and that is my main reason for including my article here.

The fourth reprinted article in the book, "Inapplicable Concepts" (from *Philosophical Studies*) is a personal favorite of mine. It doesn't fit in well or neatly with any well-known disagreements or research traditions within philosophy, but I believe it makes a point that may sometime or someday be useful. It argues that certain concepts have no valid conditions of application, are inapplicable in principle, and it concentrates most particularly on the concept of a monster—though other notions are also discussed and said to be inapplicable. Now the idea that there cannot be such a thing as a monster may seem mistaken or worse to some of you readers, but I ask you to look at the article before you make your minds up absolutely. I found the idea initially difficult to believe myself, but I think I can see now why the notion of a monster really has to be inapplicable, and that might happen with you.

If that *does* happen with you, then that can also bring up an issue that I never discussed in the original article, but that seems well-worth discussing. In *Naming and Necessity* Kripke argues (very roughly) that there couldn't have been such things as unicorns or Pegasus, but that these necessary truths are a posteriori. Well, if I am correct, the impossibility of monsters is an a priori fact, but both monsters and unicorns are fictional, and someone interested in the ontology of art or fiction might wonder whether that difference in any way affects the fictional status or reality of monsters as opposed to unicorns. Now the non existence of a particular monster like Godzilla might be a posteriori rather than a priori because it may be only a posteriori that Godzilla *is* a monster. But this last claim calls out for further critical examination; I'm not at all sure it is true or even what it means. And in any event those interested in fiction who buy into my idea that monsters are impossible in reality (as opposed to fiction) might find the question of the fictional status of Godzilla and other particular monsters as perplexing as I do and feel that the question implicitly raised by "Inapplicable Concepts" deserves serious consideration.

"Morality and Ignorance" (from the *Journal of Philosophy*) discusses the "unmasking" tradition of Marx, Nietzsche, and Freud and asks whether it is relevant to the understanding or justified status of moral claims. Those three figures argued that our moral beliefs are often crucially based on a misunderstanding or ignorance of our own motives or situation, and my article speculates that if that charge can be proved against one or another moral view, that weakens the case for its validity and may even simply *undermine* its validity. This is reminiscent of some things Bernard Williams has said about morality and ignorance, and both of us were saying these things around the same time. But the chief relevance of these ideas today seems to me to be the relevance to issues raised in the literature of feminism. Alison Jaggar has argued that an ethical view needs to be able to sustain itself in the face of facts about its own origins and milieu, and she uses that idea against the kind of Kantian ethical rationalism that seeks to insulate moral and political thought from such empirical thinking about origins and milieu. I think Jaggar is right about this and that what Williams and I said all those many years ago serves to confirm what she is saying and other feminists may want to say. That is one of the reasons for my decision to reprint this article here. But there is another.

I have in recent years defended the idea that motives are relevant to the moral assessment of actions; in fact I have probably defended that view more assiduously and single-mindedly than any other present-day philosopher. But if motives are relevant to the moral assessment of actions, how does that bear on the conclusion argued for in "Morality and Ignorance," the conclusion that any moral view or principle whose acceptance depends on ignorance is less likely to be, or can't possibly be, true? I don't think I know the answer to that question, but I think feminists and others (e.g., care ethicists) who tie morality to sentiments and motives have reason to think about that issue—as I do myself. That is another reason for reprinting the article and, of course, for writing this Introduction.

The sixth article reprinted here is "Time in Counterfactuals" (from the *Philosophical Review*). It develops a cotenability account of counterfactuals that is roughly in the tradition inaugurated by Nelson Goodman and argues that such an approach evades some of the difficulties that are known to attach to "closest possible world" accounts of counterfactuals. But my view also has its difficulties, so it is hard really to say whether it is more promising than "closest possible world" accounts, which tend to dominate the field nowadays. Still, I think it is good to for people to be reminded that cotenability approaches may be there to bail us out if the currently dominant views ever really begin to founder. The article also argues that every counterfactual makes two distinct sorts of temporal reference, and this idea may on its own be of some use to linguists and philosophers interested in (the) semantics (of counterfactuals).

"Assertion and Belief," which was published (somewhat obscurely) in *Papers on Language and Logic* from the University of Keele, has led a kind of underground cult existence. People keep referring to it and using it—and asking me for copies because it is difficult, if not impossible, to lay one's hands on the volume in which it originally appeared. The main idea evolved from Peter Unger's thought that asserting involves one in representing oneself as knowing something. Since, as I argued, a person who believes (and knows s/he believes) something needn't regard herself/himself as knowing the thing, there are things one can properly believe but not assert. That is perhaps a surprising thought, but the article sought to nail that conclusion down with a number of linguistic and epistemological arguments. It is good to be able to reprint it here, so that people can have a place to find it easily.

The next two papers represent a flurry of interest (on my part) during the late 1970's in issues about free will. "Understanding Free Will" (from the *Journal of Philosophy*) seeks to show that Frankfurt, Watson, and Neely style accounts of freedom, accounts that stress the psychological structure(s) of a free person's desires, values, and/or beliefs, leave out considerations about the *origin* of such structures that are also relevant to free will. The next paper, "Selective Necessity and the Free-Will Problem" (also from the *Journal of Philosophy*) discusses the modality involved in ascriptions of free will. If the "can" of "s/he can do otherwise" is a logically well-behaved one, then arguments by Van Inwagen, Wiggins, and others seem to indicate that free will is incompatible with determinism (at least for finitely existing beings). However, I argue that the modality involved in "can do otherwise" is much more complex and logically less well-behaved than is usually supposed, and I do this in part by showing that some other ordinary modalities—e.g., the modality of "this happened by accident"—are also not well-behaved and misbehave, in fact, in much the same way that "can do otherwise" does. If this is right, then the well-known modal arguments for incompatibilism given by Van Inwagen, et al., just don't work.

The tenth essay, "Is Virtue Possible?" (from *Analysis*) is a short piece on the implications of the (neo-)Aristotelian assumption that the virtuous individual always knows what it is right to do. Nowadays there are perplexing unresolved moral issues about children's rights, patients' rights, and a host of other topics, and it seems unlikely that we will ever run out of this sort of moral controversy, however many particular issues get "settled" in the court of "enlightened" opinion. There will always be something else we agree we don't know (the answer to), but even if such perplexing issues run out some time in the future, we have them today. Does that mean that no one is virtuous because no one knows how to resolve all the moral issues we face today? And what about ancient times? No one in the ancient classical or biblical world thought it was wrong to own slaves, yet we nowadays are all of us sure that it is. At the very least this means that no one in the ancient world was virtuous in the terms Aristotle set, and I think that present-day Aristotelians can profit from being reminded of this fact and of the general difficulty of knowing everything one needs to know ethically in order always to act morally.

"Morality Not a System of Imperatives" (which originally appeared in the *American Philosophical Quarterly*) takes its title from a well-known essay by Philippa Foot called "Morality as a System of Hypothetical Imperatives." Foot had argued that it wasn't necessarily irrational to be unwilling to act in accordance with moral imperatives one acknowledged to be valid or true; but she never questioned the assumption that specific or general moral claims/utterances are always imperatives, always practical, always action-guiding. My paper mentions some examples at the heart of morality where moral claims just aren't supposed to guide action. For example, the idea/claim that it is morally permissible to kill in self-defense isn't the sort of claim one reasonably expects a person being attacked by someone with a meat cleaver to take into account in deciding whether to respond with deadly force. Rather, it is a standard of post-hoc (and to some extent also pre-hoc) moral evaluation: someone who has killed in self-defense and without thinking about moral issues may be considered to have acted in a morally justifiable way (justifiable homicide), and it is also morally all right to anticipate the need for self-defense in various practical ways.

In subsequent work defending virtue ethics and/or the ethics of care, I have (following Francis Hutcheson and Nel Noddings) claimed that acting from certain "natural" motives like compassion is more morally commendable than acting from principle or a sense of duty. But the example of self-defense cuts across all moral theories, doesn't assume any particular take on morality except, perhaps, common sense; and so it undercuts the idea that morality is a system of imperatives better than arguments that depend on a particular theoretical approach to morality.

My review of Alvin Plantinga's *God and Other Minds* is the only review I have chosen to reprint here. My reason is not that Plantinga's book is more significant than any other I have reviewed—though it is a very, very good book. Rather, it is because I made a point in it that I think hasn't sufficiently registered in the philosophy of religion community—and I would like to give it another chance to do so. When I started writing the review I began working with the Principle of Sufficient Reason and after a while I had one brief giddy moment where I thought I had shown that everything in the world was necessary rather than contingent. Then I realized that I had only shown that the Principle was *inconsistent* with the world having any contingent history and was thus necessarily false because it is necessary that some things in the world's history (including that total history itself) be contingent. James Ross in *Philosophical Theology* had come close to these conclusions, but I still think philosophers of religion haven't taken the full measure of their significance.

The next three articles reprinted here are all on utilitarianism. I have been writing about utilitarianism since the early 1980's, and the irony is that at the very beginning of the 1980's I told some fellow philosophers that I thought utilitarianism was a ridiculously implausible doctrine. But I soon came to think otherwise, and part of the reason (I like to think) was a new sense, obtained *somehow*, of how *humane* Bentham's focus on human and sentient welfare actually was. So unlike many non-utilitarians who work on (opposing) utilitarianism, my focus, from the start, was on Bentham more than on Mill or Sidgwick. And the three articles reprinted here bear the mark of that greater interest in Bentham, as does my book of the same period *Commonsense Morality and Consequentialism*. (In more recent books, however, I have been more interested in Sidgwick.) Going back all the way to Bentham allowed me to better distinguish what is essential to utilitarianism from what holds or has held of utilitarianism because it has/had developed in a particular direction, and this knowledge is reflected in various ways in the three articles reprinted here.

"Utilitarianism, Moral Dilemmas, and Moral Cost" (from the *American Philosophical Quarterly*) seeks to show that utilitarianism allows for a richer variety of moral phenomena than is usually imagined. It has been held, for example, that our rich common-sense understanding of moral phenomena allows for the possibility of moral dilemma or, at least of moral cost, but that the utilitarian's exclusive emphasis on maximizing utility precludes these phenomena. But the just-mentioned paper attempts to show that this is not so either for maximizing versions of (act-)utilitarianism or for non-maximizing forms of the sort that, at one time, Bentham himself seemed entirely comfortable with.

"Object Utilitarianism" (from the *Pacific Philosophical Quarterly*) focuses on a particular and (somewhat) distinctive aspect of Bentham's utilitarianism and tries to measure and assess its implications. Bentham treated the utilitarian evaluation of works of art and of household objects like knives or sofas as an essential part of utilitarianism's total evaluative take on the world, but this broad utilitarian stance has been less in evidence in subsequent utilitarian philosophizing (though Sidgwick seems at least to be *committed* to it); and "Object Utilitarianism" considers whether a utilitarianism that evaluates actions, motives, laws, and societies in utilitarian consequentialist terms doesn't have to, in all consistency, do the same for the evaluation of art objects and so-called utilitarian objects like sofas or even houses. (Bentham says we should evaluate houses in utilitarian terms.) I concluded in the article that consistency does commit a utilitarian (who wishes to remain a utilitarian) to this broader range of utilitarian evaluations.

But Bentham never considered whether the same consistency might not also force the committed utilitarian to evaluate *beliefs* and *forms of inference* in utilitarian terms, and after I had written "Object Utilitarianism," this new question began to bother me, and I even suggested to Richard Hanley, a graduate student who eventually became a philosophy professor, that he might want to do a paper on this issue. But he never did, and I never took the question any further than to raise it. But having raised it here in this Introduction, let me presume to ask those who read the article in the context of this book to consider the question too. Perhaps, someone, some day will explore the possibilities of belief-utilitarianism, something which, I believe has never been done since utilitarianism emerged in the late eighteenth century. Pragmatism and various forms of reliabilism tie the truth or justification of beliefs to certain kinds of consequences, but the consequences aren't conceived in the general impartialist terms that are characteristic of utilitarianism: it is typically consequences for a given believing/inquiring individual that constitute the measure of truth or justification. But although I might myself some day want to take up this issue of belief-utilitarianism, I am no longer in any large way focused on utilitarianism, and it seems to me more promising to hope that someone else will find it worthwhile to take up this issue.

The third of the essays on utilitarianism reprinted here is called "Utilitarian Virtue." It was originally published (in *Midwest Studies in Philosophy*) at a time when people were just beginning to realize that utilitarianism doesn't have to exclusively focus on the evaluation of acts (or rules or motives), and perhaps the realization that utilitarianism has something to say about the virtues reflects (in my own case, at least) the emergence of virtue ethics as a force in Anglo-American philosophy. Virtue ethics emerged in part as a reaction to the lack of interest in or emphasis upon the virtues within recently previous Kantian and utilitarian thought, and subsequent attempts by both Kantians and utilitarians to focus on or develop the virtue-oriented side of their theories or approaches represent, more than anything else, an attempt to undercut or counteract the intellectual motivations that led people to become so interested in reviving virtue ethics in the first place. But these new Kantian and utilitarian efforts came perhaps too late. The horse was already out of the barn and nothing was going to stop virtue ethics from becoming one of the main and dominant approaches to ethical theory. However, the work that utilitarians and Kantians have recently done on the virtues from the standpoint of their own approaches may at least have prevented virtue ethics from taking over ethics as a whole, something that virtue ethics hasn't at all done and, I think, isn't likely to do.

In any event, "Utilitarian Virtue" had the particular aim of comparing what had previously been said about such traditional virtues as courage and temperance with what, again in all consistency, a utilitarian would need to say about these virtues. The article worked some of this out, but, like other work I have done on utilitarianism, never committed itself to taking a strictly utilitarian approach to the virtues or to any other matter.

The next two reprinted essays focus on anti-utilitarian, commonsensical ways in which our ordinary thought about and practice of rational choice usually or often take place. "Moderation, Rationality, and Virtue" (taken from *The Tanner Lectures on Human Values*) is an attempt to show that it can be rational to satisfice, rather than maximize or optimize, with respect to one's own good or well-being (in contexts where the good of others isn't an issue). When I originally gave this material as a pair of lectures, some members of the audience at Stanford were horrified at what I was saying. I was going further than Herbert Simon had gone in defending the intrinsic rationality of a satisficing attitude toward good things (including both appetitive satisfactions and career goals), and the professors in the auditorium were aghast. (By contrast, the graduate students seemed to like my ideas, but I always wondered whether they had liked them at least in part because their professors didn't and because the professors were not having an easy time of it saying exactly why those ideas were mistaken.)

In any event, I have to tell you that when I later went to Holland and stated the same ideas there, I was told that people thought they had wasted money bringing me there. What I was claiming, they said, was *too obviously true* to need philosophical defense. Does this say something significant about the difference between European and American attitudes toward moderation and toward self-betterment? I certainly think so.

The paper on "Rational Dilemmas and Rational Supererogation" (from *Philosophical Topics*) defends what it takes to be a common-sense approach to practical rationality that runs counter to received views about dilemma and supererogation. Those who have defended the idea of moral dilemmas haven't thought much about whether there can be such a thing as rational dilemma, and when they explicitly or implicitly have, their view has tended to be that, unlike morality, there is no such thing as a practical rational dilemma. Even if morality can leave us in a position where, through no fault of our own, we cannot avoid acting wrongly, it is usually assumed that is always possible for reason to find something for us to do that avoids our being accused of having made an irrational choice in a given circumstance. My paper argues, by examples and with a bit of theory, that this isn't the case. It also attempts to show that there is such a thing as rational supererogation, cases where, if one doesn't do what it would be most rational for one to do, one may still be acting in a rationally acceptable manner. The idea of rational supererogation hadn't ever previously been broached (as far as I know) in discussions of practical rationality, but I argued that there are good reasons why we need to take such an idea seriously, more seriously than we take such a possibility even today.

"Ethics Naturalized" (from *Philosophical Perspectives*) took the main idea for its title from Quine's "Epistemology Naturalized." (Interestingly, Andy Clark published a paper with the same title as mine a couple of years later.) The paper argues that utilitarianism can be viewed as a form of naturalistic reductionism, and though such an idea is not unfamiliar, I believe I pushed it harder than anyone else had previously done. I also tried to show that various forms of virtue ethics can also be seen as naturalized or naturalizing—and I wasn't just talking about the natural *teleology* that Aristotle in some sense presupposed in his ethical writings. But, returning to utilitarianism, the paper also made the further point that a naturalizing utilitarianism doesn't have to be seen as a form of reductionism. There is, or can be, an eliminativist version or form of utilitarianism as well, a version that, for example, eliminates talk of rightness and good consequences in favor of talk about felicificness and happiness/pleasure/desire satisfaction. Such utilitarianism doesn't forbid talk about rightness and good consequences in ordinary life (any more than reductive utilitarianism rules out the use of anti-utilitarian common-sense principles in daily life), and I have discussed this unusual form of naturalistic utilitarianism in my book *From Morality to Virtue*. But I should also add that the discussion in "Ethics Naturalized" only partially anticipates what the later book has to say about the choice between (naturalizing) reductive and (naturalizing) eliminative utilitarianism.

"Nietzsche and Virtue Ethics" (from *International Studies in Philosophy*) focuses on an issue that can arise when one tries to pin Nietzsche down a bit within the usual spectrum of philosophical isms. Nietzsche is often regarded as having taken a teleological approach to ethics, but the term "teleology" doesn't distinguish between perfectionistic consequentialism and certain kinds of virtue ethics, and when one looks at Nietzsche's works, it turns out that the issue of whether he is a virtue ethicist or a perfectionist is difficult to resolve. In fact, he seems to assert both views within the space of a single page in one of his books, and yet, as is obvious, these views are (defined as) mutually inconsistent. It is very difficult, though not perhaps impossible, to claim Nietzsche for virtue ethics, but it is not clear how many virtue ethicists would be eager to do that.

"Caring Versus the Philosophers" (from R. Curren, ed., *Philosophy of Education*) comes from a symposium Nel Noddings and I did together at a meeting of the Philosophy of Education society. She and I disagreed on some important points, as we often, but constructively, have; and the paper records my side of the disagreement. It also talks about the nature of theory-building and asks whether care ethics ought to be conceived as a theoretical approach. Given the fact that care ethicists think principles and theories are relatively out of place in the moral life, a theoretical care ethics would have to treat itself as esoteric, as something not for daily or general use, but my paper argues that this wouldn't necessarily give us reason to regard such a theory as inappropriate or mistaken in principle.

The three next papers have not been previously published. The first, "Global Justice, Global Caring," applies some of the ideas of my recent book *The Ethics of Care and Empathy* (Routledge, 2007) to international moral issues. It also responds to critics of earlier work of mine who have claimed that my virtue-ethical approach leads to or toward undue paternalism and makes sheer intention more centrally criterial to the moral value of an action than it should be. The first of these criticisms comes from Virginia Held, the second from political scientist Daniel Engster, and my reply to them focuses on the importance, on my view of caring, of the phenomenon of empathy and painstakingly describes how and why an emphasis on motives over consequences actually fits in better with our commonsense intuitions than approaches that make the actual consequences of an act more relevant to its moral assessment than I do.

The second previously unpublished paper, "Empathy and Objectivity," extends what I said about empathy in *The Ethics of Care and Empathy* (ECE) to the realm of epistemology. In ECE I argued that respect for others depends crucially on having sufficient empathy with their point of view, and in the present paper, the idea is that personal epistemic objectivity is a matter, roughly, of having sufficient empathy for the way people who disagree with one see things. Of course, people may disagree because one party is less good at understanding issues than the other, but a failure of understanding or intelligence or correct inference isn't a failure of objectivity; it involves a clearly different form of intellectual inadequacy, and the paper discusses at length what empathy involves (what empathy can be empathy *of*) and how empathy with other people's ideas and attitudes actually works.

The third previously unpublished paper, "In Place of Moral Reasoning," focuses on the implications of accepting a sentimentalist care-ethical morality that treats empathy as the engine of morality. It argues that those who think that moral reasoning is central to the moral life greatly underestimate the motivating role of empathy in leading us to make morally acceptable or good decisions. When we are moved by empathy and empathic concern for others, we needn't think in explicitly moral terms or invoke any moral principles/rules in deciding what to do and then doing it. To that extent being a moral person doesn't rest on good moral reasoning, and the paper argues that such reasoning is much less important than is usually thought throughout the whole range of moral issues and problems. It also turns out that motives based in empathy (like compassion) and motives that can work against empathy (like self-preservation) interact in ways that are highly reminiscent of so-called non-monotonic logic and reasoning; and this gives an ethics based in empathy some of the richness and complexity it needs to accurately mirror our best thinking about morality. The paper also argues that care ethics can make use of the notion of empathy to specify techniques of moral education that can be seen as absolutely crucial to becoming a morally caring individual. The ethics of care is thereby provided with moral educational underpinnings that are just as articulate and effective as—and, I argue, more plausible than—those provided by Piaget and Kohlberg for Kantian/liberal theories of morality.

"Some Thoughts for the Future" (from J. Ryberg and T. Petersen, eds., *Normative Ethics: 5* Questions) seems an appropriate end-piece for a volume like this. It discusses the present situation in the field of ethics and describes some of the difficulties that exist in getting one school or approach to pay attention to others. Kantian rationalism, for example, has given short shrift to care ethics while at the same time becoming, in recent years, more and more rationalistic, even to the point of what I would call hyperrationalism. The identification of love with placing a high value on the rational dignity of another person seems to me just one example of how recent Kantianism has to some extent metamorphosed into hyperrationalism—Kant thought (as I do) that ordinary "pathological" love *isn't* an attitude toward or about people's rational dignity. But if some Kantian thinking seems to distort the nature of ordinary emotions or feelings, care ethics for its part has ignored some of the issues that exercise Kantians and indeed worry *most* mainstream ethicists. Most ethicists are worried, for example, about how or whether one can justify deontology, but care ethicists have largely ignored this issue, and I urge them in this final paper of the present volume to pay deontology more attention.

I hope this Introduction will be useful to the reader of these papers, but for that to fully happen, the Introduction has to come to an end, and people have to look at the papers themselves.

1

The Theory of Important Criteria

Consider the following questions: can a promise be kept by accident? is philosophical doubt really doubt? is a nation that has majority rule but no minority rights a democracy? is the whale a fish? is Buffalo really a city? are tables and chairs ever solid? All these questions either are philosophical or closely resemble philosophical questions in the way they are argued about by both philosophers and nonphilosophers without seeming ever to be definitively resolved. In recent years some notable theories have been put forward to explain disagreements over questions of this sort. Most of these theories seek to explain the existence and persistence of such disagreements in terms of two, or more, meanings of the term whose applicability is in question.

In *Ethics and Language* Charles Stevenson attempts to explain disputes over such words as 'poetry' and 'justice' in terms of two meanings of those words and via his theory of "persuasive definition."[1] Stevenson's theory can be applied to disputes of the kind mentioned above. One might, for example, attempt to explain the disagreement over whether the whale is a fish by claiming that in ordinary usage 'fish' means something like "streamlined animal that lives in the water" and in biological usage something like "completely aquatic, water-breathing, cold-blooded craniate vertebrate."[2] (Let us abbreviate these definitions as O and S, respectively.) According to Stevenson's theory of persuasive definition, a biologist will insist that the ordinary

---

I am indebted to Professors R. Firth and S. Cavell and to Mr. D. K. Lewis for discussion of the ideas of this paper.

[1] See *Ethics and Language* (New Haven: Yale, 1960), chap. 9.

[2] As does Nelson Goodman, *Structure of Appearance* (Cambridge, Mass.: Harvard, 1951), p. 5f.

man is wrong to say that the whale *is* a fish, even though he knows that what the ordinary man is saying is (according to the ordinary sense of 'fish') literally true.[3] But this implies great intellectual dishonesty on the part of biologists, and there is strong reason to think that biologists are not dishonest in this sort of way. Furthermore, everything we know about biologists indicates that they typically believe that the whale is *really* not a fish and that ordinary men are speaking incorrectly when they call the whale a fish. Thus the Stevensonian explanation of the disagreement over the whale appears to be rather implausible.

One might attempt to salvage this theory by altering it so as to have it claim that the biologist is *not* aware that in ordinary usage 'fish' means O and that that is why he denies that the whale is a fish without ever mentioning the possibility of a sense of 'fish' different from his own in which whales *do* count as fish. Thus reinterpreted, the theory does not accuse the biologist of intellectual duplicity. But it does imply that biologists are ignorant of the ordinary usage of 'fish', do not know in what cases something counts as a fish according to the ordinary meaning of that word. And it seems rather implausible that biologists should be thus ignorant of the usage of an everyday term like 'fish', when one considers that they were once ordinary men themselves who, by hypothesis, meant by 'fish' O. Thus this alteration of Stevenson's theory seems also to lead to unacceptable consequences.[4]

Some of the disputes mentioned above are more easily explained in terms of two meanings within ordinary usage of the words whose applicability is in question than in terms of a divergence between ordinary and technical usage of those words. A Stevensonian explanation of the dispute over whether a nation that has majority rule but lacks (full) minority rights can still be a democracy might, for example, want to say that 'democracy' means both "nation with majority rule" and "nation with both majority rule and minority rights" in ordinary English. But such a two-meaning explanation of the dispute over 'democracy' could be shown to be open to the same criticisms we leveled at the above-discussed two-meaning theory of the dispute about the whale. All such theories are fundamentally implausible because they imply an implausible amount of duplicity *or* imperceptiveness on the part of those who participate in the disputes they attempt to explain.[5]

---

[3] See Stevenson, *op. cit.*, p. 231 ff.

[4] On the theory we have been discussing, it is understandable that the biologist should for theoretical purposes have stopped using 'fish' to mean O and started using it to mean S. But it hardly follows that his previous judgments, in which he did not use 'fish' in that new sense, were wrong. It is the fact that biologists typically want to claim that they were *always* wrong to call whales fish that renders a two-meaning theory implausible as an explanation of the debate over the whale. For, on a two-meaning theory, this fact can be accounted for only by assuming more duplicity or dull-wittedness on the part of biologists than we have any reason to suspect them of.

[5] Quite different two-meaning explanations of the sorts of disagreement mentioned above have been put forward by John Wisdom (*Other Minds*, Oxford: Blackwell's, 1956, I and VIII, *passim*; and *Philosophy and Psychoanalysis*, Oxford: Blackwell, 1957, *passim*) and by Paul Edwards ("Bertrand Russell's Doubts about Induction," in A. Flew, ed., *Logic and Language*, I, Oxford: Blackwell, 1955, *passim*). The theories these philosophers propound are subject to the very same criticisms we have directed at the two-meaning theories we have already examined. But they are subject to additional difficulties, because they claim that certain disputes are due to alterations in the meaning of certain words on the part of philosophers and others. For philosophers and others who participate in the debates Wisdom and Edwards consider typically do not *think* that they are changing the meaning of various words.

I should like to consider one other possible explanation of this sort of debate. One might claim that the dispute over 'democracy' is chiefly due to vagueness in that word. William Alston has recently argued that a term like 'religion' is vague just because there are cases where no amount of empirical evidence can definitively settle the question whether something is to count as a religion.[6] Thus Hinayana Buddhism lacks certain features of religion (belief in supernatural beings) and has others (rituals, an ethical code, etc.), and so it is hard to decide whether it counts as a religion, no matter what empirical facts we know. Alston would probably want to say that the term 'democracy' is also vague, because there are cases—e.g., where a nation has majority rule, but no (full) minority rights—where people continue to disagree about applying the term, even when all the relevant facts seem to be in.

But even if vagueness in a term may explain why it is hard for people to know when to and when not to apply it, vagueness *alone* could never explain why some people consistently apply a term in certain cases, while others just as consistently refuse to apply it in those cases. And this is just what happens with regard to 'democracy' and the other terms we have been considering. Thus one cannot explain debates over these terms merely in terms of their vagueness, even if they *are* to some degree vague. Vagueness theories cannot explain why some would never call a nation without minority rights a democracy, while others would. And so no vagueness theory could adequately explain the disagreement over whether a nation without minority rights but with majority rule can be a democracy.

Let us consider in a new light the question whether a nation with majority rule that does not grant full minority rights is truly a democracy. Some people think that, if a nation has majority rule, then whether or not it grants minority rights does not make much of a moral or political difference to the sort of nation it is. They think that a nation with both majority rule and minority rights is not very much more morally commendable than a nation that has the former but lacks the latter. But they also think that whether a nation has or lacks majority rule *does* make an important difference, both morally and politically, to the sort of nation it is. Thus the possession of majority rule is an *important criterion* of a nation's being a democracy in a way that the granting of minority rights is not, so that a nation without minority rights can be a democracy even if a nation without majority rule cannot.

Many people, on the other hand, think that whether a nation grants minority rights *does* make a crucial moral and political difference to the kind of nation it is. They think that the granting of minority rights is a great good, and that its loss is of great disvalue, even where majority rule is retained. A nation that grants minority rights and has majority rule, they would say, is a very different sort of nation from one that lacks minority rights and has majority rule. Such persons, then, will presumably maintain, against those described above, that the granting of minority rights, being a criterion of democracy whose presence or absence makes so important a difference to what a nation is like, is an absolutely necessary condition of a nation's being a democracy.[7]

---

[6] *Philosophy of Language* (Englewood Cliffs, N.J.: Prentice-Hall, 1964), p. 87 ff.

[7] The same sorts of consideration that arise in the dispute over whether a nation lacking minority rights can be a democracy could also be shown to arise in the dispute over whether a nation without female suffrage can be a democracy.

Consider next the question whether the whale is a fish. Even people who know that whales are warm-blooded air-breathing mammals sometimes say that the whale is a fish (just a very atypical sort of fish), whereas biologists will vehemently deny that the whale is a fish at all. The biologist knows that there are many criteria of fishhood, of something's being a fish: having fins, having scales, having a tail, breathing water, being oviparous, living in the water, not suckling one's young, etc. Some of these criteria are important from the standpoint of the biologist, are important for and central to the biologist's purposes of learning about and explaining the physiology, morphology, and behavior of fish and, indeed, of animals in general. Cold-bloodedness is biologically important in this way. Knowledge of whether something is cold-blooded or not tells a biologist many biologically important facts about that thing and enables him to explain certain *other* important biological facts about it. Not suckling one's young and breathing water are also biologically important characteristics. And biologists refuse to call whales fish because whales lack these important criteria of fishhood.

The possession of scales, on the other hand, is not, according to biologists, a particularly important characteristic for purposes of biological knowledge and explanation. Whether an animal has scales or not does not make a big difference to the kind of animal it is; and one cannot explain very much about an animal from the mere fact that it has or lacks scales. Having scales is thus not, according to biologists, a very important criterion of fishhood. That is why the shark, which lacks scales, is considered by biologists to be a fish nonetheless. For the shark lacks only *unimportant* criteria of fishhood.

Those ordinary people, on the other hand, who insist on calling the whale a fish despite knowing that the whale is a mammal, etc., are usually fairly ignorant of biology and thus of the reasons why biologists consider cold-bloodedness or breathing water to be of such importance. Because of their ignorance of the biological importance of cold-bloodedness, etc., they will call the whale a fish because it lives in the water, has fins and a tail, and has a generally fishy look. They will be more impressed with these superficial characteristics of fish and will consider them more important in determining what sort of animal an animal is than cold-bloodedness, etc.

What we have seen in the above two examples is this: When philosophers, scientists, or ordinary men become convinced (or are already convinced) that some characteristic x (that is a criterion of f-ness) is important, they consider nothing to be (an) f unless it has x. And when they become convinced (or are already convinced) that some characteristic y (that is a criterion of f-ness) is *not* important, they think something can be (an) f without having y.[8] And, finally, when they become, or are already, convinced that something lacks only unimportant criteria of f-ness, i.e., that it has all the important criteria of f-ness, they call it (an) f.

What I should like now to claim is that, for a large number of general terms, which we shall call "cluster terms," the following principle, the Principle of Important Criteria, holds: x is (an) f if and only if x has all the *important* criteria of f-ness. This principle is valid of cluster terms just because one can by means of it frame analytic definitions of those cluster terms as they are ordinarily used. Thus, if 't' is a cluster term and $a,b,\ldots,n$ are (all of) its criteria, then the principle "x is (a) t if and

---

[8] Unless the possession of y is entailed by possession of some criterion z of f-ness that they think *is* important.

only if *x* has whichever of *a,b,...,n* are important" is analytically valid, valid by virtue of the meaning of '*t*', definitive of '*t*'. The particular principles generated by thus applying the Principle of Important Criteria (henceforth abbreviated PIC) to cluster terms can be seen to be analytically valid by reference to the ordinary usage of those terms. Consider the word 'democracy'. The principle that something is a democracy if and only if it has whichever of majority rule, female suffrage, minority rights, etc., are important, is analytic; and part of our reason for saying so is just the fact that, whenever people think, or come to think, that, e.g., minority rights are important, they refuse, come what may, to believe something to be a democracy if it lacks minority rights. And when they do *not* consider minority rights to be so important, they do not think in this way. And the same sort of thing is true of 'fish' and 'doubt' and the other terms whose applicability is involved in the questions mentioned above.[9]

Furthermore, such claims as are formed by application of the PIC to particular cluster terms have a certain "immunity to revision" that is characteristic of those statements and principles which philosophers typically designate as a priori and "true by virtue of meaning." For it could be shown that it is only because we adhere to the principles generated by applying the PIC to cluster terms like 'fish', 'solid', and 'city' that we come to such (to common opinion) paradoxical conclusions as that the whale is not a fish, that tables are never solid, and that Buffalo (or Omaha or Kansas City) is not really a city. And surely if those particular principles *were* subject to revision, we would reject them as soon as we saw that they forced us to highly paradoxical conclusions, so as to be able to reject those conclusions themselves. But in fact we do not reject these principles in such cases. Rather, the fact that we implicitly hold on so tenaciously to principles generable from the PIC shows how deep-seated adherence to such principles is in our ways of thinking and talking, and gives us some reason to think they are not merely empirical, but analytic of the terms to which they apply.

I should like now to clarify my usage of the key terms 'criterion' and 'important'. As I am using the term 'criterion', a characteristic *x* is a criterion of *f*-ness if and only if *x* is a logically necessary condition of something's being a paradigm case of *f*-ness, of an *f* (thing). And what I mean by a paradigm case of *f*-ness is a perfect, or ideal case, or example, of an *f* (thing), a perfectly paradigmatic case of an *f* (thing), a thing displaying all the elements of *f*-ness, which could not better exemplify, or be improved as a case of, *f*-ness. These notions are all, I think, about equivalent, and since they are notions with which we are all acquainted, they should clarify what I mean by a "paradigm case," and, hence, what I mean by a "criterion" of *f*-ness.

Now that I have defined 'criterion' as I wish to use the term, I should like to say what I mean by an *important criterion*. A characteristic *x* is an important criterion of *f*-ness if and only if *x* is a criterion of *f*-ness and knowing whether *x* is or is not present in any given thing *s* is important for our disinterested understanding of or knowledge about *s*; i.e., tells us a good deal, something important, about (the sort of thing) *s* (is), about what *s* is really like, about the "nature" of *s*. A criterion is important, in

---

[9] Criteria of cluster terms that are not important *per se*, but are important relative to the other criteria of those terms also are (treated as) necessary to the application of those terms. Thus the PIC should have the phrase 'or relatively important' added on; and what is really analytic of, e.g., democracy is the possession of whichever of majority rule, etc., are (either) important or relatively important. For purposes of simplicity, this qualification will be dropped during the rest of this paper.

other words, just in case its presence or absence in any given thing s makes a good deal of difference, from the standpoint of disinterested knowledge or understanding of s, to (the kind of thing) s (is).

I believe that disputes about all the questions mentioned at the beginning can be understood in terms of the Theory of Important Criteria (henceforth abbreviated TIC). For example, consider the question whether Buffalo (or Omaha or Kansas City) really is a city. Some will want to say that it is, others that it is not. Now there are many criteria, in my sense, of cityhood. One is the possession of a large population. Others are the possession of a rich and varied cultural life and the possession of a sophisticated, cosmopolitan, urbane atmosphere. Places like Buffalo fulfill the first, but not (according to some) the latter two criteria of cityhood. But if 'city' can be defined in terms of its criteria, 'x is a city' means something like "x has whichever of large population, rich cultural life, urbane atmosphere, etc., are important." If so, it should be understandable why some people think a place like Buffalo can be a city, while others do not. Some people think that whether a place has an urbane atmosphere or rich cultural life or not, makes a great difference to the sort of place it is; for such people, urbane atmosphere and rich cultural life are important; that is why they feel that Buffalo, which they think lacks these characteristics, is not really a city. On the other hand, some people do *not* think there is so great a difference between having or lacking an urbane atmosphere (or rich cultural life); and for such people urbane atmosphere and rich cultural life are not important, nor, thus, necessary to cityhood. And so they think Buffalo *is* a city, and find it hard to imagine how anyone could believe otherwise.

The other disputes mentioned above could be given a similar sort of analysis, if space permitted. Indeed, there are a large number of disagreements about the application of various ordinary terms that can be explained via the TIC.[10] The TIC is not subject to the sorts of difficulty inherent in two-meaning theories of disputes over the sorts of question we have been discussing, and it has other advantages over two-meaning theories as well.

For one thing, anyone who wishes strongly to defend one or another side of any of the disputes we have considered has every reason to prefer a one-meaning theory to any two-meaning theory of those disputes. For someone who is totally convinced that whales are not fish or that minority rights are (or are not) necessary to democracy thinks that his claims to that effect are directly relevant to and undermine the claims of those who deny what he asserts. And it is clear that this will be true only if his opponents mean the same thing by 'fish', 'democracy', etc., as he does. Hence the advantage of belief in a one-meaning theory for anyone who feels compelled (and how many of us, really, do not?) to take sides in one or another of the (sort of) disagreements we have been discussing.

It should be clear why participants in the debates we have examined cannot and do not admit the validity of any two-meaning theory of those debates. For to admit such validity would be to admit that those debates are really pseudo-debates, and that the problems raised by those debates are only pseudo-problems arising from a lack of communication. If a two-meaning theory is true, each participant in the debates will be right according to his own meaning of the word whose applicability is in dispute,

---

[10] The TIC is especially suited for explaining disagreements between science and ordinary belief on such questions as whether the tomato is a fruit, whether glacial ice is rock, etc.

and there will really be nothing to dispute. It is no wonder, then, that participants in these debates do *not* think that they are being hoodwinked by ambiguities, and feel, rather, that they and their opponents are using the same sense, the ordinary sense, of the word under dispute. And this gives us strong reason to believe that these participants *are* using the same ordinary sense of the words whose applicability they are debating, to believe that some sort of one-meaning theory is true.

Scientists have a particularly good reason to be happy with a one-meaning theory, indeed with the TIC itself, as an explanation of their claims that the whale is not a fish, that the tomato is a fruit, etc. For our theory furnishes them with an excellent justification for such claims. According to the TIC, the biologist who wishes to justify, e.g., the claim that the whale is not a fish need only show that some of the various typical fish traits whales lack—e.g., ability to breathe water, cold-bloodedness, and inability to suckle its young—are criteria (in my sense) of fishhood and important (in my sense). But clearly the above characteristics are criteria of fishhood, since, according to the common notion of a fish, nothing could (logically) be a paradigm or perfect example of a fish without them.

And it should also be apparent that these characteristics are important. And that is just because biologists consider them to be so. Biologists believe that a great deal that is important can be explained about an animal by knowing whether or not it is cold-blooded or breathes water, etc. But what plays an important role in *explaining* an animal's behavior, morphology, etc., is important for our *understanding* of the animal's behavior, morphology, etc., and so of what the animal is really like. Thus biologists believe that the above characteristics are important for disinterested knowledge about and understanding of animals, that to learn whether some animal x has or lacks one of these characteristics is to learn something important for our disinterested understanding of x, i.e., for our knowledge of the sort of thing x is. But the beliefs of biologists about what is important in explaining, and thus in understanding, animals have a certain authority and decisiveness. The beliefs of those who think the whale is a fish because they are not impressed with the importance of the criteria of fishhood that whales lack can in some sense be overruled and dismissed, if they conflict with the beliefs of biologists. Such conflicts between common opinion and biological science typically (though not necessarily always) show only that biology goes a great deal deeper than common opinion and that common opinion is typically superficial and *unscientific*. And since biologists believe that certain of the criteria of fishhood whales lack are important, we have every reason to think that they are important, and that the whale is not a fish. Thus one who believes strongly that the whale is not a fish (or that the tomato is a fruit, etc.) has good reason to accept the TIC, which furnishes him with such a ready way of justifying beliefs of this sort.

On the other hand, the TIC also serves to explain why certain others of the disputes we have examined cannot be settled in the decisive way that biologists can claim to have shown that whales are not fish. The latter sort of dispute depends solely on questions of what is important for natural science, questions which biology can answer authoritatively. But disputes about whether Buffalo is a city or whether a nation without minority rights can be a democracy depend not on scientific but on ethical questions and on questions of taste. The question about Buffalo depends on the importance of the presence or absence of sophistication and culture. And one's beliefs about the importance of these criteria of cityhood depend in turn at least partly on such personal variables as whether one values, disvalues, or is indifferent to culture or sophistication.[11] It is no wonder, then, that disputes over what is a city or what is a democracy are so difficult to resolve, our opinions about these questions depending as they do on factors that vary from person to person, on differences in allegiances, sensitivities, conditioning, and the like. Thus the TIC allows us to explain the length and intractability of certain disputes without postulating dull-wittedness or duplicity on the part of the disputants, in the manner of two-meaning theories. According to the TIC, the persistence of these disputes depends, rather, on the difficulty of decisively resolving certain sorts of value questions about what is and is not important.[12] The TIC is not, then, subject to the failings of two-meaning theories.

Now that some support has been given to the TIC, we are finally in a position to say what sorts of terms are *cluster terms,* i.e., terms to which the PIC applies. Cluster terms are all terms with a variety of different criteria such that disagreements arise (or at least very naturally could arise) about their applicability in at least some cases where one of the criteria of their application is missing. We have seen that, where such disagreements arise, they are better explained in terms of a one-meaning theory like the TIC than via two-meaning theories. Cluster terms, then, are terms disputes over which are typically due not to ambiguity but rather to differences in the importance attributed to one or another missing criterion of the term being disputed.

It has been commonly held by philosophers that the sort of terms I have called "cluster terms" obey a logic far different from that attributed to them by the TIC. Such diverse philosophers as Alston,[13] Hospers,[14] and Wittgenstein[15] have argued that none of the criteria (in something like my sense of 'criterion') of cluster terms are ever (treated as) necessary to the application of those terms.[16] Something can lack any *one* of the criteria of some cluster term 'f' and still be (thought to be) (an) f, even if it cannot lack *most* of the criteria of 'f' and still be (thought to be) (an) f. According to these philosophers of language, furthermore, there is no fixed fraction or number of the criteria of 'f' whose presence makes things f('s) and whose absence makes them non-f('s); and a set of, say, three criteria of f-ness may suffice for f-*ness,* whereas a different set of, say, four may not.

---

[11] The fact that what one feels is important for disinterested knowledge may partly depend on one's private interests and attitudes does not mean that one means by 'important for disinterested knowledge' "important for the knowledge that I, given my particular values, and interests, am interested in," any more than the fact that we call something beautiful partly because it pleases us shows that 'beautiful' means "pleasing to my particular aesthetic sensibilities." Someone who thinks Buffalo is not a city may do so, in part, because he *likes* places with sophistication. But in thinking that Buffalo is not a city, he is committed to the belief that the presence or absence of sophistication makes an important difference to the moral or aesthetic character of a place where people live, to what such a place is *really* like, not just to what he, personally, would like a place (like Buffalo) to be like, if, for example, he were to settle there.

[12] There is surely such a thing as giving good reasons for claims about what is or is not important for disinterested knowledge, even in the case of disputes where personal factors play a role. Part of such reason giving may, e.g., involve getting people to *see* things properly, or to notice patterns or relations they had previously failed to notice. On this, see J. Wisdom's "Gods," in *Philosophy and Psychoanalysis, op. cit.*

[13] *Op. cit.*, chap. 5.

[14] *Introduction to Philosophical Analysis* (Englewood Cliffs, N.J.: Prentice-Hall, 1964), chap. 9.

[15] Cf. George Pitcher, *The Philosophy of Wittgenstein* (Englewood Cliffs, N.J.: Prentice-Hall, 1964), chap. 9.

[16] These philosophers would designate as "cluster terms" most of the terms I have been calling cluster terms, but would not imply in so doing that those terms obeyed the PIC.

Now some of these views are perfectly compatible with, indeed follow from, the TIC. It is clear, for example, that if the TIC is true, no fixed number or fraction of the criteria or f-ness will always be both necessary *and* sufficient for the applicability of any cluster term 'f'. For the only fraction or number always sufficient for f-ness is the sum total of all the criteria of f-ness, since, according to the TIC, the lack of but *a single important* criterion of f-ness makes for non-f-ness; and the sum total of the criteria, sufficient always though it be, is not always necessary, because of cases where something is (an) f even though it lacks an *unimportant* criterion of f-ness. And it also follows from the TIC that a given set of criteria may suffice for f-ness even though a larger but different set may not. For the smaller set may just contain all the important criteria of f-ness while the larger set may not. Furthermore, if something lacks *most* of the criteria of f-ness, it will almost certainly lack at least one important criterion of f-ness and so be non-f.

The trouble with the work on cluster terms done by previous philosophers, however, is that, even where they are correct about the logic of cluster terms, they give almost no explanation of why those terms behave as they do. They do not explain *why* three criteria may suffice for f-ness while four do not, why no fraction or number of the criteria of f-ness is always both necessary and sufficient for f-ness, etc. But, as we have just seen, this is just what the TIC allows us to do.

In addition, previous writers about cluster terms are simply wrong in maintaining that none of the criteria of cluster terms is necessary to the applicability of any of those terms, at least if the TIC is correct. For, as we argued earlier, cold-bloodedness, etc., are necessary (though not logically necessary[17]) to fishhood: i.e., given the importance of cold-bloodedness, etc., nothing can be a fish without being cold-blooded, etc. And it is clear, too, that the existence of majority rule is in the same sense (thought to be) necessary to democracy. That is because people are agreed that it makes an important difference whether a nation possesses or lacks this criterion of democracy.[18]

Those philosophers who have (to my mind mistakenly) claimed that criteria of cluster terms are never necessary to their applicability have, nonetheless, pointed up something interesting about those terms, namely, that they cannot be defined simply by listing a set of characteristics individually necessary and jointly sufficient for their application. But they have gone on to say that cluster terms cannot be defined at all; and in this they have been mistaken. Definitions via the PIC may be novel and unexpected, but they are analytic definitions, nonetheless.[19]

---

[17] One who says the whale is warm-blooded and a mammal, but a fish anyway, does not contradict *himself*. He is just saying what cannot be true given the discoveries of biologists.

[18] Even the word 'game', which is Wittgenstein's primary example of a word whose instances lack something in common, is correctly applicable only to rule-governed activities that are played for fun. 'Game', as applied to certain activities (and not, say, to pheasant and grouse), can be defined via the PIC as: "thing having whichever of the properties of being played for fun, being played according to rules, allowing for winning and losing, etc., are important." The reason that all games are (thought to be) playable for fun and according to rules, but not necessarily capable of being won or lost, is that the former two properties (are thought to) make a more important difference to what an activity is like than the latter.

[19] It is often said that the term 'religion' has nothing common to all its instances (cf. Alston, *op. cit.*, p. 87 ff) and cannot be defined (cf. William James, *The Varieties of Religious Experience*, New York: The Modern Library, p. 27 f). If space permitted, it could be shown that 'religion' is definable via the PIC, and that disputes about whether Marxism or Hinayana Buddhism are religions involve differences about the importance of certain criteria of religion.

One obvious consequence of the TIC is that value judgment is far more involved in the making of what are commonly thought to be factual statements than has been imagined. Every time we apply a cluster term we are committed to a judgment about what is or is not important, and such judgments either are or are very close to value judgments. For to say that a criterion is important (in my sense) is to say, or to come very near to saying, that knowledge of the presence or absence of that criterion in things is useful or valuable for purposes of gaining disinterested knowledge of those things. And, clearly, judgments about what is useful or valuable are a species of value judgment.

Of course, if certain statements thought to be purely descriptive and factual do entail value judgments, we shall either have to admit that there is no Naturalistic Fallacy (in one sense in which that fallacy has been understood) or show, somehow, that those entailing statements are not descriptive and factual. But the latter move seems unwarranted and *ad hoc*. For what possible reason could we have to call 'x is a fish' or 'x is a city' non-factual and nondescriptive—except our discovery that they did entail value judgments? One feels like saying: if these are not factual statements, nothing is. It seems, then, that, if the TIC is correct, there is, in one sense, no Naturalistic Fallacy. In recent years some philosophers, notable among them Mrs. P. R. Foot, have attempted to overcome the Naturalistic Fallacy by showing how close value judgments are to statements of fact. The TIC overcomes the supposed gulf between fact and value in the opposite direction, namely, by showing how close some factual statements are to value judgments.

It should be noted, further, that the TIC allows us to see exactly what is wrong with the Paradigm Case argument. At least one version of that argument claims that, if people commonly teach, or show that they know, the meaning of some term 'f' by applying it to things that are in fact a, b, and c, then it will be incorrect ever to say that something is *not f, because* it is a, b, or c. If this argument were sound, the fact that ordinary people teach the meaning of 'city' to children by applying it to places like Buffalo and sometimes teach the meaning of 'fish' by applying it to whales or dolphins would show respectively that Buffalo is a city and whales and dolphins fish. But one cannot validly argue from the fact that some cluster term is taught in application to certain things to the conclusion that those things possess all the important criteria of that term. And so, on the TIC, whales and dolphins are not fish, no matter how many people ignorant of the importance of cold-bloodedness, etc., teach their children to call them fish, and Buffalo may not be a city despite the fact that children are taught to call it one. Those who support the Paradigm Case argument claim to do so out of a belief that ordinary language is correct language. But the Paradigm Case argument does not, as they think, define the meaning of cluster terms, so that, in opposing it, I am not denying that ordinary language is correct, but only trying, via the TIC, to give a better picture than adherents of the Paradigm Case argument give of what ordinary language is really like. Of course, philosophers have long been suspicious of the Paradigm Case argument; but the TIC gives us a theory on the basis of which we can see, perhaps for the first time, exactly *why* that argument does not work.

Value Judgments and the Theory of Important Criteria

In the twentieth century, a number of different sorts of meta-ethical theories have been put forward to explain and clarify the meaning of value terms and to answer the age-old question whether it is possible to give (objectively) good reasons for value judgments. Older, cruder forms of ethical naturalism, emotivism, and intuitionism (nonnaturalism) have been criticized for so many different reasons and from so many points of view that most contemporary ethical theorists are convinced that such theories cannot yield an adequate account of the meaning and justification of value judgments. In recent years, R. M. Hare has articulated a modified type of emotivist theory, and this theory has been criticized by Philippa Foot and others[1] from the standpoint of a new and highly sophisticated version of naturalism. In the present paper, I shall offer some criticisms of these two recent and (to my mind) important and promising metaethical theories, and then develop a new theory of the meaning and justification of value judgments based on the Theory of Important Criteria.[2]

I am indebted to George Boolos, Samuel Coleman, Arthur Danto, and Robert Shope for discussion of the ideas of this paper.

[1] For example, P. T. Geach in "Good and Evil," *Analysis*, XVII.2, 56 (December 1956): 33–42.

[2] See my "The Theory of Important Criteria," this JOURNAL, LXIII, 8 (April 14, 1966): 211–224. Also "Empirical Certainty and the Theory of Important Criteria," *Inquiry*, x, 1 (Spring 1967): 21–37.

I

It is part of Hare's view that there are no (interesting) limitations on what can serve as an ultimate value assumption or principle.[3] And the weaknesses of this claim, have, I think, been effectively pointed out by Mrs. Foot in "Moral Beliefs"[4] and in "Moral Arguments."[5] Hare also believes that, whenever one makes a full-blown value judgment, one commits oneself to making certain choices.[6] If one calls something a good knife, one is thereby committed to choosing knives of that kind in appropriate circumstances. This, according to Hare, is a result of the evaluative meaning, or imperative force, of 'good knife'. Mrs. Foot has ably criticized this view at some length in the articles cited above and elsewhere.[7] Her main point, I think, is that, if someone calls something a good x, he does not thereby commit himself to choosing or wanting x's like it, because he may very well have idiosyncratic tastes and know that he does. In other words, he may distinguish between good x's and x's that are good for his purposes. One example of this might be the case of the ugly man who wants only flattering photographs and portraits of himself. Such a man might very well admit something to be a good likeness of himself and *for that reason* not want or choose it. He would prefer certain bad likenesses to good ones.

Hare admits that we sometimes call something a good x without committing our will (i.e., without committing ourselves to certain choices); but he claims that in such cases 'good x' is being used in an "inverted commas" or "ironic" or "conventional" sense, rather than in its usual evaluative sense.[8] Mrs. Foot has argued against this view on the ground that Hare has given us no reason to think that those who call things good x's *without* being committed to certain choices mean by 'good x' anything different from what is meant by those who call things good x's and *are* committed to such choices.[9] And in the absence of such reasons, why should we not assume that the meaning of an evaluative statement is not affected by whether the person who utters it is or is not committed to certain choices? Of course, Hare defines 'evaluative' in such a way that a statement cannot be evaluative unless one commits one's will in making it.[10] But then there is no reason to think that certain evaluative statements (in Hare's sense) differ in meaning from corresponding nonevaluative statements; or that one cannot use 'this is a good x' in its ordinary sense without committing one's will, without making an evaluative statement (in Hare's sense). And this is really all an opponent of Hare need prove.

---

[3] See *The Language of Morals* (New York: Oxford, 1952), pp. 96f, 115; and "Descriptivism," *Proceedings of the British Academy*, XLIX (1963), 128–132.

[4] *Proceedings of the Aristotelian Society*, LIX (1958–1959): 83–104.

[5] *Mind*, LXVII, 268 (October 1958): 502–513.

[6] *Language of Morals*, pp. 107f, 127; "Descriptivism," p. 131.

[7] See her "Goodness and Choice," *Proceedings of the Aristotelian Society*, supp. vol. xxxv (1961): 45–60.

[8] *Language of Morals*, p. 124f.

[9] "Goodness and Choice," p. 59f.

[10] *Language of Morals*, p. 164.

Furthermore, even when people use inverted commas around a value expression or use 'so-called' before that expression, it is by no means clear that they do so in order not to be committed to applying that expression *tout court*. Hare is correct in saying that when we do not approve of or desire some quality like beauty, we often use 'so-called' and/or inverted commas in calling someone beautiful. A religious person who for any of a number of possible reasons disapproved of beauty and did not seek beauty for himself or in others might well say something like: 'so-called beautiful women all too frequently lack moral fiber' or 'she is one of those "beautiful" women who are capable of nothing deep or serious'. Hare seems to think that such a religious person uses 'so-called' or inverted commas in order to avoid being committed to the applicability of 'beautiful' in its ordinary sense, and takes this as a confirmation of his theory that calling something beautiful ordinarily commits one's will. But actually a religious person who says the above sorts of things will typically *not* want to deny that the women he is criticizing are really beautiful. If one were to ask such a person whether he thought such women really were *not* beautiful, he would most probably reply that he certainly did think them beautiful and that their being *merely* (physically) beautiful was his reason for being so critical. The fact of the matter is that when inverted commas or 'so-called' is used in the above sort of case,[11] it is used not, as Hare thinks, to avoid commitment to the full-blown applicability of certain value terms, but rather to cancel certain connotations of approval and liking that are conventionally associated with the use of value terms like 'beautiful'. And so the use of inverted commas and 'so-called' in the above sort of case in no way supports, and indeed goes against, Hare's theory; for if inverted commas and 'so-called' are sometimes used to indicate nonapproval and nonchoice and not to avoid the ascription of certain value predicates in their ordinary sense, then such predicates can be used in their ordinary sense without committing the will.

The criticisms I have been making of Hare's views have a naturalistic flavor to them. But I do not myself want to support any form of pure naturalism. The theory I shall be defending is quasi-naturalistic at best, but it bears important resemblances to the sort of naturalism espoused by Mrs. Foot.

On the other hand, it is in certain respects quite different from her theory. In the first place, Mrs. Foot offers no explicit account of how value disagreements can occur between persons who agree on all the empirical "facts" of a situation. But John Wisdom has, I think, given us strong reason to believe that different ways of noticing, weighing, and appreciating the same "facts" may lead people to different evaluations and valuations of those facts and, thus, to different answers to such questions as whether someone really was a good friend, really was in love, or really was a good man.[12] Later on we shall examine in some detail one particular case where

---

[11] There are other cases, however, where one does use inverted commas to avoid commitment to a fullblown value judgment. One example would be Hare's own case of a man who says 'that is a "good" Carlo Dolci' in describing a painting that is said to be good, but which he himself does not really admire, or think well of (see *Language of Morals*, p. 125). But in such cases one's desire to avoid a fullblown value judgment arises from one's disagreement with the critical evaluations of certain (presumably influential) people, and not just from one's failure to be committed to certain choices. So such cases also fail to support Hare's view that value judgments commit one's will.

[12] See his *Philosophy and Psychoanalysis* (New York: Oxford, 1957), *passim*.

value disagreement seems to exist independently of disagreement about particular empirical facts. And the theory I shall be proposing will be able to explain this sort of disagreement in a way that the naturalistic theories of Mrs. Foot and others seemingly cannot.

Secondly, I shall attempt to explain in what sense terms like 'good' and 'beautiful' and 'rude' can be said to be value terms possessing evaluative or emotive meaning. Mrs. Foot seems to think that there is no real difference between the logic of "value terms" and the logic of "factual terms", and that the former do not possess any special evaluative or emotive meaning over and above their descriptive or factual meaning. I do think she is correct in believing that the special evaluative meaning of value judgments that distinguishes such judgments from "mere" statements of fact cannot consist in any commitment of the will that such judgments entail. But it does not follow that there is *no* valid distinction to be made between value judgments and nonvalue judgments and *no* such thing as evaluative meaning. After all, there does *seem* to be an intuitive difference between value terms and other terms: value terms do seem to be used to express feelings and attitudes in a way that nonvalue terms do not. And surely there must be something common to uses of 'good' in 'good man' and 'good knife' and uses of 'good' in such exclamations as "Good, I'm glad you did that" and "Good for you" where it clearly *does* seem to have some sort of pro-evaluative or emotive meaning or import. I shall, therefore, be arguing that it is possible for value terms to be quasi-naturalistically defined, and yet also have a special sort of evaluative meaning that distinguishes them from nonvalue terms.

Finally, the metaethical theory I shall be proposing will be expicitly semantical in a way that Mrs. Foot's theory is not. She has argued that there exist objective criteria for ascertaining the applicability of value terms determined by the meaning of those terms, but she has never attempted any actual definitions of value terms. I shall propose rules for the framing of definitions of value terms, and sketch definitions of a few particular value terms. The inclusion of such explicit definitions will enable the theory I shall propose to explain (as recent naturalistic theories do not) exactly what it is about the meaning of value terms that permits the existence of objective procedures for supporting and validating value judgments.

II

In "The Theory of Important Criteria," I considered the nature of such quasi-philosophical disagreements as whether Buffalo is really a city, whether the whale is a fish, and whether a state without minority rights can be a democracy, and attempted to show that:

(a) Such disagreements are disagreements over the application of a term to some kind of entity that lacks one of the criteria of that term's application—where a characteristic x is a criterion of a term 'f' just in case it is logically impossible for something to be a paradigm, or perfect, or ideal case, or example, of an f (thing) without having x. The disagreement over whether a state without minority rights can be a democracy, for example, is a disagreement over the application of the term 'democracy' to a kind of thing (namely, a state that does not grant minority rights) that lacks one of the criteria of that term. For, according to the common notion of democracy, the possession of minority rights is clearly logically necessary to a state's being a perfect or ideal example of a democracy, and is thus a criterion of 'democracy'.

(b) Disagreements of the above sort cannot be plausibly explained via previous metaphilosophical theories, like those of Stevenson, Wisdom, Edwards, and Alston, which postulate either ambiguity or vagueness in the term whose applicability is in dispute, but must be explained, rather, in terms of a single meaning, the ordinary meaning, of the terms whose applicability is in question.[13] Such terms as 'fish', 'city', and 'democracy', whose applicability is disputed in certain cases where one of their criteria is missing, I call *cluster terms*. Cluster terms can be defined in terms of their criteria. Where 'f' is a cluster term all of whose criteria are $a, b, \ldots, n$, 'p is (an) f' means "p has whichever of $a, b, \ldots n$ are important." Thus 'p is a democracy', for example, means something like "p has whichever of majority rule, minority rights, female suffrage, basic human rights, etc., are important," since the possession of majority rule, minority rights, etc., are all logically necessary to paradigm or perfect democracy, and thus criteria of 'democracy'. As I define the key word 'important', a characteristic x counts as important if and only if knowing whether x is or is not present in any given thing s is important for our disinterested knowledge about our understanding of s, i.e., tell us a good deal about (the sort of thing) s (is), about what s is really like. A characteristic is important, in other words, just in case its presence or absence in any given thing s makes a good deal of (an important) difference to the kind of thing s is.

(c) The length and intractability of disputes and disagreements over the applicability of cluster terms result not from vagueness or ambiguity in those terms, but from differences over value questions about whether certain (missing) criteria are or are not important in the above sense of the word. Thus the dispute over whether a state without minority rights can be a democracy, to revert to our old example, is basically a dispute over whether the possession of minority rights is important, i.e., is a characteristic whose presence or absence in a state makes an important difference to what that state is like.

Two questions arise in considering whether the above Theory of Important Criteria (henceforth, TIC) can be applied to value terms and value judgments. Do (some)

---

[13] Of course, some of these terms have more than one meaning in ordinary usage. 'Fish,' for example, has a different meaning as a verb from its meaning as a noun used to designate aquatic animals. In saying that the debate over whether whales are fish can be explained in terms of the ordinary meaning of 'fish', I mean the ordinary meaning of 'fish' *as it is applied to aquatic animals*. Similarly in the case of the other disputes mentioned.

value terms have criteria in the above sense of the word? And if they do, is there any reason why those value terms cannot be defined in terms of their criteria in the manner suggested by the TIC? I believe most value terms do have criteria in the sense specified above.

It is a logically necessary condition of being a perfect example of a good second baseman (under the present rules of baseball) that one be able to throw a baseball, hit a baseball, and execute double plays. It is logically necessary to being an ideally fine person that one be honest, kind, and humble. In support of these views I ask the reader to consider under what circumstances he would deny any of these entailments. I think that speakers of English treat the relation, say, between being a perfect example of a good second baseman and being able to throw a baseball in the same way that they treat the relation (discussed in "The Theory of Important Criteria") between being a perfect example of a fish and being able to breathe water. In general, people would not call any animal that could not breathe water a *perfect* example of a fish (though they might consider such an animal to be a fish *simpliciter*); and they would be shocked and surprised if anyone else did. And people seem to be just as reluctant to call someone who cannot throw a baseball a perfect example of a good second baseman, and would be just as surprised to hear someone else do so. There exists, I think, the same sort of linguistic evidence for saying that being able to throw a baseball is entailed by being a perfect example of a good second baseman as there is for saying that being able to breathe water is entailed by being a perfect example of a fish. And so there seems to be as good a reason for thinking that being able to throw a baseball is a criterion of 'good second baseman' as there is for thinking that the ability to breathe water is a criterion of 'fish'. Emotivists are fond of saying that any value judgment can be denied without committing a logical or linguistic error. But if I am correct, one really cannot deny a value judgment like 'any perfectly good second baseman must be able to throw a baseball' without falling into logical or linguistic error.

Certain value terms have criteria. And they also resemble the sort of cluster terms described in "The Theory of Important Criteria" in that disputes about their application can arise in cases where one of their criteria is absent. For example, it is sometimes a matter of disagreement whether a man who is not humble, but *is* honest, kind, intelligent, sensitive, etc., can be a fine person. And humility is a criterion of a being a fine person. Similarly, it might be disputed whether someone who could not execute double plays, but who in all other respects fielded and batted well, would count as a good second baseman. And, again, the ability to execute double plays is a criterion of being a good second baseman. So it would seem that both 'good second baseman' and 'fine person' are cluster terms and should, at least according to the TIC, be definable in the manner of such other cluster terms as 'fish' and 'democracy'. Thus the TIC as applied to value terms (henceforth to be called the Metaethical Theory of Important Criteria, or the MTIC, for short) is committed to saying that 'fine person' ordinarily means something like: person having whichever of kindness, honesty, intelligence, humility, sensitivity, etc., are important. And it is committed to a similar definition of 'good second baseman' in terms of its criteria. Furthermore, there seems to be no reason why a large number of other value terms cannot be defined in the same way. Such terms as 'good swimmer', 'good carving knife', and 'good friend' seem excellent candidates for such definition, since, if time permitted, they could all be shown to be terms about whose applicability disputes can arise in cases where one of their criteria is missing.[14]

The MTIC opposes cruder forms of emotivism in allowing for the sensibleness of talking about the truth and falsity of value judgments and also in allowing for some measure of rationality in the validation of value judgments. If 'fine person' is definable in the above way, then, in order to show that someone p is a fine person, it is only necessary to show of *every* criterion of 'fine person' that it is either present in p or unimportant. That is why 'p is kind' is relevant to and in some sense evidence for 'p is a fine person'. For to show that p is kind is to show of *one* of the criteria of 'fine person' that it *is* either present in p or unimportant, and is thus part of a rational procedure for validating or verifying 'p is a fine person'. And for the same reason 'p is not kind' is relevant to and in some sense evidence for 'p is not a fine person'. For in order to show that p is not a fine person, one must show that he lacks an important criterion of being a fine person; and one way one might try to show this would be to show that p lacks kindness and that kindness is important.

Mrs. Foot has claimed that certain claims are clearly relevant to the support or validation of certain value judgments, whereas others, just as clearly, are not. And the MTIC can given an explicit explanation of this. On the MTIC, 'p is kind' is relevant to 'p is a fine person' because of the very meaning that theory assigns to 'fine person'. 'P is kind' is also *inductively* relevant to 'p is a fine person' inasmuch as kind men are more likely than not to be honest and sensitive, i.e., to have other criteria of being a fine person. And similarly, characteristics that are not criteria of being a fine person and thus not mentioned in the definition of that concept may also be used to give inductive support to 'p is a fine person'. The fact that p is president of the Cancer Society gives us some reason to think that p is kind and honest, and so is inductively relevant to the claim that p is a fine person. It is equally clear, on the MTIC, why certain other claims are entirely *irrelevant* to 'p is a fine person'. 'P has brown hair' is irrelevant because brown hair is neither a criterion of being a fine person nor (to the best of our knowledge) inductively correlated with any such criterion. Thus if someone says that p must be a fine person because he is so kind, no one will raise any question about the *relevance* of what has been said. But if someone were to say that p must be a fine person because he has brown hair, one will want to ask what possible relevance brown hair has to being a fine person, and if the original speaker cannot show any inductive correlation between brown hair and certain criteria of being a fine person, no one will think he has given any reason for his claim that p is a fine person.

But what about cases where one wants to show that someone is a fine person despite his lacking one of the criteria of being a fine person? Here one must show,

---

[14] I think "x is a good friend to y," for example, means something like: x has whichever of loving y, seeking y's welfare, liking to be with y, being willing to make sacrifices for y, etc., are important. I do not, however, think that all value terms can be defined via the MTIC, especially terms relating to gustatory and aesthetic value and terms like 'ought', 'should', and 'good' (when not followed by a noun—as in "it is good to be here"). Nor can the MTIC define 'good' in the context of 'good second baseman' or decide the frequently debated question whether its meaning in that sort of context is the same as its meaning in other contexts, like those of 'good friend' or 'good knife'.

or in some other way point out, the unimportance of the missing criterion. And of course in cases where one wants to show that someone is *not* a fine person, one must show, or in some other way point out, the importance of some criterion that he lacks. At this point, however, someone might claim that the TIC specifies a notion of importance that is irrelevant within the value context. Someone, that is, could hold that although, for many value *and* nonvalue terms '*f*', something is *f* if and only if it has all the important criteria of *f*ness, the relevant notion of importance for value terms (though not for nonvalue terms) is that of practical importance (i.e., usefulness) to the person judging whether some value term applies (or to some group to which he belongs), rather than that of importance for (disinterested) knowledge of what things are like. Such a claim, I believe, does not square with the way value judgments are in fact used, with the considerations that actually play a part in decisions about the application of value terms of the sort we are dealing with here. If, for example, a person (or group of persons) were told on good authority that they would be rewarded by person *p* every time he (or they) could find a man who was not boastful about the athletic prowess of his children, then knowing whether any given man had this criterion of fine personhood would be of practical importance to the person (or group of persons) in question. But that would not cause him (or them) to say that no man who is boastful about his children's athletic prowess is really a fine person. And that is because nobody thinks that whether a man is boastful in this (harmless) way or not makes such a terribly big difference to what sort of person he is, to what he is like. In the light of this and easily constructible similar examples, I think we have good reason to think that, even in the value context, the relevant notion of importance is that of importance for (knowledge of) what things are like. And so we have thus far produced no reason for thinking that value terms cannot be defined in the same way as the nonvalue terms discussed in "The Theory of Important Criteria."

Of course, the notion of importance we are working with is still a value notion or something very close to a value notion,[15] and this introduces some flexibility into attempts to show the applicability of the sort of terms that the MTIC deals with. But it in no way follows that our procedures for validating value judgments are some sort of emotive grab-bag without rhyme or reason. And that is true partly for reasons already discussed above and partly because it seems possible to have good reasons for and be sure of claims about what criteria are or are not important (in the sense specified by the TIC and the MTIC). Some criteria of value terms just clearly do make a bigger difference by their presence or absence to what things are like than others. Whether a man is kind or not makes a big, an important, difference to the sort of person he is;

---

[15] My reason for hesitating about whether 'important' as I have defined it is a value term or is just very much like a value term (e.g., in the way that disputes can arise about its application) is just this. I defined an important criterion as a criterion knowledge of whose presence or absence in any given thing *s* tells us a good deal (something important) about what *s* is like. If one believes that it analytically follows from this definition than an important criterion is one whose presence or absence is *worth* determining (or ought to be determined) if one seeks to know what something *s* is like, then one must grant that 'important' thus defined is a value word. However, one might hold that although criteria that are important in my sense are worth paying attention to in certain situations, to claim this is just to make a value judgment, rather than to state an analytic truth; and in that case, 'important' would not, it seems, be itself a value word. I find it hard to decide between these two positions.

if a man who is kind grows to be unkind (or vice versa), a big change has taken place in him. And this will be obvious to anyone with a normal sort of education, even if he does not particularly like or like being around kind people. Other characteristics are just as clearly unimportant. For example, whether or not a man is humble (or modest) about the athletic prowess of his children pretty clearly does not make much of a difference to the kind of person he is.

In some cases, however, it is by no means easy to get general agreement or an authoritative decision on whether some characteristic is or is not important. And since disputes about the applicability of a value term can sometimes result from disagreements about the importance of some missing criterion of that term, it is possible for there to be long-standing and seemingly unresolvable value disputes, even where no obvious differences of opinion exist about relevant empirical facts. Thus two people may agree that p has all the criteria of being a fine person except humility (and other criteria entailed by humility),[16] and yet disagree about whether p is a fine person, because they disagree about the importance of humility. One of them might place a great deal of emphasis in his own life on humility and think that whether a man was humble or not made a significant difference to his character. He might feel that a lack of humility made a man's other virtues count for less. And as a result he might not be willing to call p a fine person. The other might be very much influenced by the fact that a lack of kindness will typically hurt other people in ways and to an extent that a lack of humility typically does not; and so he might think that the presence or absence of kindness made a far greater difference to what a man was like than the presence or absence of humility, and thereby conclude that p was really a fine person after all.

Now some disputes that hang on disagreements about the importance of certain criteria can be definitively resolved. In "The Theory of Important Criteria" (see 219) I argued that the question whether the whale is a fish, which hangs on the importance of such criteria of fishhood as the ability to breathe water and cold-bloodedness, can be definitively resolved by biologists. The biologist can authoritatively show that these criteria (which are absent in whales) are important, and thus that the whale is not a fish. On the other hand, there are no readily available and reliable scientific techniques to show the importance or unimportance of humility, and thereby resolve the dispute over whether p is a fine person. Furthermore, one's opinion on this matter would seem at least partly to depend on one's particular sensitivity and imaginativeness and on the kinds of lived and literary experiences one has had. As I mentioned earlier, John Wisdom has frequently pointed up the ways in which personal differences can affect our evaluations of human character and human beings. He has also argued, however, that reasoning and learning occur in this area. Only they are of a very subtle kind. Resolving disagreements about such questions as the importance of humility may involve getting people to see things differently, to notice and appreciate patterns and similarities that had previously gone unnoticed, to see, for example, the charm in what was recently thought only to be unfinished or callow, or to see the shallowness in what was previously thought

---

[16] Given the definition of a criterion, anything logically entailed by a criterion of a term 'f' is also a criterion of 'f'.

to be instructive or illuminating. Such changes in people's ways of seeing things typically do not come about as a result of logical argument or scientific evidence. Yet they do occur, and they often have a certain rationality or reasonableness to them. Furthermore, those who disagree about such a question as whether a fine person can lack humility may *both* have reasons for what they say and with time succeed in conveying those reasons to one another. And so their dispute may persist because so much stands for and so much against the importance of humility. Thus the fact that disagreements about the importance of certain criteria, and the value disputes that hang on those disagreements, are often so difficult to resolve in any definitive manner does not show that there is any aspect of the making of value judgments that is entirely inaccessible to rationality and to greater and greater insight and understanding. And this can be true even if some value disputes persist at least partly because of personal differences between people and cannot, at least at present, be resolved in the authoritative way that biologists can claim to have shown, once and for all, that coldbloodedness and the ability to breathe water are important and that the whale is not a fish.[17]

The MTIC is clearly committed to the existence of certain rational procedures and of objectively good reasons within the value sphere. To that extent it is clearly opposed to (older forms of) emotivism. But it is also not a strictly naturalistic theory, inasmuch as the definitions it offers of value terms crucially involve the notion of importance, itself a value notion or very close to being one. The MTIC is also clearly opposed to intuitionism (nonnaturalism) because of its claim that certain value terms can be defined in terms of their criteria. For traditional intuitionism claims that there is no more than a synthetic necessary connection between value terms and the sort of characteristics we have designated as criteria of such terms.[18]

III

But where in this whole picture of the meaning and justification of value judgments is there room for evaluative or emotive meaning? The definitions I have offered of value terms do not seem to mention or specify any familiar sort of emotive meaning as belonging to the terms they define. For example, on the MTIC, 'good second baseman' means something like: second baseman who has whichever of the ability to throw a baseball, the ability to make double plays, the ability to bunt well, etc.,

---

[17] However, questions about importance that at one time appear hard to resolve may at a later time appear to admit of an essay and definitive solution—all because of an historical increase in human sensitivity and wisdom. At one time, for example, it might have seemed difficult to decide whether a nation whose Negroes were not allowed to vote could or could not really be a democracy. Today, it does not. That is because we are now more sensitive to what an enormous difference it makes to the character of a nation whether or not it bars certain racial or religious groups from voting. We are wiser than we were. Similarly, many other questions about importance that now seem hard to resolve may with time be seen to have clear and definite answers.

[18] Except that intuitionists certainly would want to say that *certain* criteria of 'good second baseman', like being a second baseman and being a baseball player, *are* analytically entailed by being a good second baseman.

are important.[19] Now this definition does contain certain value words: 'well' and 'important'. But neither of these gives the definiens the sort of pro-evaluative or laudatory emotive meaning that I believe 'good second baseman' has. To say that someone has certain important criteria is not necessarily to praise him; for a characteristic counts as important just in case its presence or absence makes a large difference, *whether for better or for worse,* to what things are like. (To say that someone has all the important criteria of being a bad man, for example, is surely not to praise him in any way.) And secondly, our definiens of 'good second baseman' does not entail "second baseman who bunts well" (in which case that definiens would indeed have the same sort of pro-evaluative laudatory meaning as 'good second baseman'), but only "second baseman who, *if* the quality of being able to bunt well is important, is able to bunt well." In other words, the definiens only hypothetically ascribes the ability to bunt well, with its evaluative meaning, while the definiendum is categorically committed to something with evaluative meaning.

But if our definition of 'good second baseman' does not have the sort of emotive or evaluative meaning that 'good second baseman' itself has, how can it be an adequate definition of that expression? As Hare asks by way of criticism of naturalism, how could an expression *without* evaluative meaning suffice to define one that *has* evaluative meaning?[20] In order to maintain that one can provide adequate definitions of value terms via the MTIC, will I not in the end have to deny that value terms have any special sort of emotive or evaluative meaning?

I think not. 'Good second baseman' and other such value expressions can have evaluative meaning and still be defined in terms of definientia that do not, because the evaluative meaning of those terms is not part of their logical meaning or content. The evaluative or emotive meaning of 'good x' consists of the fact that when we call something a good x, our utterance carries with it a Gricean[21] implication to the effect that we like or approve or have some other appropriate pro-attitude toward (some appropriate aspect of) the thing we call good.[22] As I argued earlier, this implication is not a logical one; we are not logically committed to liking or approving, much less to choosing, the x's we call good. For we can, after calling something a good x, in all propriety disclaim any pro-attitude toward (any aspect of) the thing in question. But it is a conventional connotation, or standard implication, of calling something good that one has an appropriate pro-attitude toward the thing in question and that one means to be praising and/or commending that thing. That is, it is as a result of certain conventions of the use of value words like 'good' that those who hear one say that something is a good x have the right to conclude that one has an appropriate

---

[19] I do not think that the fact that certain criteria of value terms are themselves designated by value terms causes any special difficulty for the MTIC.

[20] *Language of Morals,* p. 85.

[21] I shall mean by 'implication' pretty much what Grice means by that term in his "The Causal Theory of Perception," *Proceedings of the Aristotelian Society,* supp. vol. xxxv (1961), 121–152.

[22] Not all uses of 'good' involve *calling* something good, nor thus involve this implication. For example, if I say 'If that is a good knife, then I have just been cut by a good knife.' I am not calling anything good, nor is there any implication that I have any pro-attitude towards the knife in question. Perhaps, then, it is best to say that 'p is a good x', rather than 'good x', has evaluative meaning.

pro-attitude toward the thing in question, *unless* one makes a specific disclaimer of such a pro-attitude or special circumstances obtain in which such a disclaimer is already understood to exist.[23] And, of course, since people tend to be influenced by what they think are the attitudes of others, someone who hears something called a good x will, in the absence of any disclaimer of pro-attitude, tend himself to have an appropriate pro-attitude toward the thing in question and to act at least somewhat differently toward the thing as a result. So our theory about the nature of the emotive meaning of value terms can give some sort of account of the so-called "magnetic influence" of value terms.

According to Grice, certain standard or normal implications of an expression may not be part of the (logical) meaning of that expression. Thus the use of 'it looks red' standardly carries with it something like the implication that the speaker is not sure that the thing in question is red. But it is not a condition of the truth of someone's utterance of 'it looks red' that the speaker be in doubt about the redness of anything (139f.). 'P is a good x' has the same sort of implication, and this implication constitutes the evaluative or emotive meaning of such an expression. But in that case the emotive meaning of value expressions is not part of the logical meaning of those expressions, has nothing to do with the truth conditions of those expressions, or thus with what is analytically entailed by those expressions. If so, then 'p is a good second baseman' may possess an emotive meaning that the definiens assigned to it by the MTIC does not, and yet it still be the case that the definiens provides a perfectly adequate analysis of the logical meaning of (or what is analytically entailed by) 'x is a good second baseman'. I believe this in fact to be the case. And what follows is that the emotive meaning of 'x is a good second baseman' is both cancelable and detachable in Grice's sense (128ff.). It is cancelable because one who says that p is a good second baseman can deny (the implication) that he has a pro-attitude toward p without taking back his original assertion. It is detachable because there is a way of saying what 'p is a good second baseman' is used to say without having what one says carry with it the clear sort of evaluative implication that 'p is a good second baseman' has, namely, by saying: p has whichever of ability to throw a baseball, ability to execute double plays,... Inasmuch as the definiens of 'p is a good second baseman' assigned to it by the MTIC is analytically equivalent to 'p is a good second baseman', the MTIC offers the sort of definitions philosophers have sought to give of value terms and value judgments. And so we have made good our promise to show how value terms could be defined and yet also possess emotive or evaluative meaning.

It should be said, further, that what separates value terms from nonvalue terms is the conventional (but nonlogical) implication of a pro- or con-attitude that attaches to certain uses of those terms. Certain nonvalue expressions like 'pleases me' are often used to make statements that *entail* that the speaker has a pro-attitude. But this is a logical implication, and not the sort of implication of which Grice is mainly talking

---

[23] Such circumstances exist, for example, if I am an atheist and anti-Catholic and call someone a good Catholic in the presence of people who know about these attitudes of mine and know that I know they know about them. The case of a man who will call people good Catholics although he detests Catholicism counts heavily against Hare's theory about commitment of the will. I am indebted for this example to Dr. S. Coleman.

or in terms of which I wish to define the difference between value terms and nonvalue terms. It is also true that in appropriate circumstances nonvalue terms can be used to make statements that express and perhaps even imply a pro- or con-attitude. If I say 'this is smooth whiskey' in the appropriate circumstances, people will (have the right to) take me to like the whiskey and to be praising it. But this will only be so because of the particular nature of human wants and the sorts of beliefs people have about those wants. It is because everyone knows that people tend to prefer smooth whiskey that people will (have the right to) infer that the person who says that a certain whiskey is smooth likes the whiskey he is talking about and is praising (or recommending) it. The implication of liking does not, in this case, arise from conventions of usage. There is nothing about the rules governing the usage of 'smooth whiskey' that dictates that we should use that expression only if we have a pro-attitude toward (some aspect of) the whiskey we call smooth (unless we make or there already exists a disclaimer of such a pro-attitude). But it *is* a matter of convention that calling someone a good second baseman implies that one has a pro-attitude toward (some aspect of) the person in question, because there is some sort of (implicit) rule governing the usage of 'good second baseman', or of any other pro-evaluative value term 'f', to the effect that one should only call someone or something a good second baseman, or (an) f, if one has an appropriate pro-attitude (unless one goes on to disclaim such a pro-attitude or such a disclaimer is already understood in the circumstances). Where 'f' is any pro-evaluative value term, those who hear one call something (an) f without hearing or knowing of any disclaimer of pro-attitude can conclude that the person speaking likes (some aspect of) the thing in question merely on the basis of their knowledge of the rules governing such value terms, that is, merely by assuming that the speaker is following the rules governing the usage of such value terms and without any assumptions about the wants or needs of human beings in general or of the speaker in particular. And, of course, the same holds true of con-evaluative value terms.

Footian-type naturalistic theories find it hard to explain why people generally have some sort of pro-attitude to the x's they call good and some sort of con-attitude to the x's they call bad. Of course, at least part of the reason for this is that such expressions as 'good knife' and 'good second baseman' are analyzable in terms of properties whose presence in things (of the appropriate kind) most people like, want, admire, or approve, whereas just the opposite is true of such expressions as 'poor knife' and 'bad friend'. But Footian naturalism cannot easily explain why this latter should be the case, cannot easily explain why such expressions as 'poor knife' and 'bad friend' are *not* used to designate properties people want, etc. Surely if the typical Naturalist belief in the nonexistence of pro-evaluative and con-evaluative meaning is correct, it is an amazing coincidence that for, so many values of 'x', 'good x' is analyzable in terms of properties people generally want, etc., while 'bad x' or 'poor x' is *not*.

It counts in favor of the theory of evaluative meaning offered here that it *can* give a plausible explanation of this fact. For if calling something a good x has a conventional implication of a pro-attitude on the part of the speaker and if calling something a bad or a poor x has just the opposite sort of conventional implication, it is both understandable and natural that 'good x' and 'bad x' and 'poor x' should be used in such a way (i.e., be analyzable in terms of properties of such a sort) that those implications were generally not misleading. Thus if the qualities in terms of which some particular value term 'good *g*' is definable become less and less desired and approved by most people, there is pressure on the usage of 'good *g*' to change in such a way that 'good *g*' will again apply to things most people like and approve and no longer have a misleading implication.[24] And it follows that, when the meaning of 'good *g*' is fairly stable (as is the meaning of most value terms today), most people will have a pro-attitude toward the qualities in terms of which 'good *g*' is defined and thus toward good *g*'s.

In some sense, then, Hare is correct in claiming that the evaluative meaning of value terms is primary and their descriptive meaning secondary.[25] For at least in the case of value terms involving 'good', 'poor', or 'bad', it is typically the descriptive or logical meaning of value terms that adjusts itself to the evaluative implications of those terms, rather than vice versa. The pro-evaluative meaning of any value expression 'good *x*' will normally stay constant over time even if its logical meaning changes.

I want, in conclusion, to mention one difficulty that faces certain metaethical theories, like the MTIC, that attempt to ascribe univocal meanings to certain value terms. According to the MTIC, the ordinary meaning of many value terms can be defined in terms of the criteria (in our sense of the term) of those terms. The MTIC claims that such terms typically have only a single meaning in ordinary usage and that disagreements or disputes over their application do not (except perhaps very rarely) arise from ambiguity or vagueness in those terms, but, rather, from disagreements about the importance of certain agreed-upon criteria of those terms.[26] But is it clear that those who dispute over the application of value terms typically *do* agree about the criteria of those terms? Is it so obvious, for example, that those who dispute about whether a man who is unchaste outside of marriage can be a fine person agree on the criteria of fine personhood? Is it not possible that being chaste outside marriage *is* logically necessary to being an ideal example of a fine person in the usage of one who thinks no one unchaste outside of marriage can be a fine person *simpliciter*, but *not* in the usage of one who thinks one *can* be a fine person without having been chaste outside of marriage? If this were so, 'fine person' would, it seems, have at

---

[24] If, for example, everyone stopped wanting to travel in cars, because they became much more frightened about the risks of driving than people usually are today and if cars started to be used as musical instruments, e.g., and people preferred those cars which made the most interesting musical noises, the meaning of 'good car' would probably change. 'Good car' might come to mean something like 'musically interesting car'.

[25] *Language of Morals*, p. 118f.

[26] In "The Theory of Important Criteria" I argued that certain factual, non-value terms (like 'fish') can be defined partly in terms of the value notion of importance. The MTIC claims that value terms are partly definable in terms of certain nonvalue terms that designate criteria of those value terms. It is my general purpose to stress the interconnectedness of value and nonvalue notions, even though I believe, as I made clear earlier, that there is a valid distinction to be drawn between value terms and nonvalue terms. For example, both value terms and nonvalue terms can have both value characteristics and nonvalue characteristics among their criteria. It is a criterion of being a good second baseman that one be able to throw a baseball and that one be able to throw a baseball well; and it is a criterion of being a fish that something be able to swim and that it be able to swim at least fairly well.

least two meanings, and the MTIC would be incorrect as an analysis of 'fine person' and (presumably for very similar reasons) of most other value terms as well.

But is it really true that some people treat chastity (outside of marriage) as logically necessary to paradigm fine personhood, while others do not? I think that many people who might at first want to say that chastity was logically necessary to paradigm fine personhood have, in fact, only empirical reasons for thinking that no one lacking this quality can be a perfect or ideal example of a fine person. They may, for example, believe that God has ordained chastity and that only one who does what God ordains can be an ideally fine person. But it is clearly a contingent matter whether God has ordained chastity, since, for one thing, God's existence is contingent. Someone else might think that unchaste people are never ideal examples of fine people, because they are always rather selfish and/or always rather lacking in temperance and self-control. But I am inclined to think that none of these things is true, much less necessarily true. And in the light of such examples I am inclined to think that there is at best only a contingent relation between chastity and ideal fine personhood, even for those people who first claim to see a logical connection here.[27]

But let us imagine that I am mistaken about the relation between chastity and selfishness. Let us imagine that it *is* logically necessary to not being selfish that one be chaste. In that case, it will be those who think chastity is not logically necessary to paradigm fine personhood who will be mistaken. For clearly not being selfish *is* logically necessary to being an ideally fine person. Now it might perhaps turn out that chastity *was* logically necessary to a characteristic that everyone knew to be necessary to ideal fine personhood, even though most people did not know that this was so. For sometimes it is very difficult to be sure of all the logical relations of a term. But the heart of the matter is this. Either chastity is logically necessary to (something logically necessary to) paradigm fine personhood or it is not. If it is, then most sexual "liberals" are mistaken about chastity, and chastity is both a criterion of 'fine person' and part of the meaning of that term. If it is not, then there may be empirical reasons for thinking that no one who is unchaste can be a (perfect example of a) fine person, but chastity will not be a criterion or part of the meaning of 'fine person'. In either case, I think, 'fine person' can and will have a single meaning definable in terms of the MTIC. (And the same will, for similar reasons, be true of the other value terms that I have claimed can be defined via the MTIC.) The only problem that remains is whether chastity should be included in that definition. But the fact that it is sometimes difficult to complete definitions in terms of the MTIC is not, I think, any reason for dissatisfaction with that theory.

Of course, what I have just said may be totally wrong. It may be that value terms like 'fine person' have many meanings, because people do, in fact, make use of

---

[27] Of course, *some* people may persist in saying that the connection between chastity and paradigm fine-personhood exists independently of any empirical reasons they give for that connection. They may insist that the connection would exist even if God did not exist, etc. Such utterances, I think, need not always be taken at face value. I think it is perfectly reasonable to explain such tenacity by saying that certain persons' devotion to chastity is so deep-seated that they cannot psychologically admit to themselves the possibility that chastity might, under certain circumstances, not be of value. Any good theory of the linguistic usage of certain terms will have to discount at least some responses people make as being due to stubbornness, unimaginativeness, unintelligence, or psychological fixations.

different criteria of those terms. But so far we have seen no strong reason for thinking that this is so, and that the MTIC is untenable. And so I think we have some reason at least tentatively to accept the MTIC, to test it, and to see where it leads us. The relation between chastity and being a fine person may present certain problems for the MTIC; but it does not seem to present it with any insuperable difficulties.

3

The Rationality of Aesthetic Value Judgments

Philosophers, aestheticians, and others have often wondered whether one can ever make reasonable or objective aesthetic, or other, value judgments. Many have thought that one could, but many others have believed that in the fine arts (at least) *de gustibus non est disputandum*, have believed that when one judges a work of art—whether of poetry, music, literature, or sculpture—to be beautiful (good, subtle, or masterful) or to be more beautiful (good, subtle, or masterful) than some other work of art, one is not saying anything that can be objectively confirmed, verified, or supported in the way that claims in science and mathematics are. And, of course, such people have also held that similar judgments about or comparisons between artists, authors, composers, etc., are equally incapable of rational or objective support or confirmation.

Let us say that such people attack the *Thesis of Rationality in Aesthetics* (TRA, for short). In recent decades philosophers have attempted to defend or to attack the TRA by means of semantic considerations. Theories of the meaning of aesthetic, and other, value terms have been proposed as a means to enabling us to decide whether something like the TRA is true. Thus far, however, no such semantic theory has found general acceptance. And in the present paper I should like to try out another approach to the issue of our ability to make rational, reasonable, objective aesthetic value judgments. I shall argue that there are scientific explanatory reasons for believing in the TRA, and I shall do so independently of any particular theory about how

---

I am indebted to Ted Cohen, Sue Larson, David Levin, and Robert Shope for discussion of the ideas of this paper.

aesthetic and other value terms are to be defined or analyzed. In the end, though, I shall argue that the sort of argument for the TRA I shall be presenting suggests and to some degree supports a rather new sort of semantical theory about the meaning of aesthetic, and possibly other, value terms.

I

There are certain facts about the way human beings have over long periods of time responded to certain works of art and to certain artists (in the broadest sense of the term 'artist') that have not, as far as I can see, been given sufficient attention by those interested in the question of the reasonableness or objectivity of aesthetic, or other, value judgments. And I think that, if we seek a scientifically reasonable explanation of those facts, we shall be led to conclude that certain aesthetic value judgments can be objectively supported and are in fact worthy of our acceptance, so that the TRA is true.

The facts about human aesthetic responses to which I wish to call attention are these. In all the arts with which I am acquainted—music, drama, poetry, etc.—there exists a certain long-term unidirectionality with respect to changes in certain kinds of aesthetic preferences. Take, for example, the field of music. There are some pairs of composers such that many people prefer a given one of them to the other, at the same time that many other people have just the opposite preference. A good example of this might be the composers Brahms and Wagner. During the period when both were alive, and ever since, many people have liked Wagner's music more than the music of Brahms and many others have had just the contrary preference. Furthermore, many people start out with a tendency to prefer Wagner to Brahms, and then, later, after continued exposure to the music of both composers, come to prefer Brahms's music. But the preferences of many other people, it seems, change in just the opposite direction. There thus seems to be *no* unidirectionality of preference change with respect to the music of Brahms and Wagner.

Consider, on the other hand, how people tend to respond to the music of Mozart and Bruckner. Almost everyone who spends a good deal of time listening to music tends to prefer the music of Mozart to that of Bruckner. In speaking here of people who prefer the music of Mozart, however, I do not mean to imply that such people would *always* choose to listen to Mozart rather than Bruckner. One may on a given occasion prefer to listen to Bruckner because one has just been listening so much to Mozart or because one wants music to serve some purpose other than that of serious listening. In talking of people who prefer Mozart or like Mozart better, I mean something like: people who in general (apart from satiation, etc.) tend to prefer Mozart's music to Bruckner's music for serious listening. Of course, some people may well start out being very moved by and happy with the "bombast" or the "schmaltz" of Bruckner's music and consequently like his music more than the "tinkling" of Mozart. Perhaps there are people who stay this way, no matter how much they study or listen to music. But on the whole, the longer people are exposed to the music of these composers and to music in general and the more they learn about the purely technical aspects of music, the more there are who come to prefer Mozart, if they haven't liked Mozart better from the start. But does anyone ever during the first period of his acquaintance with classical music prefer Mozart to Bruckner, and then later, after much greater musical experience and study, come to the conclusion that Bruckner was really the greater or generally prefer Bruckner's music for serious listening? I doubt it. I think, in other words, that there is a unidirectionality of preference change with respect to Mozart and Bruckner that does not exist, say, with respect to Brahms and Wagner. The flow of musical appreciation and liking is from Bruckner to Mozart in general; and this is not just true today, but has been true for many, many years.[1] And it is this fact of (long-term) unidirectionality, and other facts like it with respect to other pairs of artists or of works of art, with which I shall be concerned here.

Such unidirectionality exists with respect to other pairs of composers, no doubt. Glinka and Beethoven, Bruch and Beethoven, Glinka and Bach, etc., provide some likely examples. But there is also unidirectionality in the other arts. It exists in poetry, for example, with respect to, say, Robert Southey or Leigh Hunt, on the one hand, and Keats, Wordsworth, or Yeats, on the other. And similarly, in the other arts. That there is such unidirectionality in various of the arts seems to be a noteworthy and an interesting fact. And it is a fact that calls for explanation.

When scientists attempt to explain a given fact or phenomenon, they generally consider various possible alternative explanations of the fact or phenomenon, and accept one of these explanations as correct only if it is clearly more reasonable, in terms of certain standards of scientific methodology and according to the available evidence, than any of the alternative explanations that they have been able to think up. And there are many possible explanations of why it is that unidirectionality of preference change exists with respect to (the music of) Mozart and Bruckner. One might claim that this unidirectionality was due to the fact that people are generally in some way brainwashed into preferring Mozart, or to the fact that something in the human psychological make-up influences people's aesthetic likes and dislikes in favor of Mozart. Or one might deny the existence of this sort of unidirectionality. But, assuming the existence of such unidirectionality, one explanation of it is of particular importance for our purposes here: the hypothesis, namely, that the more people study and are exposed to music, the more they like what is good in the field of music and the less they like what is mediocre or bad in the field of music, and that Mozart is, in fact, a greater, a finer, a better composer than Bruckner. If we could show that *this* explanation of the unidirectionality that exists with respect to (the music of) Mozart and Bruckner is superior to all its various alternatives and also show that it is unreasonable to deny the existence of that unidirectionality, we could perhaps show that there is good reason for us to think that certain particular aesthetic value judgments are true, and this would give us good reason to believe in the truth of the TRA.

Note, however, that in thus arguing for the TRA, we shall not necessarily show that ordinary people or students of the arts are reasonable or justified in liking (or coming to like) Mozart better than Bruckner or in thinking (or coming to think) that

---

[1] M. Scriven [*Primary Philosophy* (New York: McGraw-Hill, 1966), p. 65 f.] holds that agreement in preferences and unidirectionality of preference changes over a short period of time may well just indicate the domination of a single artistic or critical school. But with respect to Mozart and Bruckner the general agreement and unidirectionality have lasted for a long time and through different critical or artistic "dynasties."

Mozart is a greater composer than Bruckner. Ordinary people and students of music who think Mozart greater certainly sometimes give arguments to that effect, without mentioning (and, perhaps, while being unaware of) the Mozart-Bruckner unidirectionality I have been pointing out. I shall be arguing here that those of us (if any) who reasonably believe in such a unidirectionality can present an acceptable argument, of the sort to be outlined in the present paper, for thinking that it is reasonable to hold that Mozart is greater than Bruckner as part of the best explanation of that unidirectionality. If I can do this, then I shall have provided the readers of this paper with good reason to believe in the truth of the TRA, the Thesis of Rationality in Aesthetics, but it does not follow that those lacking the sort of argument to be presented here ever are reasonable in believing, or possess acceptable arguments for believing, either that Mozart is greater than Bruckner or that the TRA is true. I am not saying that those, for example, who argue for the superiority of Mozart to Bruckner on the basis of a comparison of the actual character of the two men's music present defective or unacceptable arguments; I am simply remaining neutral on that question.

Let us now proceed to the task at hand and consider some of the explanations of the fact of Mozart-Bruckner unidirectionality that do not posit any difference of aesthetic worth or value between the music of Mozart and the music of Bruckner. Take the hypothesis that the unidirectionality results from some sort of brainwashing of those who listen to music. Taken literally, this hypothesis is clearly unacceptable. We all know that brainwashing of the kind employed by the Chinese during the Korean War is hardly, if ever, used in non-Communist countries in shaping opinions about the arts. Assuming only the common-sense facts about the world that all of us think we know, all the evidence points to the implausibility of the hypothesis under consideration as an explanation of the fact of unidirectionality with regard to Mozart and Bruckner, or with regard to other artists or works of art.[2]

What, then, about something subtler than brainwashing: subliminal influencing of opinion, of the kind that sometimes has been used on television? Such an explanation is surely also implausible. A giant food company might try to influence the public subliminally so that people would want a certain food product, but who cares enough about whether people like Mozart better than Bruckner to pay the advertising costs of using television or radio to influence people by subliminal means to like Mozart better than Bruckner? But then consider the possibility that critics and other prestigious people pressure and "bamboozle" people into liking Mozart more than Bruckner. Surely there is some plausibility to this possible explanation of unidirectionality, for it is pretty obvious to common sense that prestigious and socially important men exercise an influence on public opinion that most men cannot. But is it really very plausible to say that what stops people from switching their preference from Mozart to Bruckner and gets many people to like Mozart better than Bruckner in the first

---

[2] For purposes of the present argument, I am assuming the correctness of our common-sense and scientific assumptions about the world. I hope to show that skepticism about the TRA reduces to skepticism about certain commonly held non-value assumptions and about certain general principles of scientific methodology. I have already, in my "Value Judgments and the Theory of Important Criteria" [this JOURNAL, XV, 4 (Feb. 22, 1968): 94–112, pp. 105–110], attempted to show that there is a valid distinction to be made between value and non-value judgments, or concepts.

place is, basically, just what is written and said by critics and teachers of music, or by people strongly influenced by such critics and teachers? This may be true of many people, but surely not of everyone. Some people, it seems clear, have tastes and minds of their own, and decide what they like pretty much on their own, even if they also pay attention to what critics have to say. The reader need only consider his own case (with respect to music, if he is interested in music; with respect to some other art, if he is not) to see that this is so. He should consider the comparative aesthetic preferences he has. Is it at all reasonable to assume that his preferences in all, or even most, such matters are due to the influence of critics, teachers, and the like? And if his own likings or preferences do not result from such influences, is it reasonable to assume that people's preferring, or coming to prefer, Mozart to Bruckner is always or even generally due to the pressure and influence of critics, etc.? People are not all like cattle in aesthetic matters, and it surely goes against what we know to maintain that musically trained and interested people always form their preference for Mozart over Bruckner primarily on the basis of the opinions of respected others.

Furthermore, even if everyone today did get his aesthetic preferences from critics and teachers, the question would still remain where the critics and teachers got their opinions and their preferences from. Eventually, we must come to a temporally first critic or group of critics whose aesthetic preference for Mozart over Bruckner cannot be attributed to the influence of earlier critics or teachers. Thus explanations in terms of teacher or critic influence will not explain why Mozart was originally preferred to Bruckner; and since we are trying to explain the existence of unidirectionality *in general,* and not just the existence of unidirectionality today, explanations in terms of critic or teacher influence seem to be inadequate for our purposes. One might, however, attempt to explain why critics and others originally tended to prefer Mozart to Bruckner in terms of the fact that Mozart preceded Bruckner, and already had great prestige at the time Bruckner lived and composed. But such a move can easily be blocked if one considers the unidirectionality that exists between Mozart and Cimarosa (a contemporary of Mozart's), instead of that between Mozart and Bruckner. And in the end, I think earlier prestige can really do very little toward explaining various long-standing unidirectionalities in the arts.

II

Consider, then, some other possible explanations of the Mozart-Bruckner unidirectionality. It could be claimed, for example, that most people who initially prefer Bruckner to Mozart and then change their preference do so as the result of being satiated with listening to Bruckner's music, not because Bruckner's music is inferior to Mozart's.[3] But such an explanation cannot explain why those who initially prefer the music of Mozart do not eventually come to like Bruckner's music better than Mozart's music or why those who come to like Mozart better do not eventually start to prefer Bruckner again. And so such an explanation cannot completely

---

[3] Cf. Scriven, *op. cit.,* p. 66 f.

explain the phenomenon of unidirectionality regarding Mozart and Bruckner as we have described it.

Nor does any specific *physiological* explanation of Mozart-Bruckner unidirectionality seem particularly appropriate or plausible. Some day such an explanation may become available, but certainly there is none available today. But, of course, it may still be plausible to hold that there is *some* physiological (or physiological-cum-psychological) explanation of the Mozart-Bruckner unidirectionality, even if we at this point do not know exactly what it is. And one might then claim that to say that there is some sort of physiological-cum-psychological explanation of that unidirectionality is in effect to offer a (vague) explanation of that phenomenon, and that such an explanation constitutes an alternative to the sort of explanation that attributes the Mozart-Bruckner unidirectionality to a difference in the value or greatness of the two artists, indeed an alternative that is no less acceptable than the latter sort of explanation.

One might reply to such an argument that to say that there is some explanation (of a very general kind) of a given phenomenon is not to offer a real explanation of that phenomenon. But I am disinclined to make use of such a reply. If one says of someone who dies that his death was caused by something entering his heart, what one has said is very general and fairly uninformative; but one has at least ruled out *certain* causes of his death, e.g., suffocation, so that what one says has some sort of explanatory function. So I am inclined to treat the above as some sort of (vague) explanation of a man's death and to treat the claim that Mozart-Bruckner unidirectionality is due to some sort of physiological-cum-psychological mechanism (as well as to the character of Mozart's and of Bruckner's music) as a very general and unspecific sort of explanation as well. After all, such a claim does rule out *some* possible explanations of that unidirectionality, e.g., that it is due to the influence of God or ghosts or the stars.

If so, how do we rule out such an explanation as inferior to the explanation of unidirectionality that claims that Mozart is superior to Bruckner as a composer, and that people generally tend to prefer better music the longer they are exposed to and interested in music? The answer, I think, is that we cannot rule out the former explanation, but that our argument for the TRA can go through nonetheless. For notice that the hypothesis that Mozart is better than Bruckner and that people tend to come to prefer what is better music is a specification of (a more specific way of holding) the hypothesis that we have been treating as one of its alternatives. It says, in effect, that the superiority of Mozart's music to Bruckner's and people's tendency to prefer the better in music, in the long run, are, respectively, *what it is* about Mozart's and Bruckner's music and *what it is* about people's physiology-cum-psychology that creates a unidirectionality with respect to these two composers. To say that most people come eventually to prefer what is better in music is to say, in effect, that people's physiological and psychological functioning tend to make them prefer what is musically better. To point out that Mozart is better than Bruckner is to pick a possible thing about the music of those two composers which, when interacting with the human physiology and psychology, brings about the Mozart-Bruckner unidirectionality. But if one accepts a certain general hypothesis, and thinks a certain specification of that hypothesis is superior to all others, one must in all rationality conclude (other things being equal) that

that more specific hypothesis is worthy of at least tentative belief. So if, in examining various other possible explanations of Mozart-Bruckner unidirectionality, we can find no plausible hypotheses that are also specifications of the very general hypothesis-explanation we have just been considering, we shall have provided reason for believing *both* that very general hypothesis *and* the specification of it that attributes Mozart-Bruckner unidirectionality to the musical superiority of Mozart. In other words, if those two hypotheses cannot be faulted and if all the alternatives to them can be faulted, we can vindicate *both* those hypotheses, and thus the TRA.

One line of explanation of Mozart-Bruckner unidirectionality that we have not yet considered would involve fastening on some quality or aspect of Mozart's music *other than* its sheer greatness, or its superiority to the music of Bruckner, that makes people tend to prefer it to the music of Bruckner. One might explain unidirectionality, for example, by saying that Mozart is subtler (or more disciplined) than Bruckner and that, of any two composers, more people will prefer or like the subtler (or more disciplined) of them the more they are exposed to music. But is this really all that plausible? Many people would grant that Vivaldi or Richard Strauss was a subtler composer than Beethoven, and yet it is surely not the case that there is a Beethoven-Vivaldi unidirectionality *in favor of Vivaldi*. We must either hold that Vivaldi (or Strauss) is not a subtler composer than Beethoven after all—and perhaps risk identifying subtlety with greatness—or give up trying to explain Mozart-Bruckner unidirectionality solely in terms of subtlety. And the same goes with the quality of disciplinedness. The point is that subtlety, discipline, humor, etc., are only some of the qualities people look for in music, and so we cannot plausibly explain why there is a unidirectionality favoring Mozart over Bruckner in terms of subtlety, discipline, or humor, alone.

One might, at this point, attempt to salvage things by explaining Mozart-Bruckner unidirectionality in terms of the fact that Mozart is subtler than Bruckner and that people tend to prefer what is subtler *other things being equal*. But in what sense are other things equal between Mozart and Bruckner? The music of the two men is certainly not alike in all respects save subtlety, nor in all those qualities (except for subtlety) that people tend to look for in musical works. And if what is meant by 'other things equal', here, is that, aside from subtlety, Mozart's music is at least as good as Bruckner's, then one's hypothesis will be committed to a value judgment just as clearly as the hypothesis I am endeavoring to support here, in which case one would not need to choose between the two hypotheses in order to vindicate the TRA. For to rationally support their disjunction as an explanation of Mozart-Bruckner unidirectionality would be to support an aesthetic value judgment, albeit of a weak kind, as an explanation of that phenomenon.

However, consider the explanation of Mozart-Bruckner unidirectionality that claims that that unidirectionality is the result of the fact that Mozart is worse than Bruckner as a composer and that people tend to like what is worse in music the longer they study music. We could not so easily disjoin this explanation of unidirectionality with those just mentioned and have something that could be used to support the TRA. Indeed, if this explanation cannot be ruled out, our attempt to vindicate the TRA is in trouble. But consider how one would go about explaining the fact that people in the long run tend to prefer what is musically inferior to what is musically superior. The only half-way plausible explanation I can think of is that people tend to become more irrational about or ignorant of music in the long run. And this further explanation is indeed implausible, because it says that something happens in music that happens in (almost?) no other field of human endeavor and interest. In other areas, in carpentry, mathematics, biology, etc., people don't at all tend to become more irrational and less knowledgeable about their discipline or vocation in the long run. Just the reverse, if anything. But it is unreasonable, from a scientific standpoint, to hold that people are affected in one way in certain areas and in a different way in another area, unless one has a definite reason for thinking that this should be so. Since we have absolutely no reason to posit such a difference between music and areas like carpentry, biology, and mathematics, it is, I think, unreasonable to hold that people tend to become more irrational and less knowledgeable about music the longer they are exposed to and study music. And in that case we cannot give any reasonable explanation of why people should tend to prefer inferior music in the long run. The hypothesis I am attempting to support says that people tend to prefer better music the longer they study and are exposed to music; and this fact *can be* plausibly explained, namely, in terms of the fact that people become more knowledgeable about music the longer they are interested in music. What follows, then, is that the hypothesis that Mozart is worse than Bruckner and people tend to prefer the worse in the long run contains as a part of itself an assumption about human nature that cannot at least at this time be plausibly explained, whereas this is not true of the hypothesis we are trying to support; and this is a definite reason for favoring the latter hypothesis over the former, and for discarding that former hypothesis, at least tentatively.[4]

It should be pointed out, finally, that one might try to explain unidirectionality with respect to Mozart and Bruckner without making any commitments about what is good or bad in music, by attempting to list all the characteristics (other than goodness, greatness, and the like) that people tend to look for or dislike in music and explain Mozart-Bruckner unidirectionality in terms of that whole list of characteristics. That is, if the characteristics on the list turned out to be $a, b, c, \ldots n$, then one might say: unidirectionality exists with respect to Mozart and Bruckner, because Mozart's music has a, b, etc., and Bruckner's music c, d, etc., and people tend to prefer music with a, b, etc., to music with c, d, etc., in the long run. But notice two things about such an explanation. It would be difficult, if not impossible, for us now to compose a list of all desired and disliked musical characteristics, so that such an explanation of unidirectionality is really not available to us at present. And secondly, many of the characteristics on the list would be value characteristics. Any list of the characteristics people like or dislike in music would have to include subtlety, creativity, sublimity, effective handling of transitions, profundity, etc., and their opposites—even if it could avoid such more overarching characteristics as greatness, inferiority, and goodness. But at least some of this first group are value qualities whose objective applicability would be questioned by those who deny the

---

[4] This argument is based on scientific reasoning of a sort discussed in my *Reason and Scepticism* (London: Allen & Unwin, 1970), chaps. 3 and 5, esp. pp. 103–105, 161 f.

TRA. So perhaps we do not need to rule out explanations of unidirectionality in terms of the above sort of complete list of musically desired and disliked characteristics in order to support the TRA. And this will become even more apparent, perhaps, if one considers how one would at present have to explain the fact that people in the long run tend to prefer music with a, b, etc., to music with c, d, etc. If one seeks to explain Mozart-Bruckner unidirectionality in terms of certain characteristics that Mozart's music has and Bruckner's lacks and vice versa, one is still left with the question why people prefer music with the particular characteristics a, b, etc., of Mozart's music to music with the particular characteristics c, d, etc., of Bruckner's music, in the long run. And I think the only explanation we have examined thus far that has not already been seen to be implausible and that can provide some sort of plausible specific explanation of our present explanandum is just that music with a, b, etc., is superior to music with c, d, etc., and that in the long run people tend to prefer what is better in music. If so, we have, again, good reason to explain Mozart-Bruckner unidirectionality in terms of the musical superiority of the former, and thus to believe the TRA.

III

Unless we doubt the very existence of such a unidirectionality. After all, how can we be sure that people in general prefer Mozart and do not switch their preferences from Mozart to Bruckner after long exposure to and study of music? No one has ever taken a diachronic statistical survey of people's likes and dislikes regarding Mozart and Bruckner, at least as far as I know. And it is also true that we have no way of knowing *for sure* that unidirectionality of the sort I have been discussing exists with respect to Mozart and Bruckner. But given what I have seen people say about Mozart and about Bruckner, and given what I have seen about the way people's musical preferences vary and change over time and as a result of greater study of music, I believe that there is good reason to believe in Mozart-Bruckner unidirectionality as I have described it. Of course, I have been referring to *my* evidence and to what *I* have noticed over the years. Presumably, some readers will not have the sort of evidence I am claiming to have, and will as a result, perhaps, be unwilling to accept the argument of the present paper. But most people interested in music who read this paper will, I think, have the sort of evidence for unidirectionality that I have claimed to have. After all, it is pretty much a commonplace among people who are interested in and study music that people when first exposed to music tend to prefer the "schmaltzy," the "romantic," and the "bombastic" and then later, after devoting a great deal of time to music, tend to be disenchanted with such music and to prefer the subtlety, discipline, and inventiveness of a Bach or Mozart. I have never heard of anyone after lengthy study deciding that Bruckner is a greater composer than Mozart, nor do I think that most musically experienced and interested readers of this paper will have heard of such a case, and if this is so, they will, I hope, be willing to join me in accepting the (reasonableness of the) assumption that Mozart-Bruckner unidirectionality exists.

On the other hand, even if there very infrequently occurs a case of a person who comes to prefer Bruckner to Mozart after lengthy musical training or study, the very infrequency of such a conversion will perhaps permit the argument of the present paper to go through, nonetheless. For even if there are such cases, one will still have to explain why changes of preference vis-à-vis Mozart and Bruckner *almost always* go in favor of Mozart, and the explanations we have discarded above will for similar reasons presumably have to be discarded as explanations of the almost-total-unidirectionality that exists with regard to Mozart and Bruckner. Finally, those who are unwilling to accept that there is even an almost-total-unidirectionality with regard to Mozart and Bruckner, because they do not know of such a unidirectionality on their own and are unwilling to trust someone else's word for it, may still know of some *other* unidirectionality in some other aesthetic area or with regard to two other composers (or works of music). And if they do, they can use an argument parallel to that of the present paper to establish the TRA, even if they cannot accept the particular argument for the TRA we have given here.

Of course, someone might also challenge the argument, based on scientific methodology, for the TRA that we have given here on the grounds that the explanation of Mozart-Bruckner unidirectionality that we attempted to support involves a value notion, and that value notions like aesthetic superiority or aesthetic goodness cannot legitimately be used to explain various phenomena. But, in the first place, there seem to be no reasons deriving from common sense or ordinary usage why such value notions, and judgments making use of them, should not be used in explaining things. If one were in a situation where a given teacher was known to have been guilty of favoritism toward one of his pupils p, it would sound perfectly natural and seem perfectly reasonable to say: last time, p got the highest mark because teacher t liked him best, but this time he got the highest mark because he did better than any of the other students; t was no longer playing favorites, because he had been warned by the principal against doing so. Of course, someone might reply to this sort of example that the only legitimate explanation of the student's getting the highest mark the second time around would be that the teacher t *believed* his paper to be better than all the others. But why should we take such a reply to heart unless it rests on some acceptable argument for the view that the TRA is false, perhaps an argument based on some semantical theory of value terms that entails that such terms cannot be reasonably or objectively applied? As far as I know, no one has produced any such convincing, generally accepted, acceptable argument. There are well-known major flaws in emotivism as a theory of the meaning of value terms, and in all known arguments against the TRA that are based on the "facts" of the diversity of values and the irresolvability of various value conflicts. And assuming, as I wish to do here, that there are no solid arguments against the TRA available at present, the argument from scientific methodology and explanation of the present paper provides, I believe, a reason for thinking that aesthetic value concepts can legitimately be used in explanations and are even needed to provide the best explanation of various phenomena, in which case we have reason to believe that the Thesis of Rationality in Aesthetics is true. We have argued, in other words, that, in the absence of any good reasons to deny the rational supportability of aesthetic value claims, there are, on scientific methodological grounds, good reasons to believe that certain aesthetic value claims are rationally supportable (by us) as parts of hypotheses that provide the best explanations of certain unidirectionalities.[5] What would make our whole line of reasoning even more plausible, however, would be some sort of positive theory of the meaning of aesthetic value terms, in terms of which we could see *why* emotivism, etc., were mistaken and could understand *why* aesthetic value concepts can have just as legitimate an explanatory use as various non-value concepts clearly have. And I should like now to sketch the beginnings of such an explicit semantic theory.

IV

I believe that many aesthetic (and other) value properties are dispositional properties, and that many aesthetic (and other) value terms have much the same sort of meaning as such scientific and common-sense dispositional terms as 'soluble', 'brittle', 'magnetic', and 'flexible'. To say that something is flexible, for example, is not just to say that it is physically possible to bend it. What will bend only under extraordinarily great pressure is not flexible. Similarly, to say that something is aesthetically good (or great) is to say more than that it can be desired by someone with aesthetic interests. For what is desired by someone who is upset, irrational, jaded, uninformed, or unsophisticated may not be good. To be flexible is to have the disposition to bend, or flex, in *appropriate circumstances;* and similarly, for a work of art to have aesthetic value or be aesthetically good is for it to have the disposition to be responded to by desire to behold (or read or hear, etc.) it and liking for it in *appropriate* beings in *appropriate* circumstances. (Since appropriate beings can be thought of as part and parcel of appropriate circumstances, we shall henceforth speak only of appropriate circumstances.) Also, for one work x to be aesthetically preferable or superior to another work y is for the pair of works x and y to have the disposition to be responded to by greater liking for x than for y in appropriate circumstances.

Dispositional properties can be brought in to explain various phenomena. If flexibility were just the physical capability of bending, or the physical possibility of being bent, one might not be able to give an informative explanation of a given instance of bending in terms of flexibility. But something may bend (be bent) without being flexible and for reasons having little to do with flexibility, e.g., because it was subjected to an enormous force of some kind; and so to say that something bent because it was flexible (and was subjected to an ordinary sort of force of the right kind) is to offer only one out of many possible explanations of such bending, and is thus to make a genuine, informative, and possibly mistaken explanation of a phenomenon, an explanation that in certain situations may reasonably be held to be correct. Similarly, we can meaningfully and informatively explain why someone exposed to two aesthetic objects prefers one of them to the other in terms of the aesthetic superiority or preferability of the preferred object, because there are alternative explanations

---

[5] Incidentally, we have been attempting here to explain certain unidirectionalities in musical preferences or comparative likings. But as far as I can tell, we could also have talked about the unidirectionalities that exist regarding people's *opinions* about the aesthetic merit of Mozart's and Bruckner's music, and have attempted to explain why people in the long run tend to think Mozart superior to Bruckner in terms of Mozart's actually being superior to Bruckner as a composer.

of the preference, e.g., that the preferred object was inferior but more flamboyant, that the person who preferred it was an artistic neophyte, and that neophytes tend to prefer the flamboyant, regardless of quality. And in some cases, as indeed we have already argued earlier in this paper, the most reasonable available explanation of the (general and long-run tendency toward) preference of one aesthetic object or set of objects over another will be that the preferred object or set of objects is superior to, has greater aesthetic value than, the object or set of objects to which it is preferred.

Of course, to say that aesthetic value or goodness or greatness, etc., is the disposition to be responded to by liking, etc., in appropriate circumstances is hardly to offer a definition of the notion of aesthetic value, etc. One cannot, after all, define being a brother as: being a sibling of an appropriate kind. One might be able to define aesthetic value, etc., if one could replace 'in appropriate circumstances' with something more informative and complete, but this is a notoriously difficult thing to do. Of course, the same problem seems to exist for most ordinary and scientific dispositional concepts. We cannot *define* flexibility as the disposition to bend in appropriate circumstances; and if we tried to define flexibility by attempting to state explicitly just what circumstances are appropriate to (the testing or existence of) flexibility, we would probably never be able to complete our definition.[6] And the same may be true of such notions as aesthetic value or preferability or greatness, etc.

Actually, as far as I can tell, it might even be possible to define both value and non-value dispositional qualities *without* having to spell out in detail the conditions appropriate to their existence or their being verified and in a way compatible with what I am saying here (though the exploration of that possibility must, unfortunately, be left to another occasion). In any case, whether dispositional qualities (or concepts) are definable or not, I think we all have a great deal of implicit knowledge about what circumstances are and are not appropriate to their existence (or applicability). We know, for example, that something must be bendable under less than enormous pressure in order to be flexible, and that something must be capable of being desired or liked by aesthetic non-neophytes in order to be a great work of art. And it should be noted, further, that the kinds of circumstances relevant to aesthetic value, preferability, etc., are very close to those mentioned in "ideal observer" definitions of aesthetic and other value terms.[7] For to be desired in appropriate circumstances involves, approximately, being desired by those calm, reasonable, knowledgeable, unsatiated, unjaded beings who are acquainted with the thing in question. The theory about value concepts being sketched here might well be considered a version of the Ideal Observer theory, though one which differs from previous versions in emphasizing that aesthetic goodness, e.g., is a disposition of the object that has that quality, rather than of possible ideal observers, and in stressing the *explanatory* role and significance of attributions of value properties like aesthetic goodness.

People sometimes support the claim that some work of art is good or great in terms of further claims to the effect that the work of art in question is subtle, well-organized,

---

[6] Cf. my "A General Solution to Goodman's Riddle?", *Analysis*, xxix.2, 128 (December 1968): 55–58, p. 56f.

[7] See Roderick Firth, "Ethical Absolutism and the Ideal Observer," *Philosophy and Phenomenological Research*, XII, 3 (March 1952): 317–345.

etc. If such arguments are (ever) sound, it is, presumably, because subtlety, (good) organization, etc., sometimes (causally) contribute to the aesthetic value or goodness of certain works of art. It is, of course, well known that an object's various common-sense or scientific dispositions (causally) depend on various of its other features or traits. The flexibility of a given thing may (causally) depend on certain aspects of its microstructure, and those aspects of its microstructure may (causally) contribute to its flexibility. And, similarly, I think it is reasonable to believe that the aesthetic value or goodness of works of art will (causally) depend on certain other features of those works. Particular claims about which features of certain art works it is that (causally) contribute to their possession of value dispositions like aesthetic goodness, etc., may, of course, be mistaken; but on an analogy with flexibility, it seems reasonable to maintain that whenever works of art have aesthetic value dispositions, certain other features of those works—presumably, different features for different works—contribute to the existence of those dispositions. Of course, it may well be the case that a quality like subtlety sometimes contributes to aesthetic value, but sometimes *detracts from* aesthetic value. (Wouldn't a subtler *Guernica* have been less effective?) But there is no disanalogy here with ordinary dispositional qualities. Chlorine contributes to the toxicity (or inedibleness) of certain chemical combinations, but to the nontoxicity (or edibleness) of salt—the other element in salt, sodium, also being toxic or inedible. And clearly toxicity and edibleness are dispositional traits of things.

However, I would like explicitly to mention one interesting difference between most explanatory uses of dispositional concepts *like flexibility* and our earlier use of the notion of aesthetic superiority in explaining certain unidirectionalities. For, typically, when we explain bending in terms of flexibility, we assume that the thing that bends is in the circumstances "appropriate" to flexibility; but in assuming that the unidirectionality, say, with respect to Mozart and Bruckner is to be explained in terms of the superiority of Mozart as a composer, we do not and should not assume that those whose preferences change with regard to Mozart and Bruckner are in the circumstances "appropriate" to aesthetic superiority, or are "ideal aesthetes." In explaining unidirectionalities in terms of certain claims of aesthetic superiority, we are in essence explaining the way people's preferences change as they get closer to being "ideal aesthetes" in terms of the disposition or power, on the part of certain aesthetic objects, to affect the preferences of "ideal aesthetes." But this is no odder than explaining why the molecular motion in certain bodies diminishes as they get colder in terms of the disposition or tendency of all matter to have its molecular motion cease at a certain coldest point (absolute zero).

In bringing out the parallels between aesthetic value terms and run-of-the-mill common-sense or scientific dispositional terms, we have in effect been arguing for a certain kind of naturalism with respect to aesthetic value terms. I am inclined to think, furthermore, that the theory we have been outlining is appropriate not only with respect to various important aesthetic value terms (or concepts), but also with respect to such other value notions as: worthwhileness, desirability, a good life, what ought to be done, etc. And before proceeding any further, I would like to mention one rather striking piece of linguistic evidence for the naturalistic dispositional theory of aesthetic (and possibly other) value terms (or concepts) that I have been proposing. It is the fact that words like 'desirable' and 'preferable' have the same 'ble' ending that words like 'flexible' and 'soluble' have. For a long time, philosophers have thought of this fact as indicating an ambiguity in 'ble' endings. Mill in *Utilitarianism*, for example, is supposed to have confused the 'ble' of 'desirable', which supposedly means "*worthy* of being desired," with the 'ble' of 'visible', which supposedly means "*able* to be seen." If the theory proposed here is correct, there really is not so great a difference or gap between visibility and desirability as Mill's critics have supposed, and the 'ble' endings of 'visible' and 'desirable' may be much closer in meaning than they have thought. And, indeed, the fact that the same 'ble' ending is used, say, in both 'flexible' and 'desirable' (or 'preferable') is some evidence for our theory, since, other things being equal, it is better to explain such similarities in linguistic expression as due to similarities in underlying concepts, rather than as due to linguistic coincidence or accident.

It is worth noting that the naturalism proposed here for certain aesthetic (and possibly other) value terms is compatible with such terms' having emotive or evaluative meaning. For, as I argued in "Value Judgments and the Theory of Important Criteria" (pp. 105 ff.), the evaluative or emotive meaning of value terms consists in a Gricean-type conventional but nonlogical implication of certain assertorial uses of such terms. 'Desirable' or 'has value' is possessed of emotive meaning because, in saying that something is desirable or has value, one conventionally implies (but is not logically committed to saying) that one has a pro-attitude toward the thing called desirable or valuable, unless some disclaimer is made or is already implicitly understood. So I think that the possession of emotive meaning is consistent with naturalism with respect to a given term or set of terms; and, in particular, I think such terms as 'aesthetically good', etc., both possess emotive meaning and can be understood naturalistically. Indeed, I think what makes terms like 'aesthetically good' value terms, in a way that 'flexible', 'soluble', etc., are not, is just the possession of (pro or con) emotive or evaluative meaning of the sort just mentioned.

Obviously, there is much more disagreement about the application of such terms (or notions) as 'aesthetically good' and 'aesthetically preferable' than there is about such terms (or notions) as 'flexible'. But I can see no reason why one should not be able to explain this fact within the framework of naturalism, especially with reference to the differences in the "appropriate circumstances" that are relevant to value and non-value dispositional terms. And in any case, there clearly *can* be difficulty in knowing whether to apply a non-value dispositional term like 'flexible', just as there so often is difficulty in being sure about the applicability of dispositional value terms. There is much more to be said about such matters, but, unfortunately, there is no time to say it here.

In conclusion, then, our theory of the meaning of terms like 'aesthetically good' and 'aesthetically superior' enables us to understand how such terms might, in certain circumstances, be reasonably and "objectively" applied in explaining certain phenomena; and our earlier argument purports to bring out a particular phenomenon that indeed *is* most reasonably explained in terms of such a value-laden explanation. Thus the present paper not only provides an argument, based on considerations of scientific explanatory methodology, for the TRA, but also presents a theory of the meaning of certain value terms (the nature of certain value concepts) that gives us a deeper understanding of *why* the TRA is a reasonable philosophical thesis.

4

Inapplicable Concepts

I

I shall argue here that the ordinary notions of a monster and of an unnatural (or perverted) act are for similar reasons inapplicable to reality, and shall offer an explanation of how such inapplicable concepts come to be frequently used.[1]

Whatever else a monster is, it has to be terrifying or frightening. And monsters may also have to be (relatively) large. Most of us think that if creatures like those described in certain stories had actually existed, monsters would have actually existed. But do those creatures, imagined as actually existent, differ from dinosaurs like tyrannosaurus rex in any respect relevant to monster status? It appears not, and yet we do not think of dinosaurs as monsters. It is part of the modern world view that there never have been monsters, any more than wood nymphs or elves. Nor would scientists or other educated people call a creature a monster, if it today emerged from a dinosaur egg left frozen from the Cretaceous Period. The creature would be a dinosaur of a certain kind, no more, no less. Now it is puzzling that dinosaurs are not monsters, since they seem as appropriately monsterlike as many story-book monsters. Of course, someone might deny this and claim that dinosaurs are not rich enough in such 'monster-making' properties as voraciousness, sliminess, malevolence, and invulnerability to count as real monsters. But this view has the implausible implication that many putative story-book monsters, who are no richer in monster-making properties

---

[1] I am indebted to many people for helpful comments on this paper, but especially to Saul Kripke, David Lewis, and Thomas Nagel.

than the tyrannosaurus rex, are only mistakenly thought of as monsters. And it also implies that if certain dinosaurs had through evolution become sufficiently rich in monster-making properties, then some dinosaurs would have *developed into* monsters. And this seems inconsistent with our idea of what a monster is.

I think our reluctance to call dinosaurs monsters comes from our belief that they have a determinate (specific) biological place in nature. The monsters of stories—and here I may be using quantification loosely—do not have a really determinate biology or place in some natural order. It is well known that facts about fictional entities are often left indeterminate. And even if various monster stories represent certain creatures as having a determinate physiology, evolution, etc., there never is any specific physiology, evolution, etc., of which it can be truly said: "this is the physiology, evolution, etc., that the monster of this story has."[2]

This gives the sense in which story-book monsters lack a determinate (biological) nature. And I think only such a creature can be a monster. For that reason, if all the descriptions of some story-book monster had been, or turned out to be, realized in some actual creature (with an exotic biology), that creature would have as determinate a biological nature and as little claim to be a monster as a dinosaur has.[3]

Gila monsters and 'moral monsters' like Hitler are not, I think, literally monsters in the sense of the term under consideration. But it might be said that I am mistaken in thinking that 'monster' is inapplicable, because various mutants and deformed creatures represent actual examples of monsters. Now I think that various mutants and the like count as monsters in a technical biological sense of the term. But those 'enlightened' people who believe there are no monsters (in Loch Ness or elsewhere) are usually not ignorant of or sceptical about the existence of mutants (like two-headed calves or bulls). They are using 'monster' in a 'story-book' sense that does not apply to such creatures, and indeed most dictionaries distinguish (at least) two senses of 'monster' in this way.[4]

It is my belief that at least part of the ordinary meaning of 'monster' is: '(large) terrifying creature that lacks a determinate (biological) nature', or, for brevity, '(large)

---

[2] Saul Kripke has suggested that phrases like 'in this story (world)' can be treated as sentential or predicate operators, on the model of modal operators. And 'in this story creature *a* has a determinate biological nature' does not obviously entail 'there is a determinate biological nature *x* such that creature *a* has *x* in this story'. *If* a storybook monster is biologically determinate *in* the world of its story, then it is not, on our view, a monster *in* that story (world). (Consider that in that world some philosopher could arrive at the conclusion that the creature in question was not a monster via the very arguments we use in the actual world to show that dinosaurs are not monsters.) If a storyteller calls such a creature a monster, this description may not be internally accurate to the world of the story and may simply be a way of telling the reader how he or she is entitled to think of the creature *from the point of view of the actual world*.

[3] Here I have ignored the possibility of acausal creatures, since acausality seems in no way to help make a creature a monster. Incidentally, I am leaving open the possibility that something should have a determinate biological *nature* without being determinate in every respect. Thus my talk of determinacy of nature has been left somewhat vague. But it can at least be said that if a story-book creature is (described as) a tyrannosaurus rex, its nature is determinate enough so that the creature is not a story-book *monster*—even if other facts about it are left indeterminate.

[4] I think 'monster' cannot be an applicable epistemic term, roughly equivalent to 'terrifying creature whose nature is unknown', for it seems incompatible with our ordinary idea of a monster that something could become or cease to be a monster without undergoing any so-called internal or intrinsic alterations.

terrifying unnatural creature'. Since no actual creature could lack a determinate nature, the ordinary concept of a monster is inapplicable in principle to non-fiction reality.

How, then, do we explain the fact that if a person who had never heard of dinosaurs were to come across one while strolling alone in the mountains, he might well think of it as a monster to be feared? The answer, I think, is that such uses of the term are largely a reflection of terror (fear) and ignorance. It is necessary that anything in the natural world with us have a determinate (biological) nature. And because it is easy to think of 'unnatural' as meaning 'not in nature (with us)', the idea of not being in nature (with us) is what might be called an overtone of the notion of unnaturalness as we have defined it: namely, an idea that is logically implied by and tends to be associated with that notion of unnaturalness. In saying that a creature is unnatural and lacks a determinate nature, one may, then, in effect be expressing the thought that that creature is not in nature with us.[5] And, of course, when one is frightened of something, one would like to be able to think of it as not in nature with one, as outside one's world, and thus as no longer a threat. It is my speculation, then, that calling a creature a monster involves, or would involve, a kind of 'whistling in the dark' that psychologists call 'denial'. One denies the existence of danger, by thinking of a creature as a monster that is in effect outside one's world, in order to alleviate one's fear of a given creature. What one does is much like what one does when, in frightening or unhappy circumstances, one says, with momentary belief or hope: "I must be dreaming all this".

Of course, in calling a given creature an unnatural monster, one's description cannot in principle apply, on our theory. But on any depth-psychological account of such matters, one will not realize the inapplicability of one's description, and one's claim that a certain creature is a monster will at most be the expression of a necessarily false *unconscious* or *subconscious* belief that that creature is not in nature with one and thus no threat. But such an unconscious belief could function to alleviate or repress one's fear of the creature in question in a way that true beliefs, under the circumstances, could not. If this psychological picture is on the right track, then our claim that there cannot be non-fiction monsters is not tarnished by the fact that *terrified* ignorant[6] people would tend to apply 'monster' to certain actual creatures.[7]

In 'Naming and Necessity,'[8] Saul Kripke has argued for a view about species terms according to which it is impossible for there to be (non-fiction) unicorns, because there is no definite biological nature attributable to any unicorn(s). But these facts, he claims, are to be ascertained empirically. On our theory, 'monster' is no

---

[5] However, non existence in nature (with us) does not, in turn, entail indeterminacy of nature, since a story could give a determinate nature to some purely imaginary creature by specifying, for example, that it was a tyrannosaurus rex.

[6] Presumably, someone knowledgeable about dinosaurs would not think of one as a monster even if he confronted it in a dangerous situation. It is hard to think of something as unnatural when one knows its nature.

[7] For classic psychoanalytic use of the idea that unconscious beliefs can help repress certain fears, see, e.g., Freud's 'Splitting of the Ego in the Defensive Process' in his *Collected Papers*, Hogarth Press, London, 1956, vol. 5, pp. 372–75; and O. Fenichel's *The Psychoanalytic Theory of Neurosis*, Norton, N. Y., 1945, pp. 474–84.

[8] In Davidson and Harman, eds., *Semantics of Natural Language*, Reidel, Dordrecht, 1972, esp. p. 763f.

species term, and since it is analytic that there is no definite biology attributable to any monster(s), it can be known a priori that there can be no non-fiction monsters. The two views are similar, however, in their reliance on the fact that there is no determinate biology attributable to certain sorts of creatures in stories.

II

I shall now argue that the notion of an unnatural act (and of sexual perversion) is inapplicable in much the same way that the concept monster is. (For that reason, our arguments about these different concepts will be mutually reinforcing.) Philosophers have long been perplexed about what is meant by calling an act or behavior unnatural. In calling a (sexual) act unnatural, we are not just saying that it is wrong, since even those who condemn adultery do not call it unnatural. Nor is an unnatural act simply an unusual or incomprehensible one. Certain feats of sexual prowess, for example, are thought of as unusual, but not as unnatural. Since even believing Christians do not think of adultery as unnatural, unnatural acts cannot just be acts contravening the natural order of sexual morality instituted by God. Nor, finally, should we be led into the swamps of teleology to think of unnatural acts as being those that go against the purpose of sex. Even if it makes sense to suppose that there is a purpose to sex, namely, procreation, it will be hard for any teleological theory to explain how anyone could think that oral-genital sex, as part of the build-up to coitus, was any more unnatural than kissing, as part of that build-up.

My own view is that the notion of an unnatural act is inapplicable and, like the idea of a monster, only gets used through people's fear and ignorance. The words 'unnatural act' express horror just as strongly as the term 'monster' expresses terror. To say that an act is unnatural is to say, in effect, that it is outside of nature, or our world. And such a claim cannot in principle be true.

The acts we call unnatural horrify us, but why should that make us put them outside our world, beyond the pale, as it were? Idiots are pretty horrifying too, but they are not called unnatural. The difference here may be that the kinds of acts people call unnatural are those that most people have some impulse towards that they cannot admit to having. If we are to believe depth psychology, most of us have inside us at some level, desires for incest, homosexuality, and even one or another form of fetishism. But these are the kinds of impulses people almost never, without undergoing therapy, admit having anything to do with. Sexual behavior for which we ourselves have repressed impulses is typically what gets called unnatural. It is thereby thought of as banished to another world than ours, and this helps reassure us that the impulse towards such behavior is not *in us*. There is no such need to keep repressed and disarmed the thought that we have elements of idiocy within, for there is no literal idiocy in most of us, and most of us know that. Similarly, we do not call adultery unnatural, because even those who think it wrong are usually willing to admit (to themselves) that they have some desires in that direction. But desires for incest, etc., typically are repressed and so threatening that drastic means will, if necessary, be used to keep those desires unconscious. The use of inapplicable concepts is certainly drastic enough. But I think that one's claim that certain behavior is unnatural will at most be the expression of a necessarily false *unconscious* belief that that behavior is not in the world with one, and one will not consciously realize the inapplicability of one's description. And such a 'drastic' unconscious belief is one very effective means by which a person can and does defuse the thought, and allay the fear, that such behavior is something he deep down desires. Thus in saying that certain behavior is unnatural, we give ourselves the 'message' that certain behavioral tendencies are not in the world with us, and so not in us, and this helps to repress these very tendencies. Of course, in saying all this, I have used depth-psychological assumptions that will seem suspect to some people. But I also think that the most important parts of our psychological arguments can be made independent of abstruse psychological theorizing and based simply on common-sense insight about human nature.

It would seem, finally, that the ordinary notion of perversion involves the idea of unnaturalness. Perverted sexual behavior is by definition unnatural sexual behavior, and since the latter notion is inapplicable, so is the former.[9] And when we call certain behavior perverted, in the ordinary sense, we express and counteract our impulses and fears in much the same way that we do when we call behavior unnatural. Of course, the terms 'perverted' and 'perversion' also occur in psychiatric and psychoanalytic writings. But if those terms express (a) valid applicable concept(s) in such contexts, that is, I believe, only because they are used there in a technical way. In their ordinary sense, use of those terms expresses horror, because it is tied to the notion of unnatural behavior. But technical usage of 'perverted' does not express horror, because, I believe, such usage does not involve the idea of unnaturalness. Psychiatrists presumably understand and are unafraid of 'perverted behavior' more than most people, so on our theory they have less motive or need to call such behavior unnatural than most people have.[10] And what also supports the idea that technical usage of 'perverted' does not involve the idea of unnaturalness is the fact that those professionals who speak of perversions (almost) never seem to speak of unnatural behavior in any technical or non-technical sense. Of course, we have not specified the actual content of the (a?) technical psychiatric concept of perversion, and this would be difficult to do. But whatever its full delineation, such a technical notion presumably at least involves the idea of deviation from some favored explanatorily rich ideal-typic model of the development of human sexual motivation. In any event, we have in this paper seen how the ordinary notions of perversion, unnatural behavior, and monster could come to be frequently used in everyday life despite their inapplicability in principle to the actual, non-fiction world.[11]

---

[9] Even those who think the notion of perversion applies seem to believe that perversion entails unnaturalness. See T. Nagel's 'Sexual Perversion', *Journal of Philosophy* 66, 1969, 5f. One problem with Nagel's account of perversion, incidentally, is that it leaves unexplained why so many people think of homosexuality as a perversion.

[10] That is also why psychologically educated people do not usually speak of homosexuality and the like as unnatural acts.

[11] There may be other inapplicable concepts related to the ones we have discussed. Some possibly inapplicable concepts that I think deserve exploration are: 'uncanny', 'eerie', 'freak', and 'obscene'.

5

Morality and Ignorance

In this essay, I shall attempt to establish a philosophically interesting connection between obligation and valid morality, on the one hand, and (not) acting out of ignorance, on the other.* Consider the following formal principle:

> A principle has validity as a basic principle of moral obligation only if it is possible for people to be committed to it as one of their basic principles of moral obligation without that commitment being due to, or explainable in terms of, their being ignorant, or being kept ignorant, of various facts.

The above principle expresses, in a rough way, the particular connection between morality and ignorance that I shall argue for. I believe that it constitutes a valid formal condition on the validity (or truth) of a certain class of moral principles, and is in part constitutive of our common sense of morality. I shall begin by explicating and clarifying the above principle. I shall then indicate various different sources of support for it. Among them, I shall argue, is the fact that Marx and Engels and Freud make implicit use of something like this principle in some of their more persuasive arguments against traditional morality. We shall later see that the principle is also buttressed by its usefulness in dealing with the age-old problem of the relation between morality and self-interest, by its ability to strengthen and give new significance to Nietzschean moral skepticism, and by its implications for various substantive moral issues. I also believe that the principle is *intuitively* plausible, and shall have more to say in this connection later on.

---

* I am indebted to G. A. Cohen, Richard Wollheim, Arthur Danto, and Peter Williams for helpful suggestions.

I

The above principle of morality and ignorance, as we may call it, is meant to express a formal condition on a certain restricted class of moral principles, principles of moral obligation specifying what kinds of acts it is (absolutely or prima facie) morally wrong not to perform. It has been said that the term 'obligation' correctly applies only in cases where someone has, through a specific act, undertaken to do or refrain from doing something.[1] But I shall speak of principles of obligation wherever some class of actions is morally enjoined with the concomitant implication that it would be morally wrong, or immoral, to omit doing some of them. The principle of morality and ignorance speaks of commitment to a moral principle as a basic principle of obligation, and some clarification of this complex notion may be necessary. On my usage, commitment to such a principle involves more than an intellectual assent to it as true. It involves at least some tendency and desire to act on the principle, and also, I believe, the disposition to feel guilty if one acts against its dictates.[2] I am not saying that guilt is the only, or even the most important, moral emotion or sentiment. John Rawls, for example, has eloquently argued for the place of shame within the moral life[3] and has interpreted Kant as holding it to be the fundamental moral sentiment (*ibid.* 256). But, unlike shame, guilt is a *distinctively* moral sentiment. It is, of course, possible to feel guilty for something outside the moral sphere; but when, e.g., one feels guilty for losing a race or for being more (or less) intelligent than someone else, one has extended the moral beyond its proper boundaries. If, however, guilt is inappropriate in nonmoral contexts, perhaps it is also inappropriate within the area of the moral. Perhaps only shame or regret are proper or reasonable responses to one's immorality. We shall, in fact, be dealing with doubts like these later in this essay; but, whatever their force, they clearly express skepticism about our ordinary sense of morality. Most people think of guilt as the moral emotion *par excellence,* and, if ordinary principles of moral obligation are to have validity (or truth) *as moral principles,* I think guilt must be an appropriate response to the failure to live up to them. If it is not, then there is no valid morality of the sort we think there is, even if some of our moral principles may become valid when translated into some other sphere, i.e., when reconceived and reworded so as to express some different kind of principle. Thus, the principle of morality and ignorance should be thought of as treating the possibility of feeling guilty for failure to live up to a principle of obligation as a necessary condition of its moral validity.

Our principle speaks, however, of commitment to a principle as a *basic* principle of obligation and of validity as a *basic* principle of obligation. What I mean to exclude from validity as basic principles of obligation are principles whose applicability or validity depends on that of other principles of obligation and on "particular" circumstances. If I promise to make a yearly pilgrimage, then I presumably

---

[1] See, e.g., E. J. Lemmon, "Moral Dilemmas," *Philosophical Review,* LXXI, 2 (April 1962): 139–158, p. 140f.

[2] This disposition no more entails the disposition to transgress than the disposition to dissolve in water entails the disposition to be in water.

[3] See *A Theory of Justice* (Cambridge, Mass.: Harvard, 1971), pp. 443ff.

have a moral obligation to do so, but the obligation is not, I assume, basic, and the claim that I ought to make a yearly pilgrimage is not valid as a basic principle of moral obligation—if, indeed, it should count as a moral principle at all. Valid basic principles of obligation are principles—either prima facie or absolute—that in some sense stand on their own. The principle that one ought to keep promises is often conceived as having basic validity in this sense. I wish to claim that no principle can be valid as a basic principle of obligation unless it is possible for people to be committed to it as a basic principle of obligation without that commitment arising from ignorance. And, again, commitment to a principle as *basic* means, for one thing, that one's disposition to feel guilt for disobeying it must exist, so to speak, in its own right and not derive from the fact that, because of particular circumstances, one may feel guilty for going against some underlying moral principle.[4]

We have still not explained or illustrated what it is for commitment to be explainable in terms of one's being (kept) ignorant of certain matters. In order to do so, we shall have to proceed to some examples, examples which, I believe, will also provide some reason for *accepting* the principle of morality and ignorance.

II

Nothing is more typical of modern "enlightenment" and of the theories and enterprises that speak in its name than their tendency, their attempt, to undermine and unmask traditional moral ideals and standards.[5] And nothing is more typical of such attempts to undermine and unmask than their dependence on a connection between valid morality and not acting in or out of ignorance. Marx, Freud, and Nietzsche are often regarded, by their followers and interpreters, as calling traditional morality into question, and I believe it can be shown that their arguments against traditional morality either implicitly rely on something like the principle of morality and ignorance or, as with Nietzsche, can be interestingly reinterpreted as doing so. The cases that Marx, Freud, and Nietzsche make against traditional morality depend, for their full force, on something like our principle; but to the extent that they rely on the principle and we find their arguments both natural and compelling, there is evidence that the principle of morality and ignorance is inherent in our common sense of morality and has intuitive plausibility. And this, in turn, may serve to support the radical moral conclusions that one can (otherwise plausibly) arrive at by use of the principle.

There is evidence that something like the principle of morality and ignorance is implicitly involved in what Marx (and Engels) have to say about moral-legal principles and the nature of human society. Consider the Judeo-Christian injunction against

---

[4] The principle of morality and ignorance speaks only of basic validity because there seems to be no limit to what principles could be accepted as non basic without ignorance playing a role in that acceptance. (E.g., to get out of a situation endangering our species, all mankind might promise to do some morally neutral thing x henceforth, and doing x, whatever it was, might thus become an obligation for all mankind.) Marx and Freud do not worry about the basic/nonbasic distinction, and so our discussion of them will not focus on this aspect of the principle of morality and ignorance.

[5] Cf. F. Hacker, "Freud, Marx, and Kierkegaard" in B. Nelson, ed., *Freud and the Twentieth Century* (London: Allen & Unwin, 1958), p. 125 ff.; and S. Cavell, "Existentialism and Analytic Philosophy," *Daedalus* (1964): 946–974, p. 959.

stealing or the view, advocated in Hegel's *Philosophy of Right,* that citizens have a duty to obey, and not to rebel against, the state. According to Marx and Engels, such moral ideas are illusory "ideological reflexes," mere mystifications of the basic economic and social relations which produce them and which they distortedly reflect.[6] Moral and legal principles have always reflected economic relationships, and people have used them to justify such relationships without being aware of what they were doing.[7] "The jurist imagines he is operating with a priori propositions," but this is a false consciousness, a deceptive inverted reflection of the interests of certain classes. For the propositions he operates with are "really only economic reflexes." "This inversion... so long as it remains unrecognized, forms what we call *ideological outlook.*"[8]

Marx and Engels regard the Judeo-Christian injunction against stealing and the Hegelian denial of the right of revolution as merely ideological, as lacking in any objective truth or validity. The former is singled out for attack in *Anti-Duehring,* a book written by Engels, but approved by Marx.[9] Marx attacks the latter in *Toward a Critique of Hegel's Philosophy of Right,* in *The German Ideology* (74–78), and elsewhere. In addition, Engels, in *Anti-Duehring,* speaks of three kinds of morality—the Christian feudal morality of the past, the bourgeois morality of the present, and the proletarian morality of the near future—and claims that none of them is the true morality, none absolutely valid. "Morality," he adds, "has always been a class morality; either it has justified the domination and interests of the ruling class or, as soon as the opposition has become powerful enough, it has represented the revolt against this domination and the future interests of the oppressed" (271 f). Engels then proceeds to contrast such previous moralities with "a really human morality, which transcends class antagonisms" and which "becomes possible only at a stage of society which has not only overcome class contradictions but has even forgotten them in practical life" (*ibid.*). It is very difficult, he says, to know what this human morality will be like, given our position within the class struggle, but in speaking of it as he does, Engels clearly implies that it has a validity, a truth, that class moralities lack. He also says that, in the classless society, man for the first time will become fully conscious of the material conditions of his existence, and, through such consciousness, will become their master, leaping from the realm of necessity to the realm of freedom.[11] Engels's juxtaposition or correlation of valid human morality with full and nonillusory consciousness of the way things are is, I think, intended to

---

[6] See Marx, *The German Ideology* (New York: International Publishers, 1939), pt. I, p. 14. For the notion of mystification, see Marx, *Toward a Critique of Hegel's Philosophy of Right,* first published in *Deutsch-Franzoesische Jahrbuecher* in 1844, especially the section "People and Sovereignty."

[7] See Marx, *The Eighteenth Brumaire of Louis Bonaparte* (New York: International Publishers, 1963), p. 47.

[8] Quotations are from Engels's letter to Conrad Schmidt, Oct. 27, 1890, printed in L. Feuer, ed., *Marx and Engels: Basic Writings on Politics and Philosophy* (Garden City: Doubleday, 1959), p. 404. They reflect what Marx and Engels say in *The German Ideology* (though not in an inverted way).

[9] See Feuer, ed., *op. cit.*, p. 271. From the context, I do not think that Engels is saying *merely* that it would be foolish to *propound* the (valid) injunction against stealing, in the classless society.

Page references to *Anti-Duehring* will be to Feuer, unless otherwise noted.

[10] In the section "Modification of the Constitution."

[11] See *Anti-Duehring* (New York: International Publishers, 1966), pp. 309–10 (not in Feuer); also cf. *The German Ideology.*

indicate a more than accidental relationship. The implication is that a valid or true morality is possible in the classless society because and only because the morality that flourishes in such a society will not, or need not, depend on distortion and false consciousness.[12] And I believe that the correctness of this interpretation of Engels would be all the more apparent if we considered what some of his "followers" have said about the relation between ideology and valid morality.[13]

Philosophers and social historians have often emphasized the similarities between Marx and Freud. It has been said that both were products of the Enlightenment bent on tearing off masks of illusion and discovering deeper truths about mankind.[14] And it is also true that both Marx and Freud sought to use their theories of human illusion to sustain certain moral conclusions and practical enterprises. We have argued that something like the principle of morality and ignorance is reasonably seen as an implicit principle of inference in some of Marx and Engels's arguments concerning morality (and in the writings of some of their followers). And the fact that this can also be said about Freud and other psychoanalysts is some evidence of the pervasiveness of the principle of morality and ignorance in moral thinking.

In various places in his writings, Freud explicitly states and advocates something like the principle of morality and ignorance. In the *Introductory Lectures on Psychoanalysis*,[15] we find Freud saying:

---

[12] In his "Critique of the Gotha Program" (Feuer, p. 119), Marx says that the classless society will or should "inscribe on its banner" the motto: "from each according to his ability, to each according to his needs!". So perhaps a Marxist should hold that (at least) this ideal belongs to human morality and is valid (in part) because it can be adhered to by people free from false consciousness.

On the other hand, it is not entirely clear that Marx and Engels thought of all principles of class morality as invalid *simpliciter*. They might have wished to accord to such principles a certain epoch-relative validity, or, in the Hegelian mode, a certain partial validity or truth. To that extent, their thinking does not fully mesh with our way of putting things in the principle of morality and ignorance. Our interpretation of *Anti-Duehring* may thus to some degree involve a reinterpretation or translation of its doctrines into contemporary, and no doubt less obscure, modes of thought. To the extent that Marx and Engels really are as obscure as they often appear to be, any attribution we make (in relatively clear terms) will be subject to doubt. I am indebted here to Jerry Cohen.

[13] See, e.g., H. Marcuse, *Reason and Revolution* (Boston: Beacon Press, 1960), p. 319; and J. Habermas, *Knowledge and Human Interests* (Boston: Beacon Press, 1971), pp. 197f., 208–212, 284. Others have interpreted Marx and Engels in something like our way. In *A History of Political Thought* (New York: Holt, 1958), p. 778f., G. H. Sabine attributes to Engels the view that the ideology of the proletariat is superior to that of the bourgeoisie in part because the proletarian can adhere to his morality while being clear in his own mind about how his ideals depend upon his position in the class struggle. He goes on to suggest that Marx and Engels believe that "a preference rationally understood and responsibly accepted, with a clear understanding of its implications, is on a higher moral level than a mere prejudice." Indeed, one way to render the principle of morality and ignorance more idiomatic (though narrower in scope) is to make it claim that the validity of certain principles depends on whether people can be committed to those principles while understanding the main reasons why they have that commitment.

[14] Hacker, *op. cit.*, p. 126; and P. Roazen, *Freud: Political and Social Thought* (New York: Knopf, 1968), pp. 6, 234.

[15] See *The Complete Introductory Lectures on Psychoanalysis* (New York: Norton, 1966), lecture 27, p. 434.

...we have found it impossible to side with conventional sexual morality or to form a very high opinion of the manner in which society attempts the practical regulation of the problems of sexual life. We can present society with the blunt calculation that what is described as its morality calls for a bigger sacrifice than it is worth and that its proceedings are not based on honesty and do not display wisdom. We do not keep such criticisms from our patients' ears.

In speaking of the dishonesty on which traditional social morality is based, Freud has in mind the repression and consequent ignorance of sexual inclinations and fears which occur at the behest of conventional morality. And he proceeds to make it clear that he is condemning conventional morality as morality, not merely criticizing it from some other standpoint, by adding:

> We tell ourselves that anyone who has succeeded in educating himself to truth about himself is permanently defended against the danger of immorality, even though his standard of morality may differ in some respect from that which is customary in society (*loc. cit.*).

Both passages seem to come near to expressing the principle of morality and ignorance. The step from criticizing morality that is based—Freud would, I think, say *inevitably* based—on dishonesty, to explicit enunciation of our principle seems to be more a matter of rendering an idea explicit than of filling out an idea with further content. And if those who know themselves are permanently defended against the danger of immorality—and from the context and for reasons of plausibility, I assume that Freud here means only "defended against false moral standards," and not "defended against (all) immoral acts"—then it follows that no moral standard that would not (and could not) be chosen by people who knew themselves is valid or binding, just as our principle claims.

The principle also appears to be presupposed in Freud's criticisms of various particular standards of traditional morality. In *Civilization and Its Discontents*, he singles out for condemnation the Christian injunction to love one's enemy and the conventional prohibition against all sexuality outside indissoluble monogamous marriage.[16] In Christian love, he says, the impulse to genital love has become "aim-inhibited" and is unconsciously intended to satisfy genital desires (69–71). And it is impossible to obey the injunction to love (even) one's enemy or to love all mankind, because, where universal love is prescribed, aggression finds a way of expressing itself against those outside one's religious or ethnic community—without the agent's awareness of what is happening and with the help of rationalizations (e.g., "we are torturing these heretics for their souls' salvation") (91). Freud definitely takes it to be a criticism of the precept enjoining universal love or love of one's enemy that it requires of people more than they are capable of, and that, faced with such a demand, one either becomes neurotic in its service or revolts against it (139). Since, according

[16] New York: Cape & Smith, 1930, chaps. 4 and 5. Freud argues (p. 83) that the injunction to love one's enemy is not significantly different from the injunction to love all mankind or from the injunction to love one's neighbor.

to Freud, all neurosis involves being kept ignorant of internal unconscious forces by various unconscious mechanisms of defense, he seems committed to holding that the precept of universal love or of love of one's enemy cannot be served without a basis in self-ignorance, and to criticizing that precept at least partly on that ground. In the same work and elsewhere, Freud makes similar, though slightly less sweeping, criticisms of the conventional prohibition on all sex outside of monogamous marriage.[17] Adherence to something like the principle of morality and ignorance seems to guide Freud's criticisms of particular cultural standards, and the principle also appears to be employed by many other psychoanalytic writers.[18]

III

By finding evidence of the principle of morality and ignorance in the works of Marx (and Engels) and Freud, and of their followers, we may become convinced that the principle has a fairly widespread use. And when we find ourselves carried along by arguments in which Marx or Freud makes use of the principle as an implicit principle of inference, when we find such arguments compelling relative to their empirical/theoretical assumptions, the intuitiveness of the principle should become apparent. In either or both of these ways, we are given reason to believe that the principle of morality and ignorance is a valid formal constraint upon morality.[19] In addition, our findings about Freud and our findings about Marx (and Engels) tend to support each other. Our search for regularities being what it is, we should be more willing to attribute a certain pattern of thought to a given author if we find what seems to be a similar pattern of thinking in another. And the more reason there is to think that the principle of morality and ignorance is prevalent in *both* Marx and Freud, the more reasonable it becomes to believe the principle correct. By illustrating the principle within the work of these thinkers, the previous section thus also provides us with evidence of its truth.

---

[17] *Ibid.*, chaps. 4 and 5. Also in "'Civilized' Sexual Morality and Modern Nervousness," reprinted in Sander Katz, ed., *Freud: On War, Sex, and Neurosis* (New York: Arts and Sciences Press, 1947), esp. pp. 166–169. Cf. Roazen, *op. cit.*, p. 134.

[18] For two good examples, see H. W. Frink, *Morbid Fears and Compulsions* (New York: Moffat, Yard, 1918), pp. 518, 550–553; and M. Levine, "Emotional Maturity," in Linscott and Stein, eds., *Why You Do What You Do* (New York: Random House, 1956), pp. 263–265.

[19] For more on the methodological principles I am making use of, see, e.g., N. Goodman, *Fact, Fiction, and Forecast* (Indianapolis: Bobbs-Merrill, 2nd ed., 1965), pp. 63–65. Incidentally, one might suppose that the principle of morality and ignorance was trivially true or question-begging in its application, on the grounds that (1) if a principle is not valid, then commitment to it is explainable in terms of ignorance of its nonvalidity and/or that (2) it is trivial to point out that if commitment to a principle is due to ignorance of its nonvalidity, the principle is not valid. But this would be a mistake. It is *not* trivial or question-begging to say that if commitment to a principle is inevitably due to *some* form of ignorance (or to ignorance *other* than ignorance of its nonvalidity), then it is not valid. Nor is it clear that adherence to a nonvalid principle is always explainable in terms of ignorance of its nonvalidity. Was Newton's commitment to his theory *due* to his ignorance of what Einstein knew? In any event, even if adherence to nonvalid principles is always explained by ignorance of that nonvalidity, it hardly follows in any trivial way that, where adherence is inevitably explained by ignorance, the principles adhered to are not valid.

What we have just said about the reasonableness of using an interpretation of one thinker to support a similar interpretation of another may also help us answer an objection to our interpretations of Marx and Freud and their followers which may already have troubled some readers. Surely, when an argument is not set out formally, there are many possible ways to interpret it. Since Freud and Marx argue informally and without explicit mention of our principle, why say that their arguments implicitly rely on that principle and not on others? In order to amount to something more than an *exercise* in skepticism, however, this question needs to be reinforced by some particular suggestions of principles that might be attributed to Marx or Freud in place of the principle of morality and ignorance. And it is in fact not difficult to come up with such principles. Both Marx and Engels talk about man's unfreedom during the period of class struggle that precedes the classless society, so perhaps we should regard them as making implicit use of the principle that ideals that germinate in or result from human unfreedom and do not exist otherwise cannot be valid or true. And some of Freud's works may entitle us to attribute to him the principle that moral precepts that are inevitably based on neurosis, or mental illness, have no validity.

Two points can be made in response to these suggestions. It is not clear, to begin with, that we need to choose between these new principles, on the one hand, and the principle of morality and ignorance, on the other. In Freudian theory, neurosis is equivalent to a certain class of ways of being (kept) ignorant—on a conscious level at least—of various internal facts; neurosis exists when and only when these forms of "repression" do.[20] And Marx and Engels seem to have considered freedom to be equivalent, in this same sense; to acting out of knowledge of the material bases of human life. In that case, Marx and Engels and Freud may have implicitly accepted both the principle of morality and ignorance and one or the other of the "competing" principles we have mentioned. In the second place, if we do have to choose between the principle of morality and ignorance and the *pair* of principles that competes with it, surely we should prefer the former on grounds of simplicity and explanatory power. Clearly, it is (other things being equal) preferable to work with, or assume, one principle rather than two. And even if we agree that we *do not* have to reject either the principle of morality and ignorance or its alternatives, there is some reason to regard the former as more fundamental to Marx and Freud's thinking. It makes far more sense to explain their adherence to one or the other of the "competing" principles we have suggested in terms of their common allegiance to the principle of morality and ignorance and their acceptance of their own respective theoretical equivalences, than to do the explaining in the opposite direction.

Furthermore, it counts in favor of an interpretation of a given (respectable) argument that that interpretation makes the argument appear stronger than it would otherwise seem to be. Since we have already remarked that Marx's and Freud's arguments are each strengthened by being treated as instances of a *common* principle of reasoning, that is still further reason to prefer to understand what Marx and Freud are doing in terms of implicit adherence to the principle of morality and ignorance. Of course, it is a good deal

---

[20] For simplicity's sake, I ignore psychosis and certain exotica of mental illness; for use of 'repression' in the broad sense I am employing, see Freud's "'Civilized' Sexual Morality and Modern Nervousness," *loc. cit.*, p. 167.

easier to use and illustrate the concept of implicit use or acceptance, as we have done here, than to give an adequate account of what that concept involves. But we often make reasonable use of this notion, and others, without being able to provide strong theoretical underpinnings; and I hope I may be excused from providing such underpinnings here.

IV

We have seen evidence not only for the validity of the principle of morality and ignorance, but for its usefulness and interest as well. For, if it is valid, then it can be employed, in the manner we have attributed to Marx and Engels and Freud, to argue in what are at the very least interesting ways against certain traditional moral principles and views, in particular, against the precept "love thine enemy" and its variants,[21] against the prohibition on nonmarital sex, and against the (absolute) duty of obedience to the state.

The principle has, moreover, a certain intuitive plausibility of its own. It is difficult to believe that there could be valid basic principles of moral obligation binding upon mankind of such a sort that no one could ever be committed to their basic validity except through ignorance. If I may put the matter somewhat loosely and evocatively, how can we be morally bound by principles that will not stand up to the light of day, that take advantage, as it were, of our ignorance, when at the same time morality puts such a fundamental emphasis on the duty to tell the truth? Surely, there is some sort of incoherence in a morality which, together with its theoretical or formal underpinnings, decries lying, or the deliberate inducing of ignorance, and yet allows the possibility of valid basic principles of obligation that no one could accept as such save through ignorance. It would seem, then, that the principle of morality and ignorance cannot be rejected in theoretical ethics if we are to be consistent with the content and spirit of morality itself. When we reflect upon morality, it is natural for us to feel, vaguely, that any morality worthy of the name must pass intellectual muster; and the principle of morality and ignorance seems to be a plausible way to give expression and articulation to this feeling.

It is interesting in this connection to contrast the situation of morality with that, for example, of etiquette. Presumably, it is sometimes good manners to mislead people about one's boredom or annoyance. And because this sort of tact has an importance in etiquette that it lacks in morality, there seems to be no inconsistency in maintaining a code of manners that emphasizes such tact, while denying that any and all (basic) principles of good manners that we inevitably subscribe to only out of ignorance are automatically incorrect, inadequate, or suspect. I believe, further, that this partially accounts for our feeling—it is a feeling I have and one that I think others, upon reflection, will share—that there can be perfectly adequate or acceptable codes of etiquette not subject to any analogue of our principle of morality and ignorance. The principle thus serves to distinguish morality from certain other areas of evaluative thinking,

---

[21] At least, given our principle, when these express presumptive moral obligations or imperatives, not just ideals to cmulate.

and I believe that the "consistency" argument we have used to support it can help to explain why those other areas are not subject to similar constraints.

Assuming, then, that the principle of morality and ignorance is a valid formal principle on morality, I would like to point out another area in which its interest and importance can be seen. I believe that we can use the principle to give at least a partial answer to a problem in ethical theory that, perhaps more than any other, has exercised philosophers over the centuries, the problem of the relation between morality and prudence (or self-interest). Of the possible views that can be taken on this question, extremist positions—claiming that right action is always prudent or else claiming that right action has at best a merely accidental connection with an agent's interests or well-being—have received the most extensive philosophical articulation, and have been the most influential. And it is worth noting that both sorts of opposing extremist positions often have a theological cast. Of course, a strong connection between valid morality and self-interest, prudence, and the like is sometimes defended without recourse to theological assumptions—as, for example, in Plato, and, according to some interpreters, in Nietzsche. But though such theories are free of theological "taint," they run another sort of risk that has often been noted: if one argues for a very strong connection between morality and self-interest without otherworldly props, it can easily become unclear whether it is really morality—morality as we understand the term—that has been thus tied to self-interest. So it is with Plato, whose conception of virtue as a kind of health of the soul seems to stretch virtue beyond recognition in the process of linking it to prudence.[22] And so too it has seemed with Nietzsche, as I shall make clear later on in discussing his views about morality.

I believe that there is, indeed must be, a connection of some interesting kind between morality and prudence, even if the arguments that purport to prove that they always coincide are all either philosophically questionable or of dubious theological provenance. Common sense certainly inclines us in this direction, making us suspicious of those who preach duties of total selflessness, of self-punishing asceticism, or of total sexual abstinence. It is difficult for most of us to believe that morality can make such extreme demands against any person's well-being or happiness. And for this reason, too, perhaps, most of us believe that everyone has a basic right of self-defense that can remain intact even when the sacrifice of his life is necessary to the preservation of the lives of others. All this is not argument, to be sure. But if we are initially inclined to suppose that there is some interesting connection between morality and prudence less than the total coincidence that Plato and others have assumed, perhaps it is also worth trying to see whether we can use the principle of morality and ignorance to point up *one* particular way in which morality and prudence are connected.

There is a venerable tradition according to which one element of self-interest, of personal well-being, consists in the ability to act in full knowledge and not out of ignorance. According to Spinoza's *Ethics,* for example, the person who acts from ignorance (of the causes of his own behavior) lacks wisdom, freedom, and happiness. Certainly, it is arguable that ability to act without one's behavior resulting from ignorance is an element, or at least a necessary condition, of human well-being, and also

---

[22] Cf. W. E. H. Lecky, *History of European Morals from Augustus to Charlemagne* (New York: Braziller, 1955), vol. I, pp. 178 ff.

of such presumable elements of well-being as free action[23] and wisdom. But if acting out of ignorance is to some degree, other things being equal, against self-interest, then the principle of morality and ignorance, by ruling out basic moral principles that demand that sort of sacrifice of self-interest, establishes a certain connection between valid morality and prudence or self-interest. If the principle is correct, then we are required to act only on those principles (lacking deeper support) adherence to which is at least compatible with our retention of one element or necessary condition of our own well-being. This is not a very strong connection to have established between morality and prudence, but it is, I believe, a definite and significant one, one whose very weakness contributes to the plausibility of believing it exists.

Thus, independently of its use by Marx, Freud, and others in historically important moral arguments and theories, the principle of morality and ignorance has intuitive plausibility and important implications for ethical theory. It is of help to us in our search for a weak, interesting, plausible connection between morality and prudence, and to the extent that it is useful in dealing with an important, long-standing problem of ethical theory, we have even more reason to find it acceptable. Fertility favors principles and theories in ethics every bit as much as it favors methods and theories in science.

V

I would like to discuss one further area in which the principle of morality and ignorance may be of value. I believe that the principle can be used to argue forcefully for a strong form of moral skepticism: in particular, for the thesis that there are no (objectively) valid standards or principles of moral obligation. No doubt we have no desire, even as philosophers, to be skeptics, in this sense, about morality. But we also want to understand the frequent appeal and occasional compellingness of radical moral skepticism—even if only to be able deeply and convincingly to refute it; and the principle of morality and ignorance can be of help to us here.

One of the most sweeping critiques of common moral precepts, of the Judeo-Christian tradition of morality, and, it has been thought, of morality as a whole is to be found in Nietzsche's *The Genealogy of Morals*. Nietzsche is usually thought of as criticizing morality from the standpoint of other values, and much, probably most, of the Nietzschean corpus supports such an interpretation. In the *Genealogy*, for example, he explicitly questions the "intrinsic worth" of moral values and wonders whether morality might not be or become "responsible for man, as a species, failing to reach the peak of magnificence of which he is capable."[24] In the present context, however, I want to advocate the philosophical importance of understanding Nietzsche's argument in a new way—though at some cost, I think, to historical or textual accuracy. I shall reconstruct Nietzsche's reasoning in the *Genealogy* so that it makes use of the principle of morality and ignorance and criticizes morality in its own

---

[23] By "free action" I mean the kind of free action that political theorists consider desirable, rather than some sort of metaphysical free will. On the connection between such freedom and not acting in ignorance, see my "Desert, Consent, and Justice," *Philosophy and Public Affairs*, II, 4 (Summer 1973): 323–347, pp. 334, 346f.

[24] Garden City: Doubleday Anchor, 1956, p. 155.

terms. Much of the force of traditional skepticism about *empirical* knowledge comes from its use of seemingly plausible epistemological principles to undermine ordinary claims to have knowledge. And I think skepticism about morality, or our principles of obligation, becomes most compelling and significant when based on principles internal to morality itself—in conjunction with accepted or acceptable empirical claims.[25] We have argued that the principle of morality and ignorance has good claim to be treated as a valid formal condition on morality endemic to our shared moral thinking. And I shall now attempt to show how we can use that principle, along with some of Nietzsche's "empirical" assumptions and certain related claims, to formulate a philosophically interesting attack on morality from within.

Our enterprise is not entirely without precedent. In "Moral Beliefs," Philippa Foot[26] has claimed that courage, temperance, and even justice count as (moral) virtues only if they are qualities that people normally need and benefit from having. She attributes a similar view to Plato in the *Republic*, and says that "it is because Nietzsche's position is at this point much closer to that of Plato that he is remote from academic moralists of the present day." From this standpoint we can think of Nietzsche as denying the beneficial nature of what ordinarily passes for virtue and drawing upon a formal principle concerning what is to count as a virtue in order to attack Judeo-Christian views about virtue in their own terms, from within. But, as I have already indicated, the formal condition on virtue we must then attribute to Nietzsche assumes an implausibly strong connection between certain moral claims and the self-interest of moral agents. It is one thing to say that one has no *reason* to be virtuous, if virtue does not pay; this may be true, and then, again, it may not. But the claim that what does not benefit an agent is for that reason not a (moral) virtue in that agent seems to involve a serious distortion of what morality is. The point has been made quite forcibly by a number of ethical thinkers.[27] And it is accepted by Mrs. Foot, who has now retracted her claim that only qualities beneficial to those who have them are virtues.[28] To attribute to Nietzsche a (putatively) internal argument against morality, or moral virtue, based on the assumption that virtue must benefit its possessor, is to allow his moral skepticism little force or plausibility. Our own reconstruction of Nietzsche's line of thought will depend, of course, on the principle of morality and ignorance. And we have seen that, if that principle is valid, there is a definite, though weak connection between acting morally and acting in one's own interest. But precisely because that connection is much weaker than that assumed in the skeptical argument that Philippa Foot attributes to Nietzsche, our reconstruction of Nietzsche's reasoning will place his argument against morality in a far more favorable light.

---

[25] Thus any interpretation of Nietzsche that has him arguing from general metaphysical and epistemological skepticism to skepticism about moral claims as a particular instance limits the effectiveness and force of what he says, whatever its accuracy and other merits. [Such an interpretation occurs, e.g., in Arthur Danto, *Nietzsche as Philosopher* (New York: Macmillan, 1965), esp. pp. 133, 172.] For (Nietzsche's sort of) skepticism about the existence and knownness of facts and things is, if anything, even more philosophically precarious and suspect than skepticism about morality of the sort I am attributing to Nietzsche; and to base the latter on the former is to do an injustice to the *force* of moral skepticism.

[26] *Proceedings of the Aristotelian Society*, LIX (1958/59): 83–104.

[27] See, e.g., H. A. Prichard, *Duty and Interest* (Oxford: Clarendon, 1928), pp. 4–25.

[28] See her "Morality as a System of Hypothetical Imperatives," *Philosophical Review*, LXXXI, 3 (July 1972): 305–316, pp. 307 f.

In *The Genealogy of Morals*, Nietzsche distinguishes two diametrically opposed "sets of valuations": a morality of good and evil and a morality of good and bad. The morality of good and evil is identified with Judeo-Christian morality and is said to be dominant in the Western world (169). It is, he thinks, a morality of slaves and priests which has developed in reaction and opposition to the morality of good and bad that naturally develops within the aristocracy. Nietzsche finds the morality of good and evil odious and seeks its destruction in the name of something closer to the original aristocratic morality of good and bad. But what is crucial, I believe, is that Nietzsche's criticisms of good-and-evil morality constantly refer to the "fact" that it develops only in reaction to aristocratic morality and out of hate and resentment. While the morality of good and bad dominates, the people it depreciates—the poor, the powerless, the suffering, and the ugly—cannot directly vent the rage they feel against those who dominate and contemn them. But their resentment of the aristocrats finds an indirect expression through the morality of good and evil, which is established by priests in the name of the poor and powerless. In and through that morality, the resentment and hatred felt by the poor and powerless is turned inward. Man "invented bad conscience [or guilt] in order to hurt himself, after the blocking of the more natural outlet of his cruelty."[29] The new moral code preaches asceticism and sacrifice; so those who obey it are deprived of some worldly goods they would otherwise enjoy. And the code is so strict, so hard to follow perfectly, that its adherents are constantly beset by guilt, a feeling unknown to aristocratic morality, to the aristocratic set of valuations.[30] But slave morality also permits vengeance—some of it imaginary, some of it real—to be taken on the aristocrats. The imaginary vengeance is of the sort expressed in the *Book of Revelation* and in the writings of Tertullian, where one finds descriptions of the joy good Christians will feel on the Day of Judgment at the hell-fire punishment of the wicked (183–185). And there is real vengeance as well, since many aristocrats become adherents of good-and-evil morality—though Nietzsche never really explains how this could happen—and, once they accept the new morality, they too become victims of bad conscience and sacrifice much of what they would otherwise have enjoyed (167f, 225).

The resentment of the downtrodden gives rise to their morality, but that morality does not, according to Nietzsche, enable them to get rid of the original resentment. It festers within, frequently appearing in the guise of guilt. Adherents of aristocratic morality, on the other hand, get rid of any resentment they feel through direct action. According to Nietzsche, resentment is a kind of *poison*, and so both guilt and the entire morality of good and evil represent forms of *sickness* (155, 167, 171, 221). Given Nietzsche's emphasis on "sickness" and "health" as terms of criticism, it is easy to interpret him as arguing, along familiar, putatively Platonic lines, against any morality that is incompatible with human health. To do so would certainly also allow us to connect Nietzsche's views with Freud's, but we would then lose our connection, at least any direct connection, with the Marxian critique of (traditional) morality. So let us instead see what the principle of morality and

---

[29] *Ibid.*, p. 226. Also cf. p. 221. Nietzsche strikingly anticipates the Freudian idea that the very severity of conscience bespeaks its origin out of aggression turned inward.

[30] For that very reason, I think aristocratic "morality" is not morality as we understand the term, but it is not important to press the point here.

ignorance can do to tie up Nietzsche's ideas about the origins of Judeo-Christian morality with skepticism about its validity and about the validity of principles of moral obligation in general.

The morality of good and evil originates in and thrives on resentment redirected against the self. In order to use the principle of morality and ignorance, however, we must consider whether the followers of slave morality are, or can be, aware of these facts. Sometimes Nietzsche seems to be saying that they are. Slave morality, we are told, is a "consummate sleight of hand" (181), a "brilliant trick" (181), a "tartufferie" (155). In fact, the only place where I have found Nietzsche definitely indicating that the rancorous sources of slave morality are unknown to its adherents is in his remark that "the rancorous person is neither truthful nor ingenuous nor forthright and honest with himself" (172). But even if Nietzsche does not unambiguously say that the moralists of good and evil are ignorant of their own resentment and ways of dealing with it, we can, for our part, make that assumption in his behalf. It adds immeasurably to the plausibility of what he is saying, since staunch adherents of Judeo-Christian morality typically do not believe that their morality derives from hatred turned inward.

Nietzsche does explicitly say that guilt and Christian altruism come from hatred directed inward and inevitably wane when hatred is not directed inward, when aristocratic ideals dominate (220–228). And if we say that adherence to the morality of good and evil depends not only on the redirection of hatred against the self, but on the fact that that process goes on without the knowledge of those whom it affects, then we can immediately argue against the validity of that morality, using the principle of morality and ignorance. It might be thought that we would thereby have undermined only extreme forms of Christian altruism, not morality itself: not, for example, the moral obligation to be kind to others. Even if extreme forms of self-sacrifice, selflessness, and chastity can, in the proper psychological light, strike one as forms of aggression turned inward and as forms of self-punishment, this hardly seems likely in the case of kindness pure and simple. But such a rejoinder ignores what Nietzsche says about guilt. If we accept the injunction to act kindly as a principle of moral obligation, then we must assume the appropriateness of guilt for failure to live up to it. Nietzsche assumes that *all* guilt comes from hatred turned inward. If we but make the further, stronger assumption that this redirection of hatred cannot occur with the full knowledge of the person who feels guilty, the principle of morality and ignorance entitles us to conclude that the seemingly moderate injunction to be kind, understood as a (basic) principle of moral *obligation*, is not valid or true.[31] We do indeed end up with a thoroughgoing skepticism about moral obligation.[32]

Of course, this skepticism and the principle of morality and ignorance both depend on the existence of a close connection between moral obligation and guilt. I believe that any great loosening of this connection would signify a change in our moral concepts, and in our concept of morality, but I have already said all I can in support of this point

---

[31] In addition, a moral obligation of kindness may not make sense if pity makes no sense, i.e., depends on ignorant self-hatred or self-abasement. And Nietzsche attempts to establish such a connection in *Daybreak* (*Morgenroth*).

[32] I am assuming here that if there are no basically valid principles of obligation, no principles of obligation that stand on their own in the sense specified above, then there are no valid principles of obligation whatsoever.

of view.³³ The argument for moral skepticism also makes the assumption, based in part, as we have seen, on Nietzsche's ideas in the *Genealogy*, that guilt is incompatible with self-knowledge, at least in humans. And it is important to realize that this supposition is not incompatible with anything firmly and generally believed in present-day depth psychology and might even be, or come to be, defensible in depth-psychological terms. Freud and other analysts have held, for example, that the superego is built up from unconscious processes of projection and identification. A highly punitive superego, or conscience, develops from failure to resolve unconscious Oedipal, or other, conflicts, and such a superego tends to become attenuated or less severe through successful psychoanalytic therapy.³⁴ Within psychoanalysis, there is willingness to grant that a surprisingly high proportion of human guilt is based on ignorance, in a sense covered by the principle of morality and ignorance. But on the question whether a (hypothetical) completely successful analysis that completely eliminated repression would remove all capacity for guilt, psychoanalysis offers no unambiguous answer. In *Psychoanalysis and Politics* (67f), R. E. Money-Kyrle says that in the thoroughly analyzed patient the superego would be reabsorbed into the ego. There would no longer be a dissociated internal source of guilt, but "one would still be capable of experiencing guilt in his relations with external objects." The sentiment of guilt would no longer be of a "persecutory" variety, as it is when the superego is a harsh independent source of guilt, but would have something of a "depressive" character. Others have expressed belief in the persistence of guilt and conscience after the elimination of repression and neurosis,³⁵ but the view lacks the kind of currency and acceptance within psychoanalytic thinking that various other ideas possess. It is thus hardly *clear* that the above internal argument for moral skepticism must fail, even if current depth psychology may give us some reason to think so. By reconstructing Nietzsche's arguments to dovetail with the principle of morality and ignorance, the issue and possibility of moral skepticism come alive in a way that can, I believe, challenge current thinking in philosophy and psychoanalysis.

VI

We have just employed the principle of morality and ignorance to make an "internal" case for a strong form of moral skepticism based on assumptions whose truth or falsity are still open to speculation and investigation. Earlier, we saw how the principle of morality and ignorance was, or could be, used by Marx and Freud to argue against the validity of particular moral claims: the injunction to love one's enemy, the principle of unconditional obedience to the state, etc. All these arguments are open to question both on theoretical and empirical grounds; but the chief significance here of the principle of morality and ignorance lies not so much in its immediate and obvious moral consequences, as in the way it opens up substantive moral questions (and the

---

[33] Nietzsche himself sometimes speaks as if there could be "duties" in a morality beyond good and evil, in a guilt-free morality. Whether he meant this literally, and in the ordinary sense of the term, is hard to judge. See *Beyond Good and Evil* (New York: Random House, 1966), p. 221.

[34] See Freud, *The Ego and the Id* (New York: Norton, 1962), *passim*; and R. Money-Kyrle, *Psychoanalysis and Politics* (London: Duckworth, 1951), pp. 64ff.

[35] See, e.g., A. Kaplan, "Freud and Philosophy," in Nelson, ed., *op. cit.*, p. 216.

issue of moral skepticism) to empirical/theoretical investigation. Given the principle, it is possible to see how certain empirical and/or theoretical assumptions support certain important moral conclusions.

One consequence, however, of the principle, and of the "testability" it brings to moral claims, is a certain kind of moral relativity. As stated earlier, it says (roughly) that, if a moral principle is to have basic validity, humans must be capable of commitment to it that does not result from ignorance. But what sort of validity can this be? If validity for all (possible) rational beings is meant, then one must say that a principle Martians could live by without ignorance might not be binding on *them*, simply because *humans* could not commit themselves to it except on the basis of ignorance. Such intellectual parochialism is distasteful. To avoid it, we might let (basic moral) validity depend on whether *any* (*possible*) *rational being* could in full knowledge be committed to a given moral principle (as basic). But I think this would have disastrous effects on our whole present enterprise. The theories of Marx, Nietzsche, and Freud are about human beings, not about all (possible) rational beings. And it seems highly unlikely that what is impossible for humans should as a rule be impossible for rational beings generally. So, if the principle of morality and ignorance were framed in terms of what it is possible for a rational being *ueberhaupt* to accept, Marx, Freud, and Nietzsche's claims about what is humanly impossible—about what is incompatible with human nature—would no longer give it a foothold of applicability, and their ideas and theories would themselves lose the moral implications with which our principle, as originally stated, sought to endow them.[36] It would appear, then, that the principle itself can be used to draw moral implications from theories and discoveries about human beings and human nature, only if it speaks of what *humans* cannot accept save through ignorance. And if we retain the principle's original focus on what is humanly possible, then we must either let the principle speak of basic validity *for humans* or else restrict its application to principles that specify what *humans* ought to do. A certain relativity thus seems to be the price we have to pay for a nonparochial, empirically applicable, morally significant principle of morality and ignorance.[37] Such relativity offends a moral Kantianism that exists in many of us, by speaking of moral principles that do not necessarily concern all (possible) rational beings. But we are not the only ones faced with this sort of difficulty. It is, I believe,

---

[36] Unless the findings about human beings in virtue of which we can use the principle of morality and ignorance somehow turn out to be relevant and applicable to all (possible) rational beings. May it not be possible to argue, for example, that any being capable of reason who was committed to self-punishing asceticism as a basic obligation or to a basic duty of absolute obedience to the state could be so committed only through ignorance? Such general facts may be opaque to human understanding until a Marx or a Nietzsche comes along and points them out in the human instance; but, once we have recognized their human instantiation, it may be impossible for us to imagine how they could fail for any possible rational beings; knowledge of such facts may, then, begin with, but not depend on, empirical experience, and so in some sense be a priori. If some of the major ideas of Marx, Freud, and Nietzsche *did* turn out to be a priori in this sense, we could state the principle of morality and ignorance in terms of what any possible rational being could accept, and avoid speaking of validity-for-humans altogether. But although the prospects of such a priori psychology are intriguing, I am rather dubious about the whole idea.

[37] The moral significance of the principle extends far beyond the particular substantive ethical issues that we have had time to discuss thus far. For example, the principle can be used to argue against the basic validity of principles forbidding (all) homosexual activity. Freud has said that "those who deny sexuality in children are the last to relax educative measures against it" [*A General Introduction to Psychoanalysis*

a problem for Rawls and for various other recent ethical theorists,[38] though one that seems not to have been faced squarely by any of them.

In *A Theory of Justice*, for example, Rawls makes it clear that his theory is a theory of *human* social justice and his two principles of justice, valid for humans in virtue of their nature as free and rational *human* beings (138, 251–257). He also claims that his "Kantian interpretation" of justice as fairness is reasonably "faithful to Kant's intentions" (257). "It might appear," he says, "that Kant meant his doctrine to apply to all rational beings as such...I do not believe that Kant held this view, but I cannot discuss the question here" (257). Rawls's view of Kant is out of keeping with the way most philosophers interpret Kant; but, however right or wrong his interpretation of Kant may be, it is important to realize that one reason why people have been inclined to interpret Kant as requiring that moral principles apply to rational beings as such is the intuitive plausibility of such a requirement. Rawls does nothing (explicit) to justify the relativity to mankind he builds into his theory, and does not seem to recognize that such relativity is a problem for a moral theory, going as it does against some of our initial intuitions or ingrained traditional beliefs about what morality is.

Some of our problems, then, are problems for Rawls and others. I do not mean to suggest that there is philosophical safety in numbers here. But if empirical relevance really is important in ethics—and Rawls's imposing theory, which tests conceptions of justice against the facts of human psychology and economics, is some testimony to that—then perhaps we should be willing, despite lingering Kantian doubts, to accept the idea of human-relative morality. To the extent, furthermore, that the earlier-discussed arguments of Marx, Freud, and Nietzsche are *valid only if* they implicitly employ a human-relative principle of morality and ignorance, and are widespread and compelling *kinds* of arguments, there is genuine support for the principle of morality and ignorance in such a human-relative form. If we are willing,

---

(New York: Washington Square Press, 1960), p. 322]. And it is a similar psychoanalytic commonplace that those who most condemn and persecute homosexuals are unconsciously defending against their own homosexual impulses. *If* this is correct, perhaps it is also true that anyone who condemns homosexuality as *fundamentally* wrong or *self-evidently* indecent will have unacknowledged homosexual impulses within. And in that case, we could use the principle of morality and ignorance to infer that homosexuality cannot be excluded by any valid basic principle of morality. (From there it is not very far to the conclusion that there is nothing whatever wrong with certain forms of homosexuality.) Without putting our principle in human-relative terms, I doubt whether we could even begin to make the above argument, and, of course, the argument is in any case no stronger than the controversial psychoanalytic views on which it rests. But *to the degree* that the principle helps us to argue for a conclusion that we would *like* to be able to argue for, its fertility is, once again, underscored, and this gives us still further reason to believe it valid (in its human-relative form).

[38] Among such theorists, I have in mind Roderick Firth and his "ideal-observer theory," which analyzes moral judgments in terms of the dispositions of a hypothetical being with certain ideal characteristics who is otherwise (like) a normal human being. See "Ethical Absolutism and the Ideal Observer," reprinted in W. Sellars and J. Hospers, eds., *Readings in Ethical Theory*, 2nd ed. (New York: Appleton-Century-Crofts, 1970), p. 220f. I think the similarities and differences between Firth's theory and the view of the present paper are both interesting and instructive. For one thing, Firth advocates a certain *analysis* of ethical concepts, whereas the principle of morality and ignorance need not be analytic to be valid and, in

then, to accept the idea of morality that is valid relative to mankind, the plausibility and fruitfulness of the principle of morality and ignorance thus conceived may well be worth the price.[39]

---

any case, expresses only a *necessary* condition on the validity of certain moral principles. (Nor should the principle be strengthened into an "if and only if" principle; for it seems perfectly possible that there should be two *contrary* principles of moral obligation *neither* of which is excluded by the principle as it stands.)

[39] See my "The Morality of Wealth," in W. Aiken and H. LaFollette, eds., *World Hunger and Moral Obligation* (Englewood Cliffs, N.J.: Prentice-Hall, 1977), pp. 124–147, for some other considerations that might incline one to accept the idea of human-relative moral obligations. For a different way of arguing for human-relative morality, see R. Coburn, "Relativism and Morality," *Philosophical Review*, LXXXV, 1 (January 1976): 87–93.

6

Time in Counterfactuals

I would like to offer an account of counterfactuals that is strikingly at variance with the presently dominant Stalnaker-Lewis "similarity" theory of counterfactuals, that is something of a throwback to Goodmanlike "cotenability" treatments of counterfactuals, but that differs from Goodman's conception in putting a special emphasis on temporal distinctions and directions.[1] I shall begin by arguing for and illustrating the importance of two sorts of time reference in the truth conditions of counterfactuals. Thereafter, I shall attempt to show that the role of time in counterfactuals is most readily accommodated by a cotenability framework for counterfactuals, and shall offer a version of cotenability theory that avoids the circularity and some of the counterexamples that afflict earlier forms of the theory. The new version makes distinctive use of the concept of explanation both in explicating the notion of cotenability and in specifying the relation that holds between the antecedent and consequent of true counterfactuals (in English). Towards the end of the paper, I shall discuss the advantages this form of cotenability theory seems to have over current versions of similarity theory.

---

[1] See Robert Stalnaker, "A Theory of Conditionals," *American Philosophical Quarterly* Monograph #2 (1968), 98–112; R. Stalnaker and R. Thomason, "A Semantic Analysis of Conditional Logic," *Theoria* 36 (1970), 23–42; David Lewis, *Counterfactuals* (Oxford, 1973); and Nelson Goodman, *Fact, Fiction, and Forecast* (Indianapolis, 2nd edition, 1965), ch. 1. I shall speak of counterfactuals rather than subjunctive conditionals, for brevity's sake. But unlike Lewis (op. cit., p. 4), I think that considerations of theoretical simplicity and intuitions about particular cases dictate that subjunctive conditionals pertaining to the future be treated like other subjunctive conditionals, rather than like indicative conditionals.

I

Consider, to begin with, the following three counterfactuals:

(A) If I were (ever) to jump out of this window, I would not hurt myself (since I would never do so without first putting out a safety net, and since I have every means and intention of putting out such a net by tomorrow).
(B) If I were now to jump out of this window, I would hurt myself (on the pavement below).
(C) If I were now (already) jumping out of this window, I would immediately hurt myself (on the pavement below).

When the appropriate parenthetic material is understood as background, we see intuitively that these three counterfactuals could come out true together. But how is this to be accounted for? Without their parenthetic material, for example, (A) and (B) can *seem* incompatible, at least on a casual reading.[2] And the same is true of (A) and (C). I shall assume, in what follows, that the reader's reactions to (A), (B), and (C) are similar to my own. In order to explain these reactions—and reactions to other sets of counterfactuals that raise similar problems—it will be necessary to examine some varying roles that times play in our understanding of counterfactuals. I shall first focus on the examples (A), (B), and (C). In order to facilitate our discussion, I shall make free and uncritical use of the notions of nomic deducibility and cotenability; but I shall subsequently attempt to amplify and justify this reversion to pre-Lewis-Stalnaker theorizing.

Cotenability theory has typically maintained that any (tensed) "would" counterfactual is true just in case its consequent can be deduced from its antecedent and/or existent background conditions cotenable with its antecedent, together with relevant natural laws.[3] It is my belief that when we assert a tensed counterfactual, the conditions cotenable with the antecedent that are, along with the antecedent and laws, supposed to yield the consequent are implicitly thought of as existing all together at a single time, rather than diffusely at different times. I shall call that time the *base-time* of the counterfactual, and since the cotenable conditions are thought of as existing at that time, we can use the dummy letter "b" to stand for (the joint existence of) those conditions.

I think that the base-time of both statements (A) and (B), for example, is the present, the moment of utterance defined as narrowly as may be appropriate. And

---

[2] (A) is not to be read as the externally quantified and false: "for all times t, if I were to jump out of this window at t, I would not hurt myself."

[3] On such a theory, not every actual condition is cotenable with the antecedent of a counterfactual, since if the negation of the false antecedent of a counterfactual (always) described a condition cotenable with it, every counterfactual with false antecedent would count as true. Also, in true "even if" and "still" semifactuals the antecedent may not be needed for the above-described entailment. (I assume that words like "even" do not affect truth conditions. Cf. Lewis, op. cit., p. 33n.) Note, finally, that "would" counterfactuals contrast with "might" counterfactuals like "if you jumped, so might I."

both statements are about the future. But the use of "now" in (*B*) creates a difference in what I shall call the *reference-times* of the antecedents of the two counterfactuals. (*B*) says, in effect, that if I were right away to jump out of the window, I would hurt myself. The "now" of its antecedent refers not, in the usual manner, to the present moment, but to some time (period) in the immediate future.[4] (Compare the usage of "let us now speak French.") The reference-time of (*A*)'s antecedent, on the other hand, is not the immediate future, but the future in general, and the fact of the different reference-times here helps to explain how, shorn of their parenthetic material, such seeming incompatibles as (*A*) and (*B*) can be true together.

For the moment, let us say that a tensed "would" counterfactual is true if and only if there are conditions existing at its base time (cotenably with its antecedent's being true with respect to its reference-time) which, together with the antecedent's being true with respect to its reference time and with certain laws, logically entail the consequent's being true with respect to *its* reference-time. (*A*) says, in effect, that there are present conditions of such a kind that, given laws and assuming that I shall jump at some time in the future, it follows that I shall not hurt myself immediately thereafter. And (*A*) can be true when the conditions mentioned between its parentheses obtain; for then the conditions obtaining at its base-time, the present, will include: my present witting reluctance to jump out of the window right away, my ability and intention to attach a net, and the absence of factors around with the potential to disturb my reluctance to jump out of the window without assuring my safety with a net.[5]

(*B*), on the other hand, can be true in circumstances where (*A*) is, because there are conditions existing at its base-time, the present, and cotenable with its antecedent which, together with the truth of its antecedent with respect to its reference-time, the immediate future, and with certain laws, entail the truth of its consequent with respect to its reference time. Those conditions include the present absence of a net and the present hardness of the pavement below. But they do not include my present witting reluctance to jump immediately while being in circumstances where there is nothing with any tendency to destroy that reluctance. This last condition is not, presumably, cotenable with (*B*)'s antecedent; and this difference between (*A*) and (*B*) not only results from the difference in their reference-times, but is decisive for allowing them both to come out true despite their seeming incompatibility. (Our intuitively plausible claim of non-cotenability here will be justified later on when we come to define the concept of cotenability.) The truth of counterfactual (*C*)—in circumstances where (*A*) is true—can be explained in much the same way. (*C*)'s antecedent clearly refers to the present moment and not, as in (*B*), to the immediate future. But if we assume that (*C*)'s base-time is present, then the base-time conditions cotenable with its antecedent will include the conditions we said were cotenable with (*B*)'s antecedent, but will not include my present witting reluctance to jump while being in

---

[4] Sometimes such a "now" is understood from context. (*A*) minus its parenthetic material can be understood in this way, for example, so it is hardly surprising that (*A*) and (*B*) can sound incompatible. However, also see footnote 32, below.

[5] Our description of this last condition of "absence" is merely a convenient elliptical way of describing a no doubt highly complex situation in the universe, whose existence I assume and whose existence, together with laws, entails the continuation of my present witting reluctance to jump.

circumstances where there is nothing with any tendency to destroy that reluctance. And so we will be able to deduce (C)'s consequent's truth for its reference time from laws, cotenable conditions, and the truth of the antecedent for its reference-time.

The notion of reference-time has been used in accounting for the compatibility of (A), (B), and (C). But our notion of base-time and the assumption that the base-time of (B) and (C) is the present are also crucial to our explanation. If the relevant cotenable conditions for a counterfactual like (B) can exist diffusely at different (past) times or can exist all together at some given (past) time other than the present moment, a nomic deducibility theory based on cotenability will, I think, find it impossible to explain why (B) is true. If the relevant conditions cotenable with (B)'s antecedent could include my desire *yesterday* not to be hurt and my ability *yesterday* to attach a net, we could use them to argue that if I were now to jump, I would *not* hurt myself. For given enough of those actual earlier conditions and laws and the assumption that I shall now jump, we can, presumably, deduce that I shall not hurt myself jumping. And we would have the same problem explaining the truth of (C) if we allowed its cotenable conditions to include earlier circumstances. Furthermore, given the reference times of (B) and (C), conditions existing (only) after the present seem inappropriate for inclusion among the cotenable conditions by means of which one is allowed to deduce (B) or (C)'s consequent from its antecedent; so we have every reason to assume that the background conditions cotenable with (B) or (C)'s antecendent should be thought of as existing all together at the present moment. By insisting that (B) and (C) have a base-time and that that base-time is the present, we foil the above-mentioned deduction(s) of the falsity of (B)'s, and (C)'s, consequent and retain our ability to show, in the manner illustrated earlier, how the truth of (B)'s, and (C)'s, consequent for its reference-time follows from the truth of its antecedent for its reference-time together with laws and cotenable conditions.

None of the above, however, proves that (A) must have a base-time. But if we assume that (A) has the present as base-time, we can give a uniform and simple explanation of the truth and compatibility of (A), (B), and (C) in terms of interactions between their common base-time and differing reference-times. So I think there is some reason to treat all three counterfactuals as having the same, present, base-time. Of course, in arguing as we have for the importance of the concepts of base- and reference-time to understanding tensed counterfactuals in English, we have restricted ourselves to a set of counterfactuals some of whose members make temporal reference by means of the token-reflexive word "now;" and some of our discussion focused on particular referential features of that word. But distinctions of base- and reference-time are also necessary to understanding the compatibility of (A) with counterfactuals like: (D) "if I were to jump out of this window at midnight, December 31, 1976, I would hurt myself (since it is already too late to attach a safety device by that time)." Arguments parallel to those used above would enable us to show both that (D) is compatible with (A) and that (D)'s base-time is the time of its utterance or inscription—which is, given the parenthetic material included above, not long before midnight, December 31, 1976.

Our account of the truth conditions of tensed counterfactuals (in English) thus seems to be independent of particular ways in which reference-times are determined for such counterfactuals. And indeed there are a number of different ways in which reference-times can be fixed. (D)'s reference-times are, presumably, determined by its semantical features alone. The reference-times of (*A*), (*B*), and (*C*), on the other hand, depend on semantical features together with the time of utterance. Still other counterfactuals pertaining to the present or future make use of previous verbal context to fix their reference-times. Preceded, for example, by "I shall be at the window at midnight, December 31," the counterfactual "if I were to jump shortly thereafter, I would hurt myself" has shortly after midnight, December 31, as its reference-time; in another verbal context, it would have a different reference-time.

I believe it is a convention governing all tensed counterfactuals pertaining to the present or future that their base-time is present, the time of utterance or inscription.[6] Even counterfactuals whose reference-times are in the relatively distant future seem to have a present, rather than a future, base-time. Thus consider (*D*)—minus its parenthetic material—as said, for example, in June, 1976. If in June it is still possible for me to find and attach a safety net before December 31 and I have not yet decided whether to do so, then (*D*) as said in June will (I assume) be false. It will be true, instead, that I might *not* hurt myself if I were to jump at midnight on December 31, 1976, because I *might* put a safety net out by that time. But if (*D*) as said in June did have a future base-time—and the most plausible such time would be at or right before midnight on December 31—then it would count as true, as long as I in fact did not attach a net before the end of the year. For (*D*)'s base-time conditions would then include the very factors that, together with its antecedent and laws, would enable us to deduce that I will hurt myself. Since we presumably want (*D*) as said in June to come out false even if I never realize my potential for attaching a net by midnight, December 31, (*D*) as said in June should not be thought of as having a future base-time. In order to make the intuitive distinction between (*D*)'s truth as expressed right before midnight on December 31, and its falsity as expressed in June, it is best to think of (*D*)'s base-time as its (varying) time of utterance.[7]

And the same, I believe, can be said for any tensed counterfactual with a distant future antecedent's reference time. It is not, in general, sufficient for the truth of such a counterfactual that its antecedent and conditions around its antecedent's reference time nomically insure the truth of its consequent. Of course, sometimes when background conditions are relatively fixed and unalterable, the truth value of this sort of counterfactual would not be affected by treating its base-time as distant future rather than as present. But given what we have to say about cases, like (*D*), where background conditions are thought of as not being fixed, the simplest and most sensible

---

[6] Some counterfactuals that are grammatically in the present tense seem to make reference to past time and to need treatment along the lines of past-tense counterfactuals: e.g., "if I were now fifty, I would have been eligible to vote in 1948."

[7] However, someone asserting (*D*) in June may just *assume* that there will be no net up before the New Year, even though it is in fact causally undetermined whether that will be the case. And if we hold that that assumption is an implicit part of the antecedent of (*D*) as he intends it, we can count his assertion as the elliptical expression of a counterfactual *truth*. In that case, the response that he or someone else might put up a net by December 31 is no counter to what *he* means to say and elliptically asserts. But if no such qualification of the antecedent is implicitly intended, and it really is causally open whether a net will be put up, then I think his utterance of (*D*) in June is false because it *is* open to the response we have mentioned. For more on how background assumptions can implicitly qualify the antecedents of counterfactuals asserted in conversational contexts, see Lewis, op. cit., pp. 66ff.

conclusion to draw about cases where background conditions *are* fixed, is that it is (if anything) the fixity of the circumstances rather than the existence of a future base-time that allows one to assign the correct truth value on the basis of conditions as they will be. It should be noted, however, that this judgment is based on what I take to be our actual intuitive assignments of truth values to counterfactuals in English, rather than on a priori considerations about how natural languages should or will determine base- or reference-times. For all I know, other languages may differ from English with regard to some of the features I have pointed out.

We have not yet considered past-tense counterfactuals, but distinctions of base- and reference-time are also, for example, important to understanding the compatibility of such past-tense analogues of (A), (B), and (C) as: (Ap) "if I had ever jumped..., I would not have hurt myself;" (Bp) "if I had then jumped...,I would have hurt myself;" and (Cp) "if I had then been jumping...,I would have hurt myself." The arguments are of a piece with those offered for present-tense cases; and so there is perhaps no need to enter into them here. Since, moreover, the base-times of past-tense counterfactuals will clearly be past and since there are so many past then's for any given now of utterance, the base-times of past-tense counterfactuals cannot be fixed by the simple convention that determines the base-time of tensed counterfactuals pertaining to the present or future. There is no space here to investigate the full range of past-tense counterfactuals. But I think a careful investigation of cases would tend to show, for example, that if the antecedent and consequent of a past-tense counterfactual have the same single reference time, then the base-time of the counterfactual is identical with that time; and that if a past-tense counterfactual's antecedent and consequent refer to the same more or less definite *period* of time, then its base-time is the more or less definite *beginning* of that period. Thus the counterfactual "if I had jumped yesterday, I would have hurt myself" has (roughly) yesterday as antecedent's and consequent's reference-time and the beginning of yesterday for base-time. More needs to be said about other past-tense cases; and, clearly, our account of the factors governing base- and reference-times can and should be given further development. But this will have to wait upon another occasion.

II

We have been using a cotenability and nomic deducibility framework for counterfactuals. Previous attempts at cotenability theory—Goodman's most notable among them—have been stymied by their inability to define the notion of cotenability itself without running into circularity. But I believe it is possible to construct a cotenability account of counterfactuals that avoids the pitfalls of Goodman's classic treatment. I have already begun to present the main outlines of such a theory, and I shall continue to do so in the present section and in Sections III and IV. In Section V, I shall go on to argue that the new version of cotenability theory has two important advantages over similarity theory: it is better able to account for fine distinctions among counterfactuals like (A), (B), and (C) (or their past-tense analogues); and it can more readily deal with certain counterfactuals that have come to be regarded as possible *counterexamples* to similarity theory.

The development of a cotenability account of counterfactuals that did *everything but* define cotenability would not, I believe, be an empty achievement. But I think we should make an attempt to define cotenability, because, in the light of past history, any cotenability theory that leaves cotenability undefined will remain open to the suspicion that it is not merely incomplete but incompletable. Before we do so, however, I would first like to point out some other problems with previous cotenability theory, problems whose solution will be of help to us when we eventually come to define cotenability. Quite independently of their difficulties with cotenability, nomic deducibility theories of the kind we have been working with cannot account for important aspects of ordinary counterfactual usage. They do not, in particular, distinguish lawful deducibility from lawful explainability, and just this distinction is, I believe, crucial to our understanding of counterfactuals.

Consider the following example. Let us imagine that certain circumstances obtained yesterday in which having a shadow n feet long was (nomically) equivalent to being $n/2$ feet tall. How, then, do we account for the oddness and seeming falsity, for such circumstances, of "if I had had a fourteen foot shadow, I would have been seven feet tall," as compared with its obviously true counterfactual converse, "if I had been seven feet tall, I would have had a fourteen foot shadow?" Goodmanlike nomic deducibility theory cannot help us here, since all our previous apparatus does nothing to prevent the consequent of either counterfactual from being deduced from its antecedent together with laws and cotenable conditions. If, however, we revise cotenability theory and say that, for appropriate true counterfactuals, the antecedent, cotenable conditions and laws must by themselves be capable of validly *explaining* the consequent, we will be able to say why the first counterfactual above is false and the second true. A valid explanation of shadow length in terms of height does exist, but no valid explanation exists in the opposite direction.

On the other hand, one might fail to see the need for introducing the notion of explanation to deal with the above examples, if one failed to distinguish the kinds of counterfactuals we have been discussing from another sort of subjunctive conditional that David Lewis has called "that would have been because" conditionals. Even though "if I had had a fourteen foot shadow, I would have been seven feet tall" seems to be false, it may be true that: if I had had a fourteen foot shadow, *that would have been because I was seven feet tall*. The two claims are, on the face of it, different.[8]

Let me mention one further sort of case that illustrates the need for employing the concept of explanation in cotenability accounts of counterfactuals. It is sometimes said that if determinism is true, counterfactuals like "if I had been depressed yesterday, the whole previous history of the universe would have been different" are true.[9] But even assuming determinism, there is something odd about this counterfactual.

---

[8] See Lewis's "Causation," *Journal of Philosophy* 70 (1973), 565n. Neither Lewis nor I have a positive account of "that would have been because" conditionals, but I think that such conditionals, together with certain others I shall not discuss, form a natural class. Each such conditional has a consequent that itself implicitly asserts a relationship between the antecedent that precedes it and some other state of affairs that it mentions. Henceforth, in speaking of counterfactuals, I mean to exclude conditionals of this kind.

[9] See, e.g., J. Pollock, "Four Kinds of Conditionals," *American Philosophical Quarterly*, 12 (1975), 58f.; and J. Earman, "Causation: a Matter of Life and Death," *Journal of Philosophy*, 73 (1976), 10.

Nomic deducibility views clearly cannot account for that oddness. But if we assume that most of us assume that the direction of explanation is (almost) never backward in time and if we require that the consequent of an appropriate counterfactual be *explainable* in terms of the antecedent, background conditions, and laws, we can account for the oddness and seeming falsity of the above counterfactual in a way that previous cotenability theories cannot.[10]

We must, however, exercise care in bringing the notion of explanation into a cotenability theory of counterfactuals. Not every true counterfactual is true in virtue of an explanatory relationship between its antecedent and/or base-time conditions, on the one hand, and its consequent, on the other. Such trivial counterfactuals as "if I were a bachelor, I would be unmarried" are also true. And there are other true counterfactuals that are neither trivial nor true in virtue of the explainability of their consequents. The counterfactual "if we were now all dead, there would still be matter-energy conservation" seems, for example, to be true because its consequent expresses a fundamental law of nature. We shall have to take such cases into account when we come to state truth conditions for tensed "would" counterfactuals. But for the moment, we can simply say that our requirement that true counterfactuals be based on an appropriate explanatory relation can be relaxed only for counterfactuals, like those just mentioned, where one can "go" from antecedent to consequent without benefit of background conditions and where, in particular, the antecedent alone nomically implies the consequent.

III

Let us now concentrate on cotenability. If we permitted cotenable base-time conditions to be (nomically) incompatible with an antecedent, we would have difficulty accounting for the truth of counterfactuals like (*B*) and (*C*) above; for if my present witting reluctance to jump while being in circumstances...is cotenable with my now jumping, we can use it to deduce, and even explain, why I shall *not* (immediately) hurt myself. So for the moment, let us say that base-time conditions *b* are cotenable with an antecedent just in case *b*'s obtaining at the relevant base-time is nomically compatible with the antecedent. Since this definition requires *b*'s nomic compatibility with an antecedent *a*, but does not, more strongly, require that the counterfactual "if *a*, then not *b*" be false, we do not run up against circularity in defining cotenability the way Goodman does in Chapter 1 of *Fact, Fiction, and Forecast* and can use the rest of our apparatus to handle the sort of example that led Goodman to abandon his attempt to give a theory of counterfactuals.[11]

---

[10] Similarity theory also has difficulties with such counterfactuals. Lewis's reason for thinking that some such counterfactuals are false, even under determinism, is that in a deterministic world, counterfactuals like the following will sometimes be true: "if I had been depressed yesterday, the laws of nature would have been different in such a way that the world would still have had the previous history it in fact did have." (*Counterfactuals*, p. 75.) But this way we go from frying pan to fire. Our own account will make laws sacrosanct, so that bizarre counterfactuals like the one just mentioned will count as false. Cf. B. Berofsky, "The Counterfactual Analysis of Causation," *Journal of Philosophy*, 70 (1973), 568f.

[11] For convenience, I shall sometimes make sloppy use of schematic letters, and shall often substitute '*b*', 'the antecedent', and the like, for the longer '*b*'s obtaining at the base time', 'the antecedent's being true for its reference time', and the like.

Consider a match *m* that has always been dry and has never been lighted or scratched. The counterfactual "if *m* had been scratched, it would not have been dry" will then be false; but we seem to be able to deduce its consequent from its antecedent, cotenable conditions compatible with that antecedent, and laws, because the match never lighted. Goodman readily admits his inability to handle such examples noncircularly.[12] But since the match's being scratched and not lighting cannot be used to explain why the match is (was) not dry, our use of the concept of explanation enables us to account for the falsity of this counterfactual. (Clearly, it isn't the sort of counterfactual whose antecedent alone nomically entails its consequent.)[13] The counterfactual in question also suffers from difficulties of temporal structure that can be brought out by use of the notions of base- and reference-time. Its antecedent's reference-time is earlier than the past time at which the match is being supposed not to light. Lighting or failing to light is generally thought of as following (immediately) upon the scratching of a match. Now we have already seen reason to think that, when we rule out backward causation, the base-time of a counterfactual is no later than its reference-times. Thus failure to light is inappropriate for inclusion among the base-time conditions of the problematic counterfactual we are examining. And if, instead, we include among those conditions the failure to light *before* or *at* the time of the scratching, we will be unable even to *deduce* its consequent from its antecedent, laws, and appropriate background conditions. Again, there is no way, on our theory, to argue for the truth of this sort of counterfactual.

There is, however, another kind of important example that Goodman does not consider and that will force us to add to our previous definition of cotenability.[14] Imagine a branching electric circuit connecting a light to a power source with three independently controlled switches, *k*, *l*, and *m*, attached in such a way that the circuit is unbroken if and only if *k* is closed and at least one of *l* and *m* is also closed.[15] (For brevity, we can refer to the latter state of affairs as *k*-and-*l*-or-*m*.) Suppose that *k* and *l* are closed and *m* is open, so that *k*-and-*l*-or-*m* obtains and the light is on. The counterfactual "if *l* were open, the light would (still) be on" is then, presumably, false. But both this counterfactual and its seemingly true *contrary* "if *l* were open, the light would be off," come out true on our previous account. For, on the one hand, *k*-and-*l*-or-*m* is an existent base-time condition nomically compatible with *l*'s being open; and independently of whether *l* is open, *k*-and-*l*-or-*m* helps to explain *the light's being on*. But, on the other hand, *m*'s openness is another existent base-time condition nomically compatible with *l*'s being open; and if we assume that *l* and *m* are both open, it is easy to produce a valid explanation of *the light's being off*. Clearly, the

---

[12] *Fact, Fiction, and Forecast*, pp. 14–17.

[13] The notion of explanation also enables us to rule out certain problem counterfactuals that Goodman mentions and *does* handle. The consequent of "if I were in Carolina, I would be in North Carolina" cannot be *explained* in terms of its antecedent, laws, and cotenable conditions like my not being in South Carolina.

[14] I am indebted for the example to a reader for the *Philosophical Review*.

[15] Including switch *k* in our example makes things harder for us. If we omitted it, we could easily handle the case of the electric circuit by assuming that base-time conditions have to be *nomically independent* of the antecedent of a counterfactual.

theory must be modified in such a way as to render "if l were open, the light would (still) be on" false while preserving the truth of its contrary.

It seems to me that the relation between l's being open and m's being open is quite different from that between l's being open and k-and-l-or-m. Given the openness of switch m and other conditions (nomically compatible with l's being open) and laws that obtain in the situation described above, the further counterfactual assumption that l is open in no way compels us to say that m is open *despite* the fact that l is open. But given k-and-l-or-m and other appropriate conditions and laws, if we then counterfactually assume that l is open, we do have to say that k-and-l-or-m obtains—and the circuit is unbroken—*depite* the fact that l is open. This difference can be of use to us. On the face of it, "despiteness" seems to be some sort of causal-explanatory concept; and perhaps we can give an explicit (and possibly somewhat stipulative) causal-explanatory gloss of that concept that will serve to extricate us from our present difficulties.[16]

Let us say that a base-time condition has a despiteness relation to the antecedent of a counterfactual if and only if there is a valid explanation (involving no extraneous elements)[17] of the base-time condition in terms of the (internal) negation of the antecedent, other actual conditions nomically compatible with that negation, and laws.[18] The base-time condition consisting in m's being open lacks a despiteness relation to the antecedent of the counterfactual "if l were open, the light would be off," since it cannot—without the use of extraneous elements—be validly explained in terms of l's not being open, other appropriate conditions, and laws. But the base-time condition k-and-l-or-m does have a despiteness relation to the antecedent-assumption that l is open, since it can be validly (and nonextraneously) explained in terms of l's not being open, laws, and other appropriate conditions that are nomically compatible with l's

---

[16] If this gloss ultimately leads to problems, we may still be able to handle the electric circuit case in terms of the ordinary "despite" locution that we have just used to indicate the difference between k-and-l-or-m and m's being open, leaving it to future investigations to determine how to explicate that locution.

[17] Without this qualification, almost every base condition would have a despiteness relation to a false antecedent, and, in particular, we would be left with the unfortunate conclusion that m's being open has a despiteness relation to l's being open, since we can explain m's openness by saying: "it is open because you opened it last night if l is closed and l *is* closed, etc." But the fact that l is closed seems clearly to be an extraneous element in this explanation; and so I think we can use the above parenthetic qualification to avoid our present difficulty. (Note, then, that something can be an extraneous element in an explanation, even if it is, given the "artificiality" of the explanation, essential to the explanation *as it stands*. I do not, however, mean to suggest that if q explains r, then p will always be an extraneous element in an explanation of r in terms of p and if-p-then-q. It all depends on the choice of "p". For example, if John died because the knife entered his heart, we may also be able to explain his dying in terms of the fact that Jane struck with great force at his lapel and the fact that if Jane struck with great force at his lapel, the knife [must have] entered his heart. Certainly, the former fact is not extraneous here.)

It is an important problem in its own right how to define the intuitive and familiar idea of an explanation's involving extraneous elements, and a solution to this problem would certainly help to deepen our present analysis. But since my intention in this paper is not so much to analyze common explanatory concepts as to consider how counterfactuals can be understood in terms of them, I shall not enter further into these problems.

[18] Our definition of the despiteness relation needs to be expanded to cover cases where base time and antecedent's reference time do not coincide and to rule out base-time conditions to which various *antecedents* have a despiteness relation; but there is no space here to pursue the details.

not being open. And in that case, if we demand that base-time conditions cotenable with an antecedent not only be nomically compatible with that antecedent but also lack a despiteness relation to it, we can block the above explanation of the light's being on and give a univocal account of the truth of "if *l* were open, the light would be off." The notion of valid explanation thus has a second role to play in our theory of counterfactuals. Now it is time to bring the various elements of our theory into focus in a single statement of truth conditions for tensed "would" counterfactuals.

IV

Here, then, are the truth conditions I would like to propose:
A tensed[19] "would" counterfactual is true if and only if

(1) its consequent is nomically entailed by its antecedent; or
(2) there are conditions *b* that characterize its base-time, that lack a despiteness relation to its antecedent, and whose obtaining at the base-time is nomically compatible with the antecedent, of such a sort that there is a valid explanation of the consequent (solely) in terms of the antecedent and/or *b*, together with actual nonstatistical (causal) laws.[20]

Disjunct (1) of these truth conditions makes room for counterfactuals whose truth is independent of the existence of cotenable background conditions.[21] Disjunct (2) makes double use of the notion of valid explanation and bears the major weight of our theory.[22] It is worth noting, furthermore, that our truth conditions depend on the possibility of a relation of valid explanation between an antecedent and consequent

---

[19] Tenseless counterfactuals include such mathematical examples as "if three were even, four would be odd." Actually, not all tensed counterfactuals have a base-time: e.g., "if there had always been helium, there would always have been hydrogen;" and, strictly speaking, I am offering truth conditions only for tensed "would" counterfactuals with base-times. Also, antecedents and / or consequents can have what might be called "multiple reference times": as, for example, in "if I jumped today and also next Monday, I would never recover." Note, finally, that our truth conditions are easily generalized to cover truth at a (nonactual) possible world, and that, although I have presented my account as applying to counterfactuals in English, there is every reason to think that much of what I have said would carry over to sufficiently expressive languages in which time reference was made without the use of tenses.

[20] Another disjunct *may* be needed to handle semifactuals like "even if I were now in Rome, I would be wearing glasses," *if* they are true and *if* no base-time conditions cotenable with their antecedents enable us to explain their consequents. Also, I have stated our truth conditions elliptically, in the simplifying manner of footnote 11 above.

[21] One consequence of the first disjunct, however, is that unless one can make distinctions along the lines of Anderson-Belnap relevance logics, all (tensed) counterlogicals and counterlegals are true. I think we lack strong intuitions about such conditionals, so I do not mind letting them fall where the use of covenient formulations lets them. Cf. *Counterfactuals*, p. 24ff. I am also inclined to think that the notion of explanation needs to be brought in somehow to modify even the first disjunct of our truth conditions.

[22] I am not sure that counterfactuals can never be backed by statistical laws and explanations. If it is a statistical law that 99.99% of x's do y in z, do we in all accuracy have to say "if this x were in z, it would almost certainly do y" or should we relax our truth conditions to permit dropping the "almost certainly"?

that holds independently of whether that antecedent and consequent are true. In most cases, the validity of a *deductive argument* is independent of the truth of its premises and conclusion, but its soundness or correctness is not. And the theory of counterfactuals we have offered assumes that it makes sense to distinguish between valid explanations and correct explanations in much the same way that logicians distinguish between valid arguments and correct, or sound, arguments. Now the traditional nomological-deductive model of explanation clearly permits a distinction between valid and correct explanations. It can say that if appropriate premises and laws entail a conclusion, they validly explain it, even if the premises and conclusion are false and the explanation in question is thus not a *correct* explanation of any phenomenon. Of course, our own theory of counterfactuals has to reject the traditional model of explanation; otherwise we would have to say—counterintuitively and with dire consequences for our theory—that height can be explained in terms of shadow length. What I do wish to assume however, is that the eventual account of explanation will at least retain the traditional model's ability to distinguish valid from correct explanation.[23]

The above truth conditions also speak of conditions that characterize a base-time, rather than of conditions that obtain or exist at a base-time. As we shall soon see, the former is the stronger of these two notions; but if we do not make use of some such stronger notion *in conjunction with* the concept of valid explanation, we cannot preclude the truth of such unidiomatic and bizarre counterfactuals as "even if I were now unhappy, I would have been happy yesterday." Let us see why this is so.

The base-time of this last counterfactual is, presumably, the present. But then if we say that base-time conditions need only obtain (exist) at a base-time, and if, in addition, we can explain my happiness yesterday in terms of my having been very happy two days ago, we have to call that counterfactual true. For in that case, my having been very happy two days *previously* will be a condition obtaining at its base-time and the truth of its consequent will be explainable in terms of laws and the fact that that condition does obtain at the base-time.

On my usage, however, conditions *characterize* a time only if they help to constitute what the world is like at that time—or, alternatively, if their obtaining or not obtaining at that time affects our time-slice description of the world *at that time*. Intuitively, then, my being happy characterizes the times when it exists, but my having been happy two days previously does not. And because our truth conditions demand that relevant cotenable conditions characterize a base-time, we cannot use my having been very happy two days previously to explain the consequent of the just-mentioned odd counterfactual, and so preclude its truth. When counterfactuals

---

[23] A valid deductive argument has premises that, in a strict sense, cannot be *true* unless its conclusion is. So perhaps we can give a *rough characterization* of valid explanation along similar lines by saying that an explanation of a consequent in terms of laws, cotenable base-time conditions, and an antecedent is valid if it is impossible for those laws and conditions to obtain and for the antecedent to be true without all of this *correctly* explaining the consequent. Note that we can even speak of antecedents, etc., validly explaining *the truth of* a consequent, as long as we bear in mind that such talk no more entails a commitment to actual truth than does talk about the truth of one proposition being incompatible with the truth of another.

are asserted in relation to implicitly assumed background conditions existing at a base-time, the conditions assumed are, I believe, always ones that it is natural for us to think of as helping to constitute what the world is like at that time. And even if this notion cannot easily be analyzed, it may nonetheless be involved in our ordinary understanding of counterfactuals. If that means counterfactuals are not respectable, the fault may lie with counterfactuals, not with the accuracy of our truth conditions for them. And I am also inclined to think that our naive concept of helping to constitute what the world is like at a time is respectable and legitimate despite my (our) present inability to define it.

V

Even if we have defined cotenability and created a substantive, noncircular cotenability theory, we must still consider whether we ought to prefer cotenability theory thus resurrected to the sort of similarity theory that presently dominates philosophical thinking about counterfactuals. I would like now to discuss some of the advantages that our cotenability account may have over the Lewis-Stalnaker approach; our attempts in this direction will also permit us further to elucidate the structure and consequences of our own account.

Because current similarity theories lack the concept of base-time, there is some reason to believe that they would have a difficult time accounting for the truth of counterfactuals like our earlier (A), (B), and (C). Similarity theory says, roughly, that a counterfactual is true at a world w if its consequent holds in that world in which its antecedent holds that is closest, or most similar, to w. (Our subsequent arguments will not take advantage of the roughness in formulation here.)

And it is not clear how similarity theory as it stands can account for the truth of counterfactuals (B) and (C) in particular, under the sorts of assumptions about the world we made earlier in explaining their truth. Given my ability *yesterday* to attach a net, my reluctance *then* to jump, and related factors, similarity theory may have a hard time saying that I *do* hurt myself in the nearest possible world where I jump at, or right after, the present moment. Our own theory, on the other hand, can say that (B) is true because there are cotenable conditions characterizing its base-time—the absence of a net, the hardness of the pavement—which, together with laws and the assumption that I shall now jump out of this window, permit a valid explanation of my subsequently hurting myself. And a similar account can be given for (C), as well as for (A). So our use of the notion of base-time gives our cotenability theory one presumptive advantage over similarity theory.

Similarity theory also faces other difficulties. Recently, a number of putative counterexamples to similarity theory have been mentioned in print and in informal discussions. I shall now consider some of these "counterexamples"—in the process adding one of my own—and explain both why they raise problems for similarity theory and why our account—or, indeed, any standard cotenability theory—has no trouble in dealing with them.

I begin with the following, due to Paul Horwich (among others). Consider a world w where it is strictly random whether someone jumping through a certain kind of high window will hurt himself. If k is such a window in such a world, and we keep everything else about the world as "familiar" as we can, then similarity theory seems to have the implausible consequence that the statement "if John had jumped through k, he would not have hurt himself" is true at the world in question with regard to a person John who never jumps through high windows or really hurts himself in that world. For, presumably, in the *nearest* possible world where he jumps, he also does not hurt himself. Our own conditions, on the other hand, enable us to say that the Horwich counterfactual is false at w, as we would naturally think it was. There are no relevant conditions of w contenable with John's jumping at the appropriate time, which, together with the antecedent and laws of w, allow us to explain why, or deduce that, John does not hurt himself right after that time.

Similarity theory also has the consequence that every counterfactual with true antecedent and consequent is itself true. Many philosophers—including Lewis himself[24]—have worried about this result of similarity theory. And Jonathan Bennett, in particular, has recently argued at length for the implausibility of saying that all such counterfactuals are true.[25] Rather than reiterate his particular arguments, I shall simply refer the reader to his interesting discussion. But it is worth pointing out that our cotenability account has no such consequence.[26] Consider, for example, the following situation. There is a kind of particle which, when put in a cloud chamber, acts in an undetermined way, sometimes moving upward, sometimes downward. Archy knows this, but Mehitabel mistakenly believes that such particles are always caused to move downward. Suppose they both wish to learn whether one such particle was allowed into the chamber, and that in fact one was put in and moved downward for random reasons. If Mehitabel says "if a particle of that kind had been put in there, it would have moved downward; so let's see if we can find one at the bottom of the chamber," it would be perfectly natural for Archy to believe her to be mistaken in what she said—on grounds that the lawful connection her statement assumes between such particles' being in the chamber and their moving downward simply does not exist. And yet the antecedent and consequent of her statement are true, so that, on Stalnaker and Lewis's view, the counterfactual she utters is true. The fact that her utterance seems, on the face of it, not to be true thus constitutes a problem for similarity theory. But our own truth conditions readily account for the incorrectness of her assertion, again because there is no way to explain or deduce its consequent by means of its antecedent, base-time conditions, and laws.

---

[24] See *Counterfactuals*, pp. 26–29.

[25] See his "Counterfactuals and Possible Worlds," *Canadian Journal of Philosophy*, IV (1974), 381–402.

[26] But it does allow counterfactuals with true antecedents to be true. Counter-factuals almost always conversationally imply the falsity of their antecedents; but if a detective says "if he *were* guilty, his fingerprints would be all over; so let's see if we can find some," there is no such implication, or entailment. The following may illustrate the point even better. Haldeman to McCord entering the White House: "Well, if the President *were* here, and I'm not saying he is, he certainly wouldn't see *you*." The "and I'm not saying he is" makes sense only if the counterfactual does not presuppose the falsity of its antecedent, and threatens to presuppose just the opposite.

Let me mention another sort of problem that has not been previously discussed. Suppose we know that the total amount of matter, or matter-energy, in the universe is m. The counterfactual "if the amount of matter in the universe today had been between a third and a half m, it would have been nearly a half m" will then seem either false or truthvalueless; but similarity theory appears to assign it truth. For, presumably, some world where there is nearly a half m matter is more like our world than any world where there is more than a third, but not nearly a half, m matter. By contrast, our own truth conditions have no difficulty in accounting for the falsity of the above example. The universe's having nearly a half m matter simply cannot be explained by, or nomically deduced from, its having *between* a third and a half m matter and other cotenable conditions.

Let us, finally, consider a possible counterexample mentioned by Jonathan Bennett[27] and Kit Fine[28] in reviews of Lewis's *Counterfactuals*. Lewis is a Warrenite, and one of his pet examples of a false counterfactual is "if Oswald hadn't killed Kennedy, someone else would have." Yet if the assassination has made as great a difference to history as many people think, the statement seems to count as true on Lewis's own theory. A world in which someone other than Oswald kills Kennedy is, presumably, closer to our world than one in which no one does. Again, our account handles the present case without difficulty. Assuming Warrenism, there is no condition of the world at the base-time of the Oswald counterfactual that is cotenable with the antecedent and that, together with the antecedent and laws, validly explains the consequent.

It clearly stands in favor of our account that it can readily handle a number of different counterfactuals that cause trouble for similarity theory. But in saying this, I do not mean to imply that similarity theory faces insuperable difficulties. The problem counterfactuals we mentioned appear to be counterexamples only if one equates the similarity-theoretic notion of comparative similarity with our ordinary naive conception of comparative similarity. So one can take those putative counterexamples as showing that the kind of similarity relevant to counterfactuals is not ordinary similarity, but some related and perhaps more complex notion—rather than as undermining similarity theory in principle. One could then either leave the theory vague about this related notion or else attempt to spell out that notion to a sufficient extent to make it clear how similarity theory can avoid problems with the counterfactuals we have just been considering.

To adopt the former course would be to leave the theory incomplete, though not, indeed, any more vacuous on that account than a cotenability theory that did everything but analyze cotenability. Our own theory would still have the advantages of having spelled out its most central notion and of not leaving it to the chances of future inquiry to vindicate its ability to handle the "counterexamples" we have mentioned. And I also suspect that if one took the course of developing a technical notion of similarity that clearly avoided the above sorts of counterexamples—and could

---

[27] Op. cit.

[28] See his "Critical Review" of Lewis's *Counterfactuals, Mind* 84 (1975), 451–58.

help explain the truth of counterfactuals (*B*) and (*C*) above—that technical notion would involve analogues of our own notions of base-time and explanation. But if similarity theory eventually converges with our cotenability account for this sort of reason, so much the better for our account.[29]

Another possible way to modify similarity theory in the light of the problem counterfactuals we have mentioned is to use (naive) similarity *in conjuction with* the concept of explanation. In their recent, "Modal Realism: the Poisoned Pawn," for example, F. Mondadori and A. Morton have claimed, roughly, that an appropriate "would" counterfactual "if *p*, then *q*" is true (in the actual world) just in case in some possible *p*-world the explanation of why it is the case that *q* is closer to being a description of the actual world than is the explanation of why it is the case that not-*q* in any other *p*-world.[30] This analysis avoids some of the problems of ordinary similarity theory. Given Warren Commission assumptions, for example, it makes the above counterfactual about Oswald and Kennedy come out false, as we would normally think it was. Even if we obtain a greater closeness to actuality by imagining someone else killing Kennedy than we do by imagining that no one kills him, the closeness thus achieved is closeness to our world in the future and has nothing to do with the closeness of explanations of how Kennedy is killed or fails to be killed to the facts of the actual world. But Mondadori and Morton cannot readily handle the earlier-mentioned "if the amount of matter in the universe today had been between a third and a half *m*, it would have been nearly a half *m*." In (close) possible worlds where there is nearly half as much matter today as there actually is, the explanation of there being that much matter will be something like: there has been nearly a half *m* matter in the past and matter is conserved. And in (close) possible worlds where there is more than a third as much, but not nearly half as much, matter as there actually is, the explanation will be something like: there has been more than a third *m*, but considerably less than a half *m*, matter in the past and matter is conserved. Since the former explanation comes closer to describing the actual world, the Mondadori-Morton view seems to yield the counterintuitive conclusion that the above counterfactual is true.

Mondadori and Morton's revision of similarity theory gets into difficulties through its emphasis on factors of similarity in determining the truth of counterfactuals, but it also avoids some of the problems of similarity theory by using the concept of explanation. My account of counterfactuals in effect extrapolates from

---

[29] Note that Stalnaker's theory is less wedded to ordinary similarity (or, indeed, to any specific conception of similarity) than Lewis's theory in *Counterfactuals* seems to be. But in his as yet unpublished "Counterfactual Dependence and Time's Arrow," Lewis begins to develop a technical conception of similarity that can handle some of the counterexamples we have mentioned and that, indeed, does bear important resemblances to ideas introduced in this paper. Note further that the earlier example of the electric circuit seems to raise problems not only for cotenability theory, but for similarity theory as well. Given that *k* and *l* are closed, *m* is open, the circuit is unbroken, and the light is on, the counterfactual "if *l* were open, the light would be off" turns out true. But it is not obvious that the nearest possible world in which *l* is open is one where *m* is open, the circuit broken, and the light off, rather than one where the circuit is unbroken, *m* closed, and the light on.

[30] See *The Philosophical Review*, LXXXV (1976), esp. 13–16.

Mondadori and Morton's failures and successes. It relies on the concept of explanation and makes no use whatever of (ordinary) comparative similarity.

VI

We do, however, pay a certain price for employing the concept of (causal) explanation in our truth conditions. It would be nice to be able to define causation and explanation in terms of counterfactuals understood independently of these notions, and since our theory does not allow this, it makes counterfactuals seem less interesting than many of us had hoped. It is often said that laws license counterfactuals. Perhaps both laws and facts about what explains what are needed to license most counterfactuals. That may make counterfactuals seem *derivative* from other nomic or causal notions.[31] But it will be worth having a theory of counterfactuals just the same.

We have not treated counterfactuals *generally*. We have not explicitly dealt with quantification into counterfactual contexts, with "might" counterfactuals, or with counterfactuals lacking base-times. But I believe our account could be extended to these other cases. In addition, the proof of various theorems and metatheorems remains part of the task ahead. It is worth noting, however, that at least three important results of similarity theory can be obtained with our truth conditions. Stalnaker and Lewis have made it clear that counterfactuals do not permit of inference by strengthening of the antecedent, by transitivity, or by contraposition. But our truth conditions also yield these results. We have seen how "if I were now to jump out of this window, I would not hurt myself" can be false while "if I were ever to jump out of this window, I would not hurt myself" is true. But the antecedent of the former is just a strengthened version of the antecedent of the latter, and invalidity of strengthening entails invalidity of transitivity.[32] Our theory also helps to account for the invalidity of counterfactual contraposition. "If I were out in the rain, I would be getting wet" can be true while "If I were not getting wet, I would not be out in the rain" is not, because the former implies an acceptable explanatory relationship, and the latter a bizarre and nonexistent one.

Since we have not presented anything as technically developed as Lewis and Stalnaker do, the current plausibility of our theory rests on its ability to account for fine distinctions of ordinary counterfactual usage and to deal more adequately,

---

[31] I assume here that (causal) explanation and causality are involved in understanding counterfactuals, but not *vice versa*. In this limited space, I cannot defend this idea or indicate how I think causality and explanation *should* be understood. But if, on the contrary, it is perfectly in order to analyze counter-factuals via causality and explanation and to analyze causality and explanation via counterfactuality, then none of these notions will be more basic than any other. In either case, counterfactuals will be less important and central than many have hoped.

[32] However, the erroneous implicit assumption that strengthening of the antecedent is valid for any conditional comes quite naturally to most of us, and that is part of the reason why our earlier (A) and (B), or (A) and (D), can so easily seem incompatible.

or less problematically, with the "counterexamples" that have been raised against similarity theory. It has this ability by virtue of its emphasis on explanation (and its nonbackward time direction) and on the interaction between base- and reference-times. The theory may face new counterexamples of its own;[33] but on the whole, I think it comes closer to accounting for our use of counterfactuals than any contenability or similarity theory yet presented.[34]

---

[33] Sidney Morgenbesser has mentioned to me a troublesome case of a sort we have not yet considered. Imagine a completely undetermined random coin. Your friend offers you good odds that it will not come up heads; you decline the bet, he flips, and the coin comes up heads. He then says: "you see; if you had bet (heads), you would have won." I know of no theory of counterfactuals that can adequately explain why such a statement seems natural and correct. But perhaps it simply *isn't* correct and the correct retort to it is: "no, you're wrong; if I had bet (heads), the coin might have come up differently and (so) I might have lost—assuming the coin was random."

[34] I would like to thank Bernard Berofsky, George Boolos, Saul Kripke, David Lewis, Sidney Morgenbesser, Caroline Whitbeck, two readers for *The Philosophical Review*, and the editors of the *Review* for helpful criticisms and suggestions.

7

Assertion and Belief

This talk will have its messy aspects: I simply haven't been able to form a clear picture of all the phenomena I would like to speak to you about. In any event, the phenomena of belief and assertion I shall be dealing with are perhaps themselves simply messier and more confusing than one would initially suspect. And I hope to be able to make at least this much clear to you.

Philosophers have said a great deal about assertion and belief individually and in relation to one another. And there are certain nearly universal points of agreement in what they have said. They would all naturally grant, for example, that if we abstract from moral considerations that might dictate deception and the like and restrict our attention to linguistic convention and epistemic justification, we always ought to believe what we assert. With similar restrictions in force, I think most of us would also be willing to grant that there is, in general, nothing wrong with asserting what we believe and that the form of words used to assert that p will always be apt for expressing the belief that p. It may sound paradoxical, then, if I say that I believe these last two assumptions are mistaken. But I would like to try to convert you to my view of the matter. I shall present an argument to the effect that there are occasions when it is linguistically inappropriate to assert what one (more or less reasonably) believes and when, in particular, the form of words 'p' that we use to assert that p is not apt for expressing one's belief that p. But the argument will not be intended as a *roductio* of any of its premises, the very considerations that make the argument possible will, I think, help to make its conclusion seem less paradoxical than it would, and does, independently of the argument. In the end, I believe it is a conclusion we should all be willing to accept.

We all know that assertion does more than merely propel a proposition out into a conversation with assertoric force. It gives rise to various expectations and implies various things about the assertor, as the oddness of "*p*, but I don't believe that *p*" clearly attests. This particular oddness is typically explained by saying that when we assert that *p*, we imply that we believe that *p*. And that much is, I agree, undeniable. But I think we imply more, much more, when we make an assertion or statement. Would it not sound strange if someone said "it's raining, but I'm not absolutely *sure* that it is" or "it's raining, but I don't really *know* that it is"? And doesn't the oddness of such examples indicate that when we state or assert something, we represent ourselves as being sure and having knowledge about it, not merely as believing what we have asserted?[1] It seems to me that it does. Perhaps that too is why the mere unqualified assertion, e.g., that whiskey is better than wine sounds so much stronger than a more qualified utterance like "in my opinion, whiskey is better than wine." But since the latter clearly represents one as believing that whiskey is better than wine, the greater strength of the former must presumably derive from its representing one as having *more than belief* in this matter. And I think the simplest assumption would be that that greater strength consists precisely in the fact that one who states or asserts that whiskey is better than wine, represents himself as knowing and being sure that whiskey is better than wine.

Note, however, that I make this claim only about asserting and stating that *p*, not about saying that *p*. To borrow an example from Gilbert Harman, if there is a ship's pool and I make my bet with the words "I say that the ship will go five hundred miles today", then I have said that the ship will go five hundred miles. But no one knowing the circumstances would think of me as having implied that I knew how far the ship would go. I was simply betting. By the same token, moreover, no one would take me to have asserted or stated that the ship would go five hundred miles. Though it may be impossible to assert that *p* without saying that *p*, it clearly *is* possible to say that *p* without asserting that *p*, and it is only the latter, I believe, that implies knowledge and certitude on the part of the speaker.

When one asserts that *p*, the proposition that one knows (or is sure) that *p* is obviously not a truth condition of what is asserted, but neither is it a cancellable implication of one's assertion. It would be absurd to assert that *p* and go on to say: "I don't, in asserting *p*, mean, however, that I know that *p*: it may indeed be false that *p*." In this respect, the implications of asserting may resemble those that govern the use of the term "but". If I say "she was rich but she was virtuous," I will typically imply that rich females are unlikely, or less likely than conversationally-determined others, to be virtuous; and it would be absurd to attempt to cancel the implication by adding: "of course, I don't mean to imply that there is any contrast between richness and virtue." So the implication is non-cancellable, but it may not be a truth condition of what is asserted. My original claim that she was rich but virtuous may count as true (though unfelicitous) even if there is no valid contrast between richness and

---

[1] In *Ignorance* (Oxford: 1979, pp. 252–65), P. Unger attempts to show that assertion implies knowledge with the help of examples like these. He also mentions certain other arguments in this direction and says that they originated in discussions he had with me. But I find some of those arguments less persuasive now than I originally did.

virtue.² And I would want to say something similar about the general implications of assertion that I have just been arguing for.

Now if asserting that *p* conventionally and uncancellably represents one as knowing that *p*, then there is something linguistically improper about making an assertion when one does not think one knows the proposition asserted—and something even more improper when one is definitely convinced that one *does not* know that proposition.³ But in most cases where one believes, one believes that one knows. Indeed, it is sometimes maintained as an epistemic principle that if one is justified in believing, one is ipso facto in a position to know or justified in believing that one knows.⁴ But this further, stronger claim is, I think, mistaken. There are occasions when reasonable beings believe, but do not believe that they know or are in a position to know, and epistemologists have sometimes noted the existence of such cases. Thus, to borrow from H. H. Price, if I send a letter to a friend overseas, I believe that the friend will get the letter, but may not believe—or be willing to claim—that I know the letter will arrive safely. Similarly, when I fly from Chicago to Boston, I most certainly believe that the plane won't crash, but do I think that I know that it won't crash? Presumable not. Where there are *very small* but *well-known* and *unavoidable* chances of failure, it may be reasonable to believe in success while doubting or denying that one knows that one won't fail.

Of course, there are possible objections to this way of viewing the matter. It might be held, for example, that when one flies, one doesn't believe one won't crash; one only believes that it is very likely that one won't. Now I don't know about you, but if that were all *I* believed, I don't think I would fly in planes so often. Imagine that you are seated in a plane before take-off and the pilot says: "Ladies and Gentlemen, at the moment this aircraft has a minor technical defect, but we know that you are all in a hurry, and since even with the defect it is still very unlikely that we will crash, we shall proceed with the flight on schedule and not waste time on repairs." Again, as I said, I don't know about you, but I, for one, would be clamoring to be let off that plane. But most of the people who would be doing the clamoring—and how many passengers, really, would not be clamoring in such circumstances?—would in other circumstances be willing to grant that one can't ever know or be sure that a plane won't crash. So if the pilot's bizarre message in the above imaginary case makes one want to get out of the plane, it cannot be because it changes one's mind about whether one knows for sure that the plane won't crash. The reason, rather, is that it makes us no longer *believe* that it won't crash, substituting for that belief the weaker assumption that it is (merely) quite unlikely that a crash will occur. But in that case someone who takes a plane in normal circumstances will presumably

---

² A possibly parallel case. Someone who asserts that Jim is a tall nigger may uncancellably imply that he has a low opinion of Jim; but that low opinion may not count among the truth conditions of what he has asserted. Compare my Gricean account of emotive meaning in "Value Judgments and the Theory of Important Criteria," *Journal of Philosophy* 65, 1968.

³ Perhaps it is only universal principles of conversation that give rise to the implications of assertion, but even so, there will be something linguistically improper about asserting something when one doesn't believe one knows the thing asserted.

⁴ Cf. David Annis, "A Contextualist Theory of Epistemic Justification," *American Philosophical Quarterly*, 15, 1978, p. 217.

believe that the plane won't crash without believing that he knows that it won't; and it is this possibility that we have been at pains to establish. Similarly, we all know that there are inevitable minor risks associated with overseas mail and are unlikely to assert *tout court* that a given letter will arrive safely. But surely our confidence that a given letter will arrive safely amounts to more than the belief that it is *likely* to do so; if, for example, I tell someone that letters to a given country—say, Cambodia—are likely to arrive safely, he will think of our mail links with that country as *less* reliable than those with other foreign countries. And surely that is because most of us simply believe that a given letter *will* arrive safely.

Thus there are times when (reasonable) belief exists but one does not (reasonably) believe that one knows the thing believed. And if we bear in mind our previous conclusions about the implications of asserting, it will become evident how we can argue for the paradoxical conclusions I mentioned at the beginning of this talk. For if someone who asserts that p automatically implies that he knows that p, but it is possible to believe what one is not entitled to assume that one knows, then we are not always entitled to assert what we believe and the precise form of words 'p' will sometimes be inappropriate for expressing our belief that p, because to use it will be to make an assertion that misrepresents (our own opinion about) the true state of our knowledge.[5] These conclusions may now appear somewhat less strange and implausible than when I first said I was going to defend them. And I hope in what follows to be able to defuse what doubts remain through additional considerations I have not yet had time to mention.

The most immediate question that faces anyone willing to join me in accepting the initially paradoxical views that I have just, briefly, defended is this: how are we to express belief that p on those occasions where we do not feel we know that p and thus cannot without impropriety simply utter the sentence 'p'? The answer may be that we should say "I believe that p", a form of words that makes no pretension to knowledge that p. But taken most literally—or perhaps most literalistically—a sentence like "I believe it is raining" does not so much *express* the speaker's belief that it is raining as *ascribe* that belief *to* the speaker. At the very least "I believe that p" seems ambiguous between the self-ascription of a certain belief and the expression of that belief, and it would be nice if we could find some linguistic form that unambiguously served the latter function. We do not, in fact, have far to look. One of the main functions of parenthetic use of "I believe" is precisely to allow one to express a belief rather than ascribe it to oneself. When I say, for example, "It is, I believe, raining outside right now", I back the claim that it is raining outside. I may also represent myself as believing in the truth of that claim, but in any event I do not represent myself as knowing that it is true.[6] So such a form of words is precisely geared for the unambiguous expression of belief in situations where I lack sure knowledge and wouldn't simply assert, for example, that it was raining outside.

---

[5] Of course, one can use 'p' merely to put forward a proposition for consideration or in playacting, but neither use involves the expression of belief. For convenience, I am being somewhat sloppy about the use of quotation.

[6] It is not clear that someone who uses such a parenthetic locution to express belief has asserted *anything*. Is "It is, I believe, raining outside right now" something that one can assert?

The chief difference between "it is raining outside right now" and "it is, I believe, raining outside right now" is that only the former is used to imply that the speaker knows that it is raining outside. So the implication of knowledge that attaches to asserting seems to be in some sense detachable, even if it is not cancellable. And even though we can reasonably believe without believing that we know, it would seem that there is at least one form of words that is always apt for expressing belief, one making parenthetic use of "I believe". Is there any other such form?

What about parenthetic use of "I think", for example? If we believe that it is raining outside, can we not always properly express that belief in the words "It is, I think, raining outside"? Surely this locution is not open to the objection that it represents us as having more than belief. In fact, on the contrary, the problem with this form of words would seem to be, rather, that it fails to represent us as having *as much as* belief. "I think" is in general weaker than "I believe". It would be much odder to say "sometimes I believe there is a God, sometimes I believe there isn't" than it is to say "sometimes I think there is a God, sometimes I think there isn't". And that is because "believe" implies something slightly less hesitant and labile. So although it is in no way misleading or improper to express belief with parenthetic use of "I think", we thereby express something slightly less than belief. Of course, nothing dictates to us that we should be more interested in belief that *p* than in thinking that *p*, but if we seek something universally apt for expressing the full measure of belief, parenthetic use of "I believe" serves much better than a similar use of "I think".

It seems that the adverbs "probably" and "likely" also fail to express the full extent of belief.[7] If I play roulette and am at all rational, then I will believe it likely that I shall lose. But will my tendency in that direction be sufficiently strong so that I actually believe that I shall lose? I think not—judging at least from my own misadventures in this field. One is usually not *that* pessimistic, even when one is rational enough to that the odds are against one. Similarly, epistemic uses of "should" and "ought" like "She should be home by now" express something weaker than belief.

Are we, then, to conclude that parenthetic usage of "I believe" is our sole means of expressing the full extent of belief and nothing stronger? I think not. There is also the phrase "in my opinion". Although it sounds more pompous than "I believe" in certain contexts—e.g., "in my opinion it is raining outside right now"—it nonetheless seems to serve pretty much the same function that we have seen served by parenthetical usage of "I believe".

III

I think that an interesting parallel can at this point be drawn between the expression of "cognitive attitudes" like belief and of "conative attitudes" like intention. I have argued that a sentence '*p*' expresses something quite a bit stronger than belief that *p*, but that the interpolation of a parenthetic "I believe" into such a sentence allows one to express belief and no more. Something analogous exists in the area of intention,

---

[7] J. O. Urmson expresses an opinion to the contrary in his "Parenthetic Verbs", in A. G. N. Flew's *Essays in Conceptual Analysis*, p. 200f.

and I hope, by drawing attention to this parallelism, to give further support to what was said earlier about the implications of assertion and the consequent incommensurability of assertion and belief.

We have all been taught about that curious trick of grammar whereby the divergent forms of the first, second, and third persons reverse themselves when one passes from the ordinary future tense to expressions of intention. Thus "I shall be there" expresses a confident prediction, "I will be there" a firm intention, whereas "he shall be there" expresses my firm intention concerning some third party, and "he will be there" only a confident prediction. Now someone who says "I will be there" and is being sincere expresses his intention to be at a certain location, but what he says seems stronger than what he would have said by uttering the words "I intend to be there." Someone who says "I will be there" may be more or less gently reminded of various ways things might go wrong and brought to the point of saying: "Well, all right, I can't be certain that none of these problems will arise, but I can assure you, anyway, that as of this moment I fully intend to be there." The fact that this later utterance represents a way of retreating from the original expression of intention should suffice to show that "I will be there" is stronger than "I intend to be there", but in what does this greater strength consist?

I think the difference in strength here precisely parallels the difference noted earlier between assertion and the expression of mere belief. If I say "I will be there", I represent myself as entirely confident, as knowing, that I will succeed in fulfilling my intention, just as, when I say, e.g., "I shall, unfortunately, be there", I represent myself as knowing (and regretting) that my belief that I shall be there is true. But as we have seen, when I say "I shall, I believe, be there", we imply only that we believe, not that we know. And a parallel can be found with the expression of intention. We cannot, it is true, weaken an expression of intention by parenthetic means. "I will, I believe, be there" cannot be regarded as a weaker version of the intention-expressing "I will be there", and if such a phrase is uttered, it is naturally taken as the colloquial equivalent of the predictive "I shall, I believe, be there". Just why we cannot make parenthetic interpolations to weaken expressions of intention the way we do to weaken strong expressions of belief I do not know. I think it is a problem that it might prove interesting to investigate, but what is more important at the moment is that English clearly does provide an alternative way of expressing intention more weakly than "I will be there" tends to do. "I intend to be there"—understood as expressive rather than self-ascriptive of intention—is just what is needed.

Clearly, as we have seen, "I intend to be there" is weaker than "I will be there" and does not automatically convey complete confidence the way the latter does. But some of you may be wondering whether "I intend to be there" is as *strong* as I have said; for the parallelism I am arguing for requires us to hold that it is appropriate to utter these words only if one believes that one will be at the place in question, and it may be wondered whether someone who says "I intend to be there" implies so much. Can't someone intend to do something while believing only that he will attempt to do it and that it is possible that he may succeed? And couldn't such a person properly express such an intention by saying "I intend to be there"? I think not. Several recent philosophers[8] have pointed up reasons for thinking that inten-

---

[8] See, e.g., G. Harman's "Practical Reasoning," *Review of Metaphysics*, 29, 1975–76.

tion requires much more than this. If a prisoner believes that he has little chance of breaking out of prison but is going to make an attempt nonetheless, he doesn't intend to break out, he intends to break out if he can; or, alternatively, he intends to *try* to break out. No matter that the prisoner himself might use the words "I intend to break out of here tonight" to some of his fellow prisoners. This is clearly a form of braggadocio—perhaps it is a means of salving his own fears as well—and we immediately recognize the braggadocio because the words he uses express more confidence than he actually has, more confidence at any rate than he has a right to have. To take another example to illustrate the same point, if a teenager's parents have told him that he can't go to a certain party, but he hopes to persuade them to change their minds, he doesn't intend to go to the party that evening: he intends to go if he can, or if he can get his parents' permission.

I would thus want to argue that the relation between "I will be there" and "I intend to be there" is analogous to that between "I shall be there" and "I shall, I believe, be there." In each pair, the first member implies knowledge on the part of the speaker and the second member only implies belief, and the chief difference between the pairs themselves consists in the fact that both "I will be there" and "I intend to be there" automatically express intention, whereas both "I shall be there" and "I shall, I believe, be there" can be used to predict without implying any intention to make that prediction come true. Of course, I have been speaking elliptically in saying all this. It is not "I shall be there" and "I will be there" as sentences that represent the speaker as knowing he will be in the place in question; rather it is certain overwhelmingly frequent typical uses of these sentences, and of sentences like them, that have these sorts of implications. Likewise in the case of the weaker members of both pairs. My meaning should be clear enough at this point. But what should also be clear is that the very neatness of the parallelism just argued for gives us some reason to believe in the individual contentions on which it rests. And in that case, we have still more reason to accept what initially seemed so paradoxical to us, to grant that it is not always (epistemically, linguistically) proper to assert things one believes. Also more reason to put aside any doubts we may still have about whether intending to do something entails belief that one will do it. After all, someone willing to distinguish intending to do something from intending to try to do it and from intending to do it if one could might nonetheless insist that intending to do x entailed only that it was *likely* that one would do x. But the fact that the weakening involved in going from "I will do x" to "I intend to do x" seems no greater than that involved in going from "I shall do x" to "I shall, I believe, do x" supports the stronger entailment advocated above. If both "I will" and "I shall" imply knowledge, then surely, "I intend to do x" implies belief that one actually *will* do x.

IV

At this point let me mention a variety of smallish points to you by way of bringing this talk to a somewhat protracted conclusion. First, I would like you to consider a problem of language that arises out of the linguistic data we have been arguing from. Quite independently of our more contentious conclusions, most people would grant, for example, that "I shall be there" is in some way stronger than either "I believe that I shall be there" or "I shall, I believe, be there". And yet someone who says "I shall be there" can retreat to "Well, at least I believe I shall be there" in a way that he cannot, grammatically, retreat to "Well, at least I shall, I believe, be there." I have been unable to find any explanation for this difference that doesn't raise as many problems as it solves. Perhaps a plausible explanation will occur to one of you.

Next let me ask two questions that have been bothering me. First, what does someone who believes that *p* without believing that he knows that *p* say *in foro interno* at times when he has, so to speak, an occurrent belief that *p*. The usual view, I believe, is that occurrent belief involves asserting what one believes to oneself, but our earlier conclusions raise problems for this account. Unless assertion *in foro interno* differs from ordinary assertion in its implications of knowledge, it will not be appropriate for someone who believes without believing that he knows. And in that case we must ask how occurrent belief can take place in such a person. The alternative suggestion that occurrent belief is simply the conscious entertaining of a belief that one in fact (dispositionally) has avoids this problem, but has well-known weaknesses of its own. I realize, of course, that various problems about the distinction between dispositional and occurrent belief are already under discussion; I simply wish to add to their number by pointing up the difficulty of characterizing how certain occurrent beliefs can make their appearance in consciousness.

My second question concerns the universality of the phenomena we have been discussing. It may be a fact that something doesn't count as an assertion that *p* unless it represents the speaker(s) as knowing that *p*, but does this not still leave open the possibility of a language in which the form of words '*p*' could express the belief that *p* without at the same time representing one as knowing that *p*? (Of course, if this is possible, then the implication of knowledge attaching to our assertions is presumably conventional and not determined by universal principles of conversation.) I cannot see any reason why such a language should be impossible; all we may be able to say is that the users of that language would not be using the form of words '*p*' to make what we would call assertions-that-*p*? On the other hand, there may be some unsuspected incoherence in the notion of such a language, though I have no idea myself about how one would go about arguing for this.

Finally, let me try to scotch one implication that one might seek to draw from this paper. A sceptic about knowledge could use our conclusions here to argue that one should never assert anything, at least anything substantial about the world. This is the line Unger pushes in his book *Ignorance*, but I have no desire to encourage it. Quite to the contrary, I think what we have said can help us in working out an anti-sceptical theory of knowledge. In doing epistemology, there is a kind of half-way house that philosophers considering scepticism sometimes take refuge in. Though they may be unwilling to go the whole way with the sceptic, the arguments of the sceptic may nonetheless have succeeded with them to the extent of getting them, in professional contexts, to narrow down the class of claims they would say were known to be true. I have in mind, for example, the sort of philosopher who has been led, by the study of epistemological scepticism, to deny that he really knows that the departmental secretary is typing in the next room. (Assume he or she hears the *sound* of efficient typing coming from the next room.)

What we have said here about knowledge and assertion may help to provide an antidote to such half-way scepticism. For it can be pointed out to such a philosopher that he would unhesitatingly assert that the secretary was in the next room—in response, say, to a telephone query; and we may be able to convince him that by making such an assertion he would represent himself as knowing what the study of epistemology has made him claim he doesn't know. Caught in such a bind, the philosopher might, of course, become more hesitant about assertion. But I think, at least I hope, that he would be more likely to conclude that scepticism had distorted his ability to recognize instances of knowledge. And at that point he might start letting his natural inclinations to assert reinstate his previous ordinary standards for knowledge.

Understanding Free Will

In recent years, Harry Frankfurt, Wright Neely, and Gary Watson have offered accounts of free will and free agency that play down the challenge of determinism and equate freedom with a kind of rationality in action.[1]

I believe that the approach taken by Frankfurt, Neely, and Watson (FNW, for short) represents, in its conceptual sophistication and explanatory power, a genuine advance over previous rationality theories of freedom like that of Spinoza. But I also believe that FNW have themselves misunderstood, or failed to see clearly, the nature and implications of their own theories, and that the theories they present must borrow ideas from Spinoza in order to escape implausibility and attain their fullest development. In the end, however, I shall argue that no available rationality conception fully captures our intuitions about what it is to act of one's own free will.

I

Let me first give a rough sketch of some of the important features of FNW's approach, for the most part concentrating on Frankfurt's theory, which has been the

---

[1] See Neely, "Freedom and Desire," *Philosophical Review*, LXXXIII, 1 (January 1974): 32–54; Watson, "Free Agency," this JOURNAL, LXXII, 8 (Apr. 24, 1975): 205–220; Frankfurt, "Freedom of the Will and the Concept of a Person," *ibid.*, LXVIII, 1 (Jan. 14, 1971): 5–20, "Coercion and Moral Responsibility," in T. Honderich, ed., *Essays in Freedom of Action* (London: Routledge & Kegan Paul, 1973), pp. 65–86; and "Three Concepts of Free Action II," *Proceedings of the Aristotelian Society*, suppl. vol. XLIX (1975):

most elaborately and systematically developed, but indicating differences among the theories when it seems important to do so.

All three philosophers focus upon cases of irrational addiction as paradigms of unfreedom.[2] Frankfurt and Neely both characterize the typical unwilling addict as someone who (e.g.) has a second-order desire not to *desire* some drug and a second-order desire (or volition) not to *give in* to his (or her) first-order desire for the drug, but who (irrationally) gives in to his first-order desire for the drug, nonetheless.[3] In a slightly different vein, Watson characterizes the unwilling addict as someone who (e.g.) puts no (positive) value upon (getting) a certain drug, but who (irrationally) acts upon his strong desire for the drug, nonetheless. In the light of such examples, they then claim, roughly, that a person acts freely when and only when his actions flow from his higher-, or highest-, order desires/volitions, rather than opposing them; alternatively, in Watson's conception, a person acts freely when and only when his actions express his values and not just his (strongest) desires or wants. At this point, I think at least some of the connection between FNW's theories and Spinoza's rationality conception of freedom should be apparent: the addictive people that the former treat as unfree are clearly also cases of Spinozan "human bondage."

Frankfurt makes the further claim that a bank clerk who reluctantly hands over money to a holdup man who threatens him with a gun will typically count, on the account he has offered, as having acted freely.[4] Such a man, he says, would prefer not to have to make the choice that faces him; but, faced with that choice, he is satisfied to be moved by his desire to hand over the money and acts in accordance with a second-order volition. And although Frankfurt also holds that the clerk will resent the intruder and be actively discontented, presumably because he feels loyalty to the bank or to its clients, he seems to feel that such descriptions do not conflict with his characterization of the act as free by the lights of his own theory. To say that such a bank clerk acts freely has, Frankfurt admits, a jarring sound; and he thinks it a prima facie condition on the adequacy of a theory of free action that someone acting under duress in the manner of his bank clerk be judged not to have acted freely (or, presumably, of his own free will). But he attempts to mitigate the presumed implausibility of his theory not by modifying the theory, but by positing a second sense of 'free action' in which the bank clerk does *not* act freely. Neely makes the very same response to

---

113–125. Also cf. Gerald Dworkin, "Acting Freely," *Noûs*, IV, 4 (November 1970): 367–383, for a similar approach to freedom which I shall not specifically discuss.

[2] The expressions 'freedom', 'free agency', '(acting) freely', and '(acting) of one's own free will' all occur in the papers of FNW. But among such expressions, the phrase 'of one's (his) own free will' has, for English-speaking philosophers, the distinct advantage of indicating that what one is saying is relevant to the traditional problem of free will. This particular phrase, then, will be canonical for the present essay, and any other expressions I use *in propria persona* will be merely stylistic variants. Although I shall often make use of FNW's particular terminologies in reporting their views, I believe that our own canonical phraseology can be used to report those views without undue distortion. After all, they too want their ideas to be relevant to the traditional problem of free will.

[3] For Frankfurt, second-order volitions are a particular kind of second-order desire: desires that one or another first-order desire be (or not be) acted upon, i.e., effective in action. See "Freedom of the Will and the Concept of a Person," p. 8 ff.; and "Three Concepts of Free Action II," p. 114.

[4] "Three Concepts...," pp. 113–117, 122–124.

cases of duress: he does not see how his own theory can handle them and claims that there is another sense of 'free' that can.⁵

But it seems both ad hoc and self-indulgent to respond to the inability of an analysis to account for certain cases not by reformulating the analysis, but by holding on to it and claiming that the problem cases only demonstrate that there are two senses of the term or expression one is trying to define. Moreover, there is also good reason to believe that the difficulties Frankfurt and Neely think cases of duress present to their theories are themselves more imagined than real. I think it can be shown that Frankfurt and Neely's own theories, suitably supplemented, can actually *explain* why the everyday cases of duress they have in mind are not cases in which (it is natural to say that) a person acts of his own free will.

As Frankfurt and Neely describe the relevant cases of coercion, the person who reluctantly complies with a threat is reasonable to do so. So, given the emphasis their theories place on certain elements of rationality in the concept of free action, it might easily seem that they would be committed to saying that Frankfurt's bank clerk hands over the money of his own free will. But although it may be reasonable, or rational, for the clerk *to* comply with the robber's threat, he may not act rationally *in* complying with it. He may, for example, be overly frightened, or panicked; and he almost certainly will resent the intruder, if, as Frankfurt seems to assume, he has any loyalty either to the bank or to the people it serves. But does this resentment not signify a desire (or wish) for retaliation or defiance: that is, not merely a desire that the would-be robber should somehow be punished, but a desire to do something oneself to punish him or, at least, to show him what one thinks of him? Even if heroism is not widely treated as a moral obligation, most of us have a deep tendency to treat it as an ideal to be emulated. And so I think that if the clerk resents the robber, he will have various momentary/fragmentary fantasies of heroic defiance, or foiling, or retaliation, with appropriate accompanying thoughts.

But then someone who fulfills Frankfurt's description of the bank clerk and about whom the above things are also true will qualify as *ambivalent*, if he ends up complying with the intruder's threat: ambivalent, in particular, about his own compliance. On the one hand, to the very extent that the afore-mentioned resentment, wishes, and fantasies exist, he will tend, both before and after the fact, to reproach himself for saving his own skin.⁶ When he complies with the robber's threat, such a person acts from a desire by which he wishes not to be moved to act, even *given* the alternatives he confronts. There is in him a conflict between a first-order desire to comply (and play it safe) and an ultimately frustrated second-order volition that that desire not be effective and that, in particular, he should overcome that

---

⁵ "Freedom and Desire," pp. 35, 50.

⁶ It is a psychological commonplace that anger or resentment against a given person tends to displace itself onto other (inappropriate) targets when it cannot be directed against its original object. So perhaps we can draw a more direct connection between the clerk's resentment of the intruder and his later self-reproach, by arguing that if he does hand over the money and has any compunction about blaming innocent associates, his unsatisfied anger at the intruder is apt to turn inward (*sub specie* his ideals of heroism). For more on how resentment against others may be turned against the self, compare Nietzsche's fascinating speculations in *The Genealogy of Morals, passim*.

safe-playing desire through appropriate heroics or defiance. And so he will count as not having acted freely, on Frankfurt's own theory.[7] But, on the other hand, the bank clerk will also, presumably, have an opposing second-order volition that his desire to play it safe should be effective and his tendencies toward defiance and heroics restrained, based on the value he places on his own self-preservation. And it is just this conflict of second-order volitions that qualifies the clerk's attitude toward his compliance as ambivalence. Frankfurt ignores the possibility that his bank clerk might have to be ambivalent, given the descriptions he furnishes and normal human background assumptions. But once we recognize the ambivalence of the typical bank clerk in the situation imagined, we can see that there is no need to reformulate Frankfurt and Neely's theories or postulate a second meaning of 'freedom' in order to explain our reluctance to characterize most people who act under duress as acting freely.[8]

In saying that someone who is ambivalent about his own actions in the way described above does not act freely—either on FNW's theories or in actual fact—I do not, however, mean to suggest that *whenever* we choose among desires that cannot, in certain circumstances, be jointly realized, we do not act of our own free will. The choice of one out of an incompatible set of alternatives need not involve one in ambivalence about one's choice. If, for example, I have a hankering for Italian food and a stronger hankering for Chinese food that eventually "wins out," I may not in any way wish that my desire for Chinese food had not been effective, even though my hankering for Italian food has not been satisfied or entirely disappeared. For simply to have a desire for something is not, automatically, to want (wish) that other, incompatible desires not exist or be fulfilled. In ambivalence, then, we have conflicting second-order desires/volitions about a first-level desire or want: wanting the first-level desire to exist or issue in action and, at the same time, wanting this not to be so. And there seems to be no reason to suppose that this phenomenon must be present when we (simply) choose between jointly unrealizable desires on the basis, say, of the greater strength of one of those desires.

Certain kinds of ambivalence, then, disqualify one from acting of one's own free will. But that is not to say that all cases of irrational, unfree action involve ambivalence. The heroin addict may not have conflicting second-order volitions in the manner of the bank clerk; he may desire heroin, wish that desire were not effective, and in no way want the desire to be effective or even to exist. To put the matter in Watson's terminology, he may place no value on realizing his desire for heroin, whereas the ambivalent bank clerk seems to place a value both on fulfilling his desire to take no chances and on overcoming that desire in heroism. However, the bank clerk and the addict do fail to act from one of their highest-order desires. And it is this common failure that makes them seem to fall short of rationality-in-action in a way that someone who merely acts from the strongest of his jointly unrealizable desires does not.[9]

---

[7] Cf. "Three Concepts...," pp. 114, 117.

[8] If we assume that no *given* act can really express an ambivalent person's values, then Watson too can account for the lack of free agency in typical cases of duress.

[9] Neely (*op. cit.*, p. 48 f) says that anyone with conflicting desires is to that extent less free; but this very statement gives us reason to suspect that he is characterizing not our ordinary concept of acting of one's own free will, but some other, related notion, or ideal, of freedom. I shall ignore this divergence in what follows.

II

I have so far touched upon only one central case of acting under threat or duress. For ideological or personal reasons, however, some bank clerk might be quite *willing* to hand over money to an armed robber. But then he would be unlikely to be ambivalent about handing over the money, and there would be little reason to deny that he did so of his own free will.

It also seems to be possible for someone to comply with an initially unwelcome threat without being ambivalent, and this fact must be accounted for and brought to bear on the theories of free agency we have been discussing. Consider a man told by a king whom he dislikes that if he does not visit him at the palace in a month's time, he will be sent to prison. Is it not possible that the man should reasonably decide that compliance was the sensible course of action under the circumstances and should reconcile himself to the visit—so that when the time came for him to go to the palace, he neither resented the king for forcing such a choice upon him nor wished, at some level, that he could somehow defy or disobey him? Such a person responds to the king's threat, calmly and unambivalently, as if it were some sort of *physical* obstacle, and that may give us reason to say that when he finally does visit the palace, he does so of his own free will.[10] For someone who (e.g.) comes to a large lake while on a long journey may well be faced with a choice—between detouring around the lake and turning back—that he would have preferred not to have to make. But typically, when faced with such a physical obstacle, a traveler will ungrumblingly and automatically adjust his plans; and we would normally think of such a traveler as going around the lake of his own free will, even though the location of the lake clearly does make his options worse than he might have expected. And if the man whom the king threatens has an "objective" and ungrumbling attitude toward the consequent deterioration of his options—I assume that he would generally prefer not to visit such a king, even if he knows he is in no danger in doing so—then I believe he too counts as acting of his own free will if and when he finally visits the palace on the appointed day. Certainly, there is a long tradition, exemplified by Spinoza, in which the ability to reconcile oneself to the inevitable without bitterness, or personalizing, or self-recrimination, is taken as a major aspect of what is involved in being a free person. Indeed, the ability to have such an attitude to the necessities of choice, event, and circumstance that the world imposes is quite commonly considered to mark one as being "philosophical" in that widespread use of the term that everyone but philosophers seems to use.

Now although FNW pay no particular attention to cases of acting "philosophically," on their theories the man we have just described clearly counts as acting freely.

---

[10] It is less natural to say that he complies with the king's threat of his own free will than that he goes to the palace of his own free will. "Of his own free will" entails "knowingly" and "intentionally" and possesses the intensionality of these latter concepts; so although one may in doing X also be doing Y, it can still be the case that one is doing X of one's own free will but not doing Y of one's own free will. It sounds somewhat odd to say that someone complies with a threat of his own free will, because it suggests that the person involved is consciously aware that he is acting as he does because of a threat; for this, in turn, suggests rather too much dwelling on the particular source of his action to make it plausible to think that he really is reconciled and "objective" about his situation or thus acting freely. It stands in favor of our account, of course, that it can explain our tendency to make these fine distinctions. But, for ease of exposition, I shall sometimes use phrases that suggest that 'of his own free will' is not intensional.

But despite Frankfurt and Neely's mistaken opinion to the contrary, those theories allow for the possibility of free rational compliance with an (initially) unwelcome threat *only in certain cases*, the very cases about which Spinoza and, I think, we ourselves would be most inclined to say that freedom was exemplified. I would not, however, want to minimize the doubts that can arise about whether freedom really does exist in cases where someone has a "philosophical" attitude in complying with a threat. One might well feel that the king in our earlier example has so effectively intervened in the life of his "philosophical" subject, that the latter's act of visiting the palace is to a significant extent attributable to the king who has changed his options and thus not really, or fully, his own. One may feel, in other words, that however philosophical someone may be, he does not act of his own free will if the acts of another person play such an important role in determining his behavior. (One will presumably still maintain that the "intervention" of natural obstacles does not deprive people of free agency in this way, since, to ordinary ways of thinking, a person may in the course of a journey go around a lake of his own free will, even if the lake has worsened his options and led him to act as he does.)

I can see some force in these claims, but I also think that if one accepts them, one raises problems for oneself that the claims themselves are powerless to deal with (even if one grants the causal distinction between human and nonhuman "interventions" on which they are based). In particular, if we say that a threatener takes away the agency of someone who complies with his threat and that the threatened individual—whatever his inner attitude—does not, in complying, act of his own free will, we will have a problem understanding why highly attractive offers are not usually thought of as depriving us of freedom. For an attractive offer changes our options dramatically, and it seems as reasonable to attribute "ultimate agency" to someone who makes an effective offer as to someone who makes an effective threat. So I think we should be suspicious of the view that effective threats automatically deprive one of free will. What is needed, instead, is a theory of acting freely that can explain why our earlier bank clerk does not hand over the money of his own free will, but also allow for effective offers that do not deprive of freedom. And what is also needed is a theory of free agency that can accommodate our feeling that some offers are so "coercive" and humiliating that if we do take advantage of them, we act no more freely than the bank clerk—a theory, that is, that can explain why some effective offers render us less free as agents than certain others.

I believe that FNW's conception(s) of freedom can achieve these results, once we take into account the sorts of psychological phenomena mentioned earlier and ignored, for the most part, by FNW. Their theory can explain the unfreedom of the original bank clerk in terms of his ambivalence and, ultimately, of the conflict between his effective first-order desire and one of his second-order volitions. And the difference between offers that deprive of free agency and offers that do not can, I believe, be explained in similar terms. If someone offers us an opportunity that offends none of our deeply felt values and that we feel worthy of, then if we take advantage of the opportunity, we presumably do so without ambivalence and (barring other factors that might prejudice the issue) of our own free will. But consider someone who is offered a million dollars if he will lick the offerer's boots. Almost any person who took advantage of such an offer would resent the person who had made such a "coercive" offer and be somewhat ambivalent about taking advantage of it. Most of us have some ideal notion of ourselves as not being the kind of person who can be made to lower and humiliate himself for a price. So even someone who feels that it is rational and worth while for him to lick the boots will also think less of himself for being willing to be rational in this way and wish that he were somehow above this sort of thing; and it is this state of ambivalent conflict that accounts for our intuitive judgment that such a person does not lick the boots of his own free will.

The theories of FNW thus enable us to explain important intuitive distinctions concerning the freedom or lack of freedom involved in typical responses to various sorts of offers and threats. The assumption that an effective threat always deprives of freedom, on the other hand, seems, if anything, to make such distinctions impossible of explanation. Since, moreover, the FNW theories entail that certain people who are philosophical about the threats they comply with act of their own free will, the explanatory and distinction-making power of those theories give us reasons of simplicity and system to deny that effective threats always deprive of free agency. We are, instead, given reason to accept the Spinozistic view that one is free to the extent that one responds calmly and unresentfully to the necessities the world imposes and rationally, without self-recrimination, chooses the good in the light of such necessities.[11]

Of course, there are other reasons already alluded to for thinking that someone who has a philosophical attitude in complying with a threat acts freely. Such a person does, after all, depersonalize things and treat the threat he confronts in the way that most people treat ordinary physical obstacles. Since accommodation to a physical obstacle seems in no way, intuitively, to deprive an agent of his freedom, we have some reason to say the same thing about someone who complies philosophically with a threat. It is important in this connection, however, to avoid overly strong claims about the human capacity for being philosophical, and acting freely, while complying with a threat. Even someone with a capacity for philosophical calm and acceptance may not have the time to cultivate such an attitude if—like our earlier bank clerk or any robbery victim who is told "your money or your life"—he is faced with a threat that requires immediate compliance. The Stoics (and perhaps even Spinoza) seem to have thought both that it was possible to be philosophical and free even in response to such abrupt and immediate threats and that one should cultivate the capacity for such response.[12] But it is at just this point that I find myself in deepest disagreement with the Stoics—and with Spinoza, to the extent that he agrees with them.

---

[11] I here follow Spinoza in assuming that there are some occasions when a rational and self-respecting individual will comply with a threat, rather than defy it, without reproaching himself for doing so. (See the *Ethics*, Book 4, props. XX, LXV, and LXIX, proof, corollary, and note.) Frankfurt's clerk may reproach himself for not acting heroically only because he is *not* calm, unangry, and "philosophical" about his situation. Cf. footnote 6, above; and remember, too, that most of us conceive heroism as an ideal to emulate, rather than as a moral obligation.

[12] In what follows, I shall play down certain differences between Spinoza and the Stoics, but on the whole the Stoics seem much more committed than Spinoza to the idea that reason can control emotion. In fact, Spinoza explicitly asserts a difference of this kind between his own view and that of the Stoics. (In the *Ethics*, Book 5, preface; but also see Book 5, Proposition X, proof and note; Book 5, Proposition VI; Book 4, Proposition LXXIII.) On the other hand, there are major differences among the Stoics themselves about the extent to which reason can control passion and emotion. The doctrine

Consider the loyal bank clerk of our earlier example. It is a contradiction in terms to suppose that he can have an emotional attitude like loyalty and yet also be able to pick and choose among his emotional *reactions* in such a way as to (decide to) be calm and unresentful at the prospect of handing over the bank's money to an armed intruder. If someone whom we knew to have this sort of loyalty told us that he felt completely detached and emotionless in handing over money to a holdup man, we would very likely conclude that for some reason he was refusing to face his deepest feelings. And all this would also hold, a fortiori, of someone who had to give his own patiently accumulated savings to a holdup man. Faced with threats that require immediate action and that lower our expectations significantly, we cannot be completely philosophical and are incapable of free compliance. It takes time to work through resentment and reluctance, and only if a threat requires action in the relatively distant future will one's capacity for being philosophical have time to take hold. Only with such a temporal breathing space can one work through the inevitable initial reactions and come to accept the necessity of the adverse choice with which one is presented in such a way that, in complying with the threat, one acts of one's own free will.

The Stoic (or Spinoza) will claim that these considerations only show how emotionally attached to worldly things we actually are. If only we cultivated our capacity for emotional detachment, we could learn to respond to immediate threats without ambivalence or emotion and thus to act freely whether we complied with them or not. But I think that what the Stoic says is possible is not really possible, for us. Another, higher sort of being that never went through the dependency of prolonged childhood might never need or want love. But we are not beings of that sort: we seek love from the start and never really outgrow that quest or its urgency. Thus the Stoic or Spinozan ideal of emotional detachment is an illusion for us, an ideal perhaps, but one that we are simply not capable of. And if we make this assumption, then the injunction to cultivate detachment to the greatest extent possible will seem highly problematic, and the Stoic or Spinozan who claims to have achieved emotional detachment will be thought to be papering over his or her own deep (possibly thwarted) yearnings for love.

To the extent, moreover, that we love particular things or persons, we must be capable of resentment, sorrow, and anger. If threats against a loved one really leave one calm and philosophical from the start, the claim actually to love that person may be irretrievably undermined. In the abstract, the capacity to respond to threats philosophically may well be an ideal thing, a perfection. And since love for individuals by its very nature undercuts this capacity, love, as well as the need or desire for love, may constitute human weaknesses. But if these things are weaknesses, they are *basic* human weaknesses. By that I mean that they are weaknesses so endemic to our nature that if one seeks, like the Stoic, to avoid being subject to them, one is likely to get oneself into a worse position than one would have been in if one had simply accepted

---

of total control was advocated by Chrysippus, but Posidonius seems to have held that emotions and passions were in some measure autonomous and not under the direct, immediate control of reason. [On this see F. H. Sandbach, *The Stoics* (London: Chatto & Windus, 1975), pp. 59–67, esp. p. 65.]

the weakness in oneself.[13] Love and our tendency to feel sorrow and resentment may be basic human weaknesses in this sense, because if one attempts not to love anyone and not to resent or be sad at anything, no matter how badly one is treated, one may cover up these sorts of feelings, but will also, in doing so, give them all sorts of free rein for subterranean mischief and eventual destructive effect within one's life.

Of course, some of these considerations might incline one to go to the opposite extreme from the Stoics and claim that resentment at the loss of things one loves or values may sink into the depths of our minds, but never completely dissolves. I do not see why we should believe this to be true, but, even if it is, there is no need to modify the conception of free action offered by FNW. It will simply turn out that all cases of complying with an unwelcome threat will qualify as unfree on their own theories, and we will be spared the burden of having to argue for the freedom of those who have a philosophical attitude in complying with threats. On the other hand, if the Stoics are right, and someone really could accommodate himself to all threats immediately and without emotion, there will still be no need to modify the theories of FNW.[14]

III

I would like now to show that the theories of FNW, properly understood and supported, have the important consequence that acting of one's own free will—what we shall for brevity sometimes call "free will"—is not necessary to moral responsibility, blame-worthiness, and the like. In our earlier example of the reluctant bank clerk, the clerk does not hand over the money of his own free will because he acts from a desire he wishes he could rise above. But nothing in our description precludes that he acts thoughtlessly, forgetting that there is an alarm button nearby that he can push to foil the robber. And if that is his situation, then we will feel that he shouldn't hand over the money and is not only morally responsible but blameworthy for doing so.[15]

Frankfurt too believes that his bank clerk can be morally responsible and blameworthy for the way he acts under duress.[16] He also holds that it is one requisite of a good account of free action that moral responsibility should come out entailing freedom, and says that his own theory has that consequence. But it does not have that consequence, if, as we have argued, Frankfurt is mistaken in thinking that his theory commits him to calling his bank clerk a free agent. Even prescinding from

---

[13] Cf. Pascal's aphorism: "men are so necessarily mad, that not to be mad would amount to another form of madness," in the *Pensées*, ed. T. S. Eliot (New York: Dutton, 1958), sec. 414, p. 110.

[14] I shall not consider whether someone who is philosophical in complying with an effective threat must be thought to act under duress or to have been coerced into doing what he does.

[15] We may be tempted to say that he is (fully) responsible or blameworthy not for handing over the money, but only for not pushing the alarm button. However, since we would not naturally say that the clerk omits the button pushing of his own free will (cf. footnote 10, above), we are still left with a case of moral responsibility and culpability for an non-free act (omission). (I am indebted here to Bernard Berofsky.)

For a different attempt to argue for the possibility of being morally responsible for negligence or thoughtlessness in a situation where one does not act freely, see Don Locke, "Three Concepts of Free Action I," *Proceedings of the Aristotelian Society*, suppl. vol. IL (1975): 95–112, p. 109.

[16] Frankfurt, "Three Concepts...," pp. 115, 123.

Frankfurt's interpretation of his theory for cases of duress, it is not clear that Frankfurt can easily maintain that acting freely is necessary to moral responsibility. For on his account, someone struggling against a strong desire (e.g., an incipient addiction) who in the end gives in to that desire fails to act of his own free will. But nothing in this description forces us to say that the person who succumbs to his desire had to behave as he did, was compulsive rather than morally weak or, more generally, weak-willed. So, once again, Frankfurt will have to allow for cases where his definition of free will is not met but an agent is nonetheless morally responsible and even blameworthy for what he does, unless he takes the risky step of altogether denying the possibility of (blameworthy) moral weakness.

Note further that it sounds jarring and unnatural to say the (reluctant) clerk hands over the money of his own free will quite independently of any assumptions we make about whether he *had* to hand the money over or was *compelled* to do so. But this tends to show how important it is to bring in something like FNW's theories to explain our intuitive judgments about the clerk. For those theories explain why, even if he could have done otherwise, the bank clerk is judged not to act of his own free will. Of course, if the clerk for some reason really cannot do otherwise, then we may say he is not morally responsible for his actions. But as we have just seen, the judgment that someone can do otherwise does not entail the judgment that he acts of his own free will.[17] So even if being able to do otherwise is necessary to moral responsibility, that has no tendency to show that we must act of our own free will in order to be responsible for our actions.

Despite what we have said, it might nonetheless be objected at this point that moral responsibility requires freedom in *some* customary (philosophical) sense, even if it does not entail that one act *of one's own free will*. But even if such a sense of 'freedom' exists, why should it be considered immediately relevant to *freedom of will?* Perhaps the free-will problem is simply different from the problem of the conditions of moral responsibility and the contrary opinion only arises from the misconception that the importance of free will depends on its being necessary to moral responsibility.[18] More important still, if such a (further) sense of 'freedom' really were immediately at issue in the free-will question, it would follow that any proof that we sometimes (never) do things of our own free will would be itself be insufficient to show that we had (lacked) free will. And this consequence will surely seem

---

[17] Cf. P. S. Greenspan, "Behavior Control and Freedom of Action," *Philosophical Review*, LXXXVII, 2 (April 1978): 225–240, pp. 231–233.

[18] In the title essay of *In Defence of Free Will* (London: Allen & Unwin, 1967, p. 36), C. A. Campbell claims that free will is important only if it is necessary to moral responsibility. But the theories of FNW militate against Campbell's conclusion by pointing up how intrinsically undesirable certain sorts of unfreedom can be. If we accept their conception of freedom, then the cases of unwilling addiction and of "philosophical" calm-in-action both illustrate the importance free will has independently of its connection with moral action and moral responsibility.

I am not, however, proposing a complete dissociation of free will and moral responsibility. In the next section, we shall discuss a condition of autonomy in action which is necessary to free will and which seems necessary to moral responsibility as well. This common necessary condition can easily seem incompatible with determinism, and so it is also no part of my intention to deny that determinism poses a threat both to free will and to moral responsibility.

counterintuitive to philosophers in the English-speaking tradition. After all, Paradigm Case "solutions" to the free-will problem are considered objectionable because they are based on the Paradigm Case Argument, not because they assume the special relevance of the notion of acting of one's own free will to the traditional problem of free will. So it cannot perhaps be an objection to the approach of the present paper that it rests on a similar assumption.

IV

Although I have all along been defending rationality theories, I do not, in the end, think that any of them offers a totally adequate conception of freedom of will. I think they offer us necessary, but not sufficient, conditions of freedom and that the conditions they omit are among the most important for understanding why free will has been such a perennial problem for philosophers.

In "Freedom of the Will and the Concept of a Person," Frankfurt makes clear his commitment to the sufficiency of his conditions for acting freely and claims, in particular, that the existence of free will or agency does not depend on how such freedom comes about.[19] It is precisely here that I (and others)[20] disagree with Frankfurt: certain ways of coming to fulfill Frankfurt's conditions of freedom seem, intuitively, to *deprive* one of free agency. Consider the following example. Robert, who is genuinely undecided between two conflicting first-order desires X and Y, is visited by a hypnotist who decides to "solve" his problem by putting him in a trance and inducing in him a second-order volition in favor of X; as a result of having this second-order volition, Robert then acts to satisfy X, never suspecting that his decisiveness has been induced by the hypnotist. The example may bear the marks of science fiction, but it seems adequate, nonetheless, to point up the conceptual insufficiency of "rationality" conditions of free action. For we would all surely deny that Robert acts of his own free will, when he acts from the second-order volition induced by the hypnotist.

But it is important to consider why we want to say this. We would, after all, describe Robert as having *willingly* satisfied desire X; so in denying that he acts *of his own free will*, we must be implicitly assuming that so acting involves something more than willingness taken together with our previous rationality conditions. And I believe that this further condition, in simplest terms, comes down to the requirement that our actions be fully *our own*. The feeling that Robert does not, in satisfying X, act of his own free will reflects, I think, our belief that because of the particular way the hypnotist has intervened in his life, his act is not fully his own.[21] And the assumption that acting of one's own free will requires that one's actions be fully one's own also helps us to explain what the words 'one's own' are doing in the phrase

---

[19] *Ibid.*, p. 20. See also "Three Concepts...," p. 121 ff.

[20] See D. Locke, *op. cit.*, p. 105 f.

[21] Some kinds of intervention do *not* seem to deprive an agent of his freedom. If, instead of inducing a second-order volition in a given person, someone softens the force of one of his addictions—through a surgical intervention he is unaware of—so that he later finds it easier to resist the addiction, we might not want to deny that the person involved acted of his own free will in successfully resisting the addiction.

'of one's own free will'[22] and to understand the force of our intuitive distinction, in the above example, between freedom of will and mere willingness.

In order to act of one's *own* free will, then, one's actions must be fully one's own; one must in some sense act autonomously. But these locutions, however intuitive, are extremely vague, and, at this point, there are several problems that must be faced if we are to advance our understanding of free will. We will, to begin with, want to know whether anything more definite can be said about this autonomy that seems necessary to free will but not to be implied by anything in rationality theories. But we must also ask whether such a spelling out of the notion of autonomy can help us to understand the relevance of determinism to freedom of will. FNW's theories make it difficult to see how anyone could think that determinism ever presented a challenge to free will. And it is surely some sort of problem for those theories that they seem to offer no way to make sense of the age-old belief in such a challenge. (After all, for many of us "the problem of free will" is just an ellipsis for "the problem of free will and determinism.") If, however, some sort of autonomy is, as we have claimed, necessary to freedom of will, further specification of that notion may help to explain why determinism makes free will problematic by making it clear why determinism represents a challenge to autonomy thus specified.

Of course, it might turn out that the theories of FNW, even supplemented by an appropriately elaborate conception of autonomy, did not offer sufficient conditions for freedom of will, and that some further condition, e.g., being able to do otherwise, was necessary to freedom and was the aspect of free will on which the relevance of determinism depended.[23] But this suggestion must be treated with caution, since there have long been and even now continue to be important challenges to the notion that the ability to do otherwise is necessary to acting freely. Thus if what I have just been saying is correct, a good part of the free-will problem remains up in the air. The theories of FNW offer significant necessary conditions of free will, and they have an explanatory power (and important implications) that even their proponents fail to recognize. But they leave other problems untouched; and I only hope that what we have said here may give some indication of the directions we must take in order to make further progress in understanding free will.

Note too that the inducing of second-order volitions provides a much better example of an intervention that deprives an agent of freedom by rendering his actions not fully his own, than do the effective threats (or offer) we discussed earlier. I think this has something to do with the fact that someone who complies with a threat (or offer) *knows about the intervention of another person in the situation* and *himself makes a decision to do what that person wants*; neither of these things seems to be true of the person whose second-order volition is induced in the manner of our example.

[22] Cf. W. F. R. Hardie, "My Own Free Will," *Philosophy*, XXXII, 120 (January 1957): 21–23.

[23] It also might turn out that they did offer sufficient conditions for freedom of will, that those conditions were also sufficient for being able to do otherwise, and that the relevance of determinism depended on this latter fact.

9

Selective Necessity and the Free-Will Problem

A new form of argument for the incompatibility of free will and determinism has recently become prevalent. Carl Ginet, James Lamb, Peter van Inwagen, and David Wiggins have all mounted attacks on compatibilism which take inspiration from the fact that nothing can now be done about events in the (remote) past.[1] Unlike older discussions that seem to hinge on the assumption of universal causation alone,[2] these new arguments do not make the mistake of assuming that, since all actions in a deterministic universe are *necessitated by* past events taken together with (necessary) laws of nature, all our actions are themselves necessary (inevitable, unavoidable) if determinism is true. What necessarily results from past events and laws may be necessary only *relative to* those events and laws and will be necessary or unavoidable in itself only if those past events and laws are in some sense necessary. And the

---

I am indebted to Edward Erwin, David Lewis, Keith Simmons, and, especially, Sydney Shoemaker, for helpful criticisms and suggestions.

[1] Ginet, "Might We Have No Choice?," in Keith Lehrer, ed., *Freedom and Determinism* (New York: Random House, 1966), pp. 87–104; Lamb, "On a Proof of Incompatibilism," *Philosophical Review*, LXXXVI, 1 (January 1977): 20–35; van Inwagen, "The Incompatibility of Free Will and Determinism," *Philosophical Studies*, XXVII, 3 (March 1975): 185–199; and Wiggins, "Towards a Reasonable Libertarianism," in Ted Honderich, ed., *Essays on Freedom of Action* (London: Routledge & Kegan Paul, 1973), pp. 31–61. Incidentally, in calling these authors "incompatibilists," I do not mean to imply that they think that free will is logically incompatible with determinism. Various contingent assumptions enter into their arguments.

[2] Cf., e.g., Richard Taylor, *Metaphysics* (Englewood Cliffs, N.J.: Prentice-Hall, 1963), p. 46; and Roderick Chisholm, "'He Could Have Done Otherwise,'" in Myles Brand, ed., *The Nature of Human Action* (Glenview, Ill.: Scott, Foresman, 1970), pp. 295ff.

above-mentioned philosophers seek to overcome the weakness of earlier treatments precisely by insisting that the past events and laws, relative to which, under determinism, our actions are necessary or unavoidable, are themselves necessary or unavoidable. This new form of argument, insofar as it recognizes and attempts to remedy a glaring deficiency of previous defenses of incompatibilism, represents a striking improvement over those earlier arguments. But is also suffers from important weaknesses which I shall detail in what follows, weaknesses that result, in particular, from insufficient attention to a kind of necessity which, despite its prevalence in ordinary thought about the world, has rarely if ever been discussed. But our first task must be to reveal and clarify the basic structure that these new arguments for incompatibilism seem to share.

I

For a number of reasons, I shall not present anything like a formal version of the arguments Ginet *et al.* offer us. There are differences of emphasis and assumption in their reasoning, and any detailed formal argument I gave would simply be a fourth argument (or identical with one of theirs), rather than indicate the underlying assumptions they share. I shall thus restrict myself to the informal presentation of a common argument-structure, but none of the main criticisms I shall offer can be avoided by recourse to any particular one of the more or less formal presentations offered by Ginet, Lamb, van Inwagen, or Wiggins (henceforth, GLVW, for short).

As I said above, the common argument to be discerned here focuses crucially on the past. Given determinism, there will always be some much earlier set of conditions s that is connected by laws of nature to any given human action a that takes place. But nothing can be done to alter, nothing can be *done* about those laws; and neither, it may be added, can anything be done about s at any time when the doing of a is immediately in question. Since s is thus necessary (e.g., unalterable) at the time when a is in question and since a law leading from s to a is similarly necessary (unalterable) at that time, it would seem to follow that a itself is necessary (unalterable, unavoidable) at the time—however ignorant of that fact the agent of a may be. Presumably, then, the agent in question does not act freely in performing a, and, since the argument has been entirely general in its assumptions, one may conclude that no human being ever acts freely in a deterministic universe.

There are, of course, differences to be found among GLVW's specific presentations of this underlying form of reasoning. Three of the authors stipulate that the set of conditions s exist before the birth of the agent whose freedom of action is in question. This serves to underscore the unavoidability of that set of conditions for the agent in question. But David Wiggins, on the other hand, simply places the set of conditions at some earlier time whose "contents" one can no longer do anything about (at the time of the act whose freedom is at issue). Our authors also differ in the way they conceive of those earlier conditions: van Inwagen treats them as constituting a total state of the universe at some time before the birth of the person who is to act, whereas the others treat them as a more or less delimited group of conditions or events that are lawfully connected to appropriate later actions. There is also considerable variety in the modal locutions that GLVW use to express the necessity that attaches to events or conditions that pre-exist a given individual (what we can call *pre-existent events*) or (as with Wiggins) exist before the time when a given action is in question. Lamb speaks (roughly) of our inability to refrain from an action such that, if one were to refrain from it, some true proposition describing a pre-existent event would not be the case and also, more simply, of our inability to prevent such an event; Ginet, of an individual's having no choice as to whether some pre-existent instance of a certain event-kind would occur; Wiggins, of earlier conditions which at some later time nobody can do anything about, conditions which, at that later time, are (historically) necessary and inevitable; and, finally, van Inwagen (at least by implication),[3] of a person's being unable to render false some true proposition about a pre-existent state of the universe, and, again, of things one cannot do anything about.

Of course, whatever locution is chosen to express the necessity of past or pre-existent events will also be used to characterize the necessity attaching to laws of nature in relation to what humans can or cannot do, because the argument that has recently come into prominence, unlike the earlier form of argument for incompatibilism, involves a double use of modality in its premises. Thus the old form of deterministic argument against freedom of will has roughly the form:

p (where 'p' stands for a statement that posits the existence of some earlier event or circumstance)

$N(p \supset q)$ (where '$p \supset q$' stands for some law of nature)

$\therefore Nq$ (where 'q' stands for a statement that posits some human action)

And this seems clearly fallacious, whereas the more recent kind of argument has approximately the form:

$$Np$$
$$N(p \supset q)$$
$$\therefore Nq$$

And this in no way seems fallacious and in fact corresponds to an inference that is valid in the most well-known form of alethic modal logic, the logic of logical or metaphysical necessity and possiblity.[4] In that case the necessity indicated by 'N', which is clearly not a form of logical necessity, must be exactly the same for both premises and conclusion. And this means that the proponents of the more recent defense of incompatibilism are assuming that we can no more affect laws of nature than past or pre-existent events, that the laws are every bit as unalterable as the events.

---

[3] Van Inwagen explicitly says only that, if Q is a true proposition about states before S's birth and if S can render the conjunction of Q and R false, S can render R false. But his whole discussion and the direction of his argument presuppose the impossibility of rendering false a true proposition about a pre-existent state of the universe; and this assumption comes explicitly to the fore both in his subsequent "Reply to Gallois," *Philosophical Studies*, XXXII, 1 (July 1977): 107–111, and in a later, as yet unpublished manuscript on freedom of will.

[4] Cf. G. E. Hughes and M. H. Cresswell, *An Introduction to Modal Logic* (London: Methuen, 1968), esp. p. 31.

Of course, the sheer terminological force of the expression 'law of nature' would seem to rule out calling anything a law which we thought humans could alter. But there is one objection to the unalterability of laws of nature which GLVW do not consider and which may need mentioning. Could it not be held that the supposition that humans lack the ability to alter, to affect, the laws that actually obtain involves a controversial theory about the nature of laws, namely, that they are not just true universal generalizations with the right sorts of predicates or systematic interrelations, but rather involve some sort of physical necessity above and beyond these other facets? I believe the answer here can be in the negative. In assuming that we cannot affect laws, we need not assume that the laws themselves possess (a mysterious) physical necessity; for another explanation of our inability to alter them would be some weakness or lack *in us*. (Consider the theological view that God can alter the laws of nature even if humans cannot.) Our inability to alter the laws of nature may be due to the nature of law, to our own nature(s), or to some combination of the two, and the proponents of the more recent form of argument for incompatibilism need not commit themselves to any *particular* explanation of the human inability to affect natural laws which it seems so plausible to assume.

The arguments of GLVW also differ in the conclusions they seek to draw from the lemma that all human actions are necessary and in the ways they attempt to take the argument thus further. Some concentrate on free will and others on moral responsibility, but I think all their positions can be fairly summarized in the claim that if human actions are all necessary (and though they use different locutions, it is not clear that there are any important differences in the kinds of necessity they talk about), then humans lack free will or the moral responsibility that is ordinarily attributed to them. Of course, the assumption that some kind of being able to do otherwise is necessary to freedom or moral responsibility has been called into question by Harry Frankfurt[5] and others in recent years and has always been doubted within the idealist/rationalist tradition that thinks of freedom as a form of rational necessity in action. But Frankfurt's arguments and examples have been attacked by one of our proponents of incompatibilism (Lamb) and by others else-where, and the existence of free will would surely be highly problematic if the only criticism one could make of recent arguments against compatibilism was of their assumption that moral responsibility or free will entails the ability to do otherwise.

Moreover, even if we question or eliminate the step from necessity to the absence of freedom or responsibility, the recent form of argument yields the (sub)conclusion that under determinism we can never do anything but what we in fact do, and this itself seems a sufficient challenge to deeply entrenched and cherished beliefs to make it worth while to see whether the recent arguments can be attacked at some point *before* the conclusion that all actions are necessary has been drawn. And that is precisely what I shall attempt to do in what follows. For I want to argue, in particular, that the arguments of GLVW all rest on a questionable form of inference, the very inference from the double modality of 'Np' and '$N(p \supset q)$' to 'Nq' which marks the superiority of the new kind of argument to earlier defenses of incompatibilism.

---

[5] See his "Alternate Possibilities and Moral Responsibility," this JOURNAL, LXVI, 23 (December 4, 1969): 829–839.

GLVW rely on this form of inference in a variety of different ways. Ginet's argument implicitly depends on the principle/rule of inference: Np, N($p \supset q$) ⊢ Nq, for its validity, whereas Wiggins and Lamb explicitly formulate a modal principle that corresponds to that inference and use it as an assumption in their respective defenses of incompatibilism. And in our own terminology that modal principle—what can henceforth be called the *main modal principle*—can perhaps most readily be stated as: (Np • N($p \supset q$)) $\supset$ Nq (where 'N' stands for whatever form of necessity the incompatibilist argument involves).[6] On the other hand, van Inwagen makes only an indirect appeal to this latter principle or the corresponding rule of inference. Anyone who assumes the validity of arguing from 'Np' and 'N($p \supset q$)' to 'Nq' would seem to be tacitly assuming that the necessity expressed in the operator 'N' is both agglomerative (closed with respect to conjunction introduction) and closed under logical implication, so that one can, e.g., validly move from 'Np' and 'N($p \supset q$)' to 'N($p • p \supset q$)' and from the latter to 'Nq'. If we do not think about these subinferences, when we move from 'Np' and 'N($p \supset q$)' to 'Nq' or assert the main modal principle that corresponds to that larger inference, that is only because it is so natural to assume that any necessity operator will have the properties of agglomerativity and closure under logical implication or entailment. Van Inwagen does not in fact state anything directly corresponding to our main principle; but he does attribute agglomerativity and closure (under entailment) to the necessity he is dealing with. And, since these two properties seem inevitably to be presupposed in use of the main principle and together ensure its truth, it may not be unfair to say that van Inwagen indirectly appeals to that principle: it comes into his incompatibilist argument, so to speak, in pieces, rather than whole.[7]

GLVW's arguments make use of modal principles that correspond to valid principles of the most familiar form of alethic modal logic. Logical or metaphysical necessity is agglomerative and closed under entailment, and the principle

---

[6] Wiggins's and Lamb's formulations in fact differ slightly from each other and from our above statement of the main principle. What Wiggins actually states is of the form: P$p \supset$ (N($p \supset q$) $\supset$ P q), where 'P' stands for the appropriate kind of possibility. But this can be altered into our principle by contraposition and trivial logical manipulations. More significantly, Wiggins uses the main principle itself (as a principle of inference) in a less formal version of his argument which he says he prefers to the formal version (46) and also in one of his preliminary arguments (43). Lamb's assumption 4 ("can-entailment") can in similar fashion be transformed into our main principle by trivial logical means.

[7] Van Inwagen's premise (4) corresponds to the assumption of closure under entailment; his premise (5) corresponds to the principle of agglomerativity. The latter claim may not initially be obvious, but if, as we argued in fn 3, van Inwagen is assuming the impossibility of rendering false, true propositions about the past and using it to back (5) then (5) is tantamount to the assumption that if one can't falsify a law of nature L and can't falsify a proposition about the past P_0, one can't render false the conjunction of L and P_0. And this just is an agglomerativity assumption for the necessity expressed by 'can't render false'. In "Van Inwagen on Free Will and Determinism," *Philosophical Studies*, XXXII, 1 (July 1977): 99–105, André Gallois makes practically the same point about van Inwagen's need for a principle of agglomeration and gives (what amounts to) an argument against agglomerativity which is interestingly different from anything mentioned in the present paper. But, unfortunately, van Inwagen's "Reply to Gallois" (*loc. cit.*) focuses on other aspects of Gallois's article. Note finally that van Inwagen employs our main principle itself in the forthcoming manuscript mentioned in fn 3 and that Lamb's assumption 7 ("union inefficacy") is trivially transformable into a principle of agglomeration.

'$(\Box p \cdot \Box(p \supset q)) \supset \Box q$' is valid for logical necessity under any reasonable interpretation of such necessity.[8] On the other hand, the necessity at stake in the defenses of incompatibilism we are discussing is not logical necessity or what ordinarily goes under the name of metaphysical necessity (even if it represents something weaker which may also deserve to be called metaphysical necessity). And if it turned out that the necessity involved in those arguments was not closed under entailment or was not agglomerative, or (for some reason) that the modal principle '$(Np \cdot N(p \supset q)) \supset Nq$' was simply invalid for the sort of necessity involved in GLVW's arguments, then I take it that those arguments would be thoroughly undermined.

Such an eventuality may at this point seem both purely speculative and wildly implausible, since it would initially appear that anything deserving the name 'necessity' would have to be closed under entailment and agglomerative, and thus require the validity of our main modal principle. But a look in the right direction may help to persuade our second thoughts that this is not so.

II

It is generally agreed that 'A knows that p' and 'A knows that $(p \supset q)$' do not entail 'A knows that q' for appropriate substituends. People may fail to make inferences they are entitled to make. But the fact that such epistemic necessity is an exception to our main modal principle may well be thought to have little bearing on the necessity involved in GLVW's arguments. For these involve forms of situational inevitability and unfreedom that seem to be nomic and metaphysical matters, and Kripke's *Naming and Necessity* has surely taught us to be wary of arguing from epistemic or epistemological considerations to (corresponding) metaphysical or nomic conclusions. What, however, if other, nonepistemic modalities offer similar exceptions to our main principle?

Obligation is often said to be a form of deontic necessity. The very fact that we speak of someone being "released" from an obligation by the person to whom it is owed shows that we think of someone under an obligation as being in some sense bound and not at liberty. And even when an obligation is overridden by some more important moral consideration, there is still an obligation to make amends to the person one was under an obligation to, and this too is some measure of the moral necessity that attaches to the fulfillment of obligations. But, as has sometimes been noted,[9] obligations in the most ordinary sense of the term are always obligations to particular individuals (or groups) and arise from the actions of the person who puts himself under an obligation. Most typically, a person will deliberately undertake an obligation to some other person to perform in some specific way: one promises a person to do something in his or her behalf, and, if circumstances are right, one thereby comes to be under an obligation to that person to do the thing promised. By a more or

---

[8] For some doubts, however, see Martin Davies, "Weak Necessity and Truth Theories," *Journal of Philosophical Logic*, VII, 4 (November 1978): 415–439.

[9] A. John Simmons's "The Principle of Fair Play," *Philosophy and Public Affairs*, VIII, 4 (Summer 1979): 307–337, p. 317f., offers some reasons to think that a person's obligations cannot arise (entirely) from the actions of others.

less natural extension, we also speak of a father's obligation(s) to a child even when there has been no deliberate undertaking of obligations by the father in question. It is thought here that the very act of procreation can put parents under obligations of support and the like to those whom they have procreated, but once again the putative obligations arise from certain kinds of actions and are owed to specific individuals in virtue of the actions that give rise to them.

This relativity or relationality is an important feature of obligations, both intrinsically and in connection with our present investigation of modality. If I am under an obligation to one friend to return his book and under an obligation to another friend to keep a promise to meet him at a certain time, there is no one to whom I am under an obligation to *do both* of these things. Nor will my actions with respect to each of these people somehow give rise to a corporate individual to whom the obligation to do both these things would be owed. Human undertakings can give rise to obligations to collective entities only when the undertakings concern such entities. If I promise a pair of friends to attend a party they are jointly holding, then I may properly be said to owe it to the two of them to attend, and, perhaps because of their joint efforts, that obligation is owed to the pair of them considered as a (temporary) collectivity. Certainly in other cases one can undertake obligations to universities, corporations, and governments and by that means come to have obligations to collective entities. But nothing of the sort required has occurred in the situation described above where I separately undertake to return one person's book and to meet another at a certain time. And in those circumstances there is no such thing as the obligation to do both those things. I am under an obligation to return the book, and this obligation is owed to a particular friend; under an obligation to meet another friend at a certain time, this obligation being owed to that other friend; but those are the only obligations that need exist in the situation I have described. And in that case it will be obligatory that I return the book, obligatory that I meet my friend, but not obligatory that I perform the joint act of returning-the-book-and-meeting-my-friend.

Obligation (obligatoriness) thus fails to be agglomerative, and the reason why clearly has something to do with its relationality and with the specificity of the performances required to give rise to a (relational) obligation. Obligation is a moral boundness that exists only in relation to some person or collectivity owed the obligation and in virtue of certain specific kinds of performance: most typically, undertakings. And where each of two (or more) individuals is owed an obligation in virtue of some undertaking, there may have been no undertaking to do the (joint) act required by agglomerativity and thus no person or collectivity to whom the obligation to do such a (joint) act is owed. Agglomeration will thereby fail for such cases.

It is worth noting, however, that relationality alone cannot explain why a given form of deontic or moral necessity fails the principle of agglomeration. Timothy Smiley has, for example, suggested that the moral 'ought' may express relative necessity, so that 'ought p' is true if and only if 'p' follows logically from some ideal moral code, i.e., is necessary in relation to (the fullfillment of) such a code.[10] But such relational necessity is agglomerative: if 'p' and 'q' both follow classically from a code, so does their conjunction. On the other hand, some forms of relational necessity can

---

[10] See his "Relative Necessity," *Journal of Symbolic Logic*, xxviii, 2 (June 1963): 113–134.

arise only in certain narrowly circumscribed ways; and when restrictions on the way a given kind of relational necessity can come into being unhinge it from agglomerativity (or closure or our main principle), we may say that such necessity is *selective*. Thus if obligation is nonagglomerative, that is, as we have seen, because of limitations on the way (relational) obligations can arise; it is because obligations to do specific things typically derive from *undertakings* (to individuals) *to do those very things*. So obligation is not only relational, but selective. And both these factors enter into the "logic" of the notion.

The fact that moral obligation exists only when a specific kind of performance makes some act or kind of action morally necessary in relation to some individual also has implications for the closure of obligation under logical implication or entailment. Even if doing x entails doing y, I may have promised and be under an obligation to do x, without having promised or being under an obligation to do y. Thus if I promise to meet you at three o'clock tomorrow, I may be under an obligation to you to do so; but have I promised to stay alive till tomorrow? Do I have a specific obligation to be alive at that time? If I die before tomorrow, I will, presumably, have failed to fulfill a promise and an obligation to meet you at three o'clock; but not many people will be tempted to say that I (also) have an obligation to stay alive that I shall (also) have failed to fulfill, even though meeting someone may logically entail being alive.[11] And *no one*, I think, will want to say that I have promised or am under any obligation (to you) to exist at some moment in human history, though this too is entailed by my meeting you at three o'clock. Such examples illustrate the selectivity of obligations. Even promising to do something that entails doing or being x need not give rise to an obligation to do (be) x, if I am not *promising* to do (be) x and it is merely presupposed that I shall. Moreover, once we have spotted failures of agglomeration and closure under entailment in the area of obligation, it also becomes easy to find the obligatory counterexamples to our main principle. I may, for example, have an obligation to x to bring him a certain book and I may promise y to visit her if I ever bring the book to x (they are neighbors). But for reasons already rehearsed, it seems doubtful that I have an obligation to visit y outright. To whom would I owe it?

Clearly, then, the notion of obligation provides a plausible example of nonepistemic necessity failing agglomeration, closure under entailment, and our main principle.[12] But at this point the defenders of the incompatibilist arguments we

---

[11] Of course, one may be able to come under an obligation to stay alive by promising to do so. (Imagine a suicidally depressed individual and a well-meaning friend.)

[12] In "Ethical Consistency," in *Problems of the Self* (New York: Cambridge, 1973), Bernard Williams makes a tentative effort to show that (the moral) 'ought' is nonagglomerative, by adducing moral conflicts, like Agamemnon's, where two acts that cannot both be performed seem morally called for. But his argument requires him to assume that 'ought' implies 'can' and that, in the circumstances, Agamemnon really ought to kill his daughter and really ought to spare her. Many of us will wonder how both the latter 'ought's can be true—especially when, given his choice of example, we can so much more easily speak of there being two conflicting, and important, *obligations* in the circumstances (and thereby perhaps account for the need for regret/remorse and reparation, whatever Agamemnon does). Williams may be right, nonetheless, but it is harder to argue for the nonagglomerativity of 'ought' than to do so for 'obligation' just because of the relationality and selectivity that attach to obligation. We can get nonagglomeration for 'obligation' in circumstances where there is no conflict of obligations, indeed no moral conflict whatever; but such circumstances are typically ones where we feel no problem whatever about agglomerating 'ought's. And

are examining will, perhaps, have one more defense. They will grant the (perhaps initially surprising) fact that something that is reasonably thought of as a form of (nonepistemic) necessity flouts principles of inference that hold for logical or metaphysical necessity; but they will then point out that the kind of necessity involved in the incompatibilist arguments of GLVW is causal or physical. Since causal necessity is generally considered to be one form of alethic necessity among others, why, it will be objected, should we take a page from the book of deontic modal logic when we have the example of the alethic modal logic of strict or logical necessity to go by? The latter clearly does obey agglomerativity and closure under entailment, and surely it is more reasonable to hold that other forms of alethic necessity will conform to these intuitively plausible rules/principles, than to be swayed by counterexamples from the totally different realm of the deontic. But what if counterexamples to these rules/principles can be found within the alethic realm itself?

III

If we unexpectedly run across someone whom we haven't seen in years and are very pleased to see, we can naturally express our pleasure by saying or thinking: how lucky that we both should be here at the same time, what a wonderful accident! But even if it is accidental that two people should both be at a certain place at a given time, the presence of each one separately at the place (and at the time) in qustion can seem like no accident at all. Each one, for example, may have been sent by his superior to the place in question, e.g., a bank, as part of a well-known routine or plan of office functioning. (There was no last-minute substitution of the person who would go to the bank, no unusual delay in getting there: everything went normally for each of the individuals concerned.) If, then, we let 'Jules' and 'Jim' stand for the individuals in the example, it would appear to be no accident (not accidental) that Jules is at the bank when he is, no accident (not accidental) that Jim is there when he is, but a benign and lovely accident (accidental) that Jim and Jules should both be there at that time. Most people who take the trouble to think about it would recognize it to be a main feature of (non)accidentality that things that in themselves appear perfectly regular and nonaccidental may "come together" to create something that is accidental, and this feature precisely is the non-agglomerativity of the nonaccidental. And yet even in the face of such examples, it is hard to deny that nonaccidentality is a causal/nomological matter concerning how things are in the world and a form of alethic *necessity* in particular. For those who distinguish lawlike universal truths, i.e., laws of nature, from nonlawlike ones, call the latter accidental. And it is natural to equate the accidental with the contingent and to treat noncontingency as a form of necessity.[13] So it would appear that there is at least one form of alethic necessity that fails of agglomerativity.

---

that is why, in situations where 'ought's seem to conflict, it is hard to be sure that agglomerativity really fails and that paradox can best be avoided by insisting upon that failure. [Similar remarks apply to Bas van Fraassen's "Values and the Heart's Command," this JOURNAL. LXX. 1 (January 11, 1973): 5–19.]

[13] Cf. Nelson Goodman, *Fact, Fiction, and Forecast* (Indianapolis: Bobbs-Merrill, 2d ed., 1965), p. 73.

Nonaccidentality also appears not to be closed under entailment. It may be no accident that I am in a certain place right now (I was sent there by a superior in accordance with a routine plan of business operation), yet nevertheless be an accident that I am still alive right now (only an accidental and unintentional swerve on my part has prevented me from just being flattened by a runaway truck).[14] Failing that, it may at least be an accident that I ever exist at all (imagine a suitable tale of contraceptive woes), yet that too is entailed by my being where I am at the present moment. If closure thus fails for nonaccidentality, we can perhaps go on to deny that it is governed by our main modal principle, on the grounds that in the above cases where it is no accident that I am at a certain place and yet something of an accident that I still (or ever) exist, it is also (on trivial logical grounds) no accident that if I am at that place, then I still (or at some time) exist.[15]

I believe that closure, agglomeration, and our main principle all fail for nonaccidentality because of the (relational) selectivity built into that notion. When we say that some event was no accident, at least one thing that we may be saying is that that event came about according to a plan that required it. That is, nonaccidentality of the sort at issue in the case of Jules and Jim exists only in relation to a single actual plan (relationality); but the plan must also be of a very specific kind (selectivity): it must be a plan that *requires* or *calls* for the thing that occurs nonaccidentally. Thus, if Jim is at the bank at ten o'clock on the first of the month because his superior has told him (always) to go there then, it is no accident that he is there at that time. But since the presence of both Jules and Jim at the bank at ten o'clock has not in fact been planned

---

[14] It is sometimes said that, under determinism, *nothing* is accidental, and if that were so then we couldn't say that it was an accident that I was still alive or that the truck missed me. Ordinarily, however, we distinguish cases of accident from cases of nonaccident quite independently of the issue of determinism. Thus even people who believe in (macroscopic) determinism are willing to speak of traffic accidents. And since no one seems inclined to deny the possibility of *coincidences* under determinism, perhaps I can best pinpoint the ordinary usage of 'accidental' I have in mind by saying that it is a usage according to which accidentality is *entailed* by coincidentality.

Of course, ordinary claims of accidentality may be context-relative or relative to a favored standpoint, but that very fact may actually support our present position. When Jules (say) thinks it a lovely accident that he and Jim should simultaneously be at the bank, he may well be making that judgment, and the judgment that it is no accident he himself is at the bank, from his own limited point of view. But if agglomerativity holds for (non)accidentality thus relatively affirmed, Jules should also be willing to claim that Jim is (relative to Jules's standpoint) accidentally at the bank. For, on the assumption that Jim is not accidentally there, agglomerativity must commit Jules to rejecting the accidentality of the meeting or the nonaccidentality of his own presence at the bank. The fact is, however, that someone in Jules's position will not (automatically) assume that the other person is where he is by accident, even when he assumes that *their meeting* is an accident. And so it would seem that nonaccidentality, even relative to a limited standpoint, is nonagglomerative.

[15] Ordinary thought seems to treat facts of logic as nonaccidental even though no one has planned for them. But it is natural to speak of what logic "requires" in much the same way that we speak of what certain plans require, and a common sense of necessity may thus animate all our ascriptions of nonaccidentality.

Note too that, even if nonaccidentality is closed under logical implication, our main principle will be invalid as long as agglomerativity fails. For if we grant closure and our main principle, agglomerativity immediately follows: From 'Np • Nq', closure allows us to deduce 'Np • N($p \supset pq$)'; and, from the latter, our main principle allows us to deduce 'Npq'.

for, is not required by anyone's plan or intention, it is natural, on this account, to call it accidental. The particular kind of relation that nonaccidentality entails, the selectivity of the notion, may also account for nonclosure. An employer who plans for an employee to be at the bank at a certain time does not *plan* for the employee to stay alive, even if he more or less implicitly knows that being at the bank involves being alive. And similarly, even if a plan calls for someone to be somewhere at a given time, it need not call for that person to stay alive till then. The fact of aliveness may simply be presupposed by such a plan.[16] So the hypothesis that nonaccidentality is a form of selective necessity that (in the relevant cases) entails being required by and coming about according to a plan helps to explain the failure of agglomeration and of closure under entailment that we seem to find in ordinary thought about nonaccidentality.

Nor is nonaccidentality merely an isolated case of selective alethic/causal modality. Having recognized the selectivity of this one notion, we can quite easily recognize selectivity in others. To act from irresistible impulse, for example, is to be necessitated in a particular way. But even if a given person steals a trinket out of irresistible impulse (kleptomania) and the same person also burns down a house from irresistible impulse (pyromania), it will not follow—it would be extraordinarily odd to say—that the person had done the two things, had stolen the trinket and burned down the house, from irresistible impulse. Indeed, if someone did, perplexingly, say the latter, we would naturally (re)interpret him to be saying, dissectively, that each of those two things was done from irresistible impulse. For it is inherent in talk about acts done from (irresistible) impulse that those acts arise from a single impulse, and most of us assume that there is no such thing as a single, unified impulse to steal-and-burn. Thus what arises from irresistible impulse is necessary in relation to a particular kind of factor, a single impulse toward the very thing that is thus made necessary. And this selectivity is sufficient to unhinge the notion from agglomerativity, and from closure as well. (Via similar arguments similar thoughts also apply to the notion of doing something compulsively.)

IV

Given the existence of alethic/causal necessities not subject to closure, agglomeration, or our main principle, one may begin to have doubts about the incompatibilist arguments of GLVW. For these revolve around alethic/causal notions of unavoidability, unalterability, or what-have-you which may be just as selective as non-accidentality or irresistibility of impulse, and thus just as liable to failure of closure, etc.

---

[16] Just as there are unintended foreseen consequences of an intention or plan, so too, I am saying, there can be unintended and unplanned-for presupposed necessary conditions of the fulfillment of a plan or intention. (These cannot be *means* to the fulfillment of such a plan or intention.)

For material relevant to our discussion of accidentality, see Aristotle's *Physics* II 5–6 and *Metaphysics* V 30, as well as Richard Sorabji's *Necessity, Cause and Blame* (London: Duckworth, 1980), chap. 1, and Robert Hambourger's "The Argument from Design," in Cora Diamond and Jenny Teichman, eds., *Intention and Intentionality* (Hassocks, England: Harvester, 1979; Ithaca, N.Y.: Cornell, 1980), pp. 109–131.

What would, of course, more strongly recommend this conjecture would be some more definite indication of how and why the modality of GLVW's arguments might fail modal principles that operate in the case of logical or strict metaphysical necessity, some account, for example, of the form of selectivity involved in the notion of what is unavoidable or unalterable by us. And though I am not absolutely convinced that "unavoidability" and the like are selective in the way needed to unhinge familiar modal principles/rules, and it is not my intention here to give a full analysis or formal semantics of these concepts, I would like to point out one specific way in which they may plausibly be thought to be selective.

When we say that some event before our birth is something we can now do nothing about—is now unavoidable by, inevitable for, us—I think we may be saying that that event is necessary or inevitable *in relation to* a *particular kind* of factor. We have seen that the particular kind of factor "selected" in judgments of nonaccidentality is a certain sort of effective plan-requirement and that that selected in judgments of irresistible impulse and compulsiveness is a certain sort of unitary impulse (or compulsion). What (we may ask) is the corresponding factor in claims of inevitability and the like? Perhaps we should take a clue from the fact that, with the sole exception of Wiggins, all the proponents of the new form of incompatibility argument single out past events occurring before the birth of an agent, in speaking of what that agent cannot do anything about. What such remote pastness seems intended to ensure is that the event in question be beyond the causal reach of desires, beliefs, and abilities the agent *might* have acquired during his life, i.e., that whatever brought it about should not include any possible desires, etc., of the agent. And I believe similar considerations may well be inherent in *all* talk about unavoidability. When we say of any past event that we can *now* do nothing about it, I think we are saying that our *present* desires, abilities, beliefs, characters, etc., are no part of the explanation of it. And, more generally, the particular kind of factor in relation to which unavoidability exists at any given time, the factor "selected" by such necessity, is, simply, some factor (or set of factors) that brings about the unavoidable thing *without making use of (an explanatory chain that includes) the desires, etc., the agent has around that time.*[17]

A straightforward argument against the main modal principle of incompatibilist arguments then becomes available. Given the above assumptions, we cannot now do anything about past events because they are due to factors that brought them about via a causal chain that did not include our present abilities, desires, etc. And appropriate laws of nature have the same sort of necessity because whatever it is that makes them be as they are (certain deeper laws, the basic structure of the universe or what have you) is surely something that does not involve our present abilities and

---

[17] Our present gloss leaves out some factors relevant to unavoidability: e.g., unconscious compulsions. More accurately, we could specify the selectivity of unavoidability and the like as requiring (only) that what is unavoidable not be brought about by means of *accessible* current desires, beliefs, and the like. But even this is not quite accurate (there are problems, e.g., about future desires and abilities and about certain cases mentioned by Frankfurt, *op. cit.*); and one would want, in any case, to know more about the notion of accessibility.

Note further that our rough selectivity analysis of unavoidability is (at the very least) foreshadowed in Gallois, *op. cit.*, p. 103f.

desires. But even if our deliberate actions are determined, that determinism operates, nonfatalistically, by means of (causal chains involving) the approximately coeval desires, abilities, character, and beliefs of human agents. So if the necessity involved in incompatibilist arguments selects factors that bring something about (make it exist) without making use of such coeval desires, etc., then most of us *can* do something about the actions we are about to perform and the main modal principle of those arguments fails. Certain past events will be necessary in the relevant sense (necessary in relation to the right sort of factor) and certain laws leading from them to an agent's later actions will also be necessary; but it will not follow that those actions are themselves necessary at some later time when the agent is considering whether to perform them.[18] Of course, those actions will be *determined by* and presumably *predictable in terms* of factors prior to the agent's desires and abilities. But those earlier factors nonetheless bring such actions about only by means of (causal chains involving) later desires (roughly coeval with the actions they help to bring about). And what I have been claiming is that it is precisely this further aspect of the matter which is crucial to whether a given act is avoidable. There *might* be a notion of relative necessity that merely involved being determined, but I am suggesting (roughly) that the ordinary notions of avoidability, inevitability, and the like involve the idea of being determined in a particular sort of way; and such selective necessity would account for the failure of those notions to comply with the main modal principle of recent incompatibilist arguments.

However, if appropriate selectivity undoes recent defenses of incompatibilism by undermining their main modal principle, then it must also undermine either agglomerativity or closure under logical implication (or both), since the latter principles together entail or validate the former. And this we find to be so. Let 'p' represent a proposition ascribing existence in a canonical way to some (pre-existent) past event, and let '$p \supset q$' be a conditional true by virtue of the laws of nature which connects that past event with some particular about-to-be-performed action represented by 'q'. Given the selective necessity we have postulated, 'Nq' is clearly false, but 'Np' and '$N(p \supset q)$' are both true. Now, if such necessity is closed under logical

[18] After giving his defense of incompatibilism, Wiggins characterizes its notion of historical necessity/inevitability as implying that something is inevitable at t' just in case whatever anybody or anything does at t' or thereafter (consistently with laws of nature) can make no difference to that thing (45). But in ordinary usage, the latter locution has counterfactual import and entails that the thing in question would occur even if, at t' and after, people were to deliberate, choose, or act differently from the way they actually will. So when Wiggins argues from the inevitability of laws and the inevitability of the past to the conclusion that all our actions are inevitable by the time we are considering whether to perform them, his particular sense of 'inevitable' saddles him, in effect, with an argument for *fatalism*, the absurd view that we would perform the various actions we do even if appropriate initial conditions were different. And Wiggins himself not only fails to recognize this consequence of his views but seems eager to dissociate his argument from fatalism. (Cf. his discussion of 'Theaetetus sits at t', p. 59f.) Had Wiggins recognized that under determinism (something equivalent to) our main principle leads from true premises to a form of inevitability that entails fatalism, he might have rejected the main principle. For Wiggins's understanding of inevitability is in fact somewhat similar to our own: we have been *denying* the inevitability of some of our future acts, even under determinism, on the grounds that their "necessity" is *not* in the appropriate sense independent of initial conditions like desire and ability. And the fact that our sort of gloss on inevitability comes naturally even to an incompatibilist like Wiggins is surely some sort of reason for accepting that gloss and for rejecting modal principles that, on such a gloss, lead directly from determinism to fatalism.

implication, it is closed under logical equivalence, and 'N($p \cdot p \supset q$)' will be true only if 'N($p \cdot q$)' is. Our selectivity analysis suggests, however, that 'N($p \cdot q$)' is true only if (roughly but intuitively) some set of factors not operating through our desires and abilities makes p and q be true together. And since it is natural to assume that something cannot make a pair of things true without making each of them true,[19] we can reasonably conclude that 'N($p \cdot q$)' is true only if something independent of our desires, etc., makes q true, i.e., only if 'Nq' is true. But we are assuming that 'Nq' is false, so 'N($p \cdot q$)' is also false, and thus, by closure under logical implication (equivalence), 'N($p \cdot p \supset q$)' is false as well. So, given our other assumptions and a selectivity analysis of the modality involved, agglomeration fails if closure under logical implication holds. (A similar argument can be used to show that if we assume agglomeration, closure must fail.)

V

The selectivity that is plausibly attributed to the necessity involved in recent defenses of incompatibilism distinguishes between factors within and factors external to agents. For, on our rough gloss, what is effected without the "help" of an agent's (coeval) character, abilities, desires, etc. is (then) unavoidable, unalterable, inevitable, but what is brought about via a causal chain that includes appropriate internal factors is not.

Now both Wiggins and van Inwagen say that the distinction between internal and external factors, between character and circumstance, in no way affects the soundness of their arguments. Wiggins claims that "no subtleties about *in the agent* or the agent's *will*" can affect the validity of his general form of argument, and van Inwagen has been reluctant to allow that the validity of his argument in any way depends on the inadequacy of so-called "conditional analyses" of ability, analyses that highlight the importance of the internal/external distinction by explaining ability in terms of what an agent would succeed in doing if he made a certain effort or choice.[20] More recently, however, van Inwagen (at least) has been willing to concede that, if ability were conditionally analyzable and compatibilism were true, some of the modal principles he assumes would fail; but he also insists—correctly, I believe—that this fact alone hardly vindicates the compatibilist. For if van Inwagen's general modal premises are plausible before one makes any assumptions about how 'can' is to be analyzed or about the truth of determinism, then his arguments have definite force *against* compatibilism and *against* conditional analyses of ability.[21]

But at least part of the reason for thinking that the necessity involved in free will is agglomerative, closed under logical implication, and obedient to our main

---

[19] Cf. Frederic B. Fitch, "A Logical Analysis of Some Value Concepts," *Journal of Symbolic Logic*, XXVIII, 2 (June 1963): 135–142.

[20] Wiggins, *op. cit.*, p. 50; van Inwagen, "The Incompatibility...", p. 196f.

[21] See his "Reply to Narveson's 'Compatibilism Defended'" *Philosophical Studies*, XXXII, 1 (July 1977): 89–98, p. 95f.; and his "Compatibilism and the Burden of Proof," *Analysis*, XL, 2 (March 1980): 98–100, esp. p. 100.

principle comes from the powerful example of "standard" alethic modal logic, the logic of logical necessity and possibility. (I think GLVW's modal principles would seem much less compelling to educated nonphilosophers than they do to those acquainted with modal logic.) Those principles clearly hold for the most familiar forms of alethic modality, and indeed no specific example of alethic necessity flouting such principles has previously been discussed or argued for.[22] So, by unearthing plausible instances of alethic necessity that do fail those principles, the present paper may serve to weaken the feeling of inevitability and obviousness that (for most philosophers at least) initially attends the modal principles used in the recent arguments for incompatibilism. Previous suggestions that we analyze ability conditionally in order to defend compatibilism from the arguments of GLVW have seemed ad hoc in the absence of any other example of alethic necessity not subject to our main principle or agglomeration or closure; but when we supply such examples and explain how various necessities can flout those principles, the selective necessity that we have claimed may be involved in the free-will controversy is made to seem part of a plausible pattern, rather than an isolated case. None of this may absolutely demolish the recent arguments for incompatibilism, but I believe it has some force against them nonetheless, force that previous replies to GLVW, because of their and hocness and special pleading, have failed to carry.[23]

I can also think of one positive reason for claiming that the necessity involved in those arguments fails of agglomeration, closure, and our main modal principle. Consider our common-sense intuitions, what we are normally inclined to say, about the things we cannot or can do something about. Most people, when asked, would grant that we can do nothing either about the past or about (whatever) laws of nature (exist). And yet the belief that we *can* do something about what actions we are going to perform has a tendency to resist extinction in practical life, even among those who in the study or the classroom espouse determinism. Through its reliance on agglomeration, closure, or our main modal principle, the kind of argument presented by GLVW in effect seeks to undermine this "natural assignment" of truth values and to declare it and us inconsistent, as a consequence. But surely there are philosophical grounds, at least philosophical motives, for trying to avoid such a charge, and if we say that the necessity involved in recent incompatibilist arguments fails of agglomeration, etc., we can succeed in doing this. Of course, before we had any reason to believe there were forms of alethic necessity that failed these principles, we could not perhaps have deployed such a consistency argument. For the example of the alethic modal logic of logical necessity and possibility could make it appear impossible for any form of alethic necessity to fail those principles, and in that case the claim that the necessity involved in arguments for incompatibilism was an exception to the principles would enable us to avoid one inconsistency—that of our natural assignment of truth values—at the cost of embroiling us in what seemed to be another—the denial of irrecusable modal principles. The examples of nonaccidentality, of

---

[22] One exception, however, is the article by Martin Davies mentioned in footnote 8, above.

[23] I particularly have in mind Richard Foley's "Reply to van Inwagen," *Analysis*, XL, 2 (March 1980): 101–103; and his earlier "Compatibilism and Control over the Past," *Analysis*, XXXIX, 2 (March 1979): 70–74.

irresistible impulse, of compulsivity, and, even, of obligation, however, make us see that nonagglomerative, etc., alethic necessity is not only possible, but in fairly plentiful supply in our conceptual scheme; and this, in turn, allows the motive of self-consistency in our common-sense judgments about things positively to recommend the idea that GLVW's arguments involve a nonagglomerative, etc., form of alethic necessity and are thus doomed to failure.

In any event, we have pointed out some clear cases of selective necessity expressible within ordinary language and have seen that, even if some modal principles/rules are common to every form of alethic necessity,[24] others have only a limited application within the alethic realm. Recently, there has been some discussion of modal logics lacking agglomerativity and our main principle,[25] but there is an obvious need for technical investigations of the logic and semantics of the selective necessities we have mentioned and various others that are undoubtedly waiting to be discovered. I believe such projects may be worth pursuing, quite independently of any relation that exists between selectivity and the specific problem of free will, for the insights they are likely to give us into modal thinking in general.

---

[24] D. P. Snyder, *Modal Logic and Its Applications* (New York: Van Nostrand Reinhold, 1971), p. 5ff., mentions some of these common principles.

[25] See, e.g., Krister Segerberg, *An Essay in Classical Modal Logic* (Uppsala: University Press, 1971), and Brian Chellas, *Modal Logic: An Introduction* (New York: Cambridge, 1980). However, what also needs to be explored (though there is no space to explore it here) is the possibility that there are indexical aspects to (some of) the necessity operators of ordinary language, that (various) apparent failures of agglomerativity and the like involve subtle shiftings of context rather than any flouting of "normal" modal principles, and that recent arguments for incompatibilism commit some sort of fallacy of equivocation.

10

Is Virtue Possible?

Much attention has recently been paid to the nature and inter-relations of the moral virtues and to the psychology of their embodiment in particular individuals. Although it has typically been assumed that a virtuous individual knows what is right in different situations and acts accordingly, both Iris Murdoch in *The Sovereignty of Good* (London: Routledge and Kegan Paul, 1970) and John McDowell in 'Virtue and Reason' (*The Monist* 62, 1979, pp. 331–50) have laid particular stress on the (Aristotelian) idea of perception in their accounts of the epistemology of virtue. Murdoch and McDowell offer a marvellously subtle and complex treatment of virtue, and their ideas have rich reverberations for our understanding of Plato and Aristotle's ethical thought. But their account of moral virtue is also importantly incomplete. And in what follows I shall argue, in particular, that their exclusive focus on internal defects that prevent people from seeing and doing what is right makes them over-estimate the general accessibility of moral virtue and ignore the historical dimension of our attempts to understand "moral reality."[1]

I

The virtuous individual is often said to be capable of knowing right from wrong in the wide variety of circumstances that might arise in his life. This knowledge may not be embodied in any (complex) ethical precept completely formulable by him

---

[1] I shall be responding to a composite (and partial) picture of what Murdoch and McDowell say, but shall note differences of emphasis where relevant. McDowell acknowledges a debt to Murdoch and at no point

or even in principle; indeed that is part of the reason for saying, with Aristotle, that overall virtue—or any particular virtue—involves (or is) a quasi-perceptual capacity for recognizing what, in the various circumstances in which one may be called upon to act, is the right thing to do. But knowledge is nonetheless required if one is to be a virtuous person and not just someone who by benign accident or at the behest of others does what a virtuous individual is supposed to do from knowledge.

Most accounts of moral virtue treat it as a disposition to be acquired only through a proper upbringing and education. But McDowell and Murdoch place a special emphasis on another precondition of virtue. What prevents some people from being virtuous at a given time can be something about them at that time which, though it may to some extent be due to faulty training, has independent explanatory force in understanding their lack of virtue. A person can be too self-centred, too emotional, too proud to get things morally right, and because such individual defects are widespread and difficult to overcome, Murdoch and McDowell both speak of (overall) virtue as very difficult to attain.

Nonetheless, I am more struck by the possibilities of virtue McDowell and Murdoch do not rule out than by those they do. For by talking about what virtuous individuals do and are like, they both imply that there *have been* virtuous individuals, and Murdoch makes an explicit commitment to that assumption by claiming that moral virtue can be found not only in the likes of Socrates, but among peasants as well. Furthermore, Aristotle (see, e.g., *Nicomachean Ethics* 1143a: 25–35; 1144b: 30–1145a 6) appears to have believed in the existence of virtuous individuals in his own day, and McDowell not only says he wishes to defend an Aristotelian conception of the inculcation and practice of virtue, but mentions no factor that might have made it more difficult to acquire virtue in Aristotle's time than in our own.

Indeed, if the sorts of factors they mention were the sole impediments to the development and exercise of virtue, then the attainment of virtue, as traditionally conceived, might be no more problematic than McDowell and Murdoch suggest. But it seems to me that there are other, less individualistic factors that must be brought into an account of virtue, and in the light of these I think it doubtful that virtue existed in the ancient world or can ever be found among the uneducated. It even becomes questionable whether virtue is attainable today, but these difficulties are perhaps best formulated in terms of examples.

II

We now regard slavery as an unjust institution that offends the basic rights of the enslaved. But in the ancient world—in Greece, in Rome, among the Church Fathers—no one ever wrote, or is known to have spoken, against slavery as such.[2] There were occasional discussions of the abuses and justifications of slavery, but it was never held that owning slaves was simply wrong. Murdoch and McDowell say that the virtuous individual takes account of the rights of others and of what is just and fair, and they

---

indicates any disagreement with her work. Note further that my criticism will not hinge on anything either of them says, or fails to say, about *akrasia*.

[2] See M. I. Finley, *Ancient Slavery and Modern Ideology*, London: Chatto and Windus, 1980, pp. 120f. Finley mentions only Euripides as a possible exception to the above generalization.

use such moral notions *tout court*, with all the objectivity that that implies. But if we agree that slavery offends the rights of slaves, can we plausibly avoid saying that the keeping, buying, and selling of slaves not only is but was wrong; and will not that in turn commit us to saying that those engaged in such practices were not morally virtuous individuals? But such criticism will then also naturally extend beyond those who actually possessed slaves to people too poor to own slaves, perhaps even to slaves themselves. Even those who could not afford slaves would presumably have been *disposed* to own slaves if good fortune had made it possible. For slavery was simply accepted, as a natural fact, in the ancient world. No other system was known or, perhaps, even thought possible. So with benefit of hindsight, the assumption that slavery is wrong can lead one to question Aristotle's assumption that there actually were virtuous individuals to be found in his society and McDowell's seemingly unqualified endorsement of Aristotle's views about the nature and realization of virtue.

McDowell and Murdoch say that egotism, wilfulness, laziness, and bad temper can render someone incapable of seeing all that the virtuous person must see. But such variable factors of individual psychology—and various deficiencies of training—are the only barriers to virtue they mention, and if nothing else could stand in the way of virtue, then there would perhaps be no reason why virtue should not have been present in the sorts of individuals Aristotle regarded as virtuous. When, however, we consider the example of slavery—and other examples to be mentioned shortly—it can begin to seem questionable whether the above factors represent the only bars to moral virtue. If virtue requires the disposition to act justly, do the right thing, with regard to important issues, can we sensibly suppose that the failure of the ancient world to attain and act upon a correct moral view of slavery merely reflects personal weaknesses or deficient methods of moral training that, unluckily, happened to be fairly universal in those days? Presumably not.

I have never heard anyone suggest that the Greeks, ancient Hebrews, or early Christians were less able to instil moral values into their children than we are today—there is reason, in fact, to believe the contrary. And to say that the ancients were blinded to the injustice of slavery (say) by their inordinate greed would not account for the fact that those too poor to own slaves (even, I suppose, the large majority of slaves themselves) never thought of questioning slavery. Nor was ancient belief in the naturalness and inevitability of slavery (and in the existence of "natural slaves") *merely* a widespread rationalization of individual avarice. Rather, that belief is at least partly to be explained by the fact that slavery was a universal phenomenon. Just as ignorance of the alternative terms used by other languages can make matters of linguistic convention seem to be inevitable facts of nature, so too can ignorance of alternatives to a given social arrangement instil the belief that that arrangement is natural and inevitable and thus beyond the possibility of radical moral criticism. So if the ancients were unable to see what virtue required in regard to slavery, that was not due to personal limitations (alone) but requires some explanation by social and historical forces, by cultural limitations, if you will.[3] And if we today can see the

---

[3] On the distinction between individual-psychological and social/historical factors, cf. C. Ryan, "Beyond Beliefs," *American Philosophical Quarterly* 18, 1981, pp. 33–41 and references therein. On the unavailability to the Greeks of "enlightened" moral views about slavery, see T. H. Green, *Prolegomena to Ethics*, Oxford: 1883, chap. 5.

wrongness of slavery, that is in part because we have the benefit of knowledge that makes slavery seem less natural and inevitable. For unlike the ancients we know of "experiments" in living without slavery; we possess an historical record of societies, among them our own, where slavery has been absent and people have survived and flourished, nonetheless.

Similar points arise in connection with issues other than slavery. Murdoch insists (p. 1f.) that an "unexamined life" can be virtuous and that there are and can be virtuous peasants. And I believe she makes such claims because she regards personal defects as the only barriers to correct moral vision, to virtue. But there is reason to wonder whether such factors are the only ones that affect whether a peasant does the right thing. Consider, for example, a peasant father or mother who refuses to help his/her daughter leave a husband who is clearly unloving and abusive. We believe, do we not, that a woman has the right to leave such a husband (though there may be wrong *ways* of doing so), but what if the woman's own parents refuse to help her in this, telling her to stay with her husband and even rendering it impossible for her to leave him (she needs a small amount of money from them, say, in order to get away)? Such actions presumably express a failure to acknowledge the rights of the unhappy wife, and most of us would say that they are a wrong way to act towards a daughter in distress and in need. But what prevents her parents from doing right by her? Need it be envy of the new life she hopes to lead and they never had or (in the case of the father) sexist antagonism towards women generally? Need it be self-righteous anger reflecting frustration at having chosen wrongly for her (we are talking about a peasant society) or selfish discontent at having her once more dependent upon them? Can it not simply be that, despite all their love and desire to help her, they believe in *a holy book* that commands all women to stay with their husbands through thick and thin? Murdoch herself (pp. 74, 101) says that traditional religion is no barrier—is even, indeed, a positive aid—to virtue and right action. But then what can be said about the case at hand? Unless we hold, implausibly and against Murdoch's own tendencies, that only a blind or selfish person would accept the holiness of the book in question, we shall have to grant that the peasant parents may do the wrong thing for reasons having to do with social and cultural influences (as reflected of course in them) rather than through the sorts of personal, individually variable, vision-preventing defects she so exclusively focuses upon. And there are many, many other such situations where tradition and milieu would put "enlightened" views of right and wrong beyond the reach of (devout) peasants. So if Murdoch is right to insist that right action is a criterion of virtue and if modern views of the rights of women are correct, then the existence of virtue in unexamined lives seem very dubious.[4]

Nor would it be very easy for Murdoch and McDowell to evade the above conclusions by claiming that slavery was *not* wrong in the special circumstances of the ancient world or that "women's rights" *do not exist* in peasant societies. For they are self-avowed moral realists who hold that moral beings are seeking to understand an independent moral reality and, where appropriate (e.g., Murdoch, pp. 55, 59, 69;

---

[4] Murdoch says that no one is morally perfect. But my assumption that a virtuous individual should be capable of right action with regard to such important issues as slavery is hardly an insistence on moral *perfection*.

McDowell, pp. 346ff.), they have sought to distinguish their views from any form of moral relativism. Since, in addition, Murdoch and McDowell both speak freely, and in the most objectivistic terms, of justice, fairness, and rights, I find it impossible to imagine either of them being happy with the view that slavery was fair in ancient Greece or with the view that (certain) peasant women have no right to leave their husbands.

III

In that case a very real question must arise about whether overall virtue is possible even for us. We have been speaking as if the wide-ranging capacity for right action that seems problematic in relation to the Greeks or peasant societies presented no particular problem for such modern individuals as can perceive the rights of slaves and women and with proper education overcome the individual-psychological barriers to virtue that McDowell and Murdoch describe. But in fact I have no intention of being thus smug about current values and conceptions of morality. I have, for example, harped on the wrongness of slavery and the unavailability of that moral fact, and others, to the ancients, but I too admire Greek moral philosophy, and that very admiration causes me to wonder whether virtue is any more accessible nowadays than it was in classical antiquity. I assume that we now see aspects of right and wrong that the ancient world missed; but may we not also fail to see things the Greeks were able to see, and, more significantly, may there not be other moral issues on which both the ancients and we ourselves are blind? Someday, our descendants may regard twentieth century morality and moral philosophy as having been as hopelessly wrongheaded on certain issues (vegetarianism? children's rights? patients' rights?) as were ancient views about slavery. And they may have as much reason to do so as we currently have to be critical of ancient attitudes to slavery.

A natural enough induction from the history of previous *scientific* theories tells us that today's theories are very likely to turn out to be mistaken in important ways. Is there any less reason to believe the same about current-day moral thinking? If not, then there is reason to believe that moral virtue as traditionally understood is not accessible even today, but rather, like various kinds of scientific truth, is to be attained, if at all, only at the historical limit of human cultural endeavour, in a long run that no individual may ever encompass. McDowell and Murdoch have underscored the individually understandable obstacles to virtue, but because moral virtue is subject to social/historical influences and limitations that they never mention, the very possibility of virtue comes into question.

I believe, however, that I can see one reason why Murdoch and McDowell limit themselves to individualistic factors in talking about virtue and neglect the larger cultural factors I have been emphasizing. Both are wary of the scientism that holds that science can tell us everything about reality and that what it doesn't speak of doesn't exist. And they deliberately stay clear of those analogies between moral philosophy and science that moral philosophers are often so eager to develop. One such attempted analogy can be found in the idea of moral philosophy as a progressive discipline that (occasionally) arrives at new and better moral knowledge (theories) through the historical accumulation of greater non-moral knowledge—and by building on the ideas of previous (moral) philosophers. In rejecting such analogies, Murdoch and McDowell limit themselves to focusing on ontogenetic impediments to moral knowledge (vision) and right action: such limits and impediments as are due to be overcome by means of the phylogenesis of moral knowledge could be acknowledged or featured only by admitting the sort of analogy between progressing science and moral philosophy that seems repugnant to Murdoch and McDowell. [Thus when Murdoch speaks (p. 38) of the "historically conditioned" aspects of virtue, she is in fact speaking only of the history of a particular individual who is to become virtuous by overcoming his own passions and foibles. History in the usual sense remains out of the picture.]

It is clear that I am not altogether averse to the above analogy between moral philosophy (and moral ideas generally) and science. It is dangerous to speak of moral progress, but I have risked doing so with regard to certain specific issues like slavery and the right (in principle) of a woman to leave her husband. Nonetheless, the main focus of my acceptance of the analogy is not the idea of similar progress, but rather of similar historical character. There seems to be something historically *developmental* about moral philosophy, even if this does not amount to progress as science understands (and achieves) it. Such an analogy with science does not force us to the sort of scientism McDowell and Murdoch decry. For one could hold that there was (phylogenetic) historical progress in moral theory without assuming that that occurred through some sort of convergence with scientific inquiry; the progress, if it occurs, can be directed, if you like, to a moral reality of the sort Murdoch and McDowell envisage.

In rejecting the analogy with historically developing science, Murdoch (pp. 27, 76) and McDowell (pp. 346ff.) also imply that moral philosophers have no contribution to make to our understanding (knowledge) of right and wrong—they can clarify concepts and indicate the structures and processes of the moral life, but that is another matter. This, however, ignores, or perhaps rejects, some important aspects of the history of moral philosophy. When it was first discussed in the eighteenth century, Utilitarianism was an original moral idea. No one had seriously thought that right action consisted in just what Utilitarianism says it does. Similarly, to take a more recent example, Rawls's difference principle (as opposed to aspects of his argument for it) seems to be a totally new substantive moral conception. Now even if neither the principle of utility nor the difference principle is actually true (or thus represents the moral knowledge that the ancients lacked and needed for the attainment of virtue), they are ideas worth taking seriously, real contributions to the attempt to know what is right (think how much has been learned by attempts to *refute* Utilitarianism and Rawls). And if new and promising ideas not about moral concepts but about actual right and wrong can thus emerge through the individual insight or vision of particular moral philosophers (or others), does this not locate another reason why virtue may not be attainable in those too-often-neglected factors of historical development that make some sort of analogy between science and moral thinking entirely plausible?

By focusing on characteristics of virtuous individuals, McDowell seeks to give an account of morality, as he says, from the inside out (p. 331). Moral principles become secondary or drop out altogether, because the tendencies to right action that virtue requires cannot, he thinks, be grasped or formulated in any statable general moral principle(s). But if, as I have suggested, the development of moral thought and the realization of virtue wait upon the thinking up and theoretical sifting of such moral principles as the Utilitarians and Rawls introduced, then there is a place for an independent "principles" approach to moral philosophy alongside efforts to conceive morality from the standpoint of the virtuous individual.[5]

---

[5] I am indebted to John McDowell, Myles Burnyeat, John Dillon, and Edward Erwin for helpful suggestions.

11

Morality not a System of Imperatives

I

At present there exists a widespread tendency to think of morality as some sort of system or code of imperatives, precepts, rules, or principles addressed to moral agents. Indeed, I can think of no ethical thinker of recent times who has said anything explicitly or implicitly to the contrary. And despite the recent heated debate about the categorical or hypothetical status of moral claims, all parties to the debate seem agreed that (valid) moral principles are principles for the guidance of the actions of moral agents: even Philippa Foot, who sparked the recent challenge to Kantian views about the categorical status of morality, treats morality as a system of hypothetical *imperatives*.[1]

The idea that morality consists of a code, system, or whatever for the guiding of action can also be seen in the widespread assumption that moral thinking is a form (one form) of practical thinking, that moral principles are invariably practical. For the idea that morality is (a species of the) practical seems ultimately to derive from Kant, and in Kantian usage "practical" means something very close to "for the guidance of agents."[2] Thus even those who hold that moral principles are merely hypothetical imperatives that do not automatically provide reasons for action, even

---

[1] P. R. Foot, "Morality as a System of Hypothetical Imperatives," *Philosophical Review*, vol. 81 (1972), pp. 305–16. Cf. Jan Narveson's claim (in *Morality and Utility*, Baltimore, 1967, p. 105) that a principle doesn't count as ethical unless it is action-guiding.

[2] See, e.g. Kant's *Critique of Practical Reason*, Part First, Book I, Chap. I, section I.

those who would dispute the Kantian claim that morality is a form of practical *reason*, seem to agree with Kant that morality is fundamentally, invariably practical. In fact, the view that morality is a system of practical principles is both more general and more plausible than the view that morality is a system of imperatives, if the latter is taken entirely literally. But those who speak of morality as a system of hypothetical imperatives also make it clear that their notion of an imperative is not restricted to what is grammatically in the imperative mood (or what can be analyzed as being such). Statements that something ought to be done or would be good to do are also to be construed as imperatives and so, presumably, is any normative moral claim that can reasonably be expected to guide moral agents;[3] for such philosophers, then, the thesis that morality is a system of imperatives is roughly equivalent to the Kantian view that morality is a species of the practical.

Now those who share this standpoint naturally wish to allow room for the (nonpractical) after-the-fact moral appraisal of actions and agents; but such appraisal is typically seen as derivative from the role of moral principles in guiding action. We may criticize agents (ourselves included) when their behavior has been out of line with the principles we feel should have been guiding their actions or for acting in *disregard* of such principles, but it is typically held that our picture of moral appraisal should be grounded in a proper understanding of the practical aspects of morality, rather than vice versa. Thus Stuart Hampshire in a well-known article in *Mind*:

> [T]he issue is—Is the answer to the question 'What are the distinguishing characteristics of sentences expressing moral praise or blame?' necessarily the same as the answer to the question 'What are the distinguishing characteristics of moral problems as they present themselves to us as practical agents?'? Unless these two questions are identical, or unless the first includes the second, much of contemporary moral philosophy is concerned with a relatively trivial side-issue, or is at the very least incomplete. My thesis is that the answer to the second question must contain the answer to the first, but that, if one tries to answer the first question without approaching it as part of the second, the answer will tend to be, not only incomplete, but positively misleading; and that the now most widely accepted philosophical interpretations of moral judgments, their logical status and peculiarities, are radically misleading for this reason. They purport to be logical characterisations of moral judgments and of the distinguishing features of moral arguments, but in these characterisations the *primary* use of moral judgments (= decisions) is largely or even entirely ignored...If a purely critical...moral judgment...is challenged and needs to be defended and justified, it will be justified by the same kind of arguments which one would have used as an agent in practical deliberation.[4]

Though Hampshire doesn't cite anyone who actually denies the moral primacy of the practical, he holds that metaethical views like emotivism and Moorean non-naturalism at the very least obscure that primacy and put an unjustified emphasis upon moral appraisal and criticism. Hampshire may be right about this, and if so, it may be worth noting that the present eclipse of the above-mentioned metaethical views

---

[3] Cf. Foot, *op. cit.*, pp. 305–7.
[4] S. N. Hampshire, "Fallacies in Moral Philosophy," *Mind* vol. 58 (1949), pp. 466–82.

coincides rather neatly with our present tendency to accept views like Hampshire's about the fundamental agent-orientation of morality. (It is also interesting that Hare's prescriptivism, which emphasizes the practical nature of morality, emerged into prominence not long after Hampshire's article, and that Hampshire himself seems to advocate prescriptivism (pp. 479–80).) In any event, the very difficulty of finding, even among the philosophers Hampshire criticizes, an explicit defense of the non-primacy of the practical within the moral should give some indication of how deep-seated the Kantian view of the practical nature of morality has been in recent philosophy.[5]

And yet I believe this view is fundamentally mistaken, and shall endeavor to explain why in what follows. It is no part of my purpose to deny that morality can and should be action-guiding. Morality does have essential action-guiding elements, but there are other aspects of morality that I believe cannot properly be seen as derivative from or functioning in the guiding of action. And I wish in particular to question whether (as in Hampshire's words) "if a purely critical moral judgments needs to be justified, it will be justified by the same kinds of arguments which one would have used as an agent in practical deliberation." Important parts of morality do not answer to this description, and the result seems to be that morality as a whole—even that central part of morality that concerns right and wrong action—cannot properly be described as a system of precepts addressed to agents, as a system of imperatives. Let us see how this conclusion can be defended.

II

Consider what motivates, or often has motivated, the idea that the need for self-defense can justify behavior that would otherwise be wrong. It is commonly felt that it makes no sense to forbid killing in self-defense (i.e., killing of an aggressor that is necessary in order to preserve one's own life) because of the very depth and strength, in most of us, of the instinct/desire for self-preservation. No proscriptions of killing in self-defense are likely to make the least bit of difference to most people's behavior, and most of us also feel that killing in self-defense is understandable. We sympathize with the instinct of self-preservation to a sufficient extent that self-protective homicide is not condemned after the fact: not even to the extent of thinking it wrong but excusable through the mitigating circumstance of threat or attack. On the contrary, killing in self-defense is typically considered justified and permissible on the grounds that it is both unrealistic and unfair to expect people not to kill in self-defense. And the depth and strength, indeed the instinctual character, of the desire for self-preservation and/or the impulse to defend oneself against aggression lie behind our belief in the unrealism and unfairness of any contrary expectation. If people didn't value life so much, we would have less sympathy for what was done in defense of life, and the particular character of the impetus towards self-defense

---

[5] In a reply to Hampshire's article (*Mind*, vol. 59, 1950, pp. 223–29), Kurt Baier has even questioned whether Ayer, Stevenson, and Moore obscure the moral primacy of the practical to anything like the extent that Hampshire claims.

makes most of us feel the absurdity and unreasonableness of addressing an injunction forbidding killing in self-defense to ordinary human beings.

Of course, some religious traditions preach a total pacifism that effectively denies the moral legitimacy of killing in self-defense, and injunctions against self-defense presumably can at least partially inhibit the self-defensive behavior of some individuals. Those who believe in a right to self-defense might attempt to convince pacifists that self-defensive homicide was not wrong, and if they were successful, that would presumably have an effect on the behavior of some such pacifists in situations where their lives were threatened. So it *makes sense* to address the principle that self-defense is permissible to moral agents, but the sense it makes depends on those agents' having (as most of us might put it) unreasonably severe, almost "unnatural" moral inhibitions. Most of us are not pacifists and would in the normal course defend ourselves against aggression without, at those very moments, taking account of or being guided by the principle that self-defense is permissible. If acts of self-defense spring from causes as deep and insistent as we are inclined to imagine, then this helps not only to justify self-defense, but also to make it understandable that those acting in self-defense should not be paying heed to or acting from moral injunctions at such moments. And so it would seem that the very factors that make for the permissibility of killing in self-defense also make it unreasonable to address a principle or precept to that effect to human moral agents in the expectation (or hope) that they will be guided by it when they kill in self-defense. (Wavering pacifists may be guided by it, but we who believe in a right of self-defense find their inhibitions unfortunate and have no desire for other moral agents to resemble them in this respect.)

Consider the contrast with other cases. One may, through promising, incur an obligation to do something, but later learn that because of unexpected alterations of circumstances, the act one had promised to perform would cause major injury to the promisee. If the promisee is not around to release one from one's promise, one may still feel (correctly, let us assume) that one shouldn't do what one promised, that in the altered circumstances one is permitted (and perhaps even obligated by the "spirit" of the original promise) not to do what one promised. In this case, surely one's belief that altered circumstances make it permissible not to do what one promised to do is supposed to be a major part of the explanation of why one doesn't do what one promised. And because it seems reasonable to expect people to be influenced by the perception of altered circumstances in this sort of way, a principle asserting that failure to do what one has promised is permissible in certain sorts of altered circumstances can be reasonably addressed to moral agents generally and is thus properly conceived as a *practical* precept of permission. The principle that killing in self-defense is permissible cannot be conceived in this way, however, because some of the very factors that justify it make it (morally) understandable that those who kill in self-defense—even those who do so while knowing that such behavior is permissible—should not in any large way be *influenced* by the thought that morality allows them to do what they are doing.[6] And in that case the permissibility of killing in self-defense

---

[6] I do not think recourse to the unconscious will help the traditional view at this point. Even if one who kills in self-defense is unconsciously aware that what he is doing is morally justified, it is hard to believe that that belief/knowledge will affect the mainsprings of self-protective action or exert a major influence on what the self-defender does.

represents a correct standard for the moral appraisal of actions, but corresponds to nothing essentially addressable to moral agents and is thus not practical.

Consider, then, what it would be like to address such a standard of permissibility to agents as a practical precept, while holding its rationale to be as we have said. We would in effect be telling people: you are (hereby) permitted to act in self-defense in situations where this very precept will not guide you, and such a form of address is absurd and self-defeating even as exhortation. Alternatively, try to imagine what people would have to be like in order to be convinced that self-protective homicide was permissible and at the same time genuinely influenced by a principle permitting such homicide that *was* properly addressable to them. Such people would presumably have to be able to describe themselves in ways like the following: this large menacing man was coming at me with a meat-cleaver, and because I realized that it was permitted to me in such circumstances to defend myself with violent force, I picked up the gun and.... Such a description seems eerie and freakish not only because it makes the person acting in self-defense seem so unlike ourselves, but because the cold-bloodedness of the justification it gives threatens to undercut what it is intended to justify. I do not, however, wish absolutely to deny the possibility that killing in self-defense might be justified even for someone who lacked a strong desire for self-preservation. Perhaps, even a person bent on suicide could justifiably suppose that he had the right to choose his own time to die and a concomitant right of self-defense against serious aggressors. But the justification here seems much less clear-cut, much less forceful, than what we find in ordinary instances of self-protective homicide, and that very fact indicates the importance that considerations of instinctual strength have in our actual rationale for the permissibility of such homicide. The sheer overwhelmingness of our desire to defend ourselves is at least part of the reason why we think it not wrong to kill in self-defense and find it morally understandable that someone acting in self-defense should not be guided by moral considerations in so doing.[7]

We shall now see that the considerations that led us to deny the practical character of certain permissions have similar implications for various obligations.

III

Those who view morality as some sort of system of imperatives, or practical rules, typically acknowledge the need to qualify various rules of obligation, and Philippa Foot has claimed in particular that the rule (a rule) stating our obligation to help others should have built into it an exception for cases where the cost to the agent is too great. One has an obligation to help others *except when* the personal cost of doing so would be considerable.[8] Of course, this last rule is both vague and in need of further qualification, and perhaps the unavoidable cumbersomeness of any fully spelled out rule about helping others tells against this whole way of conceiving morality. But surely, on the other hand, it is entirely natural to think of moral rules and precepts

---

[7] However, none of the above should be taken to imply that our sense of what is *necessary* to our own self-defense cannot evolve in response to experience and acquired knowledge.

[8] In "Are Moral Considerations Overriding?" in *Virtues and Vices* (Oxford, 1978), p. 186f.

as having exceptions built into them, and my question, in the light of our previous discussion, is whether all appropriately-exceptioned obligations are encapsulable within precepts, rules, or practical principles.[9]

If self-protective homicide is permissible, then presumably any obligation not to kill must be qualified accordingly and we shall want to say that one has an obligation not to kill (i.e., it is morally wrong to kill) *except in self-defense*. (I ignore other qualifications, for simplicity's sake, in what follows.) But is such a principle of obligation genuinely practical? Presumably, exception-making clauses are genuine parts of a practical principle only if they qualify the practical force of the principle. So if a rule containing exception-making qualifications is properly addressable to moral agents, it must be reasonable and appropriate to expect agents to take those qualifications into account and be influenced by them in action. This is precisely what we do find with many qualified obligations. As we have seen, our obligation to do what we have promised is qualified by an exception for cases where, because of altered circumstances, doing what we have promised would cause major injury to the promisee; and it is not unreasonable to expect someone who refrained from doing what he had promised, to do so at least in part because he recognized himself to be in such an exception-making circumstance.

But our obligation not to kill except in self-defense does not function in this way. We cannot reasonably expect someone who kills in self-defense to be substantively influenced, in his actions, by the realization that he is in exceptional circumstances vis-à-vis the obligation not to kill—all for reasons rehearsed at length in the previous section. So if the principle that killing wrong is genuinely to be qualified by an exception for self-defense, that principle is not properly conceived as a practical principle, as a rule or precept for the guidance of agents, but instead constitutes a valid standard for the moral *appraisal* of human action. The person who kills in self-defense is justified in doing what he or she does, even if it is unreasonable to expect that person to take note of, much less be guided by, that fact in the heat of self-protective activity. And the unreasonableness of the expectation is indeed part of the rationale for introducing qualifications about self-defense into the obligation not to kill. Nor is the obligation not to kill the only obligation that needs to be qualified in this sort of way. Our obligation to help others presumably must also contain a qualification for self-defense, and, once again, the rationale for the qualification undercuts the practical character of the obligation. Surely it would be absurd for someone to "sign-off" from beneficent activities with the thought: "now I am permitted to stop helping because someone is threatening my life."

We thus see that various moral standards of permissibility and obligation cannot be properly conceived as imperatives in any suitably broad sense of the term. And the standards we have mentioned are clearly not outlying facets of our morality, but occupy a central place within it. Nor are exceptions to the practical nature of morality confined to the single, though important, case of self-defense. Surely it is morally permissible for parents to give special preference to their children in situations of

---

[9] I take it that rules, precepts, prescriptions, "imperatives," and injunctions are all practical by definition. But principles exist in metaphysics and pure mathematics and are not practical *ex vi terminorum*.

grave danger, and obligations to help, to refrain from violence, and indeed not to kill, clearly require qualification to accommodate parental devotion. But given the forceful character of (some) parental devotion, it would be absurd to expect a parent whose child was in danger to be guided by moral considerations in that very situation. In such circumstances, a parent will typically be beyond the reach of moral principles, and a parent who thought to himself "I am permitted to save my child because family feelings overrides my other obligations" and who acted accordingly would seem to be an unnatural parent. Even if a parent is, from a moral standpoint, justified in rescuing his child from danger, that is not a justification we expect the parent to take into account in so acting. So, once again, we have obligations and permissions (permissibilities) that are not properly regarded as practical. And in the light of these varying examples—and the examples could be multiplied if only space allowed—it should be fairly clear that morality is not simply a species of the practical, a system of imperatives however broadly construed. And we are also given a new kind of reason to deny the metaethical thesis that moral claims—in particular claims of moral obligation and permission—are all (disguised) prescriptions.[10] Hare's "descriptivist" critics have powerfully argued that moral and other value claims in general lack the categorical, will-committing force that Hare attributes to them, but have tended to agree with Hare that moral claims (at least) are always and essentially addressable to moral agents. But if, as we have argued, moral claims are not all practical in this sense, we have yet another reason to deny the universally *prescriptive* force of genuine moral judgments.

IV

I think it might be useful at this point to indicate how the views I have just been defending differ from related ideas about morality and about the practical that have appeared in recent philosophical discussions. Philippa Foot, for example, has lately maintained the anti-Kantian thesis that it can sometimes be more virtuous to act from sympathy for someone's plight than out of respect for duty; and Michael Stocker, describing a man who visits a friend in hospital and claims to be doing so from a sense of duty rather than out of fellow-feeling, argues that (the act of) such a person is lacking in moral merit.[11] Such views seem consonant with the idea that there are

---

[10] In *Freedom and Reason* (Oxford, 1965, pp. 196ff.), Hare makes it quite clear that he regards all principles of permission as prescriptive and practical. However, the assumption that moral principles must be practical might lead one to conclude that self-defense (or family favoritism) was altogether outside the scope of morality, neither morally justified (permissible, all right) nor morally unjustified (impermissible, wrong). (Cf. Bernard Williams's "Persons, Character, and Morality" in A. Rorty, ed., *The Identities of Persons*, (Berkeley, 1976), esp. pp. 214ff.) But this conclusion would force us to renounce some very plausible and deep-seated moral ideas: e.g., the belief that there is such a thing as justifiable homicide and the idea that the moral obligation not to kill needs to be *qualified* for cases of self-defense. Better to reject the original assumption.

[11] Foot in "Virtues and Vices," *Virtues and Vices*, pp. 13f.; Stocker in "The Schizophrenia of Modern Ethical Theories," *The Journal of Philosophy*, vol. 73 (1976), pp. 453–66, esp. p. 462f.

non-practical aspects of morality. If someone who visits a sick friend in hospital out of sympathy is (other things equal) more virtuous, more morally meritorious, than the man in Stocker's example, then presumably it is at least sometimes morally better not to be guided by considerations of duty in one's actions.

In that case, we could take an additional step and claim that Stocker's visiting friend would do morally better not even to be influenced by the consideration that it *is* morally better to be guided by sympathy. For if he is thus influenced, he will once again fail to act fully from sympathy and will presumably lack the merit of someone who does. So the greater merit or virtue that Foot and Stocker see in sometimes acting from sympathy is precisely not something that an agent can act upon, though Foot and Stocker do themselves not draw this natural inference from their views and, as I shall now argue, could not easily do so, consistent with other things they say.

To begin with, the idea that certain claims about what is more or less virtuous are not practical is at the very least in tension with Foot's view that morality is a system of hypothetical imperatives, and perhaps the only way one could reasonably avoid inconsistency here would be to claim that questions of greater or less virtue, though not always practical matters, are outside that essential core of morality which is constituted by questions immediately relevant to the rightness and wrongness of actions. If one then maintained that it was not actually *wrong* to visit a hospitalized friend from a sense of duty or virtue, one could perhaps consistently hold that morality was basically, essentially, a system of practical (hypothetical) imperatives with certain outlying non-practical aspects.

Stocker, however, would face even greater difficulties in acknowledging that some moral matters are non-practical. For elsewhere in his article, he inveighs at length against moral views that cannot be acted on, singling out egoism and utilitarianism in this connection; yet he fails to see that his own conclusion about the greater merit of one who acts from sympathy is not a claim that can be acted on. And since (unlike Foot) Stocker explicitly denies that questions of right and wrong are the central questions of morality, he cannot consistently urge the insignificance of the non-practical moral conclusion we have distilled from his example and his assumptions about it.

In the light of these difficulties, it is perhaps not clear whether questions of greater or less merit or virtue *are* central to morality. But in that case, the significance of our earlier examples becomes especially vivid. For these concerned issues that everyone recognizes to be of fundamental moral importance, and their non-practical character can *leave no doubt* that morality is not a system of imperatives. There are also, moreover, reasons to doubt whether Foot and Stocker are right ascribe (other things equal) greater moral merit, virtue, to someone who visits a sick friend out sympathy rather than from a sense of duty. The man who acts from duty is not the kind of friend most of us would want; perhaps he is no friend all, given his cold-blooded approach to friendship And certainly we are likely to think less well of him than of someone who acts from sympathy But even those, like Hume, who have emphasized the sympathetic underpinnings of morality also stressed the need for moral dispositions that can outlast flagging sympathies and overcome utright antagonisms, and surely the man who acts from duty may evince steadier tendencies to do the right thing than someone whose visit is primarily motivated by sympathy. So perhaps lower regard for the visitor who acts consciously from duty is a matter of finding the man less attractive as a human being than friends we hope to have, rather than of find him *morally* defective. It is thus not at all clear that Stocker's man really is less virtuous or morally meritorious than the simpatico person who acts from sympathy. And that is yet another reason to stress our earlier examples in any attempt to show that morality is not a species of the practical. For there is much more agreement about the permissibility of killing in self-defense (and even of favoring one's children) than about the greater *moral* merit of someone whose good deeds are done from sympathy.

Of course, it may seem plausible and uncontroversial to assert an obligation to visit sick friends in hospital, but there is nothing non-practical about this obligation, if it exists. Human sympathies can flag, and if we believe that people ought to visit sick friends, then we shall want someone whose friendly feeling does flag at least to be guided by (this very) moral precept. Thus circumstances that might make us invoke a moral principle concerning the *duties* of friendship are precisely those in which we would need that principle to play a practical role. The earlier-discussed principles regarding self-defense seem much less practical, by comparison, because the kind of situation that induces us to qualify the obligation not to kill is (as we have seen) typically one in which people are understandably beyond the "reach" of moral principles. So the circumstances that most clearly call for a qualification in the general obligation not to kill are circumstances in which the qualification *lacks* a practical moral function; and that is why I believe that the examples of self-defense (and to a less extent of parental favoritism) provide the best means of establishing the main thesis of this essay.[12]

V

Suggestions of a divergence between practical moral thinking and moral appraisal are also to be found among various utilitarians and critics of utilitarianism. Act-utilitarians frequently advance utilitarian arguments for holding that not everyone should attempt to follow the principle of utility and that it can be wrong to inculcate act-utilitarianism in others. And even in those favorable circumstances where a utilitarian finds it useful and right to address the principle of utility to moral agents, he may also be hoping that those agents will sometimes *not* be motivated by it. For utilitarians often maintain that one can upon occasion achieve more good by acting spontaneously (e.g., from love or friendship) than by trying to maximize utilty.[13] For all these reasons, then, the act-utilitarian principle that one has an obligation to do

---

[12] On the other hand, a duty to visit sick friends *from sympathy* would involve a failure of practicality right at the heart of morality. But it is implausible to suppose such a duty exists, partly for reasons just mentioned and in part because most of us think morality cannot properly "legislate for feeling."

[13] E.g., J. J. C. Smart in "An Outline of a System of Utilitarian Ethics" in Smart and Williams, *Utilitarianism: For and Against* (Cambridge, 1973), pp. 44ff. On the reasons against inculcating or practicing act-utilitarianism, see, e.g., Sidgwick's *The Methods of Ethics* (London, Macmillan), 1962, seventh edition, pp. 413, 469, 480–92.

what maximizes utility may embody a standard of act-appraisal that is at best imperfectly apt for the guidance of moral agents.[14]

Utilitarianism has sometimes been taken to task for allowing even a partial divergence between appraisal and the practical regulation of action,[15] but we should be suspicious of this sort of criticism because our earlier discussion makes it abundantly clear that non-utilitarians must also acknowledge a split between the critical and the practical. The examples of self-defense and parental devotion yield principles of act-appraisal that cannot reasonably be expected to govern action, and because the permissibility of killing in self-defense is acceptable over such a broad range of moral viewpoints, those earlier examples may also provide a more persuasive and more plausible demonstration of the non-practical elements in morality than any argument from act-utilitarian assumptions.[16]

On the other hand, the fact that even a utilitarian can acknowledge the value of spontaneity in action can help us to see that the divorce between practical precepts and standards of appraisal also exists outside of morality (narrowly conceived). No one doubts that it is good to be spontaneous on occasion, and yet, as has often been noted, someone who acts spontaneously cannot be acting out of a regard for the benefits of so acting.[17] Some good things are spoiled if we think about them, and their value, too much, and it seems clear enough that the value of (occasional) spontaneity cannot be properly embodied within any practical principle, moral or otherwise. So there are areas outside of moral proper where standards of evaluation and appraisal are simply not practical, and this point, in its application to questions of human welfare, may well have been appreciated for some time now. It has perhaps been less well appreciated, however, that similar considerations apply to the moral. Morality cannot be distinguished from other forms of evaluation by its universally practical character, but, like the ethics of human welfare, embodies some standards for the

---

[14] On cannot render the utilitarian principle completely practical by altering it to read: one has an obligation to seek the maximization of utility unless spontaneity would achieve better results. For the latter incoherently assumes that spontaneity can be governed by a principle recommending spontaneity.

[15] See Stocker, *op. cit.*; and B. A. O. Williams, "A Critique of Utilitarianism," in Smart and Williams, *op. cit.*, pp. 121ff.

[16] Other forms of Utilitarianism are based on principles of act-appraisal that cannot be regarded as practical. The principle (mentioned but left nameless by Williams, *op. cit.*, p. 121) that an act is right if it expresses a utilitarianly valuable character-disposition is clearly not for the guidance of action, since we cannot sensibly ask someone to *act from* a maximizing character-disposition. (But is this principle plausible? Williams doesn't appear to think so.) By contrast, typical rule-utilitarianism and the "conscience-utilitarianism" offered recently by Robert M. Adams (in "Motive Utilitarianism," *The Journal of Philosophy*, vol. 73 (1976), p. 479) do have a practical character: it makes sense to ask someone to do the things that would be demanded by a maximizing set of rules or conscience.

In the article cited, however, Adams also puts forward a "motive utilitarianism" according to which (roughly) motives are right or good to the extent that they serve utility. This principle may or may not be plausible, but in any event it is clearly not practical (as Adams himself seems well aware). However, the principle concerns the evaluation of motives, not of actions, and many of us already believe that principles for the moral appraisal of motives (or character) need not be practical. What is distinctive about the examples discussed in the present essay, on the other hand, is their tendency to show that certain (valid) standards *for morally appraising actions* cannot reasonably be addressed to moral agents.

[17] Cf. John Elster, *Ulysses and the Sirens*, (Cambridge, 1979), p. 168. Also Williams, *op. cit.*, pp. 128ff.

critical appraisal of actions that cannot sensibly be translated into precepts addressed to agents.

We found this to be true of morality in particular largely because of the way various powerful human feelings and reactions carve out a space of moral immunity that correspondingly restricts the scope of our moral obligations. Interestingly enough, however, facts about human feeling and reaction do not similarly induce us to qualify the precepts of etiquette. It is bad manners to eat peas with a knife, but no one is in the least inclined to qualify that claim into: it is bad manners to eat peas with a knife except in self-defense. Nor is it a principle of etiquette that one should not eat peas with a knife except in order to save one's own children. This difference between etiquette and morality may be of some importance and clearly calls for explanation; but for our present purposes, it chiefly serves to suggest the purely practical character of etiquette. The considerations that forced us earlier to acknowledge that morality is not a species of the practical do not seem to apply to good manners, and correct etiquette may thus well constitute a system of (hypothetical) imperatives of the kind that morality is widely thought to be.

VI

If, for the reasons given above, it is a mistake to think of morality as universally practical, then we must also reject Hampshire's claim that a proper understanding of moral problems as they present themselves to moral agents can generate a proper understanding of moral criticism. For as we have seen, some standards of moral criticism are based precisely on its being understandable that certain sorts of considerations should *not* occur to or influence moral agents. Are we to conclude, then, that in morality the critical standpoint is prior to that of the agent? Not necessarily. We would presumably not want to base such a claim on the outmoded metaethical theories that (Hampshire believes) earlier supported such a position. And there may well be aspects of moral agency that cannot properly be understood in moral-critical terms, so that neither the agential nor the critical standpoint will have clear priority. But I have, for the moment, no idea what those aspects might be, and I would like to suggest one way in which the point of view of moral agents might turn out to be derivative from that of moral appraisal.

It may be possible to think of moral criticism as containing principles with both practical and nonpractical qualifications, e.g., the principle: it is wrong to kill except in self-defense or in one's capacity as an official state executioner, etc. (It is not terribly important that this illustrative principle be plausible.) Because such a principle contains non-practical qualification, it cannot itself be thought of as practical. But since moral criticism justifies such qualifications in terms of their understandable non-occurrence to agents, it presumably also has the means to tell us which qualifications in its principles are non-practical and thus, more significantly, which qualifications in its principles need to be deleted in order to arrive at principles that *can* properly be construed as practical. Now if all practical principles of morality could be generated from critical standards in this way—and we have at this point been given no reason to believe the contrary—then critical morality would have the resources to generate and justify the principles of agential morality, and the latter would in at least one clear sense be derivative from the former.

None of this, however, would entail that we were not *chiefly* interested in correct moral appraisal for the guidance it gives us as moral agents.[18] Nor would it entail a moral intellectualism according to which the moral life was primarily a matter of making the right critical judgments, deriving the right practical precepts from them, and then acting accordingly to the latter. Quite to the contrary, one of our main points has been that people can be morally justified when they act from certain impulses and feelings without paying any attention to moral principles or justifications. We have seen that, far from simply governing human life, valid morality is itself shaped, limited, influenced, even governed by factors outside itself, and self-aware practical moral thought floats upon a deeper, fuller life that occasionally drives out all thought about morality. Indeed, there is a definite sense in which the standpoint of the present essay stresses the practical aspects of morality far more than does the widely influential Kantian tradition that holds that all aspects of the moral are reflected in the reasoning of moral agents and that morally right action should be governed by the thought of certain moral precepts. For if we understand the practical not (in the philosophically usual, Kantian sense) as entailing a regard for action-guiding principles, but rather in that everyday sense in which it contrasts with everything intellectual and intellectualistic, then surely the present essay makes morality as a whole seem much *more* practical than it is usually taken to be.[19]

---

[18] Indeed, even non-practical principles of the kind we have been discussing may have various practical *implications*. For example, the principle that it is good to be spontaneous may influence (non-spontaneous) decisions about how to educate children; and the principle that self-defensive homicide is permissible (not wrong) may persuade someone to buy a gun for his home or convince a jury to return a verdict of "not guilty." But in cases such as these, the non-practical principle involved is only useful in deciding whether to do something *not mentioned* by the principle itself. It thus has what we might call indirect practical uses, without thereby counting as practical. For on our usual understanding of the notion, practical principles (precepts, imperatives) guide an agent towards the doing of things that they themselves mention and recommend.

[19] I am very much indebted to Thomas Nagel, Joseph Raz, and Michael Stocker for helpful criticisms and suggestions.

12

God and Other Minds

A Study of the Rational Justification of Belief in God

This book is one of the most important to have appeared in this century in the philosophy of religion, and makes outstanding contributions to our understanding of the problem of other minds as well. Plantinga's chief concern is critical: to examine in detail and refute some of the most important and plausible arguments put forward by philosophers for the existence of some sort of deity and for the existence of other minds. Plantinga demonstrates great skill in argumentation and brings all the techniques of modern philosophical analysis, including modal logic, to bear on the views he criticizes.

The book is divided into three parts. In the first Plantinga criticizes what he holds to be the most significant natural theological arguments for the existence of God: the cosmological argument (as encapsulated in St. Thomas Aquinas' Third Way); the ontological argument (as stated by St. Anselm and by Norman Malcolm); and the teleological argument (as stated by Cleanthes in Hume's *Dialogues concerning Natural Religion*). In the second part, Plantinga considers what he calls "Natural Atheology," i.e., attempts to disprove the existence of any sort of deity. In particular, he examines the problem of evil and the claim that there could not be a God (of the kind believed in by the Judeo-Christian tradition) in a world with as much evil as ours contains. He also discusses the claim that God's existence cannot be necessary, since there are no necessary existents, only necessarily true propositions, and the logical positivists' rejection of religious claims on the ground that they are unverifiable.

In the third and final section of *God and Other Minds* Plantinga considers various of the most important answers that have been given to the problem of other minds. Behaviorism is rejected outright and without argument (191). Plantinga focuses principally on the argument from analogy for other minds. He considers various recent Wittgensteinian objections to that argument and various recent Wittgensteinian alternatives to it, and finds them all unacceptable. He concludes that the argument from analogy is the best available argument for other minds, but that there are grave problems even with that argument. Thus in the end, Plantinga maintains that the arguments for other minds are just as weak as those for the existence of God.

It should be clear that *God and Other Minds* is basically critical in its approach and negative in its conclusions, but, to the extent that Plantinga's criticisms are original and germane to the arguments criticized, his book makes a significant contribution to the enterprise of philosophy. Plantinga's technique is, typically, to formalize the arguments he finds in historical sources and then to work with the formal versions. An argument like the cosmological argument is stated in terms of numbered premises and conclusion, and the resultant formal argument is examined to see whether it is formally valid and has acceptable premises. When a particular formalized version of the argument turns out to be unsuccessful, others are suggested and then examined to see whether they might not be more acceptable. When all the formalized versions of the cosmological argument he discusses turn out to be unacceptable, Plantinga concludes that the cosmological argument is a failure.

Now such a technique of argumentation is convenient for a philosopher skilled in the techniques of philosophical analysis, but it is also dangerous. For how can one be sure that any of one's formal arguments corresponds to the original intent of the philosopher who originally gave the argument one is criticizing? And how can one be sure that one has tried all the possible promising ways of formalizing the original argument, or some argument resembling it? Indeed Plantinga is himself aware of the risks entailed by his own techniques of criticism. After arguing at great length against certain formalized versions of the ontological argument put forward by St. Anselm in the *Proslogion*, chapter II, he remarks:

> No doubt there are other reasonable interpretations of this Anselmian argument; I can scarcely claim to have refuted the argument überhaupt. But until other interpretations are suggested, the verdict must be that the ontological argument is unsuccessful (81 f.).

I am inclined to agree with Plantinga's summary of the fruits of his criticisms of Anselm's ontological argument. Indeed I tend to think Plantinga's criticisms of the argument are on a far higher plane than those of any previous critics of the argument. It seems to me that he suggests reasonable formalized versions of Anselm's actual argument, that he refutes those versions, and that no other interpretations of Anselm's argument readily present themselves as capable of succeeding where the arguments Plantinga examines have failed. So I think Plantinga is correct in thinking that he has at least put the burden of proof on those who would maintain that the Anselmian ontological argument can be made to work. I also find Plantinga quite convincing in his criticism of various historically influential attempts to undermine the ontological argument. For example, Plantinga argues quite surprisingly, but with great effectiveness, that the Kantian effort to undermine the ontological argument on the ground that existence is not a real predicate or property really carries no weight against the argument.

Plantinga's treatment of the cosmological argument centers entirely around the Third Way of St. Thomas. One would have liked to see him deal with the other cosmological arguments put forward by St. Thomas, but Plantinga's treatment of the Third Way gives one, I think, some idea of how he would criticize those other cosmological arguments. Nor does Plantinga deal with cosmological arguments that make use of the Principle of Sufficient Reason in order to argue from the fact that there are contingent entities to the conclusion that there is a necessary First Cause. But this is no great loss, since the Principle of Sufficient Reason *contradicts* the assumption that there are contingent entities. If *everything* has an explanation, then the whole contingent history of the universe has an explanation. But only the logically necessary choices and/or causation of a logically necessary being or thing could explain the *whole* contingent history of the universe, and if such an explanation existed, everything in the world would exist by logical necessity and *not* contingently. Thus the Principle of Sufficient Reason contradicts the assumption that there are contingent entities—and, furthermore, is necessarily false if, as I shall argue below, it is necessary that there be some contingent entity.[1] Plantinga's avoidance of cosmological arguments based on the Principle of Sufficient Reason, then, is no great omission, since such arguments are all, I believe, based on premises that are mutually inconsistent, and thus all clearly unsound.

Plantinga does, however, make one assumption in his treatment of St. Thomas's Third Way that I find questionable at best. It is the assumption that it is only contingently true that there are contingent entities. And, as Plantinga points out (20), this is an assumption that St. Thomas and the others who have attempted cosmological arguments have also made. Indeed the cosmological argument has always been thought to be an a posteriori argument just because its assumption that there are contingent entities has itself been considered contingent, and so a posteriori. Nonetheless, I think the rather surprising fact of the matter is that it is logically impossible for there not to be contingent entities, at least if one admits states of affairs as being among the entities that exist.

If there are such things as states of affairs at all, then surely, among the states of affairs that actually exist, are included: the hostility between China and Russia, Nixon's needing oxygen, and De Gaulle's love of France. There is also such a state of affairs as there being ravens. And if there were no ravens, there still would exist the state of affairs: there not being any ravens in the universe, or, what comes to the same thing, the nonexistence of ravens in the universe. Both states of affairs—there being ravens and there not being any ravens—are contingent ones, entities that exist only contingently. But it seems to be logically necessary that one or the other of those states of affairs should exist (forgetting certain problems about borderline cases that can be handled separately). Thus it is logically necessary that there exist some contingently existing entity.

---

[1] Pretty much the same views about the Principle of Sufficient Reason have been arrived at independently by James Ross in his *Philosophical Theology* (Indianapolis: Bobbs-Merrill, 1969).

A possible reply to this line of reasoning might be that states of affairs of the sort we have been discussing are contingent only in the sense that propositions can be contingent. Contingent propositions, it might be said, are contingently *true*, but necessarily exist, the way numbers and universals do. And the same might be said about contingent states of affairs. But is it reasonable to liken states of affairs to propositions in this way, assuming for the sake of argument that propositions do necessarily exist even when they are only contingently true? One reason we may have for holding that propositions are necessary existents is that it seems so odd and ridiculous to talk of bringing about or causing a proposition or of putting an end to or destroying a proposition or of a proposition that would not have *existed* if certain things had taken place. But it is quite natural to talk of bringing about a certain state of affairs, or of putting an end to one, or of a state of affairs that would not have existed if certain things had taken place. Or, to take particular examples, one can put an end to the hostility between Russia and China, to De Gaulle's love of France, or to the existence of ravens. And it is perfectly in order to say that the enmity between Russia and China would never have existed if things had been different.

If so, then our ordinary talk about states of affairs indicates that such states of affairs as we have mentioned are not necessarily existent, causally isolated entities the way propositions are often thought to be, and so there seems to be no reason to deny the surprising result that it is necessary that contingent entities exist. (Perhaps, this will not seem so surprising if one considers the rather similar case of individual entities and their accidents. Just as no contingent entity necessarily exists, but it is necessary that there be *some* contingent entity, so too no accidental property of an object is necessarily had by the object, but it is necessary that every object have *some* accidental properties.)

I have spent a good deal of time on this point because it has been neglected entirely by those who formulated the various versions of the cosmological argument, and even by so able a critic of that argument as Plantinga. But the force of the objection against the cosmological argument itself is minor. To counter it, one need only replace the assumption that there are contingent entities and that it is only contingent that there are, by the assumption that there are physical bodies (or conscious beings) and that it is only contingent that there are. Then the cosmological argument will really be a posteriori, as it was intended to be, though, of course, it will still be open to the criticisms that Plantinga has brought against it.

It would be impossible even to mention all the interesting ideas and arguments of Plantinga's book in a brief review. But I would like to say something about Plantinga's treatment of the problem of other minds. One of the most noteworthy contributions of the book is its extensive and detailed criticisms of the arguments and positions of philosophers in the Wittgensteinian tradition concerning the problem of other minds. In chapter ix of his book, Plantinga examines the attempts of such philosophers as Strawson, Malcolm, and Shoemaker to undermine skepticism concerning other minds by showing that there is a necessary connection between one's own mental states and/or suitable behavior on the part of physical bodies on the one hand, and the existence of other minds on the other. Plantinga is critical of this whole tradition, and he rejects as unacceptable all the formal reconstructions of Wittgensteinian arguments for other minds that he discusses. Here, as elsewhere, his arguments seem powerful and to the point. It is, of course, possible that Plantinga has misinterpreted the Wittgensteinian arguments for other minds; but if he has, one would like to see the authors he criticizes show *how* he has misunderstood them and *how*, correctly understood, their arguments can avoid the sorts of criticism Plantinga presents. Until such rebuttal is presented, I think we have been given good reason to be dubious about Wittgensteinian answers to the problem of other minds.

Plantinga also considers the attempts of philosophers in the Wittgensteinian tradition to undermine the argument from analogy for other minds (in chapter viii). Here again, I think he has effectively put the burden of proof on those who hold that argument to be incoherent because of the truth of certain Wittgensteinian doctrines. In the final chapter of his book, however, Plantinga goes on to present arguments of his own against the argument from analogy for other minds. Here Plantinga's criticisms strike me as less convincing than elsewhere. Plantinga considers only a very special kind of inductive-analogical argument for other minds, a kind of argument based on what he calls a *simple* inductive argument. An inductive argument is simple when it is precisely of the form: Every A such that S has determined by observation whether or not A is B is such that S has determined by observation that A is B. Therefore, probably every A is B. Plantinga claims (251) that according to the Analogical Position one can give a sound argument for other minds that makes use of a simple inductive argument. But the Analogical Position cannot in all fairness be so narrowly construed. It is possible, as I have shown elsewhere,[2] to present an analogical-inductive argument for other minds that is in no way based on a *simple* inductive argument in Plantinga's sense. And if such an argument is sound, it will surely suffice to vindicate the Analogical Position.

It must be said that Plantinga's book, for all its outstanding virtues, is marred in places by a certain philosophical cuteness or *legerdemain* that to some degree limits its ultimate effectiveness. For example, after refuting first various arguments for and against the existence of God and then various arguments for the existence of other minds, Plantinga attempts to tie the two parts of his book together and actually turn his negative criticism to positive advanage. He argues (268 ff.) that there is no way to present a sound argument for other minds any more than for the existence of God; so, since it clearly is reasonable to believe in other minds, he tentatively concludes that it is also reasonable to believe in God. Such an argument is bound to irk readers. For one thing, it throws caution to the wind in claiming that there can be no acceptable argument for other minds. Furthermore, it makes the controversial and perplexing assumption that belief in other minds can be reasonable even if totally unsupportable. Wouldn't it have been wiser of Plantinga to have assumed that since it is reasonable to believe in other minds, and since such belief must be supportable

---

[2] See "Induction and Other Minds," *Review of Metaphysics*, xx, 2 (December 1966): 341–360; this is a reply to an article of Plantinga's by the same name that appeared *ibid.*, xix, 3 (March 1966): 441–460, and that forms the basis for the last chapter of Plantinga's book.

Plantinga has recently [*ibid.*, xxi, 3 (March 1968): 524–533] put forward certain skeptical doubts concerning the argument I presented; and I can only say here that I think that his skeptical challenge can be overcome and that there is a sound argument from analogy, based on acceptable inductive reasoning, for the existence of other minds. See my *Reason and Scepticism* (London: Allen & Unwin, 1970), chap. iv, sec 3.

if it is to be reasonable, there must be a sound argument for other minds that he did *not* examine, one, perhaps, that has not yet even been discovered? And is it not also more reasonable to assume that such an argument will be found to support the claim that there are other minds than that any argument could be devised to justify belief in God? After all, for us humans, the existence of God entails the existence of another mind, but not vice versa.

In similar fashion, earlier in the book, Plantinga argues quite forcefully that God's existence as an all-good, omnipotent, omniscient being is *consistent* with the existence of the amount of evil that there is in the world, because such evil may result from human freedom, which God has reason to create, despite the fact that evil may result from it. Plantinga then considers the objection that *natural* evil is *evidence against* the existence of an all-good, omnipotent, omniscient God, because such natural evil is in no way a consequence of giving *people* free will. He replies (155) that we have *no evidence* against the view that fallen angels cause natural evil out of *their* free will and that God created angels with free will (who could fall) for the same sort of reason that he created men with free will. Such a reply to the problem of evil strikes this reader as sophistic. Most philosophers and scientists would argue that we do have evidence against the existence of fallen angels, just as we have evidence against phlogiston and leprechauns, and to say that we do not, without further ado, is to be evasive at the very crux of the problem of evil.

Despite lapses of the just-mentioned sort, however, Plantinga's book is clearly an interesting and a significant one, deserving of the attention of any philosopher seriously interested in the philosophy of religion, the philosophy of mind, or epistemology in general.

13

Utilitarianism, Moral Dilemmas, and Moral Cost

Utilitarianism has been charged in a number of different ways with oversimplifying morality and the moral life. But the present paper will confine its attention to two closely related ways in which this criticism can be made. Utilitarianism has recently been accused both of blindness to the possibility of moral dilemmas and of an inability to conceive the idea of moral cost, and in what follows I would like to respond to these charges, not, in the perhaps expectable utilitarian fashion, by admitting them but denying their destructive force against utilitarianism, but by questioning the truth of the charges. It is certainly true that (act-) utilitarian, and, more broadly, (act-) consequentialist moral theories have almost always been presented in ways that seem to preclude moral dilemmas and moral costs, but this appearance results from a tendency to overlook certain historically important forms of utilitarianism and from a failure to recognize the implications of the traditional utilitarian appeal to universal impersonal benevolence. I hope, therefore, to show that the dilemmas and costs that have recently been said to characterize ordinary moral thinking can be plausibly modelled within (act-) utilitarian moral theory. Whether this unsuspected capacity for complexity will be welcome to utilitarians and whether it will take the edge off some of the criticism that has been directed at utilitarianism by defenders of common-sense morality are questions to be discussed at the end of this essay.

I

Recent treatments of the idea of a moral dilemma have focussed on a particularly de-epistemologized version of this notion. From the standpoint of these recent discussions the existence of deep moral uncertainty is not sufficient for the existence of a dilemma; a dilemma exists only when a person (through no fault of his own) is faced with a morally tragic situation in which whatever he does will be wrong. Several recent philosophers have argued for the existence of moral dilemmas so conceived,[1] but others remain unconvinced and I shall not here attempt to settle this issue. The main point will be, rather, that *if* there are genuine moral dilemmas from the standpoint of common-sense morality, then we must also allow for the possibility of utilitarian moral dilemmas.

Recent formulations of (act-) utilitarianism and (act-) consequentialism certainly seem to leave no room for dilemmas: if the criterion of a morally right or acceptable action is that it produces as much good overall as any of the alternatives available to the agent in a given situation, then, for example, where two acts have equally good consequences and no available act would produce better consequences, both acts will be morally right and the choice between them not, therefore, dilemmatic. But why not say that an act is right only if it is *better* than any alternative, so that when two (or more) acts tie for first place neither (none) counts as morally right? The question is less obtuse than it may seem: the attempt to answer it actually helps to clear the way for a purely utilitarian version of moral tragedy. For the obvious retort would be to point out the perversity of characterizing an act with good consequences as unacceptable simply because some other act would produce just as much good—especially if either act would produce better consequences than any other act that could be performed in the situation.

But what happens when the two actions tied for first place would each on the whole have *bad* results? Utilitarian conceptions of consequences and effects make little or no distinction between commissions and omissions and allow for the possibility that every possible act in a given situation would make things worse off (than before). And though it is eminently plausible to say that where good can be accomplished, two actions tied for first place may both count as acceptable, it is less clearly plausible to speak this way of "tied least evils," of actions with overall bad consequences that are nonetheless better than anything else an agent can do in given circumstances. (Later I shall provide an illustrative example of such circumstances.) Yet on the above-mentioned typical formulations, (act-) utilitarianism makes no distinction between cases where good can be done and cases where evil consequences can only be minimized; and it is precisely with respect to the second sort of case that utilitarianism may be tempted to acknowledge the possibility of tragic moral dilemmas. There is one historically important form of (act-) utilitarianism that is in fact clearly dilemma-permitting, and once we see how the latter can be developed into a plausible alternative to contemporary versions of utilitarianism, the possibility of utilitarian moral dilemmas will come into view.

---

[1] See, for example, Bernard Williams, "Ethical Consistency," in *Problems of the Self*, (Cambridge, 1977), chap. 11; Bas van Fraassen, "Values and the Heart's Command," *Journal of Philosophy*, vol. 70. (1973), pp. 3–19; and Ruth Marcus, "Moral Dilemmas and Consistency," *Journal of Philosophy*, vol. 77. (1980), pp. 121–36. Two of the most plausible and frequently mentioned examples of dilemmatic situations are Agamemnon's tragic choice at Aulis and Sartre's example of the young man forced to choose between joining the Free French and caring for a helpless bereaved mother.

II

The dilemma-permitting version of utilitarianism I have in mind is to be found in Bentham's *An Introduction to the Principles of Morals and Legislation*. The 1823 version of the *Introduction* treats the principle of utility as requiring that one act to produce the greatest happiness of those affected by one's actions, but it does this in a prominent long footnote, and the main text of the work reads the same as the original edition of 1789 and understands the principle of utility as making the rightness or wrongness of an act depend on whether it contributes to human happiness or to human unhappiness. Now such an interpretation of the principle of utility differs from the first-mentioned version of the principle in (at least) two important respects. To begin with, it allows what I have elsewhere called moral satisficing. Instead of requiring that right acts be optimific, it treats acts as right if they merely make *some* contribution on balance to human happiness, and Bentham's original understanding of the principle of utility is thus a form of satisficing (act-) utilitarianism, as opposed to those optimizing, maximizing versions of (act-) utilitarianism that have more recently been favored and that Bentham himself introduces in the second edition of his *Introduction*.[2]

But Bentham's original principle of utility differs from recent optimizing act-utilitarianism in another important respect. The latter allows one to "flip a coin" when two or more actions are tied for first place with respect to the goodness of consequences, and it makes no distinction between consequences tied for being least bad and consequences highest in positive goodness. But Bentham's original theory requires that a right act have positively good consequences, and so entails that a moral dilemma would come about in any situation where an agent found that every possible course of action would on the whole have deleterious effects.

Now Bentham's early version of utilitarianism may well be thought inferior to now-prevalent optimizing versions. The earlier principle of utility makes any act right that has good consequences (for human happiness), and it thereby sets a ridiculously low standard for morality, allowing an act to count as right even if it produces much less good than many of its alternatives. But it is not the undemandingness of Bentham's early version of the principle of utility that makes moral dilemmas possible, but rather its *demand* that any right act have overall good consequences, a demand not made by most contemporary versions of act-utilitarianism. So Bentham's satisficing version of utilitarianism may be faulted for permitting (inappropriate kinds of) moral satisficing, without the dilemma-permitting element in the theory having thereby in any way come under attack. And in fact even an optimizing form of act-utilitarianism can lead to moral dilemmas. Thus consider the moral theory that results if one demands of a right action both that it produce consequences no less good than those producible by any alternative act available to a given agent and that those consequences be, on balance, good. Such a theory clearly demands optimific behavior; but it sets the additional requirement that right actions have good consequences on balance, and, as with Bentham's earlier view, this element of the theory

---

[2] See my "Satisficing Consequentialism," *Proceedings of the Aristotelian Society Supplementary Volume*, 1984.

just introduced entails the possibility of situations where no matter what one does, one acts wrongly. So both satisficing and optimizing forms of utilitarianism can lead to moral dilemmas.

Ruth Marcus (among others) has recently claimed that act-utilitarianism cannot lead to moral dilemmas, and has offered a particular explanation of this impossibility.[3] The explanation is not, she thinks, that act-utilitarianism makes use of only one principle for judging the morality of actions, but, rather, the fact that common-sense moral principles make the intrinsic features of an act immediately relevant to its moral status, whereas utilitarianism treats as relevant only the consequences of an action, not its intrinsic nature. (She allows, however, that many dilemmas arise, for our ordinary morality, in virtue of a conflict *between* certain intrinsic characterizations of actions and considerations of consequences.) However, if the above-mentioned dilemma-prone forms of the principle of utility are coherent, then whether or not they are as plausible as standard contemporary optimizing utilitarianism, it should be clear that Marcus's account of dilemmas is flawed. Bentham's earlier version of the principle of utility and the principle requiring acts that both optimize and have positively good consequences are both single-principle act-utilitarian moral theories that make moral status depend on consequences, rather than the intrinsic characterization of actions; yet they allow for moral dilemmas, so it cannot be the absence of morally-relevant intrinsic characterizations that prevents (the most popular contemporary form of) act-utilitarianism from generating moral dilemmas; and Marcus's more basic assumption that utilitarianism does not allow for dilemmas—an assumption shared alike by recent defenders and critics of utilitarianism—holds only for certain versions of (act-) utilitarianism, not for (act-) utilitarianism per se.

However, at this point it might be said that Bentham's early version of utilitarianism and its dilemma-prone optimizing offshoot are completely implausible and so of strictly historical interest. And it might then be claimed that any half-way plausible form of utilitarianism will be dilemma-free, whereas common-sense morality at its subtlest and most adequate precisely allows for dilemmas. But I wonder whether the two dilemma-producing versions of utilitarianism mentioned earlier can both be regarded as faulty forms of utilitarianism. Given the way act-utilitarianism has typically been conceived and justified as a moral theory, I think dilemma-producing versions of utilitarianism may have as good a claim to express the fundamental moral ideals of utilitarianism as contemporary versions.

III

The principle of utility has long been viewed as expressing the dictates of an impersonal, or impartial, benevolence. Our own benevolence is more concerned with some people than with others and concern with ourselves can hardly be called benevolence at all, but when we abstract from our own particular identities, we may imaginatively feel an impersonal benevolence that is equally interested in the welfare of every individual, and utilitarians usually regard the principle of utility as justified

---

[3] *Op. cit.*

by the fact that its dictates would recommend themselves to anyone who adopted a purely benevolent but impersonal standpoint. Thus utilitarianism treats benevolence (or sympathy) as the most fundamental moral motive, and takes a certain universalized form of ordinary human benevolence (or sympathy) as the touchstone of moral justification, whereas common-sense morality treats benevolence as only one of several forms of moral motivation and justification.

But what is benevolence? Our ordinary notion conveys the idea of wishing well and wishing to do well by, but what is supposed to underlie the principle of utility in current optimizing formulations is some sort of impersonal desire that things should somehow turn out for the best.[4] There is a disparity here that has been neglected in recent discussions, but that has great significance for our understanding of utilitarianism. The universal impersonal benevolence that is the touchstone of recent utilitarian justification is an ideal theoretical distillation of the ordinary benevolent desire that, in various situations, things should turn out for the best for certain people other than oneself. But ordinary benevolence can express itself no less in the desire to do well by people than in the desire to do the best one can for people, and these two expressions have importantly different implications with respect to situations where anything one does or does not do will make things worse for people. In such circumstances one can fulfill the desire to do the best one can but cannot in the ordinary sense do well by, or help, people; and ordinary benevolence, at least in one of its aspects, is thereby thwarted. (Even in situations where one can help people, benevolence may not be entirely satisfied if everything one can do will still leave those people fairly badly off. However, I shall ignore this complication in what follows.) But then to the extent that utilitarian moral argument is grounded in a form of universalized *benevolence*, it is subject to the same fundamental dichotomy. Impersonal benevolence will involve the impersonal desire that things turn out for the best possible in any given situation, but also the desire that, where things are not ideal, they should somehow be made better; and such benevolence will thus only be partially fulfilled through actions which on the whole make things worse for people at the same time that they make the best of a bad situation. But the question then arises why utilitarianism should require the satisfaction of only one of the two components of (universal impersonal) benevolence in order for an action to count as right. Should it not, rather, require that both elements of its foundational benevolence be satisfied in order for an act to count as morally acceptable, thus yielding our dilemma-prone optimizing version of utilitarianism rather than the less demanding version of the principle of utility recently in favor?

Nor does it seem open to the utilitarian to argue that such a requirement would be much too demanding; for the optimizing theory that utilitarians now prefer is open to the same charge, and all the moves that utilitarians have made against that charge can be made against the charge that dilemma-prone versions of utilitarianism are too rigorous. It is often said, for example, that act-utilitarianism demands too much self-sacrifice from agents, but the reply has been that self-sacrificing optimific action is required from the standpoint of disinterested benevolence and that one can in any case distinguish between an agent's acting wrongly and its being right to blame her for doing so (or wrong to praise her for doing so). A similar point can be made about

---

[4] Cf., e.g., S. Scheffler, *The Rejection of Consequentialism*, (Oxford 1982), p. 2.

the optimizing dilemma-prone version of utilitarianism introduced above. It makes it even harder to act rightly than the prevalent version of the theory, but act-utilitarianism evaluates actions from the standpoint of impersonal benevolence, judging them in terms of whether (or perhaps how well) they serve what such benevolence desires (of actions); and as we have seen, impersonal universal benevolence can naturally be expressed as desiring of actions not only that they be optimific but also that they not make things worse than they already, imperfectly, are. Such benevolence is thus more complex as a motivation and method of justification than utilitarians and anti-utilitarians have realized, and to the extent that a given action fails to satisfy both the goals benevolence has with respect to given actions, there seems no reason, from the standpoint of act-utilitarianism, to insist that the action is nonetheless morally right. One can and perhaps should say, rather, that it is wrong, but that it may nonetheless be right to praise or not to blame it, provided, again, that the latter action serves the twin goal of optimizing and generally improving (not disimproving) things for people. It is difficult to see how the act-utilitarian can claim that presently prevalent versions of utilitarianism are better or more adequate expressions of its underlying rationale than the dilemma-prone version mentioned above.

However, perhaps the best way to see how naturally dilemmas can arise within a recognizably utilitarian perspective would be to imagine circumstances that might unavoidably elicit guilt from a utilitarian moral agent in the same way that common-sense moral dilemmas are supposed to make guilt inevitable for ordinary moral agents. Imagine an impersonally benevolent person who has devoted his life to helping people, but who learns that the has contracted a particularly virulent form of plague. Wherever he moves (and even if he stays put) he will infect people (via various carriers of the disease). There is no known way of immediately isolating him or sealing him off in such a way that no one is infected, and whatever he does, people—different people in different cases depending on where or whether he moves and on how he acts—will be made worse off than they would be, say, if he could instantaneously disappear.

What will the conscientious person with utilitarian motivation feel about his actions if he learns that he has such a disease? An agent with the sort of strong benevolent motivation utilitarian theory treats as fundamental will clearly be appalled not only about what has happened to him but also about the future course of his life. He is likely to feel pain at (aghast at) the thought of what he is doing to people he would like to help (even though he may recognize that it is no fault of his own that he is in such a situation). But then, after the horrible consequences start to mount up, is he likely to feel mere regret for harming the particular people he does? Will he not also feel guilty about what he has done (and cannot stop doing), and in the circumstances is such a feeling not just as appropriate or reasonable as in those tragic situations that deontological theorists have described? I think the above example illustrates a utilitarian moral dilemma that is just as plausible from the standpoint of utilitarian moral psychology as those moral dilemmas that can be generated from within ordinary morality and *its* accompanying moral psychology. The infected benevolent person will feel horror at the things he does to people and there is nothing either about such horror or about the benevolence that underlies it that makes it imperative to interpret it as involving regret that acknowledges no wrongdoing, rather than a sense of guilt for doing wrong things. Consistently with its underlying rationale, i.e., with the impartially benevolent motivation it treats as the basis for all moral justification, there is no reason for utilitarianism to treat such cases as involving only regret and thus as illustrating the (dilemma-free) principle of utility now prevalent, rather than as exemplifying guilt (belief in one's own wrongdoing) and thus the dilemma-prone version of the utility principle introduced above. And if in addition one grants the existence of moral dilemmas under the assumptions of deontological morality, then the similarity between the present case and the usual deontological examples should tip the scale in favor of a form of utilitarianism that clearly does make room for dilemmas.[5]

IV

Some of the complexity, then, of the notion of benevolence has been left untapped by defenders and critics of (act-) utilitarianism, and this neglect has resulted in a failure to notice the possibility of (act-) utilitarian moral dilemmas. But the notion of benevolence is in fact more complex than I have yet suggested, and other elements in the notion can be shown to lead to a utilitarian version of the (deontological) notion of "moral cost." Bernard Williams has recently invoked this notion in order to illustrate a moral phenomenon in some sense intermediate between moral dilemmas and the innocent overriding of one prima facie duty by another.[6] Where, for example, an official has to harm or violate the rights of some innocent individual in order to avoid some terrible large-scale disaster or achieve some important public good, it may be appropriate for him to feel distaste at what he does even though he correctly believes that he is acting rightly. Such distaste will represent a recognition of the moral cost of doing what is right in those particular circumstances, a moral cost not present in those favorite cases of the intuitionists where one prima facie obligation simply overrides another. Where the obligation to keep a promise is overridden, for example, by the obligation to save a drowning child, one may have a subsequent duty to give some sort of explanation of the promise-breaking to the party concerned; but a disquieting sense of having done something morally distasteful will clearly be inappropriate. In cases of political necessity of the sort mentioned above, on the other hand, such moral unease or disquiet will be a sign of sensitivity to genuine moral cost. But since the cost in these cases exists despite the fact that, all things considered, one does the right thing, such cases are clearly also different from those tragic examples in which whatever the agent does is wrong.

Williams holds that the notion of moral cost indicates a subtlety, or a complexity, in (sophisticated) ordinary moral thought that cannot be matched by utilitarian

---

[5] Incidentally, even present forms of optimizing utilitarianism allow for moral dilemmas in certain logically imaginable (though highly unrealistic) scenarios. If, for any n, God will create n happy people, if one stands $1/n$ of an inch away from a given wall at a given time, then under various further simplifying assumptions, no act one can perform at the time in question will count as best (or tied-best), and by the usual utilitarian criterion one will inevitably act wrongly.

[6] "Politics and Moral Character," in *Moral Luck*, (Cambridge, 1981).

moral thinking. Utilitarianism, he claims, leaves no room for a notion of moral—as opposed to other kinds of—cost. Williams goes on to suggest that this omission results from, or is at least closely connected with, the maximizing character of utilitarian moral conceptions. But the main point to be made in what follows is that the fundamental utilitarian appeal to (a universalized form of) benevolence *can* naturally generate a utilitarian conception of moral cost and moral disquiet and can do so even within a *maximizing* act-utilitarian framework.

To understand why we must focus, once again, on the many-sidedness of the notion of benevolence. We have seen that ordinary human benevolence can involve not only a concern to do the best one can for certain people, but also a concern simply to do well by those people. But benevolence, especially universal benevolence, can (must?) also involve a concern not to harm *anyone* and not to leave *anyone's* well-being neglected. A truly benevolent person will have qualms—and why not moral qualms?—about harming some people in order to benefit a great many others, and in a world such as ours will also naturally agonize over whom or where to *help*: asking himself, e.g., whether he should give his money to famine relief in Bangladesh or in the Sahel; or whether he can do more good fighting for freedom in Afganistan or in El Salvador. But this agony will amount to more than an epistemological doubt about where he can maximize human well-being, something that is readily dispelled if and when he decides that the path he chose was indeed for the best. For he may easily retain a residue of agony, of moral shudder, for those he could not help. By the same token, a person who goes to an orphanage and adopts, from among the children there, the child who seems most in need of help and helpable, may be subsequently haunted by the thought of all the orphaned children he could not help—he may focus this feeling on particular children he remembers. And it is not likely entirely to console him to think, even if he has reason to think it, that he has done more for the child he chose than he could have done for any of the others. Benevolence aims not only to do the best it can in a given situation and to help rather than hurt people on balance, but also to leave no one—at least no object of its concern—badly off and uncared for, and this aim can leave a sense of moral consternation, when one's maximizing actions have left someone neglected or worse off than previously.[7]

This further facet of ordinary benevolence makes it possible to acknowledge a utilitarian analogue of the notion of moral cost Williams sees exemplified in ordinary (deontological) morality. It is possible for an act-utilitarian with a maximizing criterion of right and wrong nonetheless to make room for the idea of the moral cost of a particular maximizing action, because the idea of universal, impersonal benevolence naturally encompasses, in addition to the concern to maximize overall (summed-up) human welfare, a concern that no one should be harmed or neglected. (Remember that utilitarianism has traditionally made no distinction between the consequences of omissions and commissions. From a utilitarian perspective, failure to help is equivalent to harming.)

Williams treats moral cost as a fairly rare phenomenon of the moral life, but from the standpoint of universalized utilitarian benevolence, moral costs are constantly being incurred even by those who act optimifically. Helping some people

---

[7] Cf. van Fraassen, *op. cit.*

almost always involves failing to help others one could have helped instead, and so the foregoing discussion implies that if utilitarianism is correct, moral cost is a practically universal feature of moral activity. Since the acknowledgement of such costs is typically accompanied by unease or consternation, and utilitarianism seeks to promote happiness it might be thought that this result of ours is in tension with utilitarian doctrine and must somehow be incorrect. But that would be a mistake. Utilitarianism frequently invokes a distinction between moral theory and moral practice, and it has been frequently suggested, for example, that the principle of utility, which represents the theoretically correct utilitarian standard of right and wrong action, ought not (on grounds of utility) to be used or frequently used, as a guide to action in everyday life. The same kind of point can be made in regard to moral costs (as well as in regard to moral dilemmas). Utilitarian theory may properly accommodate these notions, but hold that ordinary moral agents should be ignorant of, or at least not dwell upon, the moral costs of their actions; and if this goal is best accomplished when ordinary moral thinking is conducted in largely non-utilitarian terms, then the theoretical acknowledgement of moral cost may simply give the utilitarian a further reason for encouraging (acknowledging) a split between utilitarian moral theory and the ideas that ought to govern everyday moral thinking.

Of course, the moral costs that a (maximizing) act-utilitarian theory accommodates will not turn upon the violation of deontological prohibitions, but will all be costs from the specific standpoint of benevolence, costs, therefore, in human well-being and the like. But clearly such moral costs can also be incurred from the point of view of common-sense moral thinking. It can sometimes be the right thing, in common-sense moral terms, to fulfill an obligation or duty even though (many) people will suffer as a result. But an ordinary person's sense of having done the right thing in such a case may be as appropriately qualified by a sense of moral disquiet at what she is doing (has done) as in the cases Williams mentions where deontological claims are overridden in the name of overall human welfare. And the recognition of this common-sense moral possibility may in turn make it easier to see how an entirely welfare-oriented morality like maximizing act-utilitarianism can also accommodate the idea of moral cost.

Our discussion also has implications for the Rawlsian thesis that the utilitarian injunction to maximize the sum of human happiness treats humanity as a kind of single superperson and thereby fails to respect the distinctness of moral individuals.[8] Although Derek Parfit has already countered this claim by pointing out that utilitarianism is far more naturally associated with an atomistic view of men that dissolves them into conglomerations of particular mental items than with any form of social organicism,[9] the above treatment of moral cost suggests another way in which act-utilitarians might seek to answer the charge of neglecting the separateness of persons. Just as the concern to maximize the sum of human utility represents one familiar feature of utilitarian universal benevolence (a concern with mankind's well-being *in sensu composito*), an acknowledgement of moral costs arises from

---

[8] John Rawls, *A Theory of Justice*, (Cambridge Mass., 1971), pp. 22ff.

[9] "Later Selves and Moral Principles," in A. Montefiore. (ed.), *Philosophy and Personal Relations*, (London, 1973), pp. 137–69.

another aspect of universal benevolence, from its concern that *no individual* should be harmed or neglected (its concern with mankind's well-being *in sensu diviso*). So a maximizing act-utilitarianism that acknowledges moral costs thereby does acknowledge the distinctness of individuals and give at least some moral weight to the claims of individuals as against the larger group.

V

How, then, finally, does the foregoing discussion bear on the strengths and weaknesses of (act-) utilitarianism? In particular, does the fact that (maximizing act-) utilitarianism naturally accommodates the possibility of moral dilemmas and moral cost help to undercut the prevalent criticism that utilitarianism oversimplifies the moral life?

To some extent, I think, it does. Those who have emphasized the phenomena of moral cost and moral dilemmas in ordinary morality have spoken disparagingly of the utilitarian's inability to make sense of these particular forms of moral complexity or moral subtlety; and if utilitarianism can, in fact, allow for dilemmas and moral cost, then this particular source of criticism should dry up. It would then presumably be replaced by some sort of critique of *where* utilitarianism finds its moral costs and tragedies. For all such costs and tragic dilemmas will involve some loss of human welfare and arise in connection with the idea of benevolence, whereas common-sense morality, while possibly granting the existence and force of these sorts of costs and dilemmas, will insist that cost and dilemma can also arise in connection with its deontological principles (intuitions) and with the interaction between the latter and the benevolent concern with consequences. Common-sense morality and utilitarianism will disagree, then, not about the existence of dilemmas and moral costs, but about their nature and extent. But even if common-sense morality assumes a wider *variety* of dilemmas and costs than utilitarianism does, the latter may well 1) treat certain situations (e.g. the one mentioned earlier) as dilemmatic which ordinary morality—with its somewhat less insistent emphasis on benevolence, and greater insistence on the rights of the moral agent—would not regard as such and also 2) find the moral cost involved in certain failures of benevolence (again see the examples mentioned above) more poignant, or less negligible, than common-sense might be inclined to do. So it cannot be said that utilitarianism oversimplifies by acknowledging only a small subclass of the dilemmas and costs attendant upon common-sense morality. In that case, the disagreement between utilitarianism and common-sense moral theory cannot readily confine itself to questions about the appropriate complexity or subtlety of moral theoretic structures. It is the intuitions that fill out moral structure—not the structures themselves—that constitute the main issue between utilitarianism and common-sense morality. It may be theoretically undesirable to find ourselves so much at the mercy of intuitions, but such may be our position, nonetheless, and we may have to acknowledge that fact in order to make further progress in this area.

But how welcome, in the end, will what we have been saying here be to the convinced utilitarian? Will not the utilitarian theorist be inclined to reject our offering of moral costs and moral dilemmas on the grounds that these phenomena add clutter to a theory whose greatest virtue is its simplicity? To a large extent recent developments in utilitarian moral theory have undercut the availability of such a response. Utilitarians now put great emphasis on such distinctions as that between first-level and second-level moral thinking and that between the utilitarian/consequentialistic evaluation of particular acts and the utilitarian/consequentialistic evaluation of motives (or rules), and they devote a great deal of time to attempts to show how to resolve conflicts whose possibility arises from these very distinctions (e.g., possible conflicts between acting from an optimific general motive and performing an optimific action). Thus utilitarian theorizing has now passed far beyond the defense of the principle of utility and typically attempts to elaborate a rather complex system of moral structures founded upon the familiar utilitarian touchstone of impersonal benevolence. To point out that the structures thus elaborated make room for, perhaps even demand, a recognition of moral cost and dilemmas is not to undercut some basic utilitarian-theoretic drive for simplicity.[10] Far from it: it is merely to take one or two further steps in the systematic articulation of a perennially appealing form of moral theory.[11]

---

[10] One might seek to base utilitarianism solely on the optimizing component of universal benevolence and thus, by eliminating the concern to see positive good done and see no one neglected, remove any taint of moral dilemmas or moral cost from one's theory. But what could possibly justify such a move?

[11] I would like to thank John Baker and Timothy Williamson for helpful suggestions.

14

Object-Utilitarianism

In *An Introduction to the Principles of Morals and Legislation*, Bentham claims that only pleasure and pain, happiness and unhappiness, are good or bad in themselves—everything else that is good or bad counts as such in virtue of its effects, its tendency to produce pleasure (avert pain) or to produce pain (avert pleasure). Bentham's most notable application of this idea was, of course, to the moral assessment of actions. As an act-utilitarian he held that the rightness or wrongness of actions depends on whether they cause happiness or unhappiness; no other considerations are relevant. And most subsequent utilitarian writings have focused largely, if not exclusively, on the assessment of actions or courses of action. (Even rule-utilitarians treat the consequential evaluation of rules chiefly as a means to the evaluation of actions.) But Bentham himself did not confine his evaluations to the universe of (simple or complex) actions. In the *Introduction*, not only individual actions, but motives, intentions, acts of legislation, and judicial practices are all subjected to assessment in terms of their consequences.

This broader focus on Bentham's consequentialism has recently attracted a good deal of attention. Robert Adams, for example, has helped to revive interest in the consequentialist evaluation of motives (and other traits of moral agents) along lines originally suggested by Bentham and has raised interesting problems concerning possible conflicts or tensions between motive-utilitarianism and the more familiar act-utilitarianism that has tended to dominate the recent literature of utilitarianism. But even in this new development, the full extent of Bentham's utilitarian consequentialism has remained unrecognized. In introducing his motive-utilitarianism, Bentham says: "With respect to goodness and badness, as it is with everything else that is not itself either pain or pleasure, so it is with motives. If they are good or bad, it is only on account of their effects: good, on account of their tendency to produce pleasure, or avert pain: bad, on account of their tendency to produce pain, or avert pleasure." And this statement treats motive-utilitarianism as but one instance of a general commitment to evaluate things in terms of their effects or consequences.[1] Recent discussions of motive-utilitarianism (or of utilitarianism in connection with other sorts of factors in moral agents)[2] have left the full generality of Bentham's position largely unexplored, but I hope to remedy that situation to a certain extent in what follows by examining a neglected but important aspect of Bentham's consequentialism: his commitment to evaluating the goodness and badness of functional and of aesthetic objects in terms of their actual effects on human happiness. Many of the implications of such 'object-utilitarianism' will seem bizarre at first glance, but we shall see that Bentham himself was willing to embrace them and that it is in fact very difficult for any act-utilitarian or motive-utilitarian to avoid them. Utilitarianism needs to come to terms with its own capacity for ontological spread, and something important can be learned about utilitarianism by recognizing that it can be applied not only to familiar objects of moral assessment, like acts, motives and institutions, but also to entities entirely outside the moral realm. If the idea that aesthetic and functional goodness and badness are correctly assessed in utilitarian consequentialist terms seems implausible, that implausibility is one, nonetheless, which utilitarians may have to get used to and somehow accommodate; for as we shall see, it is very difficult for the utilitarian to come up with any good reason why acts and motives, but not physical objects like knives, houses, and paintings, should be evaluated in terms of their consequences for human happiness. Both Bentham and (though he was less emphatic about it) Sidgwick seem to have been contented to apply consequentialism to the evaluation of everything other than pleasure and pain, and in doing so, I think they were following a natural tendency of utilitarian thinking and its underlying motivations.[2a] So if the utilitarian evaluation of aesthetic objects, e.g., seems a travesty of aesthetic judgment, that may redound against the utilitarian's original commitment even to act-utilitarianism. Alternatively, the fact that utilitarianism can be used to evaluate in areas where it has (at least implicitly) been thought irrelevant may indicate a recently unsuspected virtue of utilitarianism, its unifying power as a theory able to evaluate typical objects of moral evaluation, of aesthetic evaluation, and of functional evaluation all in the same consequentialist terms. The possibility of object-utilitarianism thus raises important issues about the strength or weakness of

---

[1] See the *Introduction*, J. H. Burns and H. L. A. Hart, eds., London: Methuen, 1982, p. 100. See also pp. 89, 114f., 125.

[2] See R. M. Adams, 'Motive Utilitarianism', *Journal of Philosophy* 73, 1976, pp. 467–81; and Amartya Sen, 'Utilitarianism and Welfarism', *Journal of Philosophy* 76, 1979, pp. 463–89.

[2a] See Sidgwick's *The Methods of Ethics*, pp. 105ff. It is frequently said that rule-utilitarianism, in its attempt to accommodate ordinary morality, falls into a rule worship inconsistent with the fundamental spirit of utilitarianism, and I shall presuppose this criticism in what follows. For that reason I shall not consider forms of indirect utilitarianism like rule-utilitarianism, but rather focus on views that evaluate a given kind of entity in terms of *its* effects or consequences. All such views seem very much in the spirit of utilitarianism, and the main question will be whether one can reasonably accept some forms of direct utilitarianism while rejecting others.

utilitarianism generally, but before dealing further with these questions, we must first take a closer look at what object-utilitarianism actually says.

I

Although there are places in the *Introduction* where Bentham speaks of the utilitarian evaluation of (physical) objects, he does not provide an explicit formulation of object-utilitarianism of the sort he offers us in connection with the utilitarian evaluation of motives; but since he treats motive-utilitarianism as an instance of his general consequentialism, it is natural to formulate aesthetic and functional object-utilitarianism along lines similar to what Bentham has to say about the evaluation of motives. Bentham states that motives are good if their effects are good, rather than bad, on the whole.[3] But he distinguishes between general motives like love or benevolence and particular instances of such motives (in given individuals on given occasions). On Bentham's view, particular (instances of) motives are to be evaluated in terms of their consequences rather than their intrinsic character as motives, and since no motive, not even benevolence, always has good consequences, the particular benevolence with which a person acts on a given occasion may fail to count as good motive.[4] General motives like benevolence, on the other hand, can be evaluated only through the evaluation of their instances. If benevolence, general benevolence, counts as a good motive, that can only be because the total effect of all particular instances of benevolence is more favorable than unfavorable to human happiness. So Bentham applies a consequentialistic form of evaluation to both general motives (motive kinds) and their instances, and this distinction is helpful in the formulation of object-utilitarianism. Complete criteria of the evaluation, e.g., of functional objects should presumably permit us to evaluate both single functional objects (single knives or houses) and kinds of such objects (kinds of knives or of houses) and thereby allow us to hold a particular knife to be poor, though it belongs to a kind evaluated as good. Since these distinctions parallel those Bentham makes with respect to motives, it is tempting to take over as much as possible of Bentham's theory of good motives in stating a consequentialist theory of good functional objects. So just as Bentham holds a good particular motive to be one whose effects are favorable to human happiness and a good general motive to be one whose instances' effects are on the whole favorable to human happiness, functional object-utilitarianism can say that a particular knife (functional object) is a good knife (is good of its kind) if it contributes more to human happiness than unhappiness and that a kind of knife (functional object) counts

---

[3] Bentham never considers the possibility that a motive might have to have better consequences than any other (or than any relevant alternative) in order to count as good; and such a view does not, in any event, seem very plausible.

[4] Bentham allows that some names for motives imply a positive, and some a negative, evaluation; it strains ordinary language to speak, for example, of (any particular instance of) avarice as a good motive. But he claims that we can always find some neutral term to refer to a particular or general motive: avarice, e.g., can be spoken of as "pecuniary interest." And so the issue of whether any motive is a good one need never be (linguistically) prejudged independently of consequences.

as a good kind if the effects of all its instances are over time more favorable to human happiness than unhappiness.[5] In addition, one knife or kind of knife can be said to be *better* than another if it has a better overall effect on human happiness.[6] And what we have just been saying about the evaluation of functional objects can be applied *mutatis mutandis* to the evaluation of particular and general aesthetic objects (e.g., of single paintings and of pictorial genres).

Of course it may seem that the utilitarian consequentialist evaluation of aesthetic objects makes far less sense than the application of such evaluation to what are frequently, after all, called utilitarian objects. There is some appeal in the idea that functional objects should be evaluated in terms of their contribution to human happiness, but the idea that aesthetic evaluation should proceed in similar terms will seem, by comparison, outré and ridiculous, even to some (many?) utilitarians. Surely works of art are not primarily supposed to be useful. Surely aesthetic merit can be difficult to discern and good works of art therefore sometimes neither generally pleasing nor popular. Bentham himself, however, seems not to have shrunk from the implications, in the area of aesthetics, of his commitment to evaluating absolutely everything in terms of utility. The famous remark on the comparative merits of pushpin and poetry occurs, in fact, within a long passage where Bentham criticizes all elitist attempts to base aesthetic evaluation on something other than his test of utility.

"Prejudice apart," he begins, "the game of push-pin is of equal value with the arts and sciences of music and poetry. If the game of push-pin furnish more pleasure, it is more valuable than either. Everybody can play at push-pin: poetry and music are relished only by a few. The game of push-pin is always innocent: it were well could the same be asserted of poetry. Indeed, between poetry and truth there is a natural opposition: false morals, fictitious nature." Bentham then goes on: "If these principles are correct, we shall know how to estimate those critics, more ingenious than useful, who, under pretense of purifying the public taste, endeavour successively to deprive mankind of a larger or smaller part of the sources of their amusement. These modest judges of elegance and taste consider themselves as [mankind's] benefactors...whilst they are only really the inter-ruptors of their pleasures.... There is no taste which deserves the epithet *good*, unless it be the taste for such employments which, to the pleasures actually produced by them, conjoin some contingent or future utility."[7]

Obviously not the work of someone embarrassed by the implications for aesthetics of his general consequentialism. Yet we have seen that those implications are quite bizarre from the standpoint of ordinary aesthetic evaluation. But although the idea of evaluating aesthetic objects in utilitarian terms seems far more bizarre on the face of it than a utilitarianism of functional evaluation, that appearance is in

---

[5] A version would, of course, be possible in which the happiness of all sentient creatures, rather than human happiness, was the central consideration.

[6] Cf. Adams, *op.cit.* Adams considers the view that the goodness of a motive might be a function of the average utility of any given individual's having it on any given occasion or of the utility of everyone's having it on all occasions, but I think these possibilities take us away from Bentham's actual position.

[7] See Bentham's *Works*, ed. John Bowring, Edinburgh: Tait, 1843, vol. 2, pp. 253f.

fact somewhat misleading: the inconsistency between ordinary or accepted modes of aesthetic evaluation and Bentham's proposals are more immediately obvious—more *glaring*—than the inconsistencies generated by functional object-utilitarianism; but a few examples will show that the conflict between functional object-utilitarianism and ordinary modes of functional evaluation can be very stark indeed. In the one passage in the *Introduction* where he specifically discusses the evaluation of 'objects of property', for example, Bentham says that the value of such objects ultimately depends on what we actually make of them, not on what we could do with them.[8] And what this seems to mean is that a good knife or house is not one which could be useful to people (and is perhaps never used), but rather one which actually benefits people, is of real use to people, in the long run. This clearly conflicts with the usual criteria for goodness in such things as knives and houses. Something ordinarily counts, for example, as a good knife if it is sharp, strong, rust-resistant, easily grasped, etc. But a knife lost forever in a utensil factory or accidentally destroyed before it serves anyone's purposes may count as a good knife by the ordinary criteria, while clearly not qualifying as good on Bentham's utilitarian account. Still, Bentham's account is not entirely out of keeping with ordinary evaluations of knives. Even if criteria of the sort just mentioned are ordinarily used in judging the (positive or comparative) goodness of knives, it sounds odd to call a knife good while at the same time saying that it never will serve (or has served) any useful purpose, never will do (or has done) anyone any good.[8a] And it is this aspect of ordinary thinking about the goodness of functional objects which functional object-utilitarianism elevates to the status of the sole criterion of goodness in such objects, thereby committing itself, e.g., to the highly uncommon-sensical claim that a permanently lost or unused knife is not a good knife.

Aesthetic object-utilitarianism similarly implies that a lost work of art that is of no actual use to anyone is not a good work of art, and this is certainly very odd. But what to most people will seem most outrageous about utilitarian art evaluation will not be its commitment to the latter idea, but rather its claim that goodness of art is a matter of how many people are made happy by a work of art, that aesthetic goodness can be a matter of popularity. The view that lost objects (usually) have no aesthetic value is somehow less offensive to our ordinary aesthetic sensibility and seems less of a travesty of what is distinctive about aesthetic evaluation than the view that the

---

[8] See the *Introduction*, pp. 40ff.

[8a] Cf. C. I. Lewis, *An Analysis of Knowledge and Valuation*, La Salle: Open Court, 1950, pp. 515f, 533. Lewis's own theory of value in objects focuses more on potential than on actual usefulness. Note further that the functional object-utilitarian must treat 'good' in 'good knife' and the like as a predicative adjective: a good knife, in his view, automatically counting as a good utensil (or weapon) and as a good thing. But the widespread and plausible notion that 'good' is attributive in these contexts may not be a consequence of the "logic" or meaning of 'good knife' but of the "theory" of functional goodness encapsulated in our ordinary criteria and judgments of functional goodness. One cannot easily eliminate object-utilitarianism on purely logical or semantical grounds.

Part of the effect of utilitarian object evaluation, then, is to divorce objects from their conventional categories and treat them all as things. This is rather similar to the way in which utilitarianism reduces all conventional goods/evils to the pleasure/pain they involve. (I am indebted here to helpful comments from a referee for the *Pacific Philosophical Quarterly*.)

value of works not lost is to be measured in terms of how happy how many people are made by them. Bentham may have been willing to embrace this implication along with all the others, but other utilitarians may feel, on the other hand, that the implication is too much to swallow; and they may seek for ways to retain act-utilitarianism or motive-utilitarianism without having to accept aesthetic object-utilitarianism. However, functional object-utilitarianism is in no better shape. It asserts that where an object is never used, there is an absence of functional goodness through an *absence* of effects. And we are now saying that the oddness, the real oddness, of aesthetic utilitarianism comes from its counting the *wrong sorts* of effects as relevant, treating all pleasure and pain—however indirect and however much based on misunderstanding or insensitivity—as (equally) pertinent to aesthetic goodness and badness. But in fact functional object-utilitarianism is open to quite similar objections through *its* commitment to counting all effects as relevant to the evaluation of an object. As we have formulated it, it assumes, for example, that a knife that is (accidentally or intentionally) used to hurt someone, ipso facto counts as a less good knife. Usefulness to the user may in ordinary terms be a relevant criterion of goodness in a knife, but by treating the harm an object does to others than its user as relevant to how good it is as a knife, functional object-utilitarianism seems to be counting in entirely irrelevant effects. And it seems no less offensive to common-sense to say that a knife that is used to hurt someone is, other things equal, a less good knife than to say that a painting that generally pleases by miscomprehension counts as better than one that only a few people like.

Are we then to say that both aesthetic and functional object-utilitarianism are unacceptable because they treat what are from a common-sense standpoint entirely irrelevant effects on human happiness as relevant to their respective modes of evaluation? We *may* choose to say this, but a utilitarian who takes up such a position will then, I think, find it difficult to justify holding on to act- or motive-utilitarianism. For motive-utilitarianism claims that a particular instance of malevolence may count as good, and as better than an instance of frustrated benevolence, because of the great pleasure the malevolence gives the actor and/or because it happens to lead to unintended good effects. But both these factors would ordinarily be deemed irrelevant to the moral evaluation of particular instances of malevolence and that is part of the common-sense case against motive-utilitarianism. Similarly, on act-utilitarian principles, a given malevolent act may count as morally right and a benevolent alternative act wrong simply by virtue of some unforeseeable distant or indirect consequence of one of the acts. Are the irrelevancies act- or motive-utilitarianism takes into account really less bizarre than those the object-utilitarian has to embrace?[9] The fact is that object-utilitarianism, act-utilitarianism, and motive-utilitarianism all have highly uncommonsensical implications for particular cases. Act-utilitarianism (and to a lesser extent motive-utilitarianism) has well-known ways of blunting the destructive force of such implications; but, as I shall argue in the next section, similar resources are available to object-utilitarianism. It is difficult to drive an intellectual wedge

---

[9] In *The Methods of Ethics*, p. 107, Sidgwick explicitly mentions this parallelism between act-utilitarianism and what I am calling aesthetic object-utilitarianism.

betwen these different forms of consequentialism. And once one accepts any given form of utilitarianism, it is hard to resist a slide into the absolutely general form of evaluational consequentialism both Bentham and Sidgwick seem to have favored.

II

When the act-utilitarian, through holding that distant and unforeseeable effects are relevant to the moral assessment of an action, ends up having to claim that some perfectly innocent-seeming benevolent action is wrong, she sometimes attempts to make concessions to common-sense: e.g., by distinguishing between wrong acts and blameworthy acts and saying that it may be useful, therefore right, to praise acts that are in fact wrong and to praise agents for performing such acts. A similar sort of move can be used to mitigate the common-sense implausibility of what object-utilitarianism is forced to say about particular cases. It is possible to claim a utilitarianism justification for praising the maker of the knife that is permanently lost or accidentally harms someone, and therefore fails to count as good on the object-utilitarian reckoning, on the grounds that such praise may encourage people to make similar knives and that such knives may be generally useful. But what about the kind of knife that is useful only for fighting, for war? If violence and war produce a net balance of human misery, can the object-utilitarian avoid saying that such a knife is a bad kind of knife and that there are in general no good (kinds of) weapons? Will not the sharper, stronger, deadlier weapon be treated as a less good weapon on his account?

Perhaps so, and since it seems difficult to conjure up good utilitarian reasons for praising (kinds of) weapons, the usual concession to common-sense will not be available; in such cases the conflict between ordinary criteria of functional evaluation and functional object-utilitarianism assumes its starkest form. However, the motive-utilitarian and the act-utilitarian also sometimes find it impossible to make irenic concessions to common-sense. Consider, for example, a possible act which common-sense morality considers permissible but which, because of remote unforeseeable effects, the act-utilitarian must regard as wrong. Nothing rules out the further possibility that *praise* for that act may have unforeseeable remote bad effects and so also count as wrong.

Moreover, the evaluation of weapons in terms of their effects upon human happiness is not always as uncommon-sensical and bizarre as the above examples suggest. We are living in an age when weapons, nuclear weapons, threaten the happiness and survival of our species. In these dire circumstances, it has become increasingly common to evaluate weapons more in terms of their effects on our species' well-being than in terms of their destructive power and the other usual 'intrinsic' criteria of good weaponry. On the basis of various crucial assumptions of nuclear deterrence theory, people have begun to speak of good and bad nuclear weapons systems, or better and worse ones, in terms of their effects on an ongoing balance of terror. A destabilizing weapon like the ABM thereby counts as a bad kind of weapon; and if Reagan's MX really deserved its name 'peacekeeper', then it would certainly be natural to call it a good weapons system. Given, furthermore, the uncertainty of deterrence and our consequent anxiety in the absence of nuclear disarmament, it also seems entirely natural to say that the only good nuclear weapon is a dismantled one. Thus in our present circumstances considerations of effect on human well-being have to a certain extent taken over from intrinsic criteria like explosive power, speed, accuracy, and undetectability in the evaluation of nuclear weapons.

In many ways, the situation resembles what certain defenders of common-sense morality have said about dire emergencies. While maintaining that there is a deontological restriction or side-constraint on killing the innocent—that certain intrinsic kinds of acts are morally ruled out—they have held that it may sometimes be right to kill innocent people in order to avert a large-scale disaster.[10] In such cases, but only in such cases, the reckoning of consequences for human happiness seems to override the side-constraints. And I think defenders of a common-sense view of functional evaluation can similarly admit that where the existence of certain weapons and knowledge creates a dire situation, a long-standing emergency, the usual criteria of weapons evaluation may be overridden by considerations of human welfare. Common-sense theories of functional evaluation typically focus on intrinsic criteria and ignore the influence that considerations of human welfare can sometimes have on functional evaluations; but such theories can nonetheless hold that where weapons represent less of a threat, as before the present century, it goes against common-sense and is absurd to evaluate primarily in terms of effects on human well-being. And by the same token the defender of common-sense morality ultimately can hold that in less than catastrophic cases it is absurd and wrongheaded to treat the optimific violation of side-constraints as morally permissible.

But this very analogy points up a problem for utilitarianism. For what the object-utilitarian has to say about weapons seems no further from common-sense than what the act-utilitarian has to say about the violation of side-constraints. If in the face of all common-sense moral objectionability and in the name of furthering overall human good the act-utilitarian maintains, e.g., that it can be morally all right to cut up one healthy person to save five people in need of organ transplants, how can he flinch from the view, also based on concern with human happiness, that there are no good weapons of war or that a (kind of) knife used and usable only in the kitchen may for that reason be a better knife that one used for aggressive purposes?

Now aesthetic evaluation is not usually thought to be based on the use of criteria of the sort sometimes employed in the evaluation of functional objects. A critic or connoisseur does not consult a checklist of good aesthetic features in judging works of art, the way a factory inspector might check off certain features like strength and sharpness in deciding whether certain knives were any good. It is frequently held, rather, that aesthetic merit depends on elements of originality that are available to sensitive perception but cannot be approached or codified in terms of statable, verifiable criteria. And it is in fact possible to take a similar view of ordinary *moral* judgment. Aristotle's ethical theory ties the evaluation of rightness or wrongness not to checkable criteria or statable (prima facie) principles, but to an acquired ability to perceive, to see, the noble or beautiful thing to do in a given situation. If one assumes

---

[10] See Robert Nozick's *Anarchy, State, and Utopia*, N.Y.: Basic Books, 1974, p. 30n. Incidentally, the notion of innocence must be understood somewhat technically here.

a perceptual model of common moral judgment, it is ordinary aesthetic evaluation, rather than ordinary functional evaluation, that will seem most analogous to the common-sense morality of right and wrong. But however dissimilar they may be, ordinary criteria-based forms of functional evaluation and ordinary perceptive aesthetic evaluation place a common evaluative emphasis on the intrinsic character of objects, as opposed to their effects on human happiness. And our ordinary morality of right and wrong, whether we understand it in terms of prima facie principles (moral criteria) or in terms of a quasi-Aristotelian perceptual model, also largely emphasizes the intrinsic character of intentional actions rather than their actual effects. What utilitarianism does in all three of these areas of evaluation is to replace the emphasis on intrinsic character with a reliance on effects alone. And it is this exclusive emphasis on effects that leads all three forms of utilitarianism to judgments about particular cases that are bizarre from a common-sense standpoint. However, the act-utilitarian often responds to accusations that his view has unacceptably odd implications by questioning the validity of common-sense intuition and pointing out the theoretical advantages of the utilitarian position. Common-sense and its intuitions of plausibility, he will say, are all too often based on prejudice and/or on mere habit, and considerations of theoretical clarity and simplicity favor his own position, which replaces a hodge-podge of prima facie principles and/or uncheckable intuitions with a single unequivocal criterion of act-evaluation. And by now it should be clear that the object-utilitarian can also claim that the contrary intuitions of common-sense are mere prejudices and recommend the adoption of his own view on grounds of its superior unity, simplicity and rational applicability.

III

Object-utilitarianism's structural similarities to other, more familiar kinds of utilitarianism and its ability to make similar moves in order to take the sting from its anti-common-sense implications suggest that it is as justified as these other sorts of utilitarianism and that one cannot coherently accept motive- or act-utilitarianism while rejecting object-utilitarianism. On the other hand, there may be reasons to think that however closely its structure and defense can be modelled of those of act- or motive-utilitarianism, object-utilitarianism is an *inappropriate form* of utilitarianism because of the fundamental difference between aesthetic and functional evaluation, on the one hand, and moral evaluation, on the other. The most familiar and widely accepted forms of utilitarianism apply consequentialist evaluation to acts, motives, legislative acts, social structures, and other entities to which moral evaluation can naturally be applied. Indeed, all recently familiar forms of utilitarianism are moral theories, whereas the objects of object-utilitarian assessment are precisely not the sorts of entities to which moral evaluation seems relevant. The claim that something is a good knife, the judgment that one painting is better than another or has some merit as a work of art, are not moral judgments at all. And since utilitarianism—at least act- and motive-utilitarianism—are forms of consequentialist moral theory, it seems gratuitous, a distortion of its rationale and intentions, to extend utilitarianism to objects that clearly are not subject to moral evaluation. The fault with object-utilitarianism would then be that it moralizes certain judgments, turns aesthetic and functional evaluation into forms of moral evaluation, when in fact moral assessments, on the one hand, and aesthetic and functional assessments, on the other, represent entirely different kinds of value judgment. Object-utilitarianism can be given the same structure as act- or motive-utilitarianism and made to respond to objections in similar ways, only because it mistakenly treats aesthetic and functional evaluations as if they were moral; what thus seems to be a strength of the theory is actually then a weakness, an indication that it deeply misconstrues the nature of the kinds of judgments it seeks to give an account of.

But this important objection depends, I think, on a misperception of utilitarian theories of right acts, good motives or good (just) societies. Societies, motives, and acts are indeed normal objects of moral assessment, and utilitarianism seeks to substitute a utilitarian basis for evaluating these sorts of entities for what common-sense (or other philosophies, e.g., Kantian ethics) find plausible. But the theories thus elaborated really strain our antecedent sense of moral plausibility. When the act-utilitarian tells us that an act may be wrong if in the unforeseen long run it has terrible consequences or when the motive-utilitarian tells us that ruthless capitalist expansionism may be the morally best human motive, it is natural to feel that the moral, our ordinary sense of the moral, is being gerrymandered. Motive-and act-utilitarians evaluate in consequentialist terms that can easily seem less like terms of moral evaluation than like some other sort of evaluation that is being proposed to replace moral evaluation but to be applied to the usual subjects of moral evaluation. Accepting act-utilitarianism and motive-utilitarianism (as moral theories) thus involves not only a casting aside of certain common-sense moral intuitions about particular cases, but also, I think, an altering or displacement of our ordinary sense of what moral evaluation is. And by the same token, object-utilitarianism involves a replacement of normal modes of aesthetic and functional evaluation, and a consequent shifting or displacement of our ordinary sense of what such evaluation involves. When we move from ordinary morality to act-utilitarianism, from judgments based largely on intrinsic characterizations to ones based on consequences, we make new and different particular act-evaluations, but our idea of what (kind of thing) rational moral assessment is also undergoes alteration, and the passage from ordinary aesthetic or functional evaluation to the two forms of object-utilitarianism similarly involves both different individual judgments and a shift in our sense of what aesthetic and functional evaluation are.

So it hardly seems accurate to say that the extension of utilitarianism to functional and aesthetic objects involves a moralization of functional and aesthetic evaluation. For even in its application to acts, motives, and societies utilitarianism departs from moral evaluation as normally understood and seeks to reform our sense of what moral evaluation most properly is. Object-utilitarianism gerrymanders our sense of the aesthetic in the way that act-utilitarianism gerrymanders our sense of the moral; and since act-utilitarianism takes us away from ordinary moral evaluation, there is no reason to hold that object-utilitarianism, by applying to objects the same mode of evaluation that act-utilitarianism applies to acts, is taking us towards moral evaluation as ordinarily understood, or is thus, in that sense, moralizing aesthetic or functional judgment. What seems true rather is that fully generalized utilitarian consequentialism brings moral, aesthetic, and functional evaluation closer together by shifting all three modes of evaluation, so to speak, toward the center. Object-utilitarianism no more involves subordinating the aesthetic and functional to the moral, than act-utilitarianism involves subordinating the moral to the functional or aesthetic.

Ontologically generalized utilitarianism thus replaces moral, functional, and aesthetic evaluation as they are normally conceived by a single kind of evaluation. And in that case object-utilitarianism does not so much *confuse* the aesthetic or the functional with the moral as melt all three down into a common coinage.

At this point, however, one final objection to aesthetic object-utilitarianism in particular may arise. Ordinary morality is concerned with human well-being or happiness, but art, it might be said, has no such purpose, object, or function and exists, rather, for its own sake. So although act-utilitarianism reforms morality in a direction that ordinary morality itself implicitly supports, it might be denied that anything similar can be said about aesthetic object-utilitarianism (it is more difficult, of course, to make this objection to functional object-utilitarianism).

I believe, however, that this new objection misrepresents both ordinary morality and art. Perhaps works of art make a less significant difference to human happiness and unhappiness than human actions do, but it hardly follows that art has nothing inherently to do with making life less unpleasant or that the artist as artist has no interest whatever in human well-being or pleasure. Moreover, even if ordinary morality in some sense aims at human happiness, that cannot be said to be its sole aim or concern. For ordinary morality makes it impermissible to achieve greater human happiness at the cost of violating certain deontological side-constraints. It holds up certain ideals like not killing the innocent, not torturing, and not lying, as standards that may not be violated even in the name of greater overall human happiness (or lesser overall human unhappiness). And since ordinary morality thus contains ideals whose validity is conceived as independent of any concern with human happiness, the latter can represent at most only one subject or concern of ordinary morality. Of course, art too is not exclusively concerned with human happiness: certain aesthetic ideals are valued and pursued in some sense for their own sake, for their inherent aesthetic merit quite apart from foreseen or intended effects on human pleasure or happiness. My point has been simply that in this respect, art and morality resemble one another; the view that ordinary morality is totally concerned with human well-being is as far-fetched as the view that art is totally concerned with human well-being; but by the same token, an aestheticism that claims that art is for art's sake alone seems as tendentious as a Kantianism that would rule out any concern for human happiness as being properly moral. So there seems no more and no less reason to reform ordinary moral thinking into an exclusive concern with human happiness than to seek a similar reformation of aesthetic evaluation; as far as the connection with human happiness is concerned, act-utilitarianism and aesthetic object-utilitarianism seem equally well-motivated, and indeed it is difficult to think of any way in which one could coherently accept and defend such well-known forms of utilitarianism as act- and motive-utilitarianism while objecting to the forms of object-utilitarianism we have been discussing. It is hardly surprising that the Bentham, who advocated a utilitarianism of actions should have been a utilitarian consequentialist about everything else under the sun other than pleasure or pain.

But the fact that all these forms of utilitarianism appear to rise or fall together may in fact represent a problem for the presently more well-known forms of utilitarianism and for utilitarianism generally. Up till now, and certainly in recent times, object-utilitarianism and its implications have been pretty well ignored in debates about the merits of act-utilitarianism or other forms of utilitarianism. But if the different forms of utilitarianism are theoretically interdependent, then the implications of object-utilitarianism may be relevant to the assessment not only of object-utilitarianism but also of other, better known forms of utilitarianism. Consider the act-utilitarian. If he acknowledges that utilitarianism naturally extends itself to entities other than actions, he will presumably have to reckon the implications of object-utilitarianism and of generalized utilitarian consequentialism as among the things he (probably) needs to accept in order to hold on to act-utilitarianism. Now object-utilitarianism has anti-commonsensical implications for particular cases, but of course the act-utilitarian is used to swallowing conclusions hostile to common-sense and he may not flinch from accepting conclusions that go against common-sense in the aesthetic or functional realm. But this is not necessarily the case. He may at this point say that enough is enough; that he now sees that his act-utilitarianism, via its inherent connection with other forms of utilitarian evaluation, commits him to a far greater budget of common-sense paradoxes than he ever expected and than even he is willing to swallow. And that will give him reason to rethink his commitment to act-utilitarianism.[11]

And he will have other reasons as well. For one consequence of accepting a generalized form of utilitarianism is to treat aesthetic, moral, and functional evaluation as fundamentally of a piece. And this violates our initial sense that moral, aesthetic, and functional evaluation are properly regarded as distinctive modes of evaluation. In other words, generalized utilitarianism can be said not only to have a vast array of uncommon-sensical implications for the evaluation of particular aesthetic, moral and functional cases, but also to violate our ordinary sense of the nature of these modes of evaluation, and an act-utilitarian who comes to recognize utilitarianism's natural tendency toward ontological spread may thus have two quite different kinds of reasons for questioning his own commitment to act-utilitarianism.

On the other hand, the fact that utilitarianism is not limited to moral evaluation but can function as an all-embracing evaluative theory is testimony to its theoretical fertility and unifying power. In the area of moral evaluation, act-utilitarianism has long prided itself on having substituted a simple clear principle for a hodgepodge of intuitions and principles; but it now turns out that the utilitarian can also replace distinctively aesthetic, moral, and functional evaluations with a single mode of evaluation

---

[11] The notion of an object's effects is perhaps less transparent than the idea of an act or of a motive's effects; but I assume that good sense can be made of it (possibly through reducing the idea of what an object causes to relevant claims about what events or states of affairs involving that object cause). After all, we can speak colloquially of the effects a certain mountain range has on the weather of some city or of the effects of certain labor-saving device has had on a given household; and if we believe in some version of the causal theory of (the) perception (of physical objects), then we are clearly committed to attributing causality to objects. (In any event, it would be dangerous to object to object-utilitarianism on the grounds that only events can have effects or consequences, since general and even particular motives are also not in the strictest sense events.)

that applies across all these areas. And this is perhaps an even more dazzling feat of unification than that which utilitarianism accomplishes *within* the moral realm. Sidgwick is fairly explicit about the impressive unifying power of utilitarianism in this larger sense,[12] but our recent neglect of utilitarianism's extramoral applications has long blinded us to this theoretical advantage. Still, the ability to unify different modes of evaluation under a common aegis, like so many of utilitarianism's other virtues, is something of a mixed blessing. For as we have seen, the price of evaluative unification is a merging or conflation of what intuitively seem to be distinctive modes of evaluation. This is a price many utilitarians may be willing to pay, but it is at this point perhaps too early to be sure whether the tendency towards ontological spread represents an overall advantage or disadvantage for utilitarian theory.

---

[12] *Op. cit.*, pp. 106f.

15

Utilitarian Virtue

Whatever would utilitarianism want with a doctrine of virtue or of particular virtues? Such a question may well occur to anyone reading the title of this essay who is aware of the gulf between utilitarianism—especially act utilitarianism—and the recently reviving tradition of virtue ethics, a tradition that is supposed, among other things, to represent the very opposite of the utilitarian approach. But even if present-day utilitarians have no particular interest in developing a theory of the virtues, I hope to show you that the consistent development of a utilitarianism concerned with more than the evaluation of actions calls for, or at the very least strongly suggests, a utilitarian conception of virtue. Recent work on utilitarianism has shown that optimific right actions are not the only means by which the utilitarian concern for good results may be realized; there is a separate and honorable place for the consequentialist evaluation of human motives and dispositions, and the latter naturally leads to a utilitarian view of the virtues of the sort to be introduced and considered here.

I

In this century utilitarians have focused almost exclusively on the evaluation of actions. Even rule utilitarians treat the consequentialist evaluation of rules chiefly as a means to the evaluation of particular actions. But in an earlier era, during classical utilitarianism's apolaustic succession from Bentham through Mill to Sidgwick, considerable emphasis was also placed on the evaluation of entities other than actions, and in recent years there has been a revival of interest in the utilitarian evaluation of motives, dispositions, works of art, and other potential objects of consequentialistic evaluation.[1] Even if, say, motives are not under the immediate control of the will, they can make a difference to overall human happiness and unhappiness, and a utilitarianism that is comfortable conceiving the Principle of Utility as a standard of moral assessment that may not be particularly useful as a practical guide to action needs to be open to the sorts of indirect practical consideration that lead us to evaluate motives, etc., in their own right. But once we start evaluating motives, dispositions, character traits, and the like in utilitarian consequentialist terms, we are well on our way to a utilitarian theory of virtue(s).

Bentham was aware of utilitarianism's tendency in this direction. In *An Introduction to the Principles of Morals and Legislation*, Bentham spends a great deal of time developing a theory of the evaluation of motives and dispositions (what Adams calls "motive utilitarianism");[2] but in the preface to that work,[3] he says that it is quite easy to generate a theory of virtue and vice, and of particular virtues and vices, from his views about pleasure, pain, motives, dispositions, etc. Indeed, he excuses himself from producing such a theory by claiming that given what he does say in the *Introduction*, the production of a theory of virtue(s) would be "little more than a mechanical operation." However, even working with Bentham's views about the evaluation of motives and dispositions, the attempt to elaborate a utilitarian view of virtue and the virtues raises a number of interesting and perplexing issues. And as far as I can tell, no previous attempt has been made to spell out a utilitarian theory of virtue. In the later *Deontology* Bentham dwells at considerable length on virtue and the virtues, but the view offered there is not a (consistently) utilitarian one,[4] and Sidgwick's *Methods* may offer utilitarian justifications for what we ordinarily take to be virtues, but that is a far cry (as we may soon be able to see more clearly) from offering a utilitarian conception of temperance, courage, and virtue generally. I believe, however, that a utilitarian theory of virtue(s) is well worth having, and so in what follows, I shall first sketch a utilitarianism of motives and character traits and then show how a utilitarianism of virtue(s) can naturally go forward on this by now well-marked utilitarian path.

II

In introducing his motive utilitarianism, Bentham says: "With respect to goodness and badness, as it is with everything else that is not itself either pain or pleasure, so

---

[1] See, e.g., Robert Adams's "Motive Utilitarianism," *Journal of Philosophy* 73 (1976): 467–81; and Slote, "Object-Utilitarianism," *Pacific Philosophical Quarterly* 66 (1985): 11–24. In what follows, I shall assume the correctness of recent criticisms of rule utilitarianism and shall, therefore, be discussing only *direct* consequentialist evaluation.

[2] See Adams, "Motive Utilitarianism."

[3] See *An Introduction to the Principles of Morals and Legislation*, edited by Burns and Hart (London, 1982), 3.

[4] On this point, see, of course, the *Deontology* itself (Oxford, 1983), but also Ross Harrison's *Bentham* (London, 1983), chap. 10.

it is with motives. If they are good or bad, it is only on account of their effects: good on account of their tendency to produce pleasure, or avert pain: bad, on account of their tendency to produce pain, or avert pleasure."[5] For Bentham a motive is good, rather than bad, if its effects are good on the whole.[6] But he distinguishes between general motives like love or benevolence and particular instances of such motives (in given individuals on given occasions). On Bentham's view, particular (instances of) motives are to be evaluated in terms of their consequences rather than their intrinsic character as motives, and since no motive, not even benevolence, always has good consequences, the particular benevolence with which a person acts on a given occasion may fail to count as a good, and may actually be a bad, motive. General motives like benevolence, on the other hand, can be evaluated only through the evaluation of their instances. If benevolence, general benevolence, counts as a good motive, that can only be because the total effect of all particular instances of benevolence—present, past, and future—is more favorable than unfavorable to human happiness or pleasure. And the same account is supposed to hold *mutatis mutandis* for human dispositions and their particular instantiations.

However, Bentham adds a qualification or *caveat* to the above account, which is absolutely essential to understanding the fundamental thrust of any utilitarianism of virtue(s). He points out that some names for motives strongly imply a positive, and some a negative, evaluation: it strains ordinary language to speak, for example, of (any particular instance of) avarice as a good motive. But Bentham then also claims that we can always find some neutral term to refer to a particular or general motive: avarice, e.g., can be spoken of as "pecuniary interest," and so the issue of whether any motive is a good one cannot, in one sense, be linguistically prejudged independently of consequences. It may be *de dicto* necessary that any instance of avarice be a bad particular motive—no instance of pecuniary interest counts as avarice unless it has long-run overall bad consequences. But of any particular case of avarice, it is not *de re* necessary that it have had overall bad consequences, that it have been a bad motive, that it have been a case of avarice, and this interesting complexity turns out to be very serviceable to the formulation of a utilitarianism of virtue.

Among the cardinal virtues of traditional ethics—justice, temperance, courage, and prudence or practical wisdom—only the first has been given any sort of utilitarian elaboration. And when Bentham discusses justice, somewhat briefly, in the *Introduction*, he seems to be influenced by what he has said, just a few pages earlier, about the positive or negative connotations of ethical terms. He claims that "justice, in the only sense in which it has a meaning, is an imaginary personage, feigned for the convenience of discourse, whose dictates are the dictates of utility, applied

---

[5] *Introduction*, 100. Also see pp. 96ff., 114f., 125.

[6] Bentham never considers the possibility that a motive might have to have better consequences than any other (or any relevant alternative) in order to count as good, and such a view does not, in any event, seem very plausible. Bentham uses a criterion of optimificness only for right *action*, and even here he is inconsistent; in some very prominent places he indicates that overall *good* consequences are a sufficient condition of an act's rightness. On this point, see Slote, *Common-sense Morality and Consequentialism* (London, 1985), chap. 3.

to certain particular cases."⁷ For Bentham, the dictates of justice are nothing more than "a part of the dictates of benevolence, which, on certain occasions, are applied to...certain actions." And clearly on such a conception it is always morally right to perform just actions.

But this is not the only view of justice open to a defender of act utilitarianism. Smart, in his "Outline of a System of Utilitarian Ethics," treats the dictates of justice as opposed to those of the principle of utility; that is, he takes our ordinary or commonsense views about what is just as constitutive of justice, but questions whether it is always right to perform the sorts of just actions that are morally acceptable according to common sense.⁸ Where the dictates of justice conflict with those of utility, it is the latter which determine what it is actually right to do.

It is interesting that Bentham takes such a very different line about the dictates of justice, and I believe his position on this issue is influenced, perhaps even determined, by his views about the names of motives and dispositions. It sounds just as odd to speak of an act as right but unjust as to speak of avarice as a good motive, and the desire to placate common sense that led Bentham to reserve the term "avarice" for instances of pecuniary interest whose overall consequences are bad would therefore naturally lead him to reserve the term "unjust" for actions with bad or less than optimal consequences. But this entails making assessments of justice in accordance with the principle of utility, rather than, like Smart, making such judgments in commonsense terms and leaving it an open question whether any particular just action is morally right.⁹ Smart's act utilitarianism leaves the commonsense conception (i.e., his own pre-theoretical understanding) of justice intact and as such offers no distinctive utilitarian conception of justice or of virtue generally. It is only with Bentham's approach that utilitarianism comes into its own as a view or theory of justice. Bentham, however, offers no similar treatment of any of the other traditional virtues, and I shall attempt to make up for this deficiency in what follows.

Bentham's insistence on tying (acts of) justice to the principle of utility and his assumption that human motives and dispositions are to be assessed in terms of their consequences for human happiness give justice almost definitionally the status of a virtue and force us to regard as just certain actions that are ordinarily, or intuitively, thought of as unjust.¹⁰ And we shall see in what follows that a distinctively utilitarian treatment of courage, temperance, and prudence leads to parallel conclusions.

---

⁷ *Introduction*, 120n.

⁸ See Smart, "An Outline of a System of Utilitarian Ethics" in *Utilitarianism: For and Against*, edited by Smart and Williams (Cambridge, 1973), section 10.

⁹ Using Hare's terminology, we can say that Bentham treats the evaluative meaning of "justice" as primary and changes its descriptive meaning so that it accords with his commitment to utilitarianism, whereas Smart gives primacy to the descriptive meaning and, on utilitarian grounds, modifies or seeks to modify the term's evaluative meaning.

Note further that if Bentham wants to avoid the oddness of calling unjust actions right, he may have reason to avoid the frequent utilitarian assumption that right actions may be blameworthy (i.e., right to blame). There are several maneuvers open to him, but I do not want to take up this problem here.

¹⁰ I would like to leave open the question whether all good human dispositions can be considered virtues.

But such an across-the-board approach also raises some rather interesting questions about utilitarianism generally that no "mechanical operation" can resolve for us.

III

However, before we can proceed with our discussion of courage, temperance, and prudence or practical wisdom (the treatment of other, "minor" virtues being left to another occasion), we need to become somewhat clearer about certain aspects of the utilitarian aproach to justice. Bentham holds that the dictates of justice are those of utility or benevolence, but in the statements quoted above he also indicates that the term "just" applies less widely than the term "right." However, Bentham, in the *Introduction*, never tells us anything specific about such limitations on the applicability of the notion of justice, and it is difficult to see what limitations he had in mind. In the passage quoted, he seems to want to restrict the term "just" to certain actions, which is very odd, considering how naturally it is applied to social institutions. But of course Bentham also restricts the term "right" to human actions/acts, and to that extent no divergence in usage between "right" and "just" has yet been indicated. In the *Deontology*,[11] Bentham says that the dictates of justice apply only where considerations of benevolence and/or utility give rise to an obligation. But even the familiar utilitarian distinction between right and obligatory actions is not much help to us in making sense of the restrictions on justice that Bentham apparently wishes to defend. A non-obligatory right act is certainly not "dictated" by considerations of utilitarian justice, but isn't such an act just *simpliciter* by the utilitarian's lights? I cannot for the life of me see why not, and it is worth noting here that when Rawls gives expression to what he takes to be the utilitarian conception of justice, as it applies both to social institutions and to individual acts, he seems to imply that the utilitarian regards all and only right acts as just. "The striking feature of the utilitarian view of justice," he says, "is that it does not matter, except indirectly, how this sum of satisfactions is distributed among individuals any more than it matters, except indirectly, how one man distributes his satisfactions over time. The correct distribution in either case is that which yields the maximum fulfillment."[12]

Now according to the principle of utility, it is morally wrong for a person not to maximize his pleasure or satisfactions in situations where no one else can be affected by his actions. So if the distinction between just and unjust is to apply wherever the distinction between right and wrong does, then it will in utilitarian terms be unjust for someone to neglect her own (maximal) welfare or utility. Rawls seems willing to accept such an implication of the utilitarian view of justice—after all, it may be no odder to claim that it is unjust to neglect one's pleasures than to claim, as utilitarians clearly must, that it is wrong to do so. But I am inclined to think that Bentham's vaguely expressed restrictions on justice are best defended—assuming they

---

[11] See *Deontology*, 127, 220.

[12] See *A Theory of Justice* (Cambridge, Mass., 1971), pp. 26 and also 187. The idea that utilitarian justice and injustice are applicable to every action is more explicit in S. Scheffler's *The Rejection of Consequentialism* (Oxford, 1982), p. 33.

can be defended at all—in terms of the distinction between self-regarding and other-regarding actions. If justice is to be thought of as a species of right action, perhaps it should be understood as right action undertaken in circumstances where the pleasure-pain or happiness-unhappiness of someone other than the agent (alternatively, of more than one person) is at stake.

Even if we adopted such a restriction on the domain of (the virtue of) justice, however, an anti-commonsensical *self-other symmetry* would still hold for the many cases where the notion was applicable. Ordinary intuitive morality is subject to an asymmetry regarding what an agent may permissibly do to herself and what she may permissibly do to others that I have elsewhere described at considerable length.[13] An agent is normally thought of as morally allowed to do harms or avoid goods to herself that it would be wrong for her to do or avoid to others—one is allowed to sacrifice oneself in a way one may not sacrifice others, and this commonsense asymmetry also extends to matters of justice. What it may be unjust to deny to or load upon others, it may not be unjust to deny to or load upon oneself—the idea that one cannot do oneself an injustice goes back all the way to Aristotle.

But act utilitarianism is self-other symmetric in what it regards as permissible or impermissible, and even if we restrict issues of justice to cases where more than one person's interests are at stake, the symmetry of utilitarian justice leads to stark conflict with the deliverances of commonsense talk and intuition. On any utilitarian account of justice, it is unjust to increase the happiness of others when one could have created a greater sum of happiness by enhancing one's own happiness alone, and this and a host of other examples should make it clear that the clash between common-sense morality and utilitarianism on the subject of justice is in no way eliminated—even if it is to some extent limited—by restricting the sphere of justice to certain sorts of action-situations.

In that case, one may well wonder whether there is any reason for a utilitarian to restrict the sphere of justice. Utilitarianism is fairly comfortable these days with its own clashes with commonsense intuition, and the desire to limit such clashes to the greatest extent possible is not, therefore, a very good utilitarian motive for restricting the sphere of justice. Isn't such a restriction really very anti-utilitarian in spirit; and doesn't it make more sense from the utilitarian standpoint—a standpoint from which considerations of simplicity always have their appeal—to identify the right and the just? Perhaps so, but there are other considerations which may incline the utilitarian toward limiting the sphere of justice. Such a limitation, far from being an atypical complicating move, as viewed from a utilitarian perspective, is quite similar to and no worse motivated than other limitations that utilitarians have imposed on their moral conceptions.

Act utilitarianism, for example, reserves the terms "right" and "wrong" for voluntary (human) actions/acts, rather than allowing those terms to apply to other events involving human (or other rational) beings. But consider how act utilitarianism evaluates actions as right or wrong. Something may not count as an action unless it is motivated and/or backed by some sort of intention, but utilitarianism leaves the particular motivation/intention behind an act out of account in morally

---

[13] See chap. 1 of Slote, *Common-sense Morality and Consequentialism*.

assessing it. Only the act's consequences are relevant to that assessment, and on the quite standard utilitarian view that focuses on actual rather than expectable or probable consequences, the rightness of an action may be independent of its agent's ability to foresee its consequences. But if agential motivation and reasonable belief are to be shunted aside in this fashion, so that what is right or wrong can sometimes be entirely a matter of luck (it turns out to be wrong for Hitler's mother not to have killed Hitler), then why should the utilitarian restrict the terms "right" and "wrong" to human *actions*? Why not treat an agent's involuntary slipping on a banana peel as right or wrong depending on that *event's* more or less foreseeable consequences? I think it might be very difficult for act utilitarianism to justify its restriction on the use of "right" and "wrong",[14] but in the light of that restriction, a proposal to limit the sphere of justice and injustice, say, to actions bearing on the happiness-unhappiness of people other than the agent, however difficult it may be to justify, is clearly not without utilitarian precedent. So let us remain neutral on whether the utilitarian account of justice needs to incorporate limitations on the sphere of the just. The distinctively utilitarian character of such an account remains in either case, and we are now ready, I think, to consider how best to frame similarly utilitarian accounts of the other principal virtues.

IV

What would a utilitarian conception of courage be like? From the account previously given of justice, certain conclusions fall naturally into place and certain questions inevitably arise.

First of all, if we want a distinctive utilitarian view of courage, we cannot treat courage in the way in which Smart dealt with the concept of justice: that is, we cannot concede the correctness of commonsense criteria of courage and question only whether courageous action thus conceived is always morally right or acceptable. Such a move would leave us with no specifically utilitarian view of courage—it would give us only a utilitarian position on the rightness and wrongness of (given instances of) courage. To have a utilitarian conception of courage as a virtue, I think we must follow not Smart, but Bentham: we must recognize and accommodate the oddness of speaking of courage as wrong and cowardice as right, by ruling out the possibility of immoral courage or morally good cowardice. And for a utilitarian this can be done only by making the courageousness or cowardice of an appropriate act depend solely on its overall, long-term results.

As with a utilitarian theory of justice, the implications of such a view run headlong into our ordinary notions about courage. Consider, for example, an individual who out of fear runs from the scene of battle to a position of safety. His action will presumably have to count as an instance of utilitarian courage if, for example, his actions mislead the enemy into a fatal underestimation of the courage of his comrades-in-arms and permit his side to win a victory with overall better results than if he

---

[14] It is much easier for Kantianism and commonsense morality, with their stress on factors of motivation and intention in the evaluation of actions, to justify such a restriction.

had never fled. Or if his flight so angers his fellow soldiers that they fight better and win a less bloody, optimific victory, that act of fleeing will also count as courageous by the utilitarian account. The typical utilitarian indifference to moral motivation when assessing given actions here leads to ignoring the fearfulness of the person who flees and thus to a judgment concerning his courage that is out of keeping with common sense in much the same way that it is to hold that a malevolently intended action may escape wrongness through its unintended good consequences. And the idea that an act may count as courageous because of the optimific way in which it gives others an example of what not to do is very much in keeping with more general utilitarian ideas of right and wrong: cf. Williams's "reservation" of non-utilitarians whose bad example keeps a host of others from deviating from the true utilitarian path and is therefore optimific and morally right according to act utilitarianism.[15] (Our present examples of utilitarian courage also remind one of cases where it is all right in utilitarian terms to kill one person to prevent the killing of many others.)

A utilitarian account of courage has other implications with interesting similarity to what utilitarian accounts of right and wrong have to swallow. Act utilitarianism seems to entail that it can be wrong not to use extra water during a water shortage because one's private actions will not, in fact, produce any bad results; and by the same token it may be cowardly (or at least not courageous) to join the battle and kill one of the enemy, if a victory less costly by that one death would have been achieved without one's participation; as with right and wrong, a utilitarian view of courage and cowardice allows the applicability of these notions to depend on unforeseeable quirks of circumstance and on the accidental results of confluent events. But if the utilitarian is prepared to accept such unintuitive results in morality generally, I can see no reason for her to flinch from similar results concerning the virtue of courage or of justice.

However, we have so far been considering only examples where the issue of courage vs. cowardice naturally arises, examples connected with death and danger. We must now consider whether a utilitarianism of courage should cast its net more widely and take in cases where such issues do not ordinarily arise. The question, that is, is whether judgments of courage are relevant wherever the rightness or wrongness of an action is at stake, or whether we ought, on utilitarian grounds or precedent, to limit the sphere of-courage and cowardice.

We have already seen a similar issue raised in connection with justice. But if every utilitarianly right action can be considered utilitarianly just and we make a similarly expansive move with regard to utilitarian courage (and other virtues), then we very quickly end up with a utilitarian doctrine of the unity of the virtues. Very quickly, but also, I think, very uninterestingly by comparison with the way such a doctrine is arrived at within the Platonic and Aristotelian traditions. From the standpoint of the latter, the doctrine of unity (to the extent it really does follow from their assumptions) is the rather surprising fruit of approaches that take seriously the conceptual and moral differences we normally assume to exist among courage, justice, temperance, and prudence. But a utilitarian unity of the virtues would build that unity into its views on justice, courage, etc., in the most painfully obvious way. Let us not make utilitarian virtue uninteresting by such a step. If there is any excuse to think of

---

[15] See Williams, "A Critique of Utilitarianism," in *Utilitarianism: For and Against*, p. 130.

justice as absorbing all of morality and thus as applicable to any situation of right or wrong, there is much less excuse to conceive courage and cowardice in this fashion. We need an account of courage that is distinctly utilitarian (this rules out Smart's approach), but that avoids the triviality and uninterestingness that result from treating all virtues alike. And we can achieve this by narrowing the sphere of courage in line with common opinion and philosophical tradition, while at the same time applying a rigorously utilitarian self-other symmetric criterion of courageous action with respect to those actions about which the issue of courage properly arises.

If we limit the applicability of courage and cowardice to actions in response to danger, then we can avoid treating every optimific or beneficent action as an instance of courage, and the sphere of courage will be differentiated from that justice, whatever we say about the latter's relation to rightness generally. The limitation just indicated is certainly inadequate to the precise contours of one's commonsense views about courage—e.g., it fails to distinguish courage from what David Pears calls "darage."[16] But given the way utilitarianism typically prides itself in caring more about good consequences than about fine distinctions of ordinary language, I doubt whether the utilitarian would or should feel a need for further narrowing or complication of the above-mentioned conditions for applying the courage-cowardice distinction. And having said as much, I think we have said all we need to or can say about the utilitarian virtue of courage within present limitations of space. It is time to turn to the remaining cardinal virtues.

V

As far as I can tell, the virtue of temperance presents no special obstacles to utilitarian treatment. Just as it seems natural for utilitarianism to limit application of the term "courageous" to acts in response to (or motives and dispositions pertaining to) danger, the utilitarian may wish to think of temperance as including only actions responsive to (or motives and dispositions pertaining to) an agent's (own) appetites. Alternatively—and as Bentham seems to suggest in the *Deontology*—any action having to do with pleasures of the (agent's) senses might be deemed to fall within the sphere of temperance, and where pleasures, say, of sight and sound are not objects of (bodily) appetite, this latter stipulation would diverge from that first mentioned.[17] On either stipulation—and we need not decide between them here—the realm of the temperate (or moderate) and intemperate (or immoderate) will not include all actions and motives which bear on human happiness. However, on any utilitarian account, an action falling within the sphere of temperance and intemperance will be assessed by the usual consequentialist criteria, counting as temperate or intemperate according as its consequences for human happiness are overall good or bad.

Such a view of temperance has, of course, a number of counterintuitive implications. Because a truly utilitarian view must regard effects on others as just as relevant to the assessment of an act as effects on the agents, what would ordinarily

---

[16] See Pears, "Aristotle's Analysis of Courage," in *Midwest Studies in Philosophy* 3 (1978): 273–85.

[17] See *Deontology*, 213.

be regarded as an act of intemperance will have to be treated as temperate, if its consequences serve overall human happiness—perhaps by giving errant humanity a powerfully instructive example of how certain behavior can harm the person whose behavior it is. But such results will presumably not be disturbing to utilitarians, and we are clearly now in a position to formulate a utilitarian conception of temperance that can take its place alongside similarly utilitarian views of justice and courage. But prudence raises—or appears to raise—some special problems for any attempt to find utilitarian versions of the cardinal virtues. Analogues of these problems can arise in regard to temperance and even courage, but they emerge most forcefully in connection with prudence, and we must consider them next.

As ordinarily conceived, temperance, courage, and, of course, justice, have rather obvious other-regarding aspects. They are not exclusively, or even primarily, valued for the way they serve their possessors; and indeed their status as virtues in good part connects with the good they do for a larger community, for people other than those who possess these virtues. But prudence seems different; it appears to be exclusively concerned or connected with the good of its possessors, and if that appearance is not misleading, then it will be a fundamental error to aim for a utilitarian conception of this virtue that treats the good of other people as directly relevant to whether an agent is acting prudently.

On a utilitarian view, an action may count as imprudent if it best serves its agent's interests but does so at the expense of overall human good, most particularly, the good of others. And this is decidedly odd. But if there is an error involved here, is it a conceptual one? Can a utilitarian account of prudence be ruled out *a priori*, or are we not rather faced here with another sharp moral disagreement between utilitarianism and ordinary ethical intuitions? It also sounds odd to speak of failures to serve one's own ends as instance of injustice, but utilitarianism wants to hold that such talk is not symptomatic of conceptual error, but, rather, of the greater moral clarity and vision that can be achieved by shuffling off the weight of moral tradition, together with its sediment of intuitions, and making moral assessments from a more rational and impersonal standpoint. And I can see no reason why a utilitarian should not say the same about a utilitarian theory of prudence. It may seem odd to conceive of prudence in terms which give so much weight to the interests of people other than its possessor(s), but, according to utilitarians, that may have little or no force against the validity of such a conception.

But are those objecting to a utilitarianism of prudence even correct about the self-regarding focus of prudence as ordinarily or traditionally conceived? (In the ordinary sense of the term, "prudence" connotes a certain kind of long-range playing it safe. This connotation is largely absent when philosophers regard prudence as equivalent to the notion of practical wisdom, and I shall be assuming the latter equivalence in what follows.) In calling an act prudent, do most people, e.g., simply mean that it (expectably) serves the interests of its agent? I think not. We do not typically regard it as imprudent when someone acts against his own self-interest in order to do the just or honorable thing.[18] And an act that flies in the face of justice or honesty but serves the interest of its agent is not naturally thought of as prudent (we are not likely to regard it as imprudent either): if a bank teller, knowing he will not

---

[18] On this point, see Foot, "Are Moral Considerations Overriding?" in *Virtues and Vices* (Oxford, 1978), p. 187.

be caught, helps himself to a better life by stealing from his bank, we are reluctant to call him or his actions prudent even if we share his assessment of the chances of his getting caught. So other-regarding considerations and moral justifications play a direct role in what is ordinarily regarded as prudent or imprudent. But, of course, the moral claims that affect ordinary judgments of prudence are made from a commonsense moral standpoint, and utilitarianism disputes the validity of commonsense morality. So it should now be clear how the utilitarian can reply to those who object to the idea of a utilitarian account of prudence.

We have seen that the conceptual tie between prudence (practical wisdom) and acting in one's own self-interest is much less direct than might initially be supposed. In ordinary terms, a self-sacrificing act may not count as imprudent if it is morally required and/or praiseworthy, and a successfully self-interested act may not be regarded as prudent if it is seen as dishonorable or otherwise immoral. So the moral justification of an action is *on conceptual grounds* relevant to the question of its prudence, but the moral claims that we ordinarily treat as relevant to such questions are most typically commonsense ones whose validity the utilitarian would dispute. And if we substitute utilitarian moral justifications for ordinary ones in determining what is or is not prudent, we end up with a utilitarian theory of prudence. In summary then: if, as our ordinary judgments about prudence implicitly allow, moral justification is directly relevant to judgments of prudence and imprudence, and if, as the utilitarian holds, the only valid kind of moral justification must ultimately be cast in utilitarian terms, there can be no objection to a utilitarian account of prudence which treats acts as prudent or imprudent depending on whether they serve overall human happiness, and so are morally justified, or oppose such happiness, and so are morally unjustified.

As a result, any act which serves the (maximal) good of its agent but not (maximal) overall human good will then lack a utilitarian moral justification and therefore fail to exemplify the utilitarian virtue of prudence. But the violence this does to our ordinary intuitions is, as we now can see, primarily attributable to the assumptions of utilitarian morality, rather than to any violation of the meaning of "prudence." The relevance of moral constraints and justifications is built into ordinary usage of this term, and cannot be regarded as the alien imposition of a utilitarianism overleaping its proper boundaries. So if act utilitarianism is the correct view of right action, a utilitarianism of prudence and other virtues is entirely appropriate and will bear to more traditional treatments of the virtues something like the relation act utilitarianism bears to commonsense views about right and wrong action. A utilitarianism of virtue and of the particular virtues can be as strong as other forms of utilitarianism, and at this point, therefore, the case for and against utilitarian virtue seems to blend with the case for and against more familiar forms of utilitarianism. In the next, and final, section of this essay, I want to talk about some considerations that threaten commonsense ethical views and may well strengthen the general utilitarian position.

VI

I earlier made brief reference to the self-other asymmetry of the common-sense morality of right and wrong and of justice and injustice. But the discussion we have just concluded allows us to see that the commonsense ethics of *virtue* in fact contains a *pair* of symmetrically related asymmetries. We know that certain ways of failing to help others count against the justice of one's actions in a way that relevantly similar failure to help oneself does not. And so our commonsense understanding of justice is structured by an agent-sacrificing self-other asymmetry. On the other hand, commonsense prudence seems subject to a precisely opposite, agent-favoring asymmetry. For certain ways of failing to help oneself would ordinarily be taken to count against the prudence of one's actions in a way that parallel failures to help others would not. (It is true that morality and justice are ordinarily taken to permit agents to give preference to their own good, but such agent-relative agent-favoring permissions do not give rise to an agent-favoring self-other *asymmetry* with respect to justice, because ordinary justice and morality also allow agents to give preference to the good of *others*.)

By contrast, a utilitarianism of virtue sweeps away both the above-mentioned asymmetries and treats prudence, justice, courage, and temperance as uniformly self-other symmetric. The unity and simplicity thereby achieved is, however, counterbalanced by the many clashes with ordinary intuition such a uniform account entails. And so it might seem at this point that a genuine stand-off exists between utilitarianism and intuitive accounts of the virtues. But I think the situation is actually worse for commonsense ethical views than their defenders have realized. Self-other asymmetry seems irrational and unmotivated, to be sure, from the impersonal perspective of utilitarian ethics, but problems arise for such an asymmetry even from within the perspective of commonsense ethical thinking. Commonsense morality itself has a difficult time making sense of its commitment to a self-other asymmetry of right and wrong (or justice and injustice).

To begin with—and I have argued the point at much greater length elsewhere—the difference between what we may do to ourselves and what we may do to others is not attributable to the factor of consent. It is morally worse negligently to harm another than negligently to harm oneself, but in neither case is consent likely to be present. But apart, for a moment, from whether we can explain or justify the asymmetry—after all, it may represent a ground-floor intuitive assumption—there is the difficulty of *reconciling it with other aspects of commonsense morality*.

Unlike act utilitarianism, ordinary morality treats our obligations to others as dependent on how near they stand to us in relations of affection or special commitment: obligations to our immediate family (other things being equal) being stronger than to our relations generally, obligations to friends and relations being stronger than to compatriots generally, and obligations to the latter, in turn, being stronger than to the people of other countries. To that extent, ordinary morality reflects the normal structure of an adult's concerns. We are naturally more concerned about and have more reason to be concerned about the well-being of friends and relations than of more distant others, and commonsense morality seems to build such differences into the varyingly strong duties it assigns us to concern ourselves with others' well-being. However, by means of its self-other asymmetry, commonsense morality also superimposes an absolute moral discontinuity on the structure of concern in which each agent is normally situated. On the one hand, it encourages the idea that strength of obligation weakens as one gets further from the agent, but on the other hand, and in seeming opposition to the first idea, it assumes that there is no moral obligation whatever (except indirectly) for the agent to benefit *himself*. Once one leaves the agent behind, the agent's obligations vary in proportion to his reason for concern, but where he has greatest reason for concern in the natural course of things, he has no direct obligation whatever. And this appears odd and unmotivated even apart from any utilitarian or consequentialist perspective (though the latter provides a way out of the oddness, the seeming inconsistency or discontinuity).

In fact some well-known attempts have been made to explain away or justify the self-other asymmetry (or some aspects of it), but in the light of what has just been said, those attempts make the picture appear even bleaker for commonsense morality by making it appear impossible to make sense of the above-mentioned discontinuity in commonsense thinking. Let me explain.

Both Butler and Kant point out that one can (attempt to) account for the (apparent) lack of moral duties to provide for one's own good in terms of normal human desires and instincts and plausible assumptions about their influence on our actions. We can be expected to take care of ourselves most of the time, and that, according to the account, is why there is no need for morality to impose obligations or duties to do so.[19] But such an explanation immediately gets into trouble if we consider (as Butler and Kant do not) the facts about our relations to other people that we mentioned above. We can normally be expected to take better care of our spouse and children than of distant others, yet our obligations to the former are stronger than to the latter, and this is just the opposite of what one would expect if the above account were correct about duties to seek one's own good. But it is commonsensically very natural to try to explain and justify the self-other moral asymmetry, and more particularly the absence of duties to seek one's own good, in terms of what is normal and expectable, and I think this is additional proof of how much common sense is at odds with itself in this general area. What seems like the only possible and sensible explanation of the self-other asymmetry makes nonsense out of another aspect of commonsense morality, and these internal difficulties of ordinary thought about right and wrong offer some reason, I think, to favor a utilitarianism or consequentialism that eliminates the difficulties by insisting on complete self-other symmetry in its account both of right action and of particular virtues.[20]

Nor are these internal difficulties the only ones that can be pointed to in commonsense morality. In his recent *The Rejection of Consequentialism*,[21] Samuel Scheffler shows that the most natural and appealing explanation of why it is (ordinarily considered) wrong to kill one person to prevent a greater number of persons from being killed actually undercuts what it attempts to justify. If the wrongness is attributed (roughly) to the sheer badness of killings, then the difficult question arises how it

---

[19] See Butler's "A Dissertation upon the Nature of Virtue," in *The Analogy of Religion*, (London 1736); and the Preface of Kant's *Metaphysical Elements of Ethics*. Butler is skeptical about the account, but for reasons which, I believe, are ultimately less telling against commonsense morality than those offered here.

[20] It is an interesting question just how much self-other asymmetry Aristotle wishes to admit into his views on justice, practical wisdom, and right action.

[21] Scheffler, *Rejection of Consequentialism*, esp. chap. 4. Commonsense morality also seems to be inconsistent on the subject of moral luck. See, on this point, Slote, *Common-sense Morality*, chap. 7, and various works cited there.

can be objectionable to act in such a way as to minimize the occurence of such bad (or horrible or objectionable) actions. Common sense thus here again seems at odds with itself, because the reasons it is inclined to offer in its own support actually tend to cast further doubt upon it.

Some moral philosophers have recently told us that theory is out of place in ethics and that an intuitive approach to ethics makes more sense than consequentialism or utilitarianism, with their self-styled theoretical aspirations. But this assumes that an entirely intuitive approach can give us what we need in this area, and the situation turns out to be less favorable to such an approach than this attitude presupposes. Rather, the situation in ethics is much more like what we find in the area of confirmation—to take just one example—where our intuitive gropings toward general principles and explanations of our ordinary judgments about what confirms what have been shown (by Hempel) to lead to inconsistency. Such a result is an invitation to philosophical theorizing of a sort empowered *to discard some strong intuitions*. And the situation in ethics seems, in the light of what has been said above, to be somewhat similar. Commonsense ethics, when fully and consistently followed out, leads to inconsistencies and/or glaring inadequacies, and that is an invitation to theorizing about right and wrong and virtue. To the extent utilitarianism takes up that invitation and can avoid commonsense morality's problems it may meet a challenge that common sense itself presents, and to the extent it does not fall prey to similar inconsistencies, its rejection of ordinary intuitions may be vindicated and a strong prima facie case is made for its superiority to the commonsense ethics both of right and wrong and of the virtues.

Moderation, Rationality, and Virtue

The Tanner Lectures on Human Values

Delivered at Stanford University
April 17 and 22, 1985

I

In these lectures I shall be discussing some central features of practical rationality. The focus will largely be on extra-moral, or individualistic, practical rationality—though what I shall have to say about such rationality will frequently be supported by comparison with analogous claims that can be made about morality and about practical reason as swayed by moral, and not just individualistic, considerations.

It is usually assumed by philosophers (and of course by economists and others as well) that practical rationality is subject to a condition of maximization: that the rational egoist, or the average non-egoist under conditions where the welfare of or commitments to others are not at issue, will seek to maximize her own good, or well-being. Both utilitarians like Sidgwick and anti-utilitarians like Rawls seem to assume that it is egoistically, individualistically, irrational not to maximize one's satisfactions and seek one's own greatest good.[1] More recently, however, some explicitly non-maximizing conceptions of personal well-being over time have been suggested by Amartya Sen and Charles Fried, who have, with differing degrees of vehemence, defended the notion that considerations of equality in the intertemporal distribution

---

I am indebted to the official discussants of these Tanner Lectures—Alan Donagan, Barbara Herman, Peter Railton, and Donald Regan—for helpful comments and criticisms. I would also like to thank the Stanford philosophy faculty and students (most especially, Michael Bratman, Julius Moravcsik, and Jean Roberts) for their many suggestions; and W. V. Denard for helpful points about Aristotelian usage.

[1] See *The Methods of Ethics*, 7th ed. (London: Macmillan, 1907), pp. 119ff., 381f., 497ff., and elsewhere; and *A Theory of Justice* (Cambridge: Harvard University Press, 1971), pp. 23ff., 416ff., and elsewhere.

of goods in a single life have some independent weight in the reckoning of the goodness of lives.[2] The rational individual will wish to consider how much good for himself given courses of action will produce but also how evenly or equally the resultant good or satisfaction will be distributed across different times of his life; and he will allow for trade-offs between total amount of satisfaction and equality of distribution of satisfaction in deciding what courses of action to follow.

But even in such non-maximizing conceptions of human good and the rational planning of lives, there is no suggestion that the egoistic individual, or the non-egoistic individual in situations where only his own well-being is at issue, should ever do anything but seek what is best for himself; what gives way in such conceptions is the idea that the course of action yielding the most good or satisfaction is always best for a given individual, but the assumption that the rational individual seeks what is best for himself remains unscathed. Fried and Sen in effect tell us that human well-being must be more complexly reckoned than simple maximizing accounts permit, but there is no suggestion that the rational egoistic individual, in sometimes seeking *less than the most* available good or satisfaction for herself, might also seek what is *less than best* for herself. It will, however, be my purpose in these lectures to argue for just this sort of possibility. This will not be the first time I have attempted to defend the notion that, both at an isolated given time and over a lifetime, a rational individual may seek what is less than best for herself. But I do hope to have an opportunity to expand on arguments and examples offered elsewhere in defense of views which must undoubtedly, in the light of unbroken philosophical tradition, at first seem bizarre and implausible. I think that a variety of examples drawn from ordinary life will help to clarify how we may rationally seek less than the best for ourselves and sometimes even reject what is better for ourselves for what is good enough. But a number of conceptual and other objections naturally arise in connection with these theses, objections that I have in fact not had a chance to consider and respond to elsewhere, and I hope that by providing answers to these objections I may persuade you that we are not going to fall into conceptual confusion or contradiction by rejecting the view that individualistic rationality requires doing the best one can for oneself. This first lecture will attempt to show that there is a space on our moral–psychological map, and a place in our lives, for a non-optimizing form of egoistic rationality. Lecture II will attempt to advance a step further and argue that optimization, while not itself irrational, can nonetheless be faulted on a number of other grounds.

1

The idea that a rational individual might seek less than the best for himself was originally developed, I believe, in the literature of economics. The term "satisficing" was coined for the discussion of such behavior, and I shall make use of the term here. What the economists have done, however, is point to an aspect of human behavior

---

[2] See Sen's "Utilitarianism and Welfarism," *Journal of Philosophy* LXXVI (1979): 470f.; and Fried's *An Anatomy of Values* (Cambridge: Harvard University Press, 1970), pp. 170–76.

(both individually and in groups) that philosophers have traditionally ignored, and I shall be discussing and articulating the idea of satisficing from the perspective of an attempt to give an adequate philosophical account of this phenomenon. The emphasis will be on conceptual and moral–psychological issues, rather than on the sort of technical economic–theoretic development of the notion of satisficing that can be found in the literature of economics.

Consider an example borrowed from the economics literature.[3] An individual planning to move to a new location and having to sell his house may seek, not to maximize his profit on the house, not to get the best price for it he is likely to receive within some appropriate time period, but simply to obtain what he takes to be a good or satisfactory price. What he deems satisfactory may depend, among other things, on what he paid for the house, what houses cost in the place to which he is relocating, and on what houses like his normally sell at. But given some notion of what would be a good or satisfactory price to sell at, he may fix the price of his house at that point, rather than attempting, by setting it somewhat higher, to do better than that or to do the best he can. His reason for not setting the price higher will not, in that case, be some sort of anxiety about not being able to sell the house at all or some feeling that trying to do better would likely not be worth the effort of figuring out how to get a better price. Nor is he so rich that any extra money he received for the house would be practically meaningless in terms of marginal utility. Rather he is a "satisficer" content with good enough and does not seek to maximize (optimize) his expectations. His desires, his needs, are moderate, and perhaps knowing this about himself, he may not be particularly interested in doing better for himself than he is likely to do by selling at a merely satisfactory price. If someone pointed out that it would be better for him to get more money, he would reply not by disagreeing, but by pointing out that for him at least a good enough price is good enough.

Such a person apparently fails to exemplify the maximizing and optimizing model of individual rationality traditionally advocated by philosophers. But I think he nonetheless represents a possible idea of (one kind of) individual rationality, and much of the literature of economics treats such examples, regarding both individuals and economic units like the firm, as exemplifying a form of rational behavior. Though one might hold on to an optimizing or maximizing model of rationality and regard satisficing examples as indications of the enormous prevalence of irrational human behavior, this has typically not been done by economists, and I think philosophers would have even less reason to do so. For there are many other cases where satisficing seems rational, or at least not irrational, and although some of these are purely hypothetical, hypothetical examples are the stock-in-trade of ethical and moral–psychological theory even when they are of little or no interest to economists.

---

[3] For relevant discussions of satisficing in the economics literature, see, e.g., H. Simon, "A Behavioral Model of Rational Choice," *Quarterly Journal of Economics* 69 (1955): 99–118; Simon, "Theories of Decision Making in Economics and Behavioral Science," *American Economic Review* XLIX (1959): 253–83; Simon, *Administrative Behavior*, 2d ed. (New York: Macmillan Co., 1961); and R. Cyert and J. March, eds., *A Behavioral Theory of the Firm* (Englewood Cliffs, N.J.: Prentice-Hall, 1963).

Imagine that it is mid-afternoon; you had a good lunch, and you are not now hungry; neither, on the other hand, are you sated. You would enjoy a candy bar or Coca Cola, if you had one, and there is in fact, right next to your desk, a refrigerator stocked with such snacks and provided gratis by the company for which you work. Realizing all this, do you, then, necessarily take and consume a snack? If you do not, is that necessarily because you are afraid to spoil your dinner, because you are on a diet, or because you are too busy? I think not. You may simply not feel the need for any such snack. You turn down a good thing, a sure enjoyment, because you are perfectly satisfied as you are. Most of us are often in situations of this sort, and many of us would often do the same thing. We are not boundless optimizers or maximizers, but are sometimes (more) modest in our desires and needs. But such modesty, such moderation, need not be irrational or unreasonable on our part.

Of course, moderation has been exalted as a prime virtue in many religious and philosophical traditions. But when, for example, the Epicureans emphasized the rationality of moderation in the pursuit of pleasure, they recommended modesty in one's desires only as a means to an overall more pleasurable, or less unpleasant, life, and in the example mentioned above, moderation is not functioning as a means to greater overall satisfaction. One is not worried about ruining one's figure or spoiling one's dinner, and the moderation exemplified is thus quite different from the instrumental virtue recommended by the Epicureans. The sort of moderation I am talking about, then, is not for the sake of anything else. If one has the habit of not trying to eke out the last possible enjoyment from situations and of resting content with some reasonable quantity that is less than the most or best one can do, then one has a habit of moderation or modesty regarding one's desires and satisfactions, and it may not be irrational to have such habit, even if (one recognizes that) the contrary habit of maximizing may also not be irrational.

But if there is nothing irrational or unreasonable about maximizing, isn't the moderate individual who is content with less a kind of ascetic? Not necessarily. An ascetic is someone who, within certain limits, *minimizes* his enjoyments or satisfactions; he deliberately leaves himself with less, unsatisfied. The moderate individual, on the other hand, is someone content with (what he considers) a reasonable amount of enjoyment; he wants to be satisfied and up to a certain point he wants more satisfactions rather than fewer, to be better off rather than worse off; but there is a point beyond which he has no desire, and even refuses, to go. There is a space between asceticism and the attempt to maximize satisfactions, do the best one can for oneself, a space occupied by the habit of moderation. And because such moderation is not a form of asceticism, it is difficult to see why it should count as irrational from the standpoint of egoistic or extra-moral individual rationality.[4]

Now the kind of example just mentioned differs from the case of satisficing house-selling in being independent of any monetary transaction. But the example

---

[4] *Rational* satisficing seems to involve not only a disinclination to optimize, but a reasonable sense of when one has enough. To be content with much less than one should be is (can be) one form of *bathos*. Moreover, as Peter Railton has pointed out, to be willing to satisfice only at some high level of desire satisfaction is to fail to be moderate in one's desires. In speaking of satisficing moderation, I shall assume the absence of these complicating conditions.

differs importantly in another way from examples of satisficing mentioned in the literature of economics. Economists who have advocated the model of rational satisficing for individuals, firms, or state bodies have pointed out that, quite independently of the costs of gaining further information or effecting new policies, an entrepreneur or firm may simply seek a satisfactory return on investment, a satisfactory share of the market, a satisfactory level of sales, rather than attempting to maximize or optimize under any of these headings. But this idea of rational satisficing implies only that individuals or firms *do not* always *seek* to optimize and are *satisfied* with attaining a certain "aspiration level" less than the best that might be envisaged. It does not imply that it could be rational actually to *reject* the better for the good enough in situations where both were available. In the example of house-selling, the individual accepts less than he might well be able to get, but he doesn't accept a lower price when a higher bidder makes an equally firm offer. And writers on satisficing generally seem to hold that satisficing only makes sense as a habit of not seeking what is better or best, rather than as a habit of actually rejecting the better, when it is clearly available, for the good enough. Thus Herbert Simon, in his "Theories of Decision Making" (see note 3), develops the idea of aspiration level and of satisficing, but goes on to say that "when a firm has alternatives open to it that are at or above its aspiration level, it will choose the best of those known to be available."

However, the example of the afternoon snack challenges the idea that the satisficing individual will never explicitly reject the better for the good enough. For the individual in question turns down an immediately available satisfaction, something he knows he will enjoy. He isn't merely not trying for a maximum of satisfactions, but is explicitly rejecting such a maximum. (It may be easier to see the explicitness of the rejection if we change the example so that he is actually offered a snack by someone and replies: "No, thank you, I'm just fine as I am.") And I think that most of us would argue that there is nothing irrational here. Many of us, most of us, occasionally reject afternoon snacks, second cups of tea, etc., not out of (unconscious) asceticism, but because (to some degree) we have a habit of moderation with regard to certain pleasures. The hypothetical example of the afternoon snack thus takes the idea of rational satisficing a step beyond where economists, to the best of my knowledge, have been willing to go.

At this point, however, it may be objected that the example may be one of rational behavior but is less than clear as an example of satisficing. The individual in question prefers not to have a certain enjoyment and certainly deliberately rejects the maximization of his enjoyments. But it is not clear that the moderate individual must think of himself as missing out on anything *good* when he forgoes the afternoon snack. For although he knows he would enjoy the snack, the very fact that he rejects such enjoyment might easily be taken as evidence that he doesn't in the circumstances regard such enjoyment as a good thing. In that case, he may be satisficing in terms of some quantitative notion of satisfaction, but not with respect to some more refined or flexible notion of (his own) individual good, and the example would provide no counter-example to the idea that it is irrational to choose what is less good for oneself when something better is available.

However, even if the enjoyment of a snack does count as a rejected personal good for the individual of our example, that fact may be obscured, both for him and for us, by the very smallness or triviality of the good in question. And so in order to deal with our doubts, it may be useful at this point to consider other examples, more purely hypothetical than the present one, where the good forgone through satisficing is fairly obvious.

How do we react to fairy tales in which the hero or heroine, offered a single wish, asks for a pot of gold, for a million (1900) dollars, or, simply, for (enough money to enable) his family and himself to be comfortably well-off for the rest of their lives. In each case the person asks for less than he might have asked for, but we are not typically struck by the thought that he was irrational to ask for less than he could have, and neither, in general, do the fairy tales themselves imply a criticism of this sort; so, given the tendency of such tales to be full of moralism about human folly, we have, I think, some evidence that such fairy-tale wishes need not be regarded as irrational. (In not regarding them as irrational, we need not be confusing what we know *about* fairy-tale wishes with what the individual *in* a given fairy tale ought to know. In some fairy tales, people who ask for too much fail to get their wish or have it realized in an unacceptable way. But there is no reason to suppose that we consider the person who in a given fairy tale asks for enough to be comfortable not to be irrational only because we mistakenly imagine him to have some evidence concerning the possible risks of asking for more than he does.)

Now the individual in the fairy tale who wishes for *less* than he could presumably exemplifies the sort of moderation discussed earlier. He may think that a pot of gold or enough money to live comfortably is all he needs to be satisfied, that anything more is of no particular importance to him. At the same time, however, he may realize (be willing to admit) that he could do better for himself by asking for more. He needn't imagine himself constitutionally incapable of benefiting from additional money or gold, for the idea that one will be happy, or satisfied, with a certain level of existence by no means precludes the thought (though it perhaps precludes *dwelling* on the thought) that one will not be as well off as one could be. It merely precludes the sense of wanting or needing more for oneself. Indeed the very fact that someone could actually explicitly wish for enough money to be comfortably well-off is itself sufficient evidence of what I am saying. Someone who makes such a wish clearly acknowledges the possibility of being better off and yet chooses—knowingly and in some sense deliberately chooses—a lesser, but personally satisfying degree of well-being. And it is precisely because the stakes are so large in such cases of wishing that they provide clearcut examples of presumably rational individual satisficing. But, again, the sort of satisficing involved is not (merely) the kind familiar in the economics literature where an individual seeks something other than optimum results, but a kind of satisficing that actually rejects the available better for the available good enough. Although the individual with the wish would be better off if he wished for more, he asks for less (we may suppose that if the wish grantor prods him by asking "Are you sure you wouldn't like more money than that?" he sticks with his original request). And if we have any sympathy with the idea of moderation, of modesty, in one's desires, we shall have to grant that the satisficing individual who wishes, e.g., for less money is not irrational. Perhaps we ourselves would not be so easily satisfied in his circumstances, but that needn't make us think him irrational for being moderate in a way, or to a degree, that we are not.[5]

But at this point some doubt may remain about our description of the moderate individual's response to being granted a wish. It is not obvious that an individual who wishes for less than the most money (or comfort or well-being) he could ask for is satisficing in the strong sense defended earlier. He may make the seemingly modest wish he does because he is afraid of offending the wish grantor or in order to avoid being corrupted (or rendered blasé) by having too much wealth, and thus motivated, he will not exemplify the sort of satisficing moderation whose non-irrationality I have tried to defend: he *will* be seeking what is best for himself under a refined conception of personal good that goes beyond mere wealth or material comfort.[6]

With this I can absolutely agree. An individual who asks for less than she could may indeed be motivated by factors of the above sort. My main point is, and has been, that there is no reason to insist or assume that such factors are always present when an individual asks for less than the most or best he can obtain. From the standpoint of the phenomenology of our own lives, it doesn't seem as if such factors are always present—we find it humanly understandable and not unreasonable that someone should choose the good enough when better was available. Why insist that some other factor(s) must always be present to turn putative cases of satisficing into cases, fundamentally, of optimization or maximization of the individual's (perceived) good?

The situation here resembles what is often said for and against psychological egoism. Many people—even philosophers—have argued as if it were practically a matter of definition that individuals seek their own greatest good, even when they appear to be sacrificing that good for the good of others. But nowadays philosophers at least seem to recognize that altruism and self-sacrifice cannot be ruled out a priori. Nonetheless, it in some sense remains empirically open that human altruism may turn out to be an illusion. It is conceivable, let us suppose, that a powerful enough psychological theory that entailed the universal selfishness (or non-unselfishness) of human behavior might eventually be adopted. But in the absence of such a theory, philosophers have been, I think, quite right to insist upon taking altruistic motivation seriously. Any moral psychology that wishes to remain true to our common or everyday understanding of things, to life as most of us seem to lead it, will assume that there is a phenomenon of altruistic motivation to explore and better understand, both conceptually and in its ethical ramifications.

---

[5] In fact, it is hard to see how any specific monetary wish can be optimizing if the individual is unsure about his own marginal utility curve for the use of money. To that extent, we are *necessarily* satisficers in situations where we can wish for whatever we want, unless, perhaps, we are allowed to wish for our own greatest future well-being in those very terms. If satisficing were irrational, would that mean that anything other than such an explicitly optimizing wish would be irrational?

[6] Some of these points are made by Philip Pettit in reply to an earlier paper of mine. See his contribution to the symposium "Satisficing Consequentialism," *Proceedings of the Aristotelian Society* (supplementary volume, 1984), p. 175.

And similar points can, I believe, be made about satisficing, or moderation in the sense delineated earlier. Perhaps it will someday be definitively shown by economists and/or psychologists that the best explanation of why humans act as they do requires us to assume that they are always maximizing or optimizing and thus that apparent examples of satisficing or moderation are illusory. But until and unless that happens, we should recognize—something philosophers have not previously noticed or admitted—that the common-sense understanding of our own lives leaves a definite recognizable place for occasional, perhaps even frequent, satisficing moderation. For in fact the phenomenon of moderation is not limited to fairy-tale examples, though I believe such examples allow one to see certain issues large enough and in sufficient isolation as to make it easier to recognize the phenomenon of moderation in the more muddied waters of everyday life. Even the example of the person selling a house and moving to a new location need be altered only in minor ways in order to turn it from an example of not seeking the best for oneself into an example of actually rejecting the expectable better for the expectable good enough.

Imagine, for instance, that the person selling the house has an agent and that the agent has received a firm bid on the house that falls within the range the seller considers good enough. The agent tells the prospective buyer that it may take him three or four days to get in touch with the seller because he believes the latter is temporarily out of town; the buyer says he is in no hurry; but in fact the seller has not gone away and the agent conveys the bid to him on the same day it is made. The seller then tells the agent to let the prospective buyer know that his offer is acceptable, but the agent, who we may assume is no satisficer, tells the seller that he really ought to wait a few days before accepting the offer that has been made. After all, he says, the offer is firm, and if we wait a few days before telling the prospective buyer that you agree to his terms, a better offer may come in.

Now in the circumstances as I have described them, the seller's net expectable utility is greater if he waits—we are assuming that the offer already made is firm and that there is no reason to worry that the person who has made the offer may get cold feet, since the latter doesn't expect his offer to be received for a couple of days. Yet the seller may tell the real estate agent to convey his acceptance of the terms on offer without delay. Again, the reason may simply be that he considers the offer good enough and has no interest in seeing whether he can do better. His early agreement may not be due to undue anxiety about the firmness of the buyer's offer, or to a feeling that monetary transactions are unpleasant and to be got over as quickly as possible. He may simply be satisficing in the strong sense of the term we have been defending. He may be moderate or modest in what he wants or feels he needs.

And one cannot at this point reasonably reply that if he doesn't want the (chance of) extra money for his house then that cannot represent a good thing, a personal good, that he gives up by immediately accepting the offer that has been made. There is an important distinction to be made between what someone (most) wants and what advances his well-being (or represents a personal good for him). And, once again, a comparison with issues that arise in connection with altruism and moral behavior generally may help us to see the point. If altruism makes sense, then presumably so too does the notion of self-sacrifice. But the idea of deliberate self-sacrifice involves the assumption that what a person (most) wants need not be what advances his own personal well-being, what is (in one everyday sense) best for him. And this conceptual point carries over to discussions of moderation and satisficing. Just because the moderate individual asks for less wealth than he could doesn't, for example, mean that additional wealth wouldn't be a good thing for him. The wishing and house-selling examples—as well as the earlier example of the rejected afternoon snack—indicate, instead, that an individual who does not want or care about something and who chooses not to have it, need not automatically regard that thing as not a personal good.[7]

There is conceptual space for and human understandability in the idea of a personal good or element of one's own well-being that one simply doesn't care about or wish to have—and that one actually rejects—because one considers oneself well enough off without it. It is a mere confusion, therefore, to say (as I have heard it said) that the person who turns down a certain good is nonetheless inevitably seeking his own good in some more refined sense, because the person is maximizing the satisfaction of his preferences on the whole, among which, after all, is presumably the preference not to have that unnecessary good (and/or the general preference not to have much more than he needs). The same form of argument would be laughed out of court if applied in the area of morality and altruism: we all know by now that it would be absurd to argue that the individual who sacrifices his life for others must be seeking his own greatest good in doing so, because in doing so he is maximizing his weighted preferences, a very powerful one of which is the preference that he should die so that others should live.[8] The only reason why a similar move is not instantly rejected in the area of individualistic rationality in connection with putative examples of moderation is that moderation as described earlier is a much neglected moral–psychological phenomenon. But once we get our sea legs on this topic, I think the sorts of objections to the phenomenon that naturally arise will be seen (at least in the cases mentioned above) to be as groundless as the sorts of objections to psychological altruism that abounded in earlier periods of philosophy but are now largely discredited.

---

[7] A quite similar point, that the virtuous individual who forgoes something that can only be obtained unjustly need not deny that he is forgoing a good thing, is made in my *Goods and Virtues* (Oxford: Clarendon Press, 1983), chap. 5. On the present view, a person may reasonably turn down the chance of getting more money (say, $90,000) for his house and simply accept what he takes to be a good price (say $80,000). Does it follow (as Alan Donagan and Jonathan Glover have both suggested) that the moderate individual might (should) turn down a firm $90,000 when $80,000 is on offer? Certainly not. If $80,000 really is a good and sufficient price, then holding out for and striving after a higher amount may seem a form of "grubbing" with little to recommend it (more on this in the second lecture). But no such grubbing is involved when the higher price is firmly on offer, and in such a situation nothing need stand in the way of accepting the higher price. Note too that in the normal course of events it will never be clear that one won't need the extra $10,000, so the case where both $80,000 and $90,000 are firmly on offer is also different from the fairy-tale example, where one can wish for enough money to be moderately well-off for the rest of one's life and where it is assumed that there will definitely be no need for any more than one is actually wishing for. Once again, there may be reason to take the firm $90,000, even if the moderate individual has no reason to ask for more than moderate wealth in an idealized fairy-tale situation.

[8] Cf. Amartya Sen, "Rational Fools: A Critique of the Behavioral Foundations of Economic Theory," *Philosophy and Public Affairs* 6 (1977): 322ff.

2

However, we are not yet finished with objections that cast doubt on moderation and satisficing as I have described it. We have examined and, I hope, answered some objections to the very possibility of moderation occurring in the way I have described it. But it is also possible, while not denying the existence of moderation, to hold that the rejection of the better for the good enough is, when it occurs, irrational. In response to my account of satisficing moderation, for example, Philip Pettit has argued that the person who rejects what is better for himself in favor of what he considers good enough may have a reason for choosing what he chooses—what he chooses is, after all, good enough—but has no reason to choose what he chooses in preference to what he rejects. There may be a reason to wish for or choose moderate wealth or well-being, but there is no reason for the moderate individual I have described to choose moderate wealth over great wealth, and for that reason, according to Pettit, his choice counts as irrational or unreasonable.[9]

This objection, however, is extremely problematic. It is not, to begin with, a general condition of rationality that in choosing between two options one has (a) reason to choose one of those options rather than the other—otherwise, we would sometimes really be in the position of Buridan's ass. When two equally good or self-beneficial options present themselves, it need not be irrational to choose one of them, even though one has no reason to prefer it to the other. (I have somewhere read that Arthur Balfour once spent twenty minutes trying to decide whether there was any reason for him to ascend via a staircase to the left or via one to the right in order to join a soirée to which he had been invited.) In the second place, reasons can be relative to an individual's concerns, her world view, or even her habits; and from the distinctive standpoint of the moderate individual, there may well be a reason to prefer moderate wealth (well-being) to great wealth (well-being). The fact that great wealth is much more than she needs (or cares about) can count, for such an individual, as a reason for rejecting great wealth and choosing moderate wealth, but of course such a reason will not motivate, or even occur to, someone who always seeks to optimize. The moderate individual will thus sometimes have a reason to prefer what is less good for herself, but a reason precisely of a kind to lack appeal to the maximizing temperament.[10]

But this is not to claim that the moderate individual *always* chooses less than the best for himself. Other things being equal he will prefer what is better for himself

---

[9] See Pettit, "Satisficing Consequentialism," p. 172.

[10] Similarly, the non-egoistic reasons there are for helping others or doing the honorable thing will not appeal to the egoistic temperament, but this hardly shows that such reasons are illusory. Cf. John McDowell, "The Role of *Eudaimonia* in Aristotle's Ethics," in A. Rorty, ed., *Essays on Aristotle's Ethics* (Berkeley: University of California Press, 1980), pp. 359–76.

The moderate individual's reasons for taking less for herself are non-consequentialist, non-moral, non-egoistic, but nonetheless self-regarding. Michael Bratman has pointed out that there may be other non-consequentialist, non-moral, non-egoistic, self-regarding reasons that have nothing (directly) to do with moderation: e.g., the desire not to vote for oneself in a club election. This whole class of reasons needs to be further explored.

to what is less good for himself; but from his particular standpoint, other things are not equal when what is less good for himself is good and sufficient for his purposes and what is better for himself is much more than he needs or cares about. In such circumstances he can articulate a reason—a reason I think you and I can understand and empathize with—for choosing what is less good for himself. But faced, e.g., with the choice between great wealth and dire poverty, he would have reason to choose the former (the moderate individual is not an ascetic) and indeed with respect to most choices between better and worse for himself he would (be able to) prefer the better-for-himself to the less-good-for-himself.

However, we are not yet quite out of the woods. We must consider one final objection to the rationality of satisficing moderation based on Donald Davidson's recent influential discussion of the notion of weakness of will. In his essay "How Is Weakness of the Will Possible?" Davidson characterizes weakness of will, or incontinence, as involving, roughly, the intentional doing of some action x, when the agent believes that there is some available alternative action y which it would be better for him to do than to do x.[11] Davidson points out that the Aristotelian account of incontinence (sometimes) makes reference to the idea of an agent's going against some (prior) decision or choice, but Davidson wishes to allow us to speak of incontinence even when the agent who performs some act other than the one he judges to be best never actually decided or intended to do that best act, and he mentions passages in Aristotle that lend support to such an understanding of the concept of incontinence or weakness.

Now as we have seen, the moderate individual in a moment of moderate choice may choose an option that benefits him less, is less good for him, than some alternative available in the circumstances. But if he chooses the less good option, does he not in fact fall under Davidson's seemingly reasonable definition of incontinence and thus count as acting irrationally?

I believe we have a confusion here, one that turns in part, but not entirely, on an ambiguity in the notion of an option. When we speak of an individual's deciding between options, the options spoken of may be certain choices, acts of choosing, or the assured results (assuming an absence of uncertainty) of those choices. In the situation where someone chooses between (having) great wealth and (having) moderate wealth, we can think of her options either as choosing great wealth vs. choosing moderate wealth, or as having great wealth vs. having moderate wealth, and small as this difference appears to be and in most circumstances actually is, the distinction is crucial to the existence or non-existence of incontinence in cases of satisficing moderation. Davidson (rightly) characterizes incontinence in terms of actions, not results of actions; it is only when we perform the less good action that weakness of will is said to be involved. But when the moderate individual chooses the option that is less good for himself in the sense that it involves him being less well off than he would be under some other option, we are comparing the results of certain choices. We are saying that (the act of) choosing moderate wealth will

---

[11] Davidson's essay is reprinted in his *Essays on Actions and Events* (Oxford: Clarendon Press, 1980), pp. 21–42.

result in his being less well off than if he had chosen great wealth. Nothing has yet been said about the comparative merits of the choices themselves, in the sense of the acts of choice that are involved here. It is a mistake, therefore, to slide, in the way I illustrated earlier, from the claim that a certain option is less good for someone than some other to the claim that the first option is less good, and thence to the claim that the individual who takes the first option has acted incontinently in Davidson's sense. And if we distinguish between options as states of affairs that result from certain choices and options as choices (or acts of choosing) we shall be less likely to imagine that moderation involves weakness of will. Of course, some philosophers—most notably G. E. Moore in *Principia Ethica*—have assumed as obvious and even as definitional that it is always best to produce the best consequences one can.[12] But deontological moral theories precisely deny this connection, and it gravely misconstrues the character of such theories to assume that they can be reformulated without alteration of content so as to advocate the production of best consequences suitably understood.[13] Since deontological theories are coherent, the connection between best action and action with best results is neither self-evident nor, presumably, definitional; and in any event, it is even less plausible to maintain a tight connection between the best action an individual can perform and the action that benefits *him* most. Just as the individual who sacrifices her well-being for the benefit of others may coherently claim to have done the best she could, to have performed the best act available to her in the circumstances, there is no reason why a moderate individual who rejects dazzling levels of well-being for moderate contentment must hold that it would have been better for him to act otherwise. He has his reasons for rejecting, e.g., great wealth and there seems to be no reason why he should not be willing to stand by what he has done and hold (though he need not proclaim it from the rooftops) that he has done the right thing in the circumstances (given his own tastes and interests). He has done (what he considers) the best thing for him to do, even though he has not acted to insure his own highest or best level of well-being. There seems nothing amiss in what he has done, and there is no reason to suspect him of incontinence once we distinguish the evaluation of results from the evaluation of actions (including choices) and notice that the term "option" is ambiguous as between actions and results.[14]

Now that I have defended satisficing moderation, let me conclude this first lecture by saying something about the directions in which our discussion of moderation can or will take us. The idea that self-seeking rationality may be moderate in its aims and intentions finds a notable parallel within the sphere of morality that I would like at this point to mention briefly. I have argued elsewhere for the existence and defensibility of a kind of "moral satisficing" that is in many ways analogous to the satisficing

---

[12] Cambridge: Cambridge University Press, 1959, p. 25.

[13] Cf. Samuel Scheffler, *The Rejection of Consequentialism* (Oxford: Clarendon Press, 1982).

[14] A similar ambiguity in our usage of "alternative" can similarly lead to confusion and an unwarranted slide from the ascription of moderation to the accusation of incontinence. Cf. Sen, "Rational Fools...," pp. 329, 336.

we discover in the sphere of individualistic rationality.[15] The individualistic rational satisficer does not seek the best for herself and may sometimes deliberately reject the better for the good enough, and I think common-sense morality permits something rather similar within its sphere. Consider an occasion when a moral agent can choose to do either more or less good for others and where the choice of greater good entails no (relative) personal sacrifice to the agent and no violation of deontological restrictions or side-constraints. In such a situation ordinary individuals sometimes do the lesser good for others and yet act in a way that ordinary morality would not condemn or find unacceptable. I have elsewhere provided lengthy illustrations of these sorts of situations, and I shall not repeat the descriptions here. The main point is that rational individualistic satisficing finds a parallel in common-sense moral satisficing, and the latter phenomenon, in turn, evokes the further possibility of satisficing forms of (act-)utilitarianism and (act-)consequentialism. A consistent consequentialist can hold, for example, that an act is morally right if and only if its consequences are good enough in comparison with the consequences of the other acts open to the agent. An act may be morally acceptable, even when there are alternatives whose consequences would be better, if its consequences are very good and close enough to the best that can be accomplished in the circumstances. And such a satisficing version of (utilitarian) act-consequentialism gains support not only from the prevalence and plausibility of moral satisficing within everyday morality, but also from any support we are able to give to the idea of rational individualistic satisficing. Satisficing act-consequentialism has distinct advantages that I have described elsewhere over prevalent optimizing forms of act-consequentialism, but there is no time here to pursue this purely moral-theoretic development of the idea of satisficing moderation. I mention it so that we can see where the idea of moderation can take us, but for present purposes I think it will be best to focus primarily on satisficing and moderation as features of individualistic rationality.

In the second lecture there will be two aspects of such moderation occupying our attention. One emerges from our discussion just now of the reasons an individual may have for deliberately choosing what is less good for herself. I believe our examples of moderation illustrate two fundamentally different kinds of reasons that may lie behind and motivate individual satisficing, and at the beginning of the next lecture I would like to distinguish these two sorts of reasons and explain their significance. I shall then go on to examine another issue that has been almost palpably omitted from our previous discussion: the question whether moderation in our present sense represents any sort of virtue or admirable trait and the connected question whether the tendency, in extra-moral contexts, to optimize with regard to one's own well-being represents a desirable or an unfortunate habit of mind and action. In this first lecture I have defended the rationality of satisficing; but in the next, I shall argue that the optimizing mentality, while not necessarily representing any failure of practical *rationality*, can nonetheless be criticized for its failure to embody certain (other) deep-seated human ideals.

---

[15] In my own contribution to the symposium "Satisficing Consequentialism," and at greater length in chapter 3 of *Common-Sense Morality and Consequentialism* (London: Routledge & Kegan Paul, 1985).

II

1

In the first lecture, I used the expression "satisficing moderation" to refer to a kind of moderation not engaged in for the sake of an overall greater balance of satisfactions, a moderation, therefore, that occupies a sort of conceptual middle ground between asceticism for its own sake and the instrumental virtue of moderation recommended by the Epicureans. But you will also recall that satisficing moderation as I have understood it goes considerably beyond the satisficing that has been defended by Herbert Simon and others in the economics literature of the firm and elsewhere. The satisficing individual may not only fail to seek the best results for himself, but may in certain circumstances actually reject the better or best for the good enough; and I last time argued that there need be nothing irrational about such a choice.

Today, I would like to discuss two quite different reasons for satisficing moderation that can be elicited from our previous examples. To begin with, someone who rejects what is better for himself may feel, as I put it last time, that a certain option will give him much more than he needs, and from the standpoint of a genuinely moderate individual, that will be a reason to reject the option—at least when there is an alternative that provides him with what he feels he does need. A reluctance to go greatly beyond what one (feels one) needs is thus a mark of the moderate individual, the individual modest in her desires or wants, and, at the same time, a locus, for such an individual, of reasons for choosing less than the best for herself or failing to aim for such an optimum. Such reasons are familiar and understandable, though sometimes their expression is a bit more informal and colloquial than anything indicated earlier. If someone keeps pressing me to accept great wealth, lavish accommodation, or an extra dessert, and I, being a moderate individual, keep turning down these things, I may end up saying with some emphasis, in exasperation, "who needs it?" And that will be an expression of the kind of reason mentioned earlier, of the moderate individual's desire not to go way beyond what he actually needs.

Of course, if a host is pressing one to accept an extra dessert, good manners—if not on the host's part, then at least on the part of the guest—might dictate to the moderate individual that he simply accede and take the unwanted extra dessert, but if we imagine a situation where there is less reason to mask one's feelings by forms of politeness, the expression "who needs it?" seems precisely fitted to convey an exasperated reluctance to take much more than one needs, and a moderate individual will naturally express himself in this way either to himself or to others when such circumstances arise. But not just the moderate individual. We can, roughly, characterize the moderate individual as someone whose wants are more modest than those of others and who thus finds herself more frequently than most of us in a situation where she fails to seek or actually turns down good things. But the moderate individuals among us are not some moral–psychologically isolated though understandable subpopulation of our species. There are elements of moderation in most or almost all of us, and a full appreciation of the rational understandability of satisficing moderation requires us to see that this is so.[16] We all say things like "who needs it?" sometimes, and we all turn down afternoon snacks or second desserts or cups of tea on at least some occasions whose underlying circumstances are basically the same as those assumed in the examples mentioned earlier.[17]

In case, however, there are any lingering doubts about how an individual can have reason to reject something good on the grounds that he has no need for it, it may be helpful, at this point, to consider a case where lack of need counts as a reason quite independently of any effect upon the individual's (or anyone else's) well-being. Why is it that if offered a choice between having one copy and having two copies of the morning paper gratis, many of us would prefer to take just one copy? Need it be because we don't want to deprive someone else of a copy or because it is harder to carry around and get rid of two copies of a newspaper?

Surely there are circumstances where neither of these considerations, or anything similar, is relevant, but where, nonetheless, we would be inclined to take one copy rather than two. But why should this be so? The obvious answer, not only in the light of what has already been said but also on grounds of sheer common sense, is that some of us are quite naturally reluctant to take more than we need, when we can have everything we need without doing so. One takes the single paper because it answers one's need for information; one has no need for two newspapers. (I am assuming that one is not worried about losing the single newspaper and/or that the difference between the chance of losing two and the chance of losing one is negligible.) But in the circumstances I have described one is equally well off whether one has one newspaper or two, so if the absence of need moves one to reject the offer of two newspapers it does so quite independently of any consideration of well-being and of the whole issue of optimizing or satisficing. This may help us to see that the fact that something is absolutely unnecessary or much more than one needs really is a reason for action and choice that has force and validity with most human beings—even people who are initially dubious about satisficing will presumably see the point of rejecting the offer of two copies of the morning paper.

However, it might be possible to grant total lack of need a rational status in cases of the sort I have just mentioned, while denying the rationality of satisficing as described earlier. One might say that considerations of well-being are always lexically prior to considerations of non-need, so that the fact of non-need can be used to break ties in situations, like that of the morning newspaper, where one is (by hypothesis) equally well-off whichever way one chooses, but cannot overcome differences of well-being. The fact that a certain level of well-being or enjoyment is much more than one needs would then fail to justify rejecting such well-being or enjoyment in favor of what was (merely) good enough, and satisficing moderation as we have

---

[16] It is also possible, I suppose, for there to be isolated areas of satisficing (optimizing) tendency within a predominantly optimizing (satisficing) personality.

[17] The notion of need at work in satisficing moderation is not basic human need, the requirements of life itself, but some more flexible notion. If someone offers us dinner, we would not ordinarily refuse on the grounds that (given that we have already had two meals that day) dinner is much more than we need (to stay alive and keep functioning). What we take to exceed what we need may therefore be relative to social circumstances and individual background.

described it would remain an irrational phenomenon, despite the fact that the appeal to a lack of need can *sometimes* justify rejecting an alternative.

Such a move is highly reminiscent of the treatment of considerations of equality in Sidgwick's utilitarianism. As Rawls and others have noted, Sidgwick allows considerations of equality to have an influence on moral choices only to break ties among choices with equally good (pleasant) consequences.[18] Considerations of aggregate well-being are lexically prior to reasons of equality, and this in effect gives equality a minimal role in Sidgwick's theory, a role far less than defenders of the moral importance of equality would be willing to accept. It has always struck me, however, and I am sure this will also have occurred to others, that Sidgwick's compromise theory represents a somewhat unstable solution to the problem of giving adequate weight to considerations of aggregate welfare and to considerations of equality within an acceptable total moral theory. Sidgwick's idea that equality has enough weight only to break ties seems to be an extraneous imposition, in the name of reconciliation with common-sense intuitions, upon an underlying utilitarian moral conception. Utilitarianism itself and what motivates utilitarianism according to traditional conceptions can provide no source of support for an independent factor of equality even as a means of breaking ties. Consistent with the motivation underlying utilitarianism, then, it would seem more appropriate to say that equally felicific (optimific) acts are both entirely permissible and right, even if one of them tends towards more equality than the other, and indeed more recent versions of act-utilitarianism have tended to drop any suggestion that equality ought to be used to break ties. Either equality counts for nothing intrinsically in the moral assessment of actions, or it should have a weight far greater than that allowed it by Sidgwick.

My own feeling, for what it is worth, is that the situation with regard to lack of need is quite similar. If one really grants that the fact one doesn't need two newspapers can represent a sensible reason to take a single paper, then considerations of non-need have and must be admitted to have a force independent of considerations of greater or less well-being. But if they do, then in those numerous satisficing cases where those considerations at least *seem* to have force sufficient to overcome certain kinds of considerations of well-being, we have, I think, no reason to doubt that such force exists. If we grant the independent existence of reasons of non-need, it seems implausible and untrue to our own best sense of things to hold that such considerations have force enough only to break ties and can never stand up against considerations of well-being. So once it becomes clear that non-need can function as a reason *independently* of well-being, as with our newspaper example, it should become easier to accept the idea that non-need can have force *against* the idea of well-being, and satisficing moderation may seem less perplexing and outré as a phenomenon.

We have, so far, been concentrating on a single kind of rationale that can lie behind and motivate satisficing moderation. But our examples in fact reveal another quite different kind of consideration that can motivate the moderate individual and each and every one of us in her more moderate moments. In the first lecture, in

---

[18] See Rawls, *A Theory of Justice*, p. 77; Sen, "Utilitarianism and Welfarism," pp. 469f.; and Sidgwick, *The Methods of Ethics*, pp. 417, 447.

discussing the standpoint of someone who turns down an afternoon snack or an extra slice of cake, I characterized such an individual not only as feeling no need for some additional good thing, but also as feeling perfectly satisfied as she is. Lack of need, of course, is the sort of reason for satisficing we have just been describing in some detail, but the idea that someone is perfectly satisfied as she is invokes a new sort of satisficing consideration that is worth examining. In the situation where one is being asked to choose between one and two newspapers, or between great and moderate wealth, there is no issue of retaining the status quo, either newspaperless or lacking wealth altogether; but in the case where one is offered an afternoon snack or a second dessert, retaining the status quo is a considered option and is actually preferred to a good-yielding change. And I believe such cases contain a distinctive reason for satisficing precisely in virtue of the fact that the status quo is involved as an option. The very fact that some satisfactory or satisfying state is the one actually enjoyed at a given time may at that time yield a reason for preferring to remain in that state rather than make some transition to a satisfactory alternative state; and a certain primacy of the actual may thus be part of what lies behind the rejection of a second dessert or afternoon snack. Part, I want to suggest, not all, because such examples also gain support from the fact that the individual involved feels no need for the dessert or snack. But the absence of need cannot, I think, be all that is involved in making the examples plausible. An individual turning down a second dessert might idiomatically express himself by saying "No, thank you, I'm fine as I am," and such a remark implicitly refers not only to the absence of any felt need for an additional dessert but also to the acceptability of the status quo. However, there are other cases where the same idiomatic remark would be made, but where there was nothing either to be gained or lost by abandoning the status quo, and I believe such cases give the clearest indication of the independent status, as a reason, of the sheer fact of actual (present) satisfactoriness.

Consider another harmless example concerning newspapers. Imagine that you are staying at a hotel and are one morning reading one of the newspapers the hotel provides gratis to its guests. Imagine further that one of the hotel's employees, newly arrived on the job, is so nervous and so eager to please that he offers you a different copy of the same paper in exchange for the one you have. "Perhaps you'd rather have this copy of the paper instead, sir," he says. Let us imagine that it is perfectly clear that this other copy is in no way superior to the one you have, and also that there is no issue of your keeping both copies—every available copy is needed for the use of the guests. We have a clear example of misplaced attentiveness and recognizing this, but not wanting to hurt the feelings of the overeager employee, you simply say: "No, thank you, I'm doing just fine with the copy I have."[19]

What will be the motivation for rejecting the offered paper? Surely not the energy it takes to switch papers—it also takes energy to turn the offer down and a quick

---

[19] Of course, if one wanted to humor the employee, one might accept the exchange. But it seems perfectly reasonable to reject the exchange and in that case the reason will be as I have said. Also, I am not denying that we sometimes go against the status quo in the name of variety. But where variety is not an issue, as with the present example, the status quo can play a role in motivating our choices.

comparison of energies expended is highly unlikely to lie behind the rejection. But neither, as in so many of our other examples, can the motivation derive from the fact that the newspaper offered in exchange is seen as much more than one really needs or cares about. We are supposing one does really want to have a paper. In the circumstances mentioned there can only be one reason for turning down the exchange, the fact that one is fine, or doing fine, *as one is*, and I believe that the motivating force of the status quo is clearly evidenced in the just-mentioned example. But if the satisfactoriness of the status quo is a motivating factor in cases where the issue of going beyond what one needs is irrelevant, I see no reason to deny it a (reinforcing) role in those cases where the issue of need or lack of need is also present. The person who turns down an afternoon snack would seem to have two sorts of motivation for doing so: the fact that he doesn't particularly need or care about the snack in question; and the entirely satisfactory nature of his present state, of the status quo; and when someone uses an expression like "I am perfectly satisfied as I am" to turn down such a snack, he invokes both of these factors.

We have thus discovered two different sorts of reasons for moderate choice within the array of examples I have been using to defend the non-irrationality of satisficing moderation. There may well be other sorts of considerations that are capable of motivating moderation, but for the moment, at least, I am unable to detect them. It is at any rate worth mentioning that the two factors we *have* pointed out bear a rather surprising, and even eerie, analogy to considerations that are thought to influence scientists in the selection and evaluation of hypotheses. Simplicity as methodological desideratum involves a preference for explanations that minimize assumed principles or posits, that do not multiply entities or assumptions beyond necessity. But this tendency in scientific theorizing clearly resembles the moderate individual's rejection of options that bring her much more than she needs or cares about.[20] By the same token, methodological conservatism, the theoretical preference for already-familiar satisfactory theories or hypotheses, is strongly reminiscent of the preference for the satisfactory status quo that seems to animate a good deal of ordinary practical rationality.

I do not, however, want to place too great an emphasis on these parallels or to attempt to derive the validity of reasons for satisficing moderation from the acceptability of parallel reasons within the theoretical or scientific sphere. For one thing, the analogy is quite limited, and there are actually some striking disanalogies between scientific methodology and satisficing moderation. Not everyone is a satisficer, is moderate in his wants, and people differ greatly in regard to the frequency with which they act in ways deemed to be moderate; but it is not clear that there are any parallel differences among scientists in regard to the emphasis on theoretical simplicity or the conservation of principles and hypotheses. Perhaps there are; quite possibly there are not; and in any event discussion of that issue lies outside the main focus of these talks and is well beyond my competence. But the partial analogy between satisficing practical rationality and two important aspects of scientific methodology is nonetheless worth noting. Having done so, I would like now to focus on the main question to be

---

[20] An individual who preferred moderate wealth could be said to have a preference for simplicity in his life.

considered in this second lecture, whether there is anything particularly praiseworthy about satisficing moderation. I think, however, that we shall be in a position to make a proper evaluation of moderation only if we put the opposing tendency towards optimizing into proper perspective. The widespread tendency to treat optimization as the only mode of practical rationality has blinded us, I think, to some negative features of the tendency to optimize, and once we recognize the non-irrationality of satisficing, it becomes easier to see how unfortunate the tendency to optimize really is and to place a proper evaluation on the contrary tendency towards moderation.

2

It has sometimes been pointed out that the optimizing tendency may be in some measure self-defeating. A person bent on eking out the most good he can in any given situation will take pains and suffer anxieties that a more casual individual will avoid, and it is hardly clear that the pains and anxieties will (on average) be compensated for by goods garnered through optimizing alertness and energy. Moreover, it may be a psychological truth that an optimizing individual, someone who always seeks to make the best of the situations she is in, will tend to be unhappy when things are not going well, i.e., when she has to make the best of a bad situation; and the more moderate individual might, as a matter of empirical fact, be more likely to remain contented when things were not going well. But the above points turn on psychological assumptions and contingencies which, though plausible, do not reflect our deepest reasons for questioning, and even deprecating, the optimizing temperament. The habit of optimizing has intrinsic, essential features in the light of which I think we shall inevitably think less well of those who have that habit. It is no accident—though the matter has been obscured by the univocal preference for an optimizing form of practical rationality—that optimizing cannot be regarded either as a desirable or as an admirable trait.

Consider, first, how much more planful and self-conscious the continual optimizer must be in comparison with the satisficer who does not always aim for the best and who sometimes rejects the best or better for the good enough. The satisficer need not consider and compare as many possibilities as the optimizer—indeed, quite typically, the satisficer will pursue the first option he notices; if it seems reasonably satisfactory, he will not bother even to consider other possibilities. Now the optimizer will see such a failure to consider alternatives as an irrational, perhaps even a wilful, refusal to consider one's own best interests; and from the standpoint of such interests, as they define the perspective of the optimizing individual, the satisficer does seem irrational. But we are not restricted, in considering the merits of optimization and satisficing, to the internal standpoint of the optimizer. Nothing dictates its preference or preferable status as a reference point for evaluation. We should also be interested, perhaps even be primarily interested, in how optimization can be seen and understood from a more impersonal perspective, most particularly, in how the optimizer *looks to others*.

Planfulness, self-consciousness, circumspection are all (noncontingent) enemies of spontaneity and of a plucky adventurousness that most of us think well of, even admire. Prudence and the possession of a long-range life plan, for example, have sometimes been granted the status of virtues in almost grudging, and certainly in lukewarm, terms, and the reason has typically been a countervailing sense of the spontaneity and boldness that on purely conceptual grounds must be missing from the life governed by prudence and life-planfulness.[21] Optimizing at given different times need not, I suppose, involve any sort of spelled-out life-plan nor even the playing-it-safe so characteristic of prudence in the ordinary sense. But the habit of optimizing does share the aspect of unspontaneous and constrained living that is characteristic of these other traits, and it is in all these cases a conceptual fact, not an accidental psychological generalization, that these negative features should attach to what are sometimes presumed to be virtues. We, to some extent, feel sorry for, think less well of, someone lacking in spontaneity, and the optimizing individual, who lacks spontaneity in a very high degree, can hardly seem admirable when regarded under that aspect. But that is not all.

The optimizing person is possessed of other negative features that further serve to undercut our antecedent sense that optimizing rationality is a desirable or admirable human trait. The optimizing individual—again, as a matter of conceptual necessity, not of accidental psychology—seems lacking in self-sufficiency. Now self-sufficiency as I shall be describing it is a much-ignored trait, partly, I think, because the claims of self-sufficiency were so thoroughly overemphasized and exaggerated by philosophers in the ancient world. The Stoics in particular exalted self-sufficiency, *autarkeia*, to the status of an absolute and practically exclusive standard for evaluating human good and virtue, and we have every reason to shy away from their excesses. For the Stoic, the wise man or sage would be absolutely self-sufficient in his well-being, depending neither on loved ones nor on the fortunes of this world for his ultimate happiness. Nothing subject to loss or risk can feature in such a conception of happiness. But the Stoic ideal is not ours, and we have grown wary, and more than wary, of attempts to seal off human excellence or well-being from the risks and taints of the world, and of our less-than-ideal human nature.[22] We are very much in danger, as a result, of throwing out the baby with the bathwater and failing to recognize elements in the Stoic ideal that touch us very deeply and cannot be characterized as some sort of neurotic attempt to make human life absolutely safe. The ideal of self-sufficiency need not be carried to Stoic extremes, and indeed the notion has great currency in ordinary thinking about the world. We value, we admire self-sufficiency in the ordinary sense of the term, and a soberer ideal of such self-sufficiency can in fact be used as a touchstone for the criticism of optimization. Consider, again, how the optimizer appears to others. Will not his tendency to eke out the most or best he can in every situation strike someone who witnesses or hears about it as lacking in self-sufficiency? Will not the optimizer appear needy and grasping and his persistent efforts a form, practically, of desperation, by contrast with the satisficer who accepts the good enough when he gets it. Modesty in one's desires and/or needs is, and is as a matter of conceptual fact, an expression of self-sufficiency as ordinarily understood. A person eager for and intent upon the best (for himself) automatically appears (other things equal) less self-sufficient than a satisficer satisfied with less than the best, and so I

---

[21] See my *Goods and Virtues*, chap. 2 *passim* and p. 118.

[22] On this topic, see *Goods and Virtues*, chap. 6.

am saying, among other things, that there is an inherent connection between aiming for what one takes to be sufficient, rather than for what is best, and a kind of personal self-sufficiency that most of us think well of.[23] To the extent the optimizer thus seems needy and somewhat desperate, as well as cramped and unspontaneous, we shall feel sorry for him and find it difficult, if not impossible, to think well of him. If anything, the habit of optimization will have to be taken as an anti-virtue, an unfortunate and lamentable human character trait. And the habit of moderation would then naturally take its place as a desirable trait, a (non-moral) virtue—a minor virtue perhaps, not the most admirable trait known to man, but a trait, nonetheless, in whose absence a human being becomes somewhat unfortunate and pitiable.

It is worth going back and considering how we have managed to arrive at this conclusion—I am sure those initially in favor of optimizing will suspect some sleight of hand or fallacy in the argument. We have arrived at the above (re) evaluation of the merits of optimization and satisficing moderation by deliberately refusing to judge the issue from the standpoint of the optimizing rational (and I have not questioned his rationality) individual. From such a standpoint optimizing choice must invariably seem not only rational, but ideal, and the "strategy" (as the optimizer might put it) of the satisficer irrational, pathetic, absurd. After all, from the optimizer's standpoint (and barring all moral issues for the limited purposes of this discussion) the whole point of action is to serve one's own interests and well-being, and for the optimizer it must seem self-evident that such an aim involves serving those interests, that well-being, to the greatest extent possible. It is only when one gets outside the optimizer's way of seeing things and tries to empathize with the satisficing temperament—seeing things from the satisficer's standpoint—that one may begin to recognize that optimizing is not an inevitable or inescapable rational tendency. Once satisficing is understood sympathetically, we have the wherewithal to take a disinterested or objective look at the underlying personality structure or character of both the optimizing and the satisficing individual. And, as we have seen, a comparison of these two ideal types enables us to recognize some desirable features the satisficer possesses but the optimizer lacks.

The insistence on going outside a given point of view in evaluating those who have that point of view is hardly a new thing in philosophy. We all know that we cannot hope in most cases to justify an attribution of insanity by appeal to, or while remaining within the perspective of, the insane individual, yet most of us believe some people are and can be known to be insane—the man, for example, who thinks he is Catherine the Great. However, we have not always gone beyond the recognition of such extreme cases, beyond the idea that the evaluation of certain traits must transcend the perspective of those who have the traits, to apply this notion in other cases where it cries out for application.

Consider, for example, the long history of the "subjective turn" in post-Cartesian epistemology. Sceptical doubt has a much-honored place in such epistemology, and from the standpoint of someone who wishes to answer but finds it difficult to answer such doubts, it may naturally seem as if all further philosophizing, all other areas of

---

[23] In emphasizing appearances here and elsewhere, I am not raising epistemological doubts, but rather conveying the assumption that personal traits need to be evaluated at least in part from a social perspective (and from a perspective at least partly external to that imposed by the traits themselves).

philosophy, must be held in abeyance until skeptical doubt has been answered. Moreover, since epistemological doubt calls into question the whole external world and all our ordinary assumptions about that world, it may seem reasonable, to someone in the grip of such doubt, to suspend or consider questionable those daily activities which play down or ignore (the validity of) such doubts. An ordinary person will not usually display doubts about whether his home will still be there when he returns from work, for example, but from the perspective of unanswered epistemological doubt, such doubts are in some sense more reasonable, deeper, and more admirable, than the ordinary unquestioning confidence that one's house is still there, or that some other fact relevant to practical thinking and action is as we normally would assume it to be. The epistemological perspective from which the difficulty of answering skepticism is of paramount importance thus defines a point of view from which a certain sort of hesitancy in practical affairs is some sort of (intellectual or rational) virtue, but when we leave epistemological skepticism behind, such hesitancy or doubt in practical affairs appears, as it would ordinarily appear to most of us, as an undesirable trait, a failure of efficiency or adaptation, a neurotic lack of self-confidence, or whatever.[24]

Recently, of course, epistemology has been increasingly naturalized. And one crucial aspect of the naturalization has been the tendency to stop seeing epistemological problems and concepts from the traditional internal, or subjective, perspective of someone trying to overcome skepticism and (so to speak) reestablish contact with the world, and rather to view them as arising or not arising for an individual inextricably and essentially tied to his environment—an individual who registers an environment through sensation and perception and who affects that environment through deliberation, choice, and volition. The naturalized epistemologist is thus encouraged to evaluate traits of thinking and acting in terms of their likelihood of enabling successful representation of or action upon an individual's (or a group's) environment, and judged from this new standpoint, it should be clear why epistemological doubt, however valid and admirable from the standpoint of traditional epistemological concerns, should appear less desirable and more questionable than it does from that other perspective. Again, once we assume an environment with people interacting in it, the tendency to doubt such an environment and the people in it may easily begin to appear undesirable and, even, absurd. And the reevaluation of epistemological doubting and of the philosopher's sense, deep down, that there is something quite admirable about the person who hesitates or doubts about whether his house is still there requires us to leave the internal perspective of skepticism and view matters more externally or environmentally, in much the same way that a more objective approach calls the value of optimization into question.[25]

---

[24] Cf. the title essay in John Wisdom's *Philosophy and Psychoanalysis* (Oxford: Basil Blackwell, 1957).

[25] For examples of the naturalizing approach, see D. M. Armstrong, *Belief, Truth, and Knowledge* (London: Routledge and Kegan Paul, 1973); W. V. Quine, "Epistemology Naturalized," reprinted in R. M. Chisholm and R. Swartz, eds., *Empirical Knowledge* (Englewood Cliffs, N.J.: Prentice-Hall, 1973): pp. 59–74; and E. Sosa, "The Raft and the Pyramid," in *Midwest Studies in Philosophy V* (1980, *Studies in Epistemology*), esp. p. 23, where Sosa states: "In epistemology, there is reason to think that the most useful and illuminating notion of intellectual virtue will prove broader than our tradition would suggest and must give due weight not only to the subject and his intrinsic nature but also to his environment and to his epistemic community."

Something similar to what happens in the case of optimizing also occurs within moral philosophy. Conscientiousness in the ordinary sense—meticulous attention to whether one is doing the right thing and to questions about what would be the right thing to do—is a trait that has sometimes been singled out for praise by ethical theorists.[26] And from the standpoint of someone who is highly conscientious, it can seem that since one wants to do the right thing, the more time spent carefully considering what is right the better. Any diminution of attention to the rightness or wrongness of one's actions will then seem morally slapdash or sluggish, proof of a deplorable lack of seriousness about morality. However, when we consider how meticulous conscientiousness looks in comparison with a less pervasive attention to the rightness and wrongness of one's actions, its justification and admirability can easily come into question. Conscientiousness can seem anxiety-ridden and compulsive in comparison with a less pervasive (more satisficing) concern with how morally well one is acting, and such a comparison essentially depends on leaving conscientiousness's own perspective and attempting to find a more objective or environmental perspective on that phenomenon. But having discussed at some length the general usefulness of getting outside the perspective generated by a certain trait when that trait is itself the subject of evaluation, let me return to the issue of optimizing vs. satisficing and clarify our previous conclusions in that area by means of a comparison, yet again, with similar conclusions that can be reached about morality and concern for others.

3

Our previous discussion has tended toward the conclusion that we should think less well of the (purely) optimizing temperament than of the disposition towards satisficing moderation. (Of course, I am not assuming that the moderate individual will never seek the best—I am speaking of moderation as a tendency, as a major element in personality, and contrasting this disposition with the disposition to optimize whenever there is an issue for rational deliberation and choice.) However, in comparing satisficing and optimizing to the detriment of the latter, I have said nothing against the rationality of optimizing. I have treated both satisficing and optimizing as forms of practical rationality. We shall perhaps be less surprised by this set of conclusions if we consider the rather parallel set of conclusions that can be reached on the subject of altruism, the concern for others. Those who would defend altruism often seek to show that egoism, exclusive devotion to one's well-being, is self-stultifying and that one is likely to be better off, happier, if one devotes oneself to others. But such arguments are not always convincing and, in any case, usually depend on empirical assumptions that may be denied or fail to hold for a given individual. But independently of the possible benefits, to an agent, of an altruistic attitude and altruistic deeds, we non-egoists (and even perhaps many egoists) find something attractive and admirable in an attitude of concern for others, and pure egoism, by contrast, seems repellent and inhumane. Most of us tend to think less well of someone who

---

[26] See James Wallace, *Virtues and Vices* (Ithaca, N.Y.: Cornell University Press, 1978), p. 91.

is incapable of concern for others, and this opinion in no way depends, I think, on a belief that an egoist's egoism prevents him from doing as well as he can for himself. There is something inherently unattractive, even pathetic, about total egoistic self-concern, but in reacting thus to the image of the egoistic individual, I do not think we are necessarily imagining that there is anything irrational about the egoist. We may deplore the limitation of his practical concerns, but that failure does not typically strike us as a failure of practical rationality—we have other words, and we have just used some of them, for describing what we object to in such an individual—and of course in the actual pursuit of his limited objectives, there need be no failure of practical rationality on the part of the egoist.[27] On the other hand, it is difficult to show that there is anything irrational about altruism either. Altruism seemingly requires a willingness to sacrifice one's own well-being for that of others, but unless the moral point of view is itself a form of irrationality, an illusion, it is difficult to see why self-sacrifice should not be a rational option for an individual with genuine concern for others.[28] So the area of morality yields, in connection with the opposition between altruism and egoism,[29] a situation rather similar to what we have uncovered in the opposition between individualistic satisficing and individualistic optimizing. Although neither individualistic satisficing nor individualistic optimizing can be faulted on grounds of rationality, we have a better opinion of the satisficing tendency; and by the same token, although we have no reason to hold that either egoism or altruism is a form of practical irrationality, we do have reason for thinking more highly of the altruistic tendency—and in fact our higher regard for altruism is at least partly based on considerations paralleling those that actuate our better opinion of satisficing moderation.

There is something cramped and constrained not only, as we have seen, about the tendency to optimize, but also about an exclusive concern with one's own interests and well-being. And like the optimizing individual, the egoist will appear lacking in self-sufficiency—as Nietzsche reminds us, benevolence towards others is a characteristic expression of a sense of satisfaction with oneself or with what one has; the ungenerous individual conveys an unavoidable appearance (relative, at least, to any recognizably human psychology) of dissatisfaction and insufficiency. So at least some of the reasons for our low opinion of egoistic individuals—the reasons deriving less from our moral and altruistic feelings and more from our sense of what is properly and self-respectingly human—mirror our earlier criticisms of the optimizing temperament, and I believe the interplay and analogy between what philosophers

---

[27] It is traditionally assumed that the egoist must be an optimizer, but our discussion should make clear the possibility of a satisficing form of egoism. On this see my *Common-Sense Morality and Consequentialism*, chap. 3, section 4. Incidentally, I have tried to simplify the discussion by focusing on egoistic reasons to promote one's own well-being and on altruistic or moral reasons for action, to the exclusion of certain desires for achievement, e.g., the desire to solve certain problems in mathematics. But even our desires/reasons for achievement can be realized in a satisficing manner. On the relation between desires for achievement and egoism, see Derek Parfit, *Reasons and Persons* (Oxford: Clarendon Press, 1984), Part Two.

[28] See Sen, "Rational Fools...," esp. pp. 241ff.; and Parfit, *loc. cit.*

[29] But also in connection with the opposition between egoism and moral ideas/imperatives not particularly tied to altruism.

find it natural to say about the opposition between egoism and altruism and what I have here suggested about the opposition between moderation and optimization may help to clarify and support the picture I have been offering.

Both altruism and moderation are traits requiring cultivation within the individual. In some sense they do not come naturally, and parents, teachers, and others have a difficult task on their hands when they attempt to overcome or mitigate children's insatiable selfishness and greed. The typical simplified picture of how a child develops intrinsic concern for others involves the assumption that children need to go through an intermediate stage where they see a concern for others as furthering their own interests; and a similarly simplified picture of the attenuation of childhood demandingness and greediness might well depict the child as having to go through a stage where moderation was seen (in the Epicurean manner) merely as a means to greater overall satisfaction (the cake will spoil your dinner or give you a tummy ache). But just as the development of some degree of intrinsic concern for others is typically regarded as a form of moral progress, I believe that the development of some degree of non-instrumental moderation is also a good thing, a kind of human progress.

This is not, of course, to deny that moderation for its own sake can be overdone or that instrumental moderation is useful and sometimes admirable. Asceticism, certain forms of puritanism, and the Stoic indifference to the goods of this world all seem examples of moderation gone haywire; and what I have been recommending, or at least commending, is something soberer that sticks closer to the facts of human psychology. The Stoics elevated self-sufficiency to the be-all and end-all of virtue and assumed a capacity within our nature to remain genuinely unconcerned with all those this-worldly things which might compromise the highest degree of self-sufficiency; but a life free of need and risk seems in fact to be impossible for us; and total self-sufficiency, the Stoic *autarkeia*, appears to be an illusory ideal for us to strive after: the purported Stoic sage who claims indifference to all people and things is nowadays naturally suspect, if not worse, in our eyes.[30]

On the other hand, the merely instrumental moderation recommended by the Epicureans, although it may constitute some sort of practical virtue, contains none of those elements of self-sufficiency that make *autarkeia* initially so appealing. By contrast, the non-instrumental satisficing moderation I have been describing does embody an ideal, part of the Stoic ideal, of self-sufficiency, and if, as I believe, such moderation is a typical product of normal individual psychological development, then we may have succeeded here in characterizing a soberer ideal of self-sufficiency than anything to be found in Stoicism.[31] Moreover, just as it is possible to overdo

---

[30] Cf. *Goods and Virtues*, chap. 6.

[31] According to Aristotle and many, many others, a (morally) virtuous individual may feel pleasure or satisfaction at having done what virtue requires, even if she was not aiming at such pleasure in acting virtuously. Aristotle sometimes implies that the satisfaction of acting virtuously will always exceed the satisfactions one has to forgo in the name of virtue (see, e.g., the *Nichomachean Ethics*, 1169a 2–25). But there is absolutely no reason to make this assumption or the more general assumption that the virtuous individual is never required to sacrifice her own well-being or self-interest. (On this see my *Goods and Virtues*, ch. 5.) Similar points apply to satisficing moderation. If what has been said in the text above is on

moderation, altruism too can be overdone and distorted. There is perhaps nothing immoral about total selflessness, about giving one's own well-being no weight at all in deciding what to do, but it is difficult, e.g., to admire a Père Goriot who compulsively sacrifices everything to the advancement of his daughters. And so we have yet another interesting parallel between altruism and satisficing moderation.

To complete our discussion of the virtue of moderation, we must say something, finally, about how satisficing moderation as described here relates to the Aristotelian virtue of moderation or temperance. Aristotle actually uses two terms that can be translated as "moderate." One of them, *sōphrōn*, designates one of Aristotle's main moral virtues and represents a habit of "medial" choice and desire with respect to bodily pleasures. The temperate or moderate individual, in this sense, desires and chooses the right or reasonable amount of food or sex in the various changing circumstances of his life, where this right amount lies in a mean between extremes. This concept of moderation is part of Aristotle's general *theory* of the virtues, but in canvassing received opinion and common-sense ethical views, Aristotle sometimes uses another term, *metrios*, which also can be translated as "moderate." In his discussion of justice, for example, he points out that those who take less than they deserve and give others more than they strictly deserve are sometimes praised for their moderation or modesty (*Nicomachean Ethics*, 1136b 15–24). Here, and in a few other places in the *Nicomachean Ethics*, Aristotle uses the term *metrios*; the more frequent term for moderation (or temperance) is *sōphrōn*, and the latter conveys Aristotle's theoretical view about the virtues. *Metrios*, by contrast, is used to express an ordinary Greek idea of moderation, and as such I believe it comes very close to the concept of moderation delineated in these lectures.

It is easy enough to confuse, or be confused about the relation between, these two notions, not only because in English one and the same term can be used to convey either of them, but also because there is at least some common conceptual basis for the identical translation. Both notions strongly convey the idea of a mean between extremes. But the notions diverge in other respects, and by pointing out how, we shall be in a position to see that the account of moderation offered here is not just some variant upon or inchoate version of Aristotle's theory of moderation. The two are essentially alternative and possibly incommensurate pictures of what is admirable, or virtuous, in human character.

If we restrict our attention to the pursuit of bodily pleasures—an area to which Aristotle explicitly limits the term *sōphrōn* and to which the present account of moderation is in the first instance most naturally applied, then two related salient differences arise with respect to these two conceptions of moderation. For Aristotle, moderation entails the taking of the *right* amount, let us say, of food (for the moderate individual to take in various different circumstances); and the perception or recognition of what is the right amount on a given occasion involves, for such an

---

the right track, then a moderate individual may derive a pleased sense of self-sufficiency from satisficing; but in satisficing he is not aiming at this satisfaction, nor is there any reason to assume that the satisfaction involved is always greater than those forgone through satisficing. Satisficing need be no more illusory than self-sacrifice.

individual, a display of practical wisdom. So the right amount is the one and only amount it is *rational* for the individual to take.

To that extent, Aristotle's view of moderation as a virtue differs essentially from the account offered here. The present view involves no concept of the right amount of food or whatever for an individual to desire or take, and if we look into the phenomenology of the ordinary moderation I have discussed it is easy to see why. The individual who refuses a second cup of tea or a snack (or an extra pot of gold) may support what she is doing by saying she is fine as she is, but we would not expect such an individual to have the further thought that there is a right amount of tea, snacks, or money (for her) and that taking anything more (or less) would push her beyond (leave her short of) that right amount. Ordinary moderate satisficing is typically less rationalistic (or moralistic) than that, and that fact leads us to the second feature of difference between the Aristotelian view and that offered here. Just as our ordinary sense that moral individuals are more admirable than egoists need not lead us to say that the former are inherently more or less rational than the latter, so too our ordinary sense of the greater admirability, or virtue, of the moderate individual, as contrasted with the optimizer, involves no assumption that either sort of individual is essentially more rational. Even if the exercise of moderation in our sense involves choosing somewhere between extremes, some level that counts as good enough short of the best possible, it should not be concluded that our sense of what is good enough involves the perception of what level of good is uniquely dictated by reason. It may involve a sense of what is good enough that cannot be codified by principles and that may thus require something naturally called perception, and, like Aristotle's notion, it may involve essential variability from individual to individual and from situation to situation; but it will be different from the perception Aristotle requires for temperance in being focused specifically on what is good enough and fine rather than on what it is right or rational for an individual to choose. Thus for Aristotle what is admirable about moderation is that it is a unique exercise and expression of rationality, but the present view bases its high regard for moderation on its characteristic lack of constraint and its characteristic self-sufficiency, although it has been essential to the view presented that there at least be nothing irrational in what we ordinarily call moderation.

We began these lectures by considering whether philosophers, economists, game-theorists, and others may not traditionally have had too narrow a conception of rational choice and action. I attempted to argue that satisficing (both in forms familiar to economists and in forms that go well beyond what the economists have been willing to allow) is in fact a prevalent, even a pervasive, phenomenon of human life; but I attempted to argue that such satisficing should not be considered a form of human irrationality, but rather an exception, a widespread exception, to the received view that practical rationality involves some sort of optimization. Certainly there are many egregious, and frightening, examples of pervasive human irrationality to be cited, but it seems to me, and I have argued, that in the present instance the accusation of irrationality does not fit; what must be adjusted, rather, is our antecedent theoretical notions about what rationality is.

In some sense, the optimizing model of rationality is already somewhat attenuated by the admission that moral and, in particular, altruistic considerations can limit someone's rational pursuit of his own well-being. For the implication is that egoism—the pursuit of one's own well-being—may be rationally limited from without, i.e., by considerations extrinsic to egoism. What has not been realized—though it might have been expected to present itself at least as a purely formal possibility—is that the pursuit of one's well-being may also be rationally limited from within. Egoism, individualistic extra-moral rationality, may be inherently *self-limiting*, and our entire discussion of satisficing moderation as rational and as a virtue has been intended to show that this formal possibility can be fleshed out to enrich and correct distortions in our moral–psychological understanding of human beings.

Rational Dilemmas and Rational Supererogation

The recent literature of philosophy contains many discussions of moral dilemmas. The idea that there may be situations where (through no prior fault or guilt of one's own) one finds it impossible to avoid guilt, to avoid wrongdoing, has been defended, criticized, and mined for its implications: with increasing frequency, the idea of moral dilemmas has become a focus of ethical discussion. In this essay, I would like to consider a related issue which may be useful in casting light on the merits of the case for moral dilemmas, but which is of considerable independent interest. We are by now familiar with the ways in which issues concerning morality and concerning practical rationality can run parallel, and although I would not want to suggest that rationality and morality are in every way analogous, it seems to me we have devoted insufficient attention to a possible major parallel: the case for the possibility of rational dilemmas has yet to be explicitly made. In what follows I would like to consider how that case might be made and to what extent it differs from what may be said in favor of the existence of moral dilemmas. In the course of doing so, we shall find ourselves having to consider the unsettling possibility that, in parallel with what is frequently said about morality, there may be such a thing as rational supererogation, i.e., supererogatory degrees of practical rationality. But the latter topic is perhaps best left alone till our unfolding discussion of rational dilemmas forces us to consider it.

I

What would count as a rational dilemma? Presumably, and there is no reason to question this, a situation in which through no practical fault of her own, an agent found it impossible to act rationally, to make a rational choice among two or more alternatives. Let us see whether we can model such a situation on considerations in the area of practical rationality that parallel the factors that are said, by defenders of moral dilemma, to give rise to moral dilemmas.

In the most frequently-discussed putative case of moral dilemmas, Agamemnon has to choose between violating his duty as a parent and violating his duty as the leader of a military expedition, and defenders of the view that his situation is truly (morally) tragic have held that each of these duties applies with undiminished force despite the existence and applicability of the other.[1] That is, neither duty overrides the other so as to make it right not to fulfill the other; rather both have their full force as duties, all things considered, and for that reason Agamemnon must incur guilt (not just an obligation to make amends) whatever he decides to do.

Those advocating the existence of a moral dilemma in such a case as this hold that each of the conflicting obligations or duties has moral force of its own, and that it is a superiority of common-sense morality over consequentialism that it allows for such varying sources of moral obligation and thus can accommodate the complexity of the moral life. The existence of dilemmas is but one illustration, according to this view, of the richness, subtlety and difficulty of the moral life. Now whether consequentialism or utilitarianism is really banned from the enjoyment of this intellectual bounty is a question to which we shall return a little later. For the moment let us consider whether any structure similar to what arguably exists in Agamemnon's situation of tragic choice can be found in any case of rational decision making. Can precepts or principles of practical rationality conflict for a given agent in a given situation in such way that there is no way for the agent to act rationally, no action which it would be rational for the agent to choose?

We can see what such a situation would have to be like in order to represent a convincing analogue of Agamemnon-type moral dilemmas. There are precepts like "one ought to give weight to one's future interests" and "one ought not take unnecessary chances with one's own life" which can readily be seen as common-sensical *prima facie* principles of rationality. A Rossian-type view of such precepts would treat them as mutually adjustable and balanceable in such a way that whenever they conflict, one or another (or some group) of them always takes precedence over, overrides, or outweighs, those in conflict with it, with the result that there is at least one rational or rationally justified thing for one to do. But one could question this view by claiming, in parallel with what has been said about Agamemnon's tragic situation, that there is no guarantee that amid the welter of conflicting rational principles there will always be a decision, choice, or action which is rationally justified or rational. The accumulating effect of the rational principles in force in a given situation may be to prescribe *a* without qualification and prescribe *b* without qualification, even though they cannot both be performed, thus leaving the aware intelligent agent with the sense that he cannot act in a rational or justified way in the situation he is in.

This, then, is what a defense of rational dilemmas analogous to what has been said of the Agamemnon example would have to look like. But that still leaves us without a

---

[1] See, e.g., Bernard Williams, "Ethical Consistency," *Problems of the Self*, Cambridge University Press, 1973, Chap. 11.

plausible example of such a dilemma. And we have to ask ourselves whether we can plausibly give life to the structure of a rational dilemma based on the Agamemnon choice paradigm of a moral dilemma. Can we suggest any plausible or vivid example where, say, two precepts of rationality conflict and where an agent finds it impossible to fulfill the requirements of rationality, to act rationally? And can we do so without relying precisely on the moral examples that are used to support the idea of moral dilemma? For, of course, the idea that moral precepts or requirements are rational requirements, reasons for action, might allow us to turn examples of moral dilemma into examples of rational dilemma.[2] If Agamemnon is wrong whatever he does, then it is natural (in the light of our own belief in the rationality of acting morally) to characterize his plight as one where whatever choice he made would have been unjustified, where nothing could count as a reasonable practical answer.

But when we began by speculating about the possibility of rational dilemmas, we were looking for a form of dilemma arising outside the usual area of morality and having to do with the impossibility of acting rationally, or justifiably. A practical dilemma based in a moral dilemma was not what we had in mind. What would really interest us would be a case where it was impossible for an individual to act rationally with regard to her purely egoistic or self-regarding aims, a case of individualistic rational dilemma. And the Agamemnon example is not of this sort.

Foot mentions a non-moral prudential case where "pressing business has given one overriding reason to go to town" but "one nevertheless *ought* to be at home nursing a cold."[3] But it seems appropriate to treat such a case (Foot herself seems to treat the case) as understandable in fundamentally Rossian terms, as a case where one rational precept or imperative overrides another, and where, therefore, there is at least one thing it is rational for one to do.

In order to have an example of a rational dilemma, we need to describe a situation where, all things considered, every practical solution is fatally flawed and rationally unacceptable. And I have been unable to come up with a plausible example of a rational dilemma in this strong sense that possesses anything like the structure of the Agamemnon example, and not just what we find in Rossian examples of moral or other overriding. But it would be a major, though it might be a natural, mistake at this point to give up on the idea of rational dilemma until some rational parallel to the Agamemnon example could be unearthed. The Agamemnon example involved conflicting principles or precepts, the injunction: protect your daughter, and the injunction: as commander do what is necessary to ensure the success of your enterprise.

But as Ruth Marcus has pointed out, a conflict of obligations can arise from a single principle, like the obligation to keep promises, when it turns out that through no fault of one's own one cannot keep all the promises one has made; the promises may be of sufficient weight so that guilt is appropriate whatever one one breaks.[4] Here wrongdoing is inevitable and there is a conflict of obligations, but a single moral principle is behind the conflict: particular obligations derived from application

---

[2] See P.R. Foot, "Moral Realism and Moral Dilemma," *Journal of Philosophy* LXXX, 1983, pp. 394f.

[3] *Op. cit.*, p. 383.

[4] In "Moral Dilemmas and Consistency," *Journal of Philosophy* LXXVII, 1980, pp. 125f.

of a single principle cannot both be fulfilled. So not every conceivable or putative example of moral dilemma is based on conflicting general principles.

Marcus goes on to argue that although there can be moral dilemmas based on a single principle like that enjoining promise-keeping, act-utilitarian and act-consequentialist moral theories advocating a single principle of right or obligatory action cannot yield dilemmas because such theories base the moral characterization of actions solely on their consequences. For a dilemma to occur, according to Marcus, at least one moral principle that bases the moral assessment of actions on their intrinsic character must be in play, and this of course is ruled out by strict consequentialism.

I have elsewhere argued that this is a mistake.[5] There are single-principle versions of utilitarian act-consequentialism which allow for dilemmas, for situations in which, in the light of the principle, one cannot avoid wrong-doing. Thus consider the principle of utility as put forward in the 1789 original edition of Bentham's *An Introduction to the Principles of Morals and Legislation* (and retained in the 1823 version through implicitly qualified—or contradicted?—in footnote, by a different and to us more familiar version of the principle). Bentham says that the rightness or wrongness of an act depends on whether it contributes (overall) to human happiness or to human unhappiness. This principle allows for dilemmas, because it seems in no way impossible for a person to be in a situation where whatever she does (including doing nothing) will (in one way or another) be harmful to overall human happiness. (Some examples of historically possible situations where an agent faces this sort of dilemma are mentioned in my article.)

I believe that it is from utilitarian moral dilemmas that we can best learn how to construct a plausible example of (non-moral) rational dilemma. The natural self-regarding rational analogue of the above example of moral dilemma would be one based on the single principle that an act is (self-regardingly) rational if and only if it contributes to the well-being or happiness, increases the well-being or happiness, of the agent. Such a principle would allow of rational dilemma if true, because where an agent cannot help but make his situation worse whatever he does, nothing he does will count as rational according to the principle, even if he chooses the least self-damaging option available to him. But the principle is not plausible and neither, as a form of utilitarianism, is the original Bentham principle that allows for dilemmas. Nevertheless the principle does allow us to see that intrinsic non-consequentialistic characterizations need not figure in every set of principles that permits dilemmas. And having seen as much, perhaps we can find a more plausible act-consequentialist utilitarian principle that allows for dilemmas—perhaps, even the usually accepted present version(s) of the principle of utility have unsuspected capacity for dilemma. And this in fact turns out to be the case. At least in principle, there can be situations in which it is impossible to optimize utility, to perform an act with consequences at least as good as those of any other available act. And on contemporary versions of act-utilitarianism or act-consequentialism such a situation would constitute a moral dilemma.

But how is such a thing even in principle possible? Will there not always be some act with consequences better than or at least as good as those of all the other

---

[5] In "Utilitarianism, Moral Dilemmas, and Moral Cost," *American Phil. Quarterly* 22 (1985), pp. 161–68.

acts available to the agent? Not if the agent is capable of doing any of an infinite number of acts and no one of them is first or tied-first in the goodness of its consequences. Consider the following logically coherent science-fiction scenario (it may be possible to think of more mundane cases illustrating the same point but I have not been able to think of any). If, for any n, one can stand $1/n^{th}$ of an inch from a given wall and God will create n happy people (or add n happy days to the life of already existent people) if one stands $1/n^{th}$ of an inch away from that wall at a given time, then under various simplifying assumptions, any act one performs will have less good consequences than some other act one could have performed; no act one can perform at the time in question will be either best or tied-best and by the usual act-utilitarian criterion one will inevitably act wrongly.

So even under plausible contemporary interpretations of the principle of utility, moral dilemma is coherently imaginable, and this result may encourage us to look for analogous cases in which self-regarding rational dilemma is unavoidable. After all, egoistic, individualistic, extramoral practical rationality is often, is paradigmatically, understood in terms of an optimizing, maximizing model. The rational individual (in a situation where only her own well-being or satisfactions are at stake) seeks to maximize her satisfactions, does what she believes will have the best, most satisfying, consequences for herself. And if situations are imaginable in which no action one can perform has better overall consequences than any other action one can perform, is it not likewise possible to conceive a case where no action a given individual can perform has optimal consequences for that very individual, a situation where there is no way for the agent to achieve what is best for herself, because, for any given act she performs, there is available to her some alternative action with better consequences for herself?

This possibility does exist and it can be illustrated along the lines of our just-mentioned example of utilitarian/consequentialist moral dilemma. The examples of rational dilemma to be mentioned are purely hypothetical: they all involve unrealistic, or science-fictional, assumptions about human powers and opportunities. But they are nonetheless relevant to the issue of principle we are considering. If rational dilemmas are distinctly conceivable that will have important conceptual and philosophical implications for the way we understand practical rationality.

Imagine a science-fictionalized fountain of youth with some very special properties. This fountain emits life-and-happiness-giving rays and can work for a given person only once and at a certain precise moment. Depending on how far from the fountain one is at the exact time when its rays bombard one, one will be given additional days of life and happiness. Assume further that one is capable of standing as close as one pleases to the fountain. For any n, one is capable of standing $1/n^{th}$ of an inch away from the fountain, and if one stays a $1/n^{th}$ of an inch away one will receive n extra days of happiness (if one touches the fountain all bets are off). In such a case, any proximity one chooses will be less than some other proximity one could have chosen, and so however many happy days one adds to one's life, one could have added many—equally many, twice as many, etc.—more. Assuming that one has reason to prefer more to fewer happy days, one inevitably performs some act of standing at a certain distance from the fountain such that there was a better act to perform: for example, one stands at $1/n^{th}$ of an inch from the machine, and it would have been better if one had stood $1/2n^{th}$ of an inch from the machine. One has more reason on balance to stand $1/2n^{th}$ inches away than to stand $1/n^{th}$ inches away and so for any action one performs there is some alternative in one's power which one had more reason to perform. If it is irrational to do one thing, when one has more reason to perform some alternative, when it would have been better for one to have performed some definitely available alternative, then one has, inevitably, acted irrationally in the circumstances just mentioned. We have described a rational dilemma.

But just as the idea of moral dilemma invariably evokes a great deal of opposition, there is something inherently, or at least initially, repugnant in the idea of a rational dilemma.[6] It is usually held, and it is natural to hold, that an intelligent person always has it within her power to figure out at least one rational course of action in any given situation, or at least that within any given practical context there is always at least one rational, reasonable course of action which it is in principle possible for a rational agent to discern.[7] But the above examples, together with some seemingly innocuous assumptions and inferences about rationality, have led to the denial of what we usually take for granted, and, as so often occurs with putative examples of moral dilemma, it may be suspected at this point that some subtle fault in our assumptions about rationality may have led us astray.

Perhaps our problems arise, for example, from relying on an optimizing/maximizing model of rational choice and action, on the assumption that a rational agent must (in appropriate self-regarding contexts) choose what is best for herself. The recent literature of economics suggests the possibility that in some situations where one cannot figure out what course of action is best, it may be rationally acceptable to satisfice, choose some good enough course of action, rather than attempting to optimize. And even where what is better or worse is known to the agent, it may not be irrational to choose one course of action even when there is some other available action that one knows would allow one to do better for oneself. There is a clear conceptual distinction between an act with best results for oneself (or for all concerned) and a best act, and we learn this distinction from moral theories that make room for rational altruism (or for the rational non-optimific honoring of certain deontological restrictions). But even in purely self-regarding or individualistic contexts where the results of every alternative are known we can distinguish between what it is best (most rational) for an agent to do and what would allow an agent to do best for herself. I have elsewhere argued at some length that our ordinary conception of moderation allows it to be rational, or not irrational, for an individual modest or moderate in his desires deliberately to choose a given course of action while knowing that he

---

[6] The possibility of undeserved tragic moral dilemma entails the possibility of one kind of moral luck, and, of course, the idea of moral luck is offensive to (one side of) common moral opinion. But act-utilitarianism treats luck as essential to moral evaluation, through its exclusive emphasis on (foreseen and unforeseen) consequences, so perhaps act-utilitarianism has *less* reason to recoil from the moral dilemmas it treats as possible than common-sense morality has with regard to the Agamemnon example and others like it.

[7] One reason for the qualification: Joel Feinberg's well-known example of an agent prevented from making a decision by a coughing fit: perhaps such an agent never had it in his power to act rationally in that particular situation. See Feinberg's "Problematic Responsibility in Law and Morals," in *Doing and Deserving*, Princeton University Press, 1970.

could do better for himself by another.[8] A person may turn down a second cup of tea or an afternoon snack which he thinks he would enjoy, which he thinks of as a good thing, because he considers himself well enough off as he is; and in the fairy-tale situation where one is offered as much wealth as one wishes, and one chooses to be moderately well-off, the moderate individual may choose as he does, not because he fears asking for more or because he thinks himself constitutionally incapable of benefiting from greater wealth, but because such great wealth represents much more than he thinks he needs (much more than he cares about). Reasons like "I'm fine as I am" or "That's much more than I need" are, for certain moderate individuals,[9] reasons for not choosing what (admittedly) would be best for themselves (their own greatest well-being). But to that extent, such individuals need not be considered to act irrationally. Although they sometimes choose what is less than best for themselves, on such occasions, according to their lights, the balance of reasons favors making such a choice; so they can hold it is better for them to do what is less good for themselves, a distinction already familiar from moral contexts.

There is thus, even in individualistic contexts, a distinction to be made between best actions (choices) and actions (choices) that are best for (have the best results for) oneself.[10] And if we find this distinction at all convincing, then we must be careful not to fudge it in attempting to show the possibility of rational dilemma. In the putative example of rational dilemma mentioned above, a rational individual must inevitably make a choice which is less good for himself than certain definitely available alternatives. But it may not automatically follow that he makes a less good choice than he might. And if that further inference requires us to assume an optimizing model of rationality that rules out rational moderation as described above, then I think we have at best a doubtful argument for the possibility of rational dilemmas.

However, although I have strong doubts about whether individualistic rational choice (under certainty) universally requires optimization and would like to leave room for the possibility of rational moderation as described briefly above, I think the example of adding happy days to one's life naturally invites the optimizing model of rationality.[11] Satisfaction with less than immortality, or with a shorter rather than a

---

[8] See "Moderation, Rationality, and Virtue," in *The Tanner Lectures on Human Values*, VII, 1986; also, more briefly, *Commonsense Morality and Consequentialism* (Boston and London Routledge and Kegan Paul, 1985), pp. 38–44.

[9] These individuals are not moderate as a means to an overall greater balance of happiness or well-being, in the manner recommended by the Epicureans; but neither are they ascetics: they are not seeking to avoid satisfactions whenever possible. On these points, see "Moderation, Rationality, and Virtue."

[10] Although one who performs best actions can in some sense be said to optimize, that is not the usual sense of the term nor the sense I am making use of here.

[11] Indeed, it was chosen for that very reason. Somewhat similar examples occurring in the recent philosophic literature raise somewhat similar problems about the nature of rationality. (See, for example, John Pollock, "How Do You Maximize Expectation Value?," *Noûs* XVII, 1984, pp. 409–21; my *Common-sense Morality and Consequentialism*, pp. 44, 144f.; and "Utilitarianism, Moral Dilemmas, and Moral Cost," p. 168n.) But the previous examples were not used to support the possibility of rational dilemma (indeed Pollock explicitly denies the possibility of dilemma); and in fact those examples may yield dilemmas only if we assume the universal applicability of the optimizing model of rationality, thus denying the rationality (non-irrationality) of non-instrumental moderation. For some of the examples seem to involve choosing among an infinite number of better and worse results where it doesn't seem to make much difference whether

longer life, is not part of our ordinary conception of moderation, or modesty of desire: the moderate individual may be indifferent (at a certain point) to more happiness in the sense of greater or more intense happiness, but there seems to be no element of moderation in a willingness to allow one's life to end sooner rather than later.[12] (Perhaps it is irrational for us humans not to *accept* our unavoidable mortality, but it hardly follows that we would have reasons of moderation, or of any other kind, to reject immortality if it were ever on offer.) And so in the fountain-of-youth example it is very difficult to block the move from "choice with better results for oneself" to "better choice." It would appear that for any distance one chooses to stand from the fountain, there are other closer positions which he had more reason to choose. And since it seems self-evidently irrational to make a given choice when a better, more rationally supported choice is clearly available, we appear to have a rational dilemma.

Of course, we could easily evade the dilemma if, with Bernard Williams,[13] we held that immortality was not a good thing and attempted to infer that there was some (vaguely specifiable) finite length of life beyond which it is worth no one's while to live. But such a way out would be as paradoxical as the idea of rational dilemma itself, and it seems that the latter fairly forces itself upon us in our attempt to describe the example we have been focusing on. If one is really pleased at the prospect of n additional happy days of life, one will have reason to prefer $2n$ additional days, and it seems undeniable not only that the person who stands $1/n$ inch away and get n extra happy days would have been better off if she had chosen to stand $1/2n$ inches away, but that she would have done better to stand $1/2n$ inches away. She was capable of standing at the latter distance and there was reason for her to stand at that distance rather than at the distance she actually chose (she has no reason of moderation to be reluctant or indifferent about choosing to stand closer and have the longer life). So whatever she chooses to do, it would, on the balance of reasons have been better for her to choose otherwise.

Moreover, even if, in this case, the existence of dilemma depends on an assumption about the goodness of indefinitely long pleasurable existence, it is possible to construct a rather similar example requiring no such assumption. Imagine that God has condemned some wine connoisseur to an infinite life with only as finitely much of his favorite wine, Château Effete, as he asks for on a certain occasion. How many bottles of Château Effete should he ask for as a consolation for the unpleasant tedium of his largely wineless immortality? Since no finite amount is an immoderate quantity when consumed over infinite time, the man will have reason to specify as large a finite amount as possible; and whatever amount he actually specifies, there will be (more) reason for him to choose some larger amount.

---

one chooses the better or less good results and where a rational but moderate individual might not care about, be influenced by, such differences in utility. The examples I have used and will be using here are not naturally thought of in terms of "diminishing returns," and as we shall see, they allow no ready foothold for the idea of non-optimizing moderation.

[12] About an additional pleasure or increment of wealth one may say "who needs it?," but this is not the response one would expect to an offer of happy longer life. And "I'm fine as I am" may be a reason for turning down an additional enjoyment, but is irrelevant, of course, to the offer of a longer life.

[13] See "The Makropulos Case: Reflections on the Tedium of Immortality," in *Problems of the Self*.

Practical rational dilemma thus seems inevitable in the case of our wine connoisseur, and given some rather plausible assumptions about the desirability of indefinitely long (happy) life, in the fountain-of-youth case as well. Even if we may wish to hold that it can be self-regardingly rational to choose less than the best (results) for oneself, it seems self-evidently irrational to make a given choice when, as in our examples, a better, a more rationally supported, choice is clearly available.

But there is another possibility. Even granting that whatever a given person chooses, there will be some other better choice, we may still hold that there are degrees of rationality in the cases we have described. Clearly, it would be irrational in our first example for someone to stand only a quarter of an inch from the "fountain of youth" (or, in our second example, for the connoisseur to ask for only five bottles of Château Effete). To stand one billionth of an inch away from the fountain would be a much better thing to do, and perhaps there are degrees of proximity that it would be rational (not irrational) to choose, even though it would have been better, more rational, to have chosen some even greater degree of proximity. In other words, it may be possible for an act (choice) not to count as irrational or bad, even if it is less than ideally rational, less than the best available.

But such a way out of rational dilemma involves one in denying an assumption that, as far as I am aware, has been always accepted as obvious by philosophers discussing practical rationality, the assumption (roughly) that it is irrational to act one way when one believes there is some alternative action which one has, on balance, more reason to perform, which it would be better (and the sense of "better" here is in no way limited to moral considerations) to perform. One finds this assumption in recent works by such philosophers as Donald Davidson and David Pears, but it is taken for granted, as far as I can tell, by everyone who has dealt with practical reason and practical rationality.[14]

Taking it for granted amounts to a denial of the possibility of rational supererogation. The morally supererogatory exists, we know, if there are some moral or non-immoral acts that are morally less good than some of their alternatives. For an act is morally supererogatory if it is morally better than some alternative that would not have been wrong. However, even if common-sense morality seems to make abundant room for supererogation, there are moral theories which rule it out. Act-consequentialists and Act-utilitarians, for example, rank acts according to their consequences and nowadays typically hold that right actions must have optimal consequences relative to their alternatives, and thus be better than (or as good as) any of their alternatives. So for such a utilitarian no act can be right unless there is no alternative open to the agent which is morally better than it. But this is not in general true of moral views, and common sense allows for the moral acceptability of behavior to which there are morally superior, e.g., heroic and saintly, alternatives.

However, on the topic of rational supererogation there has been no such division of opinion, or perhaps we should say that there has simply never been such a topic as rational supererogation, because everyone has taken it for granted that it is irrational to do one thing when from a rational standpoint it would be better for

---

[14] Davidson, "How is Weakness of the Will Possible?," in J. Feinberg, ed., *Moral Concepts*, Oxford Univ. Press, 1969; Pears, *Motivated Irrationality*, Oxford Univ. Press, 1984.

one to do something else. But perhaps we have motive and reason to question this assumption, once we realize that only by doing so can we avoid another assumption that philosophers would tend to question and reject out of hand, the assumption that through no rational fault of one's own, one may end up in a position where one cannot avoid acting irrationally. If we allow for rational supererogation, if we allow that an act may be rational (non-irrational) or be a good (or not a bad) act to perform, even though there is more reason and it would be better to perform some alternative, then we may be able to avoid the initially and perhaps persistently repugnant idea that there can be rational dilemmas.[15] Further, once we have been given a motive for questioning the assumption that rationality requires doing what is rationally best (or what is rationally not less than the best),[16] we may begin to notice reasons for questioning that assumption that are quite independent of any felt need to rule out rational dilemmas.

What I have in mind is perhaps best introduced via recent discussions of akrasia. Unlike most discussions of akrasia, Donald Davidson's "How is Weakness of the Will Possible?" makes it abundantly clear that more than two alternatives can be at issue in cases of akrasia. According to Davidson, if act b is believed better than act a and the agent chooses b, she is not off the akratic hook if there is some further action c which she thinks is better than b. And I think we can produce some good reasons to doubt whether this must always be the case. In certain complex cases of what must on standard accounts be regarded as akrasia, it is not unnatural or strained to speak of degrees of rationality, to regard less than ideal or maximum rationality as rational enough, as not simply irrational.

Let us consider two examples. A man and his wife have quarreled and in a fit of pique the wife has gone back to her mother's, threatening to stay there indefinitely. The man is disconcerted, hurt, angry; he feels greater and greater frustration as the situation drags on, but he believes his wife will come back to him and hopes to be able to help bring this about. However, right now, his wife being still away, he is at a party and one of the female guests begins to flirt with him, indeed suggests her sexual availability, and the man is tempted. But he believes it would be wrong and a (prudential) mistake for him to get physically involved with her in any way. He also believes that it would be possible, though very difficult, for him entirely to resist her advances. In his state of frustration and anxiety he gives in to the blandishments to a certain extent, engages in what used to be called "heavy necking." Somehow the lesser physical intimacy takes the edge off his frustration and actually helps him resist greater intimacy. But he may know, and we may assume, that most men in his position would have completely succumbed to the blandishments, and, in particular, that most men who had gone as far as he has would have gone all the way. So although he has not done what he deems best, has fallen short of what his own conception of ideal rationality dictates in the circumstances, his feelings after the fact may be more those of relief and even pride, than of shame or regret. He may feel

---

[15] Later on, we shall see that certain non-optimizing forms of act-consequentialism allow one to avoid the utilitarian moral dilemma described above.

[16] The qualification in parentheses rationally permits one to choose between tied-best actions and between incommensurable actions, but still rules out the less-than-best actions described in the text.

that although going as far as he did was not the best available action, it was not, in the circumstances, a bad thing for him to do.[17] What he did was not ideally rational, but neither, he may feel, was what he did simply irrational: although it demonstrated some weakness of will, it demonstrated considerable strength of will as well. If he exerted more rational control than we can reasonably expect of most people, then perhaps his act of going-as-far-as-he-did-but-no-farther is rational enough so that it would be a mistake simply to call it irrational.

Take another example. A man is angry at his boss and believes (for good reasons we needn't enter into) that it would be in his own interest and on the whole a good thing to tell the boss off when they next meet. He believes it would be best to do so in a loud enough voice so that everyone in the office will know what is happening. But both he and his fellow employees have long been intimidated by the boss, and the employee knows it will be difficult to stand up to the boss and tell him what he thinks, and even more difficult (though not impossible) to do so in the loud and angry tones he thinks most appropriate. When the time comes to confront the boss, he manages with considerable effort to speak his mind, but allows himself to be intimidated to the extent of not daring to do so loudly and angrily; and indeed from a rational standpoint and relative to the man's own values, it would have been better for him to speak angrily to the boss than to express his opinion in conversational tones. But the latter may have been difficult enough so that on the whole the man is more proud than ashamed at his performance. Even though his performance may be less than the best that lay within his power, it may be good enough for him and for us not to regard it as simply irrational. So again we seem to have a rational analogue of what common-sense morality requires for supererogation. Moral supererogation is possible if there can be (extended) action which from a moral standpoint is less than ideal, less good than it could be, but which is nonetheless good enough from a moral standpoint not to count as immoral or wrong. And our above examples seem, analogously, to involve less than ideally rational choice and action that need not be regarded as irrational *simpliciter*.

We have two sorts of reasons, then, for admitting the notions of rational supererogation and of less-than-ideal practical rationality (non-irrationality): the linguistic and phenomenological *naturalness* of conceiving certain examples in those terms and the desire to avoid rational dilemmas. And we must now consider how the idea of supererogation can help us to evade dilemma in the fountain of youth case (or the case of accumulating Château Effete).

It seems outright irrational for someone with the powers we have assumed to stand at certain distances, e.g., 1/4 of an inch, away from the science-fiction fountain of youth,[18] but how much closer does one have to choose to stand in order for one's

---

[17] I cannot think of any other area where "good (not bad) *f*" entails "best (available) *f*." Wouldn't it in fact be odd if this entailment held with respect to good choice and action, but nowhere else?

[18] Optimizing assumptions about rationality lead to problems in the cases Pollock mentions, but in the light of those problems, Pollock goes to the opposite extreme of holding that in the problem cases, anything one does (chooses) is rationally permissible, non-irrational. For reasons already mentioned, this seems an implausible solution for the sorts of cases mentioned here (and indeed it seems implausible for Pollock's examples as well, though that implausibility is less obvious if, like Pollock, one doesn't consider questions of degree, what it would be *more* or *less* rational to do). What I have sought to do is take a middle

choice no longer to count as irrational? In the supererogation-friendly examples of yielding partially to sexual temptation and of failure to speak loudly to the boss, the agent accomplishes most, the most important part, of what ideal rationality requires, but it would be difficult to apply this notion to the fountain of youth case, where one inevitably gains only an (infinitesimally) small fraction of the number of extra happy days one had reason, and the power, to obtain. In order to treat such examples as dilemma-free, we must borrow another feature of our "natural" paradigms of rational supererogation.

The performance of the man who does everything but speak loudly need not be regarded as simply irrational, because of the great difficulty of doing (rationally) better than he has done. (It may be unreasonable, for example, to expect others to do as well as he has done.) And we can similarly imagine in the fountain of youth case that, even though one can stand at any finite close distance, still the closer the distance the more difficult it would be to summon the concentration and the intelligence required to stand at that distance. The difficulty of standing at closer and closer distances thus approaches the limits of the agent's power and skill. In that case, an agent who through great effort and concentration chose to stand at a distance so near that it would have been very difficult (for him or for anyone else) to choose to stand any nearer, may count as having chosen rationally, or at least not irrationally.[19] And we can see how to avoid the admission of rational dilemmas by allowing for rational supererogation, for a gap between rationality and ideal rationality.[20]

On the other hand, someone—even someone who finds the idea of rational dilemma initially objectionable—may regard our "natural" examples of rational supererogation as more convincing than the above attempt to avoid dilemmas, and so end up accepting both rational supererogation and rational dilemmas. But the issues widen at this point, because what one wants to say about rational dilemmas and supererogation is understandably influenced by what one wants to say about moral dilemmas and supererogation. There is a long ethical tradition of drawing analogies between rationality and morality, and this tendency, and the fact that the usual direction of influence has been from conceptions of rationality to moral views or theories, may serve to explain some features of recent and traditional moral theory and suggest some possibilities for the future.

Act-utilitarianism is often seen as basing morality on a rational extension of the principle of egoistic rational choice. Self-regarding rationality involves maximizing the agent's well-being or satisfactions, and in its most familiar form, the principle

---

path between the view that everything is rationally permissible in our problem cases and the view that they should be treated as dilemmas where no rational choice is possible. This makes them more like what under ordinary assumptions the moral life is like, with impermissible, non-supererogatory permissible, and supererogatory courses of action all available to one.

[19] For the interesting application of similar notions to the problem of free will, see Patricia Greenspan's "Unfreedom and Responsibility," forthcoming in a collection of essays on moral responsibility edited by F. Schoeman. Note that in the fountain-of-youth case it is quite natural to assume that the personal costs of greater efforts are less than the benefits to be gained through greater efforts.

[20] The idea of dilemma for such an example could then be resuscitated only if one could make coherent sense of the supposition that (in other possible cases) standing nearer and nearer (without touching) the fountain need not get, or tend to get, more and more difficult.

of utility requires agents to maximize the satisfactions or well-being of all mankind or of all sentient beings. Although many other features of rationality have served as bases for moral theorizing and although many disanalogies between rationality and morality have also been asserted and defended,[21] one particular aspect of rationality that has influenced moral theory is of particular concern to us. The most popular forms of act-utilitarianism and of act-consequentialism more generally bear the imprint of another feature commonly ascribed to practical rationality, the absence of supererogation. As I mentioned earlier, the principle of utility requires agents always to perform the morally best act they are capable of performing at a given time.[22] But of course the analogous feature is familiar in the case of practical rationality and as far as I know, no one has doubted that for an act/choice to count as rational there can be no known better alternatives: that much has always seemed self-evident to the extent that philosophers have even considered the issue.

Ordinary act-utilitarianism and act-consequentialism thus seem to model their notion of what is morally good enough to be morally acceptable on the accepted view of what rationally good enough to be rationally acceptable. Sometimes this analogy has been based on the assumption that morality (moral obligation) is nothing more than what is rational (what one must choose on pain of being irrational) or that all moral distinctions can be reduced to (supervene upon) distinctions about what one has more or less reason to do. But whatever its sources or inspiration, it has led act-consequentialists to regard the supererogation that ordinary morality allows for as some sort of illusion.

Even those who have defended (common-sense) moral supererogation would not have been willing to defend rational supererogation. But although this difference of view concerning morality and rationality will seem suspect to those who think morality ought as much as possible to be understood on the model of rationality, defenders, e.g., of common-sense morality will certainly be able to reply that significant differences ought not to be glossed over or denied in the name of an illusory ideal of theoretical simplicity. If there are no supererogations of practical reason, that fact, they may say, ought not to be allowed to attenuate the strong and obvious intuition that in morality at least it is possible to avoid wrong-doing without doing the morally best act available.

For the most part, then, (implicit) total views of rationality-cum-morality have come in two forms. Either they have accepted moral supererogation, but implicitly denied the possibility of rational supererogation, or (out of a desire to model morality as closely as possible on rationality) they have not allowed either rational or moral supererogation. Almost all act-utilitarians have been in the latter group, and defenders of deontology or common sense have been in the former. But it is possible to advocate a form of act-utilitarianism or act-consequentialism that falls or lets one fall into the first group. Bentham's original version of the principle of utility considers an act right if it produces more happiness than unhappiness on balance, and this principle and various other (and as I have argued elsewhere, more plausible) versions

---

[21] Cf. Derek Parfit's *Reasons and Persons* (Oxford, 1984).

[22] For utilitarians, the question what kind of person is morally best is not rigidly tied to the question which actions are morally best.

of act-utilitarianism allow for supererogation.[23] Familiar optimizing utilitarianism is often considered too demanding precisely because it always requires an agent to do what is morally best. And even if one believes that objectively good consequences are the only thing relevant to the moral assessment of actions, one may also feel that room needs to be made for moral supererogation and that an act with good enough consequences may be morally acceptable even when better consequences (a better act) could have been produced. And that feeling, as with defenders of common-sense morality, may be strong enough so that one wants to allow for moral supererogation even while denying the possibility of rational supererogation. (If one allows for moral supererogation one may be able to avoid utilitarian moral dilemmas of the kind described earlier; this is one motive for holding a supererogation-allowing non-optimizing form of utilitarianism that is quite independent of one's views about rational supererogation or one's knowledge of the possibility of rational dilemmas.)

But once we see the possibility of rational dilemmas and the various examples mentioned in the text above are brought into view, a third and unaccustomed position on rationality-cum-morality begins to emerge, one which allows for rational supererogation and moral supererogation both. Its advocacy permits one to retain the hope of basing morality in practical rationality without falling into the typical utilitarian's anti-common-sensical denial of moral supererogation.[24] And the utilitarian who allows for moral and rational supererogation may also be able to evade both the utilitarian moral dilemmas discussed earlier and the rational dilemmas we have focused on. But any such view is, for all these possible advantages, both unexpected and unprecedented, and it will take a good deal more careful examination and exploration before anyone can be confident that this third way of construing rationality-cum-morality really does represent a viable alternative to traditional views.[25]

---

[23] See *Common-sense Morality and Consequentialism*, Chap. 3.

[24] From the standpoint of this emerging position, a fundamental mistake of supererogation-denying utilitarianism may lie not in its attempt to model morality on rationality, but in the way it understands the structure of rationality itself. I am indebted for this way of putting things to Gregory Trianosky.

[25] For interesting exploration of the idea of less-than-ideal *epistemic* rationality see, e.g., Earl Conee's "Utilitarianism and Rationality," *Analysis* 42 (1982), pp. 55–59; Frederick Kroon, "Rationality and Paradox," *Analysis* 43, 1983, pp. 156–60; Christopher Cherniak, *Minimal Rationality*, Bradford Books, forthcoming. My greatest debt, in the present paper, is to the work of Herbert Simon. I would also like to thank Jonathan Adler, Earl Conee, Carl Cranor, Patricia Greenspan, and Gregory Trianosky for their helpful suggestions.

18

Ethics Naturalized

Philosophers who have discussed or advocated naturalized epistemology have often called attention to analogies between ethics or moral theory, on the one hand, and epistemology or theory of knowledge, on the other. And utilitarianism in particular has been singled out as an ethical analogue of a naturalistic or naturalizing approach to questions of epistemic justification.[1] Both BonJour and Firth make the latter point, and since both also regard utilitarianism as ethically unacceptable, they make use of the epistemic/ethical parallelism to cast doubt on naturalizing epistemology.

It is certainly possible, however, to doubt that utilitarianism can readily be dismissed simply on the basis of counterintuitive implications of the sort Firth and BonJour allude to; for it has (for one thing) become increasingly recognized that our intuitive moral thinking can lead to counterintuitive results quite on its own—we have reason to believe, in other words, that commonsense moral intuitions conflict with one another, are incoherent as a class.[2] And this seems to give new life to the

---

[1] See, e.g., Laurence BonJour, "Externalist Theories of Empirical Knowledge," in *Midwest Studies in Philosophy* V (*Studies in Epistemology*), 1980, pp. 53–73; Roderick Firth, "Epistemic Merit, Intrinsic and Instrumental," *Proceedings and Addresses of the American Philosophical Assn.* 55, pp. 5–23; and Hilary Kornblith's Introduction to *Naturalizing Epistemology* (Cambridge, Mass.: Bradford/MIT, 1985), pp. 1–29.

[2] Arguments to this effect can be found in Thomas Nagel's "Moral Luck," in *Mortal Questions* (Cambridge University Press, 1979), pp. 24–38; in Samuel Scheffler's *The Rejection of Consequentialism*. Oxford, 1982; and in my "Utilitarian Virtue," in *Midwest Studies in Philosophy* XIII (Ethical Theory), 1989, pp. 393 ff. These discussions focus on different aspects of common-sense morality's incoherence or self-conflict.

philosophical impulse toward theory and system that has been so clearly exemplified in utilitarian ethics. But quite apart from the merits of utilitarianism or naturalistic epistemology, recent discussions connecting these two may give a false impression of that connection by seeming to imply that any epistemological naturalist will inevitably want to adopt some form of utilitarianism if she seeks a coherent overall philosophical view. Utilitarianism naturally lends support to and gains support from naturalized epistemology. But utilitarianism is not the only ethical view that naturally "goes" with a naturalizing approach in epistemology, and in this paper my main purpose will be to point out another, less familiar ethical approach that goes well with naturalized epistemology and show how differences between the less familiar approach and utilitarianism correspond to interesting differences in the ways we can seek to naturalize epistemology. It would not be correct to claim that virtue ethics in general harmonizes with a naturalizing approach to epistemology: quite the contrary, there are standard forms of virtue ethics that seem most plausibly associated with traditional, internalist epistemology. But there is another, less familiar kind of virtue ethics that can very plausibly be seen as analogous to epistemological naturalism in one of its guises, one whose present-day relevance and importance is further underscored by its ability to deal in a coherent fashion with the exasperating problem of moral/ethical luck. But Utilitarianism also has an interesting way of dealing with this problem, and I propose to begin our discussion by saying something about the paradoxes involved in our ordinary thinking about moral luck.

1. Moral Luck, Kantian Ethics and Reductionist Utilitarianism

One of the unnerving accomplishments of recent discussions of moral luck is to point to a nest of inconsistencies at the heart of our intuitive moral thinking. Consider, for example, our everyday moral reactions to the unforeseen consequences of people's actions. Ordinary moral thinking distinguishes the moral status of attempted murder from that of murder, for example, and quite apart from legal distinctions between murder and attempted murder, we think much worse of someone who has killed an innocent victim than of someone who accidentally fails to kill an intended innocent victim. And we are inclined to heap greater blame on an actual murderer than on an unsuccessful one.

To that extent common-sense morality allows actual unforeseeable consequences a role in determining moral judgment, thus making room for a certain kind of "moral luck". But as has been frequently pointed out, the very idea of moral luck affronts our common-sense moral intuitions. So our moral intuitions about cases taken singly are in conflict with a general common-sense conviction that judgments of morally better and worse, or greater or less culpability or blameworthiness, cannot properly be subject to luck or accident. And the cases where such inconsistency arises are quite numerous and varied.

To take an even clearer example, imagine someone driving a car along a country road and pointing out noteworthy sights to his passengers. As a result of his preoccupation, the car suddenly swerves to the middle of the road; fortunately there are no cars coming in the opposite direction and no accident occurs. However, in another scenario the person is similarly preoccupied, and because a truck happens to be coming, has a major accident. He is then responsible for a great deal of harm to others and would normally be accounted blameworthy or culpable in a way that he would not be thought blameworthy or culpable in the first-mentioned case. This example is borrowed from Thomas Nagel's paper "Moral Luck". But as Nagel also points out, something in us revolts against the idea of moral luck, inclining us to the view that the driver must have the *same* degree of culpability in the two cases mentioned above.[3] There is something repelling in the idea that one can be more or less culpable depending on events outside one's ken or control. And in regard to the just-mentioned pair of examples, therefore, it may seem as if we should be able to insert some kind of probability estimate into the example, so that whether the driver who swerves is culpable and the degree, if any, of his culpability would depend solely on whether he was sufficiently aware of the likelihood of an accident and on how likely an accident was, given his preoccupation with the scenery—judgments that are constant between the two imagined cases and that might allow us to say the man was culpable (or not culpable) in both cases to the same extent for having paid attention to the scenery while driving.

But (following Nagel) I think that no such solution really squares with the moral judgments we make in the ordinary course of events, before we begin to worry about moral luck in a self-conscious way. I think no matter how constant one imagines the (awareness of) probability in the two situations, common-sense morality sees some difference in the culpability, blame-worthiness, or reprehensibleness of the agent. (Actually, it doesn't matter whether the two situations are viewed as counterfactually possible relative to one another or are viewed as involving similar persons—or one person at different times—facing relevantly similar situations.) Common sense appears to subscribe to a mutually contradictory set of assumptions with regard to putative cases of inattention, carelessness, or negligence, and we therefore need to go beyond our ordinary moral thinking.

We have just spoken of one particular form of moral luck: luck with respect to results or consequences of one's actions or inactions. But moral luck can also come about in other ways. Thus if some of us would have done nothing to stop the Nazis, had we been living in Germany before and during the Second World War, then arguably any lesser or negligible guilt we have through not having in fact been in Germany during that period is attributable to moral luck in our *circumstances*. And such assumptions of circumstantial luck lead to inconsistencies that resemble those uncovered in connection with luck in *results* or *consequences*, though I don't want at this point to dwell on these difficulties.

The issue of blameworthiness (or culpability or reprehensibility) is at the very heart of the issue of moral luck, because it is the idea that luck or accident can make a difference to blameworthiness, etc., that most grates against our antecedent moral intuitions. If we concentrate on praiseworthiness the clash of intuitions is less evident, because there is such a thing as non-moral praiseworthiness—we can praise an artistic performance or work that it would make no sense to regard as culpable or

---

[3] See Nagel, *op. cit.* The first discussion of the problem of moral luck I am aware of occurs in Adam Smith's *The Theory of Moral Sentiments*.

blameworthy—and because it is therefore not odd at all to suppose that non-moral praiseworthiness can sometimes depend on accident. Of course, we could distinguish moral praiseworthiness from praiseworthiness in general and claim that it grates on our intuitions to suppose that moral praiseworthiness can be subject to luck; but it is just easier to focus on blameworthiness, where ambiguity seems less capable of misleading us because all blameworthiness seems to be moral blameworthiness. And so in what follows I shall frame the issues of moral luck largely in terms of the notion of blameworthiness.

The two dominant ethical traditions of recent times—Kantianism and utilitarianism—have different and indeed distinctive ways of avoiding the paradox and inconsistency our intuitive thinking gets into in the area of moral luck. (That is not to say that all, or even most, utilitarians and Kantians have been *self-consciously aware* of the problem of moral luck or that they have adopted their main views in *response* to that problem.) It is fairly clear that Kant wishes to preclude the possibility of moral luck and thus to avoid those judgments about individual cases that jointly imply that someone's (degree of) blameworthiness can depend on factors of luck or accident. The utilitarians, by contrast, make room for the phenomenon of moral luck, but enunciate a theory or conception of praise- and blameworthiness which, if correct, takes the sting from moral luck, i.e., makes it seem unproblematic (despite our ordinary intuitions) that differences in blameworthiness should depend on accidental factors. Let me therefore say a bit more about the ways in which Kantians and utilitarians respectively elude, or seek to elude, the intuitive tangle known as the problem of moral luck.

Kant, as I said, denies the possibility of moral luck, but he has recourse to the metaphysics of noumenal will(ing) in his effort to establish conditions of moral evaluation entirely free from contamination by luck or accident. Nowadays most of us, even many Kantians among us, would tend to resist a noumenal metaphysics—even one in which the noumenal is regarded merely as an inevitable *postulate* of the moral point of view—as the price to be paid for luck-free moral judgment. But if the idea of the noumenal is left to the side, it is difficult to see how the this-worldly determinants of moral evaluation—the factors of circumstance, constitution, and causation that give actuality and substance to moral thought—can reasonably be conceived independently of all luck and accident. And in that case the Kantian still owes us an account of how morality *without* luck is possible.

Utilitarianism, on the other hand, makes the entirely different move of *allowing* for moral luck by conceiving moral predicates in such a way as to make the possibility of moral luck seem less problematic. For the utilitarian, an act is right if it has overall better, happier consequences than any of its alternatives, and an act counts as blameworthy if the further act of blaming it is right in the aforementioned utilitarian terms. (Praiseworthiness is treated in parallel fashion.) In that case the blameworthiness of a person's act amount to nothing more than (reduces to) the fact that blaming it would have better consequences that not blaming it, and since the goodness of consequences is one of the things in this world and this life which are most subject to luck or accident, such a view makes it easy to see how blameworthiness can depend on factors of luck, if only (or once) the view itself is accepted. Of course, the utilitarian conception of blameworthiness is far from our intuitive ideas about blameworthiness (however muddled the latter may be—for the utilitarian conception is at least not *muddled*). But relative to the acceptance of utilitarian views at least, moral luck becomes fairly unproblematic.

Let us then dwell for a moment on the differences between Kantianism and utilitarianism viewed as attempts to evade the incoherence/paradoxes endemic to our ordinary thinking about moral luck. Kant seeks, in effect, to avoid (our) having to assume the existence of moral luck through the idea of a noumenal realm where human reason and activity are purified of all those empirical factors that so clearly connect with matters of luck or accident. Morality is thereby taken out of the empirical world and construed as pure (inner?) rational willing that bears only an indirect or non-constitutive relation to things and events in the external or phenomenal world. Such a move is clearly reminiscent of and is arguably analogous to the way traditional internalistic/Cartesian epistemology treats epistemic rationality and justification as a function solely of the inner states of the would-be knower.

By contrast, the utilitarian solution to the problem of moral luck is to treat the crucial notions of blameworthiness and culpability as understandable in "externalistic" or naturalistic terms in the light of which the idea of moral luck loses its intuitive unacceptability. We ordinarily think of blameworthiness or culpability as in some sense attaching deeply rather than through luck or accident to moral agents, but a utilitarianism that regards blameworthiness and culpability as matters, respectively, of what it has good/optimal consequences to blame and to treat as guilty considers such matters to be largely *extrinsic* and *accidental* to the agent/act thus deemed blameworthy or culpable. And if, e. g., a person's blameworthiness (for doing x) is a matter of its being the case that blaming the person (for doing x) will have better results for overall human (sentient) happiness than not doing so, then blameworthiness treated as an external property of this kind will also be reducible to non-evaluative empirical terms (assuming that happiness is cashed out in terms of empirically measurable preference satisfaction or pleasure, etc.).

In fact, standard utilitarianism reduces all its ethical vocabulary to supposedly empirical notions/terms—e.g., rightness is just a matter of having consequences for human happiness as good as those of any alternative action—and those who have compared utilitarianism with naturalistic accounts of epistemic terms have seen or come close to seeing that both involve a form of naturalistic *reductionism*. Thus a naturalizing approach that construes epistemic justification in terms of the use of some type of reliable belief-forming process reduces the evaluative epistemic notion of justification to nonevaluative natural/empirical terms, and this is clearly parallel to the way in which utilitarianism reduces all ethical evaluative notions to natural/ empirical ones.[4] But reduction of this sort is not the only procedure open to an epistemological naturalizer, and that fact has, in ways to be discussed shortly, been well

---

[4] I am assuming—with Putnam, Hempel, and many others—that the reduction of terms/properties can occur non-analytically, as, for example, when we say that water is nothing more than H_2O. One can most plausibly equate epistemic justification with the use of some appropriately reliable belief-forming process if one doesn't insist that this equation/reduction obtains *ex vi terminorum*. And, similarly, utilitarian reductionism needn't commit any sort of naturalistic/definist fallacy. For further comparison of the role of reductions in science and ethics, see my *From Morality to Virtue*, Oxford University Press forthcoming, Chaps. 4, 11, 13.

known to various recent participants in epistemological debates over the merits of the naturalizing tendency. What has not, however, been known or mentioned is the fact that an ethics aware of the problems of moral luck and conceiving itself as intellectually allied or associated with naturalized epistemology need not assume a utilitarian form. Perhaps it will be easier to see how this is possible, if we now consider an epistemic phenomenon that has received some attention in the literature, but not nearly as much as its ethical analogue: the problem, namely, of epistemic luck.

2. Epistemic Luck and Eliminative Utilitarianism

Many of those who have written on the nature and prospects of naturalized epistemology have pointed out that reductions of epistemic warrant or justification to non-evaluative "natural" concepts introduce a kind of unfairness and/or arbitrariness into attributions of warrant or justification. If, for example, epistemic justification is a matter (very roughly) of arriving at certain beliefs via a reliable (e.g., a typically truth-producing or truth-preserving) cognitive process, then whether or not a given person is (epistemically or rationally) justified in holding a certain belief may depend on factors he has no way of knowing about, on facts beyond his ken and unavailable to him. Thus in two different possible worlds there may be two people making the same inference about their environment on the basis of exactly similar perceptual data; but if the inference is generally reliable in one of the worlds, but not in the other, then on a reductive account of justification, the two individuals differ in the justification of their inferential beliefs. One of them will be justified in believing what he does about his environment, and the other will not be, even though neither has any view about the reliability of the process that underlies his own belief-acquisition. And it seems epistemically unfair and, from an epistemological standpoint, implausible to suppose that the individuals should thus differ in epistemic warrant, when from the standpoint of their mental activity they are (we may assume) exemplifying exactly similar perceptual and inferential processes.

Reductive, naturalizing reliabilist (or related) accounts of epistemic rationality or justification have frequently been objected to in terms like these,[5] and if we may put matters in terms closer to those we have been using here, but quite naturally invoked in regard to the example just mentioned, we can say that the idea that epistemic rationality or justification can depend on factors of luck or accident totally outside the ken of those being epistemologically evaluated is counterintuitive. Just as it is intuitively repellent to have to suppose that the moral justification of an agent's performing some act can depend on factors of luck or accident outside the ken or control of the agent, it at least initially seems implausible to hold that someone's epistemic justification should depend on factors outside her ken or control. And that explains some of the reluctance to adopt a reliabilist or any similarly externalistic naturalist account of epistemic evaluations.

---

[5] See, e.g., Hilary Kornblith, "The Psychological Turn," *Australasian Journal of Philosophy* 60 (1982): esp. p. 244, and Alvin Goldman, "Strong and Weak Justification," in J. Tomberlin, ed., *Philosophical Perspectives* 2 (1988): esp. pp. 64f.

However, the matter is somewhat more complicated than anti-reliabilists and anti-naturalists seem to have realized. We have seen that our intuitions about moral luck are not all on the side of denying the possibility of such luck, and something similar seems to be the case with regard to epistemic evaluations generally and most particularly with regard to claims about epistemic or rational justification.

Thus imagine a pair of examiners who have just had the unenviable task of telling a dissertation candidate that his dissertation is unacceptable and requires the most extensive revision. We may imagine that at the dissertation interview, the examiners were in substantial agreement about the defects of the dissertation, and that the candidate himself, when told of their objections, admitted their force and validity with a rather dejected air of resignation. At the point, however, when the examiners emerge from this meeting, one of them says to the other: I wonder whether he'll appeal the decision to higher university authorities. And the other immediately counters by pointing out that there is no reason for the candidate to appeal, since he himself agreed with the strong and shared objections of both examiners. Hearing this reply, the examiner making the original conjecture about an appeal may well feel that he was being irrational, possibly somewhat paranoid, to suggest the possibility of an appeal. But what happens if out of the blue, a few weeks later, it turns out that the student has gone on to appeal—totally unreasonably, let us assume—the examiners' decision on his dissertation? I think the examiner who originally conjectured that he might do so will tend to revise his view about the irrationality or paranoid quality of his own original conjecture. He will feel, instead, that the course of events has in some measure (perhaps completely) *vindicated* his original opinion about the real possibility of an appeal.

However, this is a case of rational luck only if we imagine that the conjecturing examiner does not attribute his vindication to some sort of intuitiveness on his part in the original situation where he made his conjecture. If he, or we, imagine that in the original situation he had some clue about the possibility of an appeal from the way the student was behaving (from the peculiar quality of his dejectedness, for example), a clue which he received subliminally but which was nonetheless functioning *as evidence* affecting the conjectures he was willing to make, then we do not have a putative case of rational luck so much as one of subliminal evidence only subsequently recognized as such.

But I don't think there is any need for the conjecturing examiner, or for us, to see his situation, and his subsequent loss of a sense of being slightly paranoid and irrational, as reflecting the existence of subliminal evidence and the subsequent recognition of its presence. The man himself may be led to revise his estimation of his own earlier rationality or irrationality by the mere fact that his conjecture turned out to be correct. His fears may seem to be (somewhat) justified *by subsequent events*, rather than by a subsequently acknowledged earlier bit of evidence, and this description may indeed be the best expression of the man's own sense of how he is (turns out to be) justified (or less unjustified and certainly not paranoid) in his original assumption. Certainly we ourselves, looking at his situation from the outside, have a tendency to withhold the judgment of paranoidness and irrationality with regard to his original conjecture in a way we would not have been inclined to do if we had simply imagined a case in which no appeal was ever lodged. Even assuming that the candidate provided no subliminal clues to his subsequent behavior, our judgment as to (degree of) irrationality and paranoidness is commonly affected by how we imagine things actually turning out, and this provides for a possibility of (epistemic) rational luck that is quite similar to what we said earlier about the common-sense possibilities of moral luck.

On the other hand, something in us recoils at the idea that epistemic or rational justification (or vindication) in cases like that just mentioned can hinge on subsequent events. And so it would seem that as with moral luck, our initial intuitions and judgments in the area of epistemic or rational luck are not entirely consistent with one another; in that case, again as with moral luck, we cannot simply remain on the level of intuitions, but are in need of theory to tell us which intuitions ought to be abandoned. Since *some* intuitions must be dropped, it cannot be a decisive objection to reliabilist and other naturalistic, reductionist accounts of epistemic justification that they go against some of our intuitions. Rather, the question must be whether, with due weight given to overall considerations of intuitiveness, the total theory arrived at by one or another naturalizing tendency or project is superior to our best internalist, anti-naturalistic, anti-reductionist epistemologies, and this question presumably cannot and should not be closed prematurely.

However, epistemological naturalizers need not end up being reductionists. Some, instead, have advocated that epistemology should be replaced by or turn into a form of psychology (or psychology-cum-neuroscience-cum-biology, etc.). And under such a development epistemic evaluations would presumably be eliminated altogether, rather than reduced to other terms. In explaining human thought and action, we might still be interested in questions of reliability and the like, but an eliminative naturalistic epistemology or psychology would have no (further) interest in whether certain cognitive mechanisms yielded or allowed for rational or justified beliefs or inferences. A thoroughgoing eliminativism would permit of no such epistemic evaluations (let us assume it would eliminate claims about knowledge along with claims about justification) and would presumably hold that there is no good *theoretical* reason to countenance the making of such evaluations (though there might be no reason to forbid them to everyday life).

I have mentioned the possibility of eliminativism, not because I wish to defend it against naturalistic reductionism or anti-reductionism in epistemology, but because its very possibility can give us a clue to some previously unsuspected ways in which ethics can be naturalized. Standard utilitarianism is the only form of naturalized ethics that (to my knowledge) has been recognized as analogous to a naturalizing trend in epistemology. But once we see that eliminativism is a possible direction for the naturalizer in epistemology, we may be encouraged to look for similar possibilities in (naturalizing) ethics.

Utilitarianism as standardly formulated is a reductionistic form of ethical naturalism, but it is also possible for utilitarianism to present itself in an eliminativist mode, and as such it represents a new and, I believe, interesting way in which ethics can seek to naturalize itself. Moreover, once we see how a thoroughly eliminativist ethical naturalism parallel to eliminativist epistemological naturalism is possible, it will be easier to recognize the possibilities of a naturalistically eliminativist virtue ethics, and the possibilities for naturalizing epistemology will in turn be enriched. But let us begin this process with an account of utilitarianism as a form of eliminativist ethical naturalism.

Eliminative utilitarianism stands to familiar reductive utilitarianism as, say, eliminative materialism stands to reductive materialism (I shall not try to respond to those, like Quine, who hold that the theoretical difference between elimination and reduction is nil or negligible). So just as an eliminative materialism claims there are no mental entities or (realized) mental properties, only physical entities and properties functioning in certain complex ways, an eliminative utilitarianism will deny that anything is right or obligatory or intrinsically good, will deny that there are any exemplified ethical (or evaluative) properties or facts. And the reasoning behind such conclusions will in fact, as in other cases where there is a choice to make between reduction and elimination, follow the reasoning for reductive utilitarianism till it reaches an ultimate parting of the ways with it. Like reductionist utilitarians, the eliminative utilitarian will point out the incoherent, or at least intellectually unsatisfactory, thinking that lies, for example, behind our ordinary moral thinking. She will hold that when one properly strips away or otherwise removes the irrational or unjustified elements in our ordinary usage of "right" and "wrong", one will be left with the clear and humanly significant core idea of producing (a net balance of) pleasure or satisfaction for sentient beings. But here, parting ways with ordinary reductive utilitarianism, the eliminativist will argue that the sheer enormity of the error and confusion in our ordinary beliefs about moral rightness justifies us in claiming that there is no such thing as moral rightness, etc. By contrast, the reductivist utilitarian holds that rightness turns out to be conduciveness to pleasure or desire-satisfaction and that ordinary moral thinking is simply very much in error about (what) rightness (is).

Clearly, the issue here between eliminative and reductive utilitarianism is familiar from our experience of other disputes regarding the respective merits of an eliminative and a reductive approach. And since the most familiar of these, probably, is the long-standing debate between eliminative and reductive materialism, it is perhaps worth mentioning one possible advantage that eliminative utilitarianism (or eliminative ethics more generally) has over eliminative materialism. It is not obvious that sense experience and thinking are merely posited hypothetical entities, and there may be some force to the claim, therefore, that what eliminative materialism eliminates (among other things) are some of the very data which reasonable abductive thinking must seek to account for. But the idea that we immediately experience certain ethical data or properties is, I believe, an (even) harder thesis to defend than what we have just allowed as a possibility in the area of mind and body, and to the extent, therefore, we have better or more immediate knowledge of our own experience(s) than of ethical facts and properties, utilitarian eliminativism may well be in better shape than (or have at least one advantage over) eliminative materialism.

But even apart from this consideration, it seems difficult to find any reason to prefer reductive to eliminative utilitarianism *as a form of naturalism*. If the traditional, reductive utilitarian protests, for example, that the eliminative approach does away with ethics altogether and therefore with utilitarianism itself as a form of ethics, it can be pointed out that this pair of claims is either simply false or altogether begs the issue against eliminativism. After all, eliminative utilitarianism, like eliminative materialism, makes a distinctive claim of its own. It doesn't remain silent or somehow render it impossible for claims to be made, but rather comes out openly and asserts that nothing is good or virtuous or obligatory—or, if you prefer, that "good", etc., do not denote any properties of things. To be sure, problems can arise here about how the negative claims of eliminative utilitarianism are most properly formulated, but there are similar problems about how to express eliminative materialism, and there is no reason, in either case, to say that the eliminativist eliminates the philosophical field he or she is supposed to be working in. Just as the eliminative materialist holds a metaphysical position and is naturally regarded as a materialist of one particular stripe, the eliminative utilitarian subscribes to a particular ethical view, and one, moreover, that is for similar reasons naturally regarded as a form of utilitarianism.

On the other hand, what one may mean by saying that the eliminativist does away with ethics is that the eliminativist does away with, in the sense of denying the existence of, ethical properties or facts. But even granting that there is a sense in which this charge is true, it hardly seems to constitute an intelligible reason for preferring reductive utilitarianism over eliminative. In the sense presumably intended, the claim that the latter does away with ethical facts or properties simply points out the essential difference between the two forms of utilitarianism. And one cannot treat that as an argument against eliminativism without essentially begging the question against it.

Certainly, if one denies the existence of good things or right acts in favor of the (mere) existence of pleasure and things conductive to it, that may have an effect on those who hear the denial(s), an effect which the reductivist may wish to call bad and that even the eliminativist can say goes against overall human happiness or pleasure. But because the eliminativist may care as much about the advancement of human happiness as any reductionist, he may have equal reason or motive to keep his theoretical views from becoming known. If, as so often happens, a reductive utilitarian can defend the validity of his views while disavowing their practical usefulness and recommending that they remain esoteric, the eliminativist can do something entirely analogous even without making use of specifically ethical or evaluative notions. And so eliminative utilitarianism cannot readily be undercut as a theoretical option by pointing to the consequences of its being adopted by people generally.

The choice between reductionist and eliminationist utilitarianism is not an easy one. And likewise it is unclear for naturalizing epistemology whether it is better to reduce terms like "justified" and risk the consequent unintuitiveness of certain judgments that then have to be made about particular examples[6] or to eliminate such intuitive judgments by the draconian method of forbidding or deeming false all epistemic value claims. At least there is considerable diversity of opinion on this question among naturalizing and even anti-naturalist epistemologists. And by the same token I don't know how to say anything definitive about the choice between reductionistic and eliminativistic utilitarianism. To be sure, accepting the former

---

[6] Note that a reliabilist view of justification will hold that in possible worlds (assuming they are possible) where a solitary person is given some totally illusory set of experiences that is exactly like someone's experiences in our actual world the former will lack the latter's *justification(s)* for belief in external things, not merely her *knowledge* of such things.

guarantees a commitment to counter-intuitive moral judgments and, in particular, to the possibility of moral luck, but eliminative utilitarianism makes its own counterintuitive judgments, and in any event both forms of utilitarianism avoid the *inconsistencies* involved in our intuitive judgments concerning moral luck.

However, another way of avoiding the problems of moral luck needs to be mentioned at this point. This alternative ethical approach is very different from any form of utilitarianism, though it resembles eliminative utilitarianism at least to the extent of advocating the elimination of certain ethical properties/epithets from our ongoing ethical theorizing. What I have in mind is a form of virtue ethics that seeks to avoid the paradoxes of moral luck by being *selectively* eliminative in regard to ethical properties/terms. It will turn out that selective eliminativism is also an attractive possibility in naturalizing epistemology, and our brief sketch of the virtue-ethical approach I want to bring to your attention may help to bring to light some previously neglected possibilities in naturalizing epistemology.

3. Naturalizing Virtue Ethics

Some paradigmatic forms of virtue ethics seem totally opposed to any naturalizing approach to ethical theory. It is sometimes said that an emphasis on inner motivations/dispositions and a primary reliance on aretaic, as opposed to deontic, ethical terms typify any virtue ethics worthy of the name, and given these criteria an ethical view like James Martineau's, which defines a hierarchy of morally better and worse motives and claims that actions are to be evaluated solely in terms of their (previously or independently evaluated) motives, is paradigmatically a form of virtue ethics. Yet its primary and exclusive emphasis on inner motivation seems to ally it with epistemological Cartesianism and the latter's "subjective turn" rather than with the kind of naturalizing epistemology that refuses to base its evaluations solely on accessible and inner mental factors. Indeed, an ethical theory like Martineau's—and I mention this unfamiliar view because it is so simply formulated and such a clear-cut instance of virtue ethics—seems to lie at the opposite end of the ethical spectrum from utilitarianism, and if all virtue ethics had to resemble Martineau's view in the relevant respects, it would make no sense to mine the field of virtue ethics for a naturalizing example.[7]

But whereas Martineau's virtue ethics seems capable of making use, in its distinctive way, of all the main concepts/terms of standard ethical theory, there is another, quite different form of virtue ethics—historically familiar from Spinoza's *Ethics*—which *restricts* its ethical terminology in the light of problems raised by a more extensive ethical vocabulary. Spinoza denies the possibility of metaphysical human freedom and on that basis refuses to allow attributions of moral praise- or blameworthiness into his theoretical account of ethical phenomena. But he is willing to speak of certain character traits as virtues or vices, and as admirable or not

---

[7] For Martineau's views, see his *Types of Ethical Theory*, 2 volumes, 3rd edn., 1891. Given Martineau's comparative obscurity, it is perhaps worth noting that Sidgwick devoted more space in *Methods of Ethics* to Martineau's ideas than to those of any other of his contemporaries.

admirable, because he assumes we can make sense of these notions independently of any assumptions about metaphysical freedom of will.

For Spinoza some people can be better or more excellent than others in various respects—e.g., one person might be a lovely person, another a vicious human being—though those judged worse in these ways are not thereby be deemed blameworthy or more blameworthy than those judged to be better. The absence of freedom undercuts moral evaluations that inherently assume some sort of metaphysical freedom on the part of human beings, but other sorts of evaluation do not entail such freedom and thus, according to Spinoza, apply to the sort of metaphysically determined but rational creatures we humans are or can be. A person who frequently turns on people unexpectedly—someone who acts angrily and aggressively toward people, without having been given any provocation—can be regarded as vicious and be avoided as such independently of any commitment to blame the person for being vicious and acting or interacting badly with others (after all, a dog can be called vicious for similar reasons). So Spinoza holds, and we can follow him in holding, that ethical evaluations need not commit us to freedom of will or (therefore) to ascriptions of moral blameworthiness, moral praiseworthiness, or moral responsibility generally.

Nowadays, we are less confident than Spinoza was that causal/metaphysical determinism makes human free will impossible, but we have another motive for wanting to avoid moral/ethical language that commits us to ascriptions of moral praise- and blameworthiness that Spinoza lacked. For we have seen that it is precisely with respect to ascription of blameworthiness and the like that ordinary intuitive thinking ties itself up into knots; the paradoxes of moral luck most closely concern such ascriptions, and so one way to avoid the paradoxes is simply to avoid ascribing blameworthiness, etc., altogether. An ethics of virtue that speaks of admirable and deplorable traits of character and of virtues and vices (or anti-virtues) in the manner indicated by Spinoza can avoid the paradoxes of moral luck by simply eliminating those ethical/moral terms whose ordinary use gives rise to the paradoxes. And this way of dealing with moral luck is quite different both from eliminative and from reductive utilitarianism.

Unlike eliminative utilitarianism, Spinoza-like virtue ethics is only selectively eliminative of moral/ethical concepts/terms, and the concepts/terms it eliminates are (among) those utilitarianism retains, but (re)interprets, reductionistically, in empirical, naturalistic terms. We have thus uncovered three different ways in which naturalizing ethical views can seek to take the sting out of the problem of moral luck. But since it may not yet be clear why I want to hold that virtue ethics of the sort just described should be viewed as a *naturalizing* alternative to utilitarianism, we have some more explaining to do, and the further explanation will help us, in turn, to identify a promising form of naturalizing epistemology that has not yet received the attention it deserves.

One of the most important aspects of naturalizing epistemology has been its typical commitment to externalism in regard to epistemic/evaluative attributions. For the Cartesian epistemologist epistemic rationality and/or justification is a matter of the thoughts, perceptual experiences, and inferences of the would-be knower, and thus concern only the internal mental states of that knower. But an externalist will treat rationality and/or justification as at least partly involving matters external to the mind or subjectivity of the person whose rationality/justification is in question. And a form of externalism like reliabilism with respect to epistemic justification, by making such justification depend in part on how reliable certain inferential processes actually are in representing our environment to us, makes epistemic justification depend on relations between the mind and the (rest of) the natural world. By contrast, internalism may or may not locate the mind at a point in the natural world but it leaves epistemic justification having nothing to do with (the rest of) the natural world, and this illustrates, I think, the clear sense in which externalism is a typical and exemplary feature of naturalizing epistemology.

But one of the thoughts that help to give rise to the paradoxes of moral luck is our ordinary belief that moral blameworthiness, badness, and goodness are a matter of inner willing or intention, not of possibly accidental and/or unforeseeable extra-subjective effects or circumstances. And to the extent, for example, that a Kantian or intuitionist places a primary emphasis on moral evaluation and sees such evaluation as based in the inner or mental life of rational agents, such an approach to ethics seems highly analogous to Cartesian epistemological internalism, and it is not surprising, therefore, that Kantian epistemology is a paradigmatic (though of course highly distinctive) example of Cartesian epistemological subjectivism.

So an ethical emphasis on the moral as inner parallels Cartesian epistemological internalism, but both these positions emphasize only one side of our ordinary ethical and epistemic evaluations. As we have seen, another part of our thinking seems to want to allow for luck, and both reductionist utilitarianism and reductionist naturalizing epistemology rely on and develop this other side of our ethical and epistemic thinking. Each of the latter focuses on extra-subjective factors that may be thought relevant to ethical or epistemic evaluation(s), and so reductionist naturalizing epistemology and standard reductionist utilitarianism represent antitheses to anti-naturalistic epistemological and ethical internalism.

But there is another way of dealing with the tensions and contradictions in our evaluative thinking than by emphasizing one element of the contradiction or paradox at the expense of the other(s). One may find reasons in the contradiction and paradox to drop the terms that give rise to them, and this, we have seen, is how a naturalistic but eliminative utilitarianism and an eliminative naturalizing epistemology-as-psychology both think we should proceed. Or, as a virtue ethics influenced by Spinoza would urge, we can be selectively eliminative: eliminating the (moral) terms whose dependence on luck seems (to some of our strong intuitions) so objectionable in favor of ethical terms/concepts whose dependence on luck or accident or the unforseen seems much less problematic and which (therefore) are less problematically understood in externalist fashion than such specifically moral terms as "blameworthy," "reprehensible," and "morally good."

Thus a person who was maltreated as a child and who (let us assume) became subsequently incapable of getting along well with others can be regarded as being the way he is as a result, in large part, of external, unlucky factors outside his control or ken. But that is no reason to deny that the person gets on badly or poorly with others if the latter notion is understood—as it seems quite natural to do—as entirely independent of the supposition that the person in question is morally blameworthy or reprehensible or responsible for being as he is. And so a Spinoza-inspired ethics of virtue can make use of evaluations that clearly and unproblematically depend on factors external to the agent (her will and knowledge).

Consider a further example. One component of being a good father and, as we may now assume, a good mother as well is to be a good provider for one's family. Imagine, therefore, a father who is laid off work after many years on the job, but who, after several weeks of vain searching for another, comparable position, finds such a position through the sheerest luck (imagine, if you will, that thousands of people with his skills have been laid off and that they are in competition for the small number of positions requiring those skills that are available or opening up). In that case, if he takes the position and is again able to provide for his family in the manner to which they had been accustomed, he will eventually be considered to have been a good provider. But if, on the other hand, he had failed to find any good job and were never again able to provide his family with any sort of comfort, then the overall claim that he is or has been a good provider would be irremediably undercut. Circumstances of the sort just described are familiar from the historical example of the Great Depression of the 1930's, and in regard to such a period it seems in no way odd or problematic to claim that factors of luck played a (considerable) role in determining who was and who was not (able to be) a good provider for his family. (Similar points can be made about the notion of taking good care of one's children/spouse/family.)

The people who were unable to find jobs in the Depression through no fault of their own cannot be considered to have been good providers, but in evaluating them thus we need not condemn or blame them; in fact it is difficult to see how anyone *could* blame them for failing, in such circumstances, to provide well for their families. (It is tragic that a whole generation of men and women should so largely have lacked access to this kind of normal human role-ethical attainment, but that is another matter.) And it is the absence of any implication of blameworthiness or reprehensibility here that allows judgments of good providerhood to depend so plausibly and unproblematically on extra-subjective factors external to the (consciousness of) the evaluated agent. So a Spinoza-inspired ethics of virtue (and in the next section we shall see, as perhaps already obvious, that such an ethics need not be fundamentally egoistic like Spinoza's) removes those ethical concepts that push one toward internalism and relies on other concepts (at least some of) which are understandable in an externalist manner similar to (though not exactly the same as) what we find in reductionistic utilitarianism. And though such virtue ethics doesn't propose to reduce the terms it uses to purely naturalistic terminology, its freedom from internalism and frequent emphasis on external factors of luck give it a definite and substantial resemblance to naturalizing epistemology.[8] What will make the attribution of naturalizing to virtue ethics more plausible, however, will be the fact that naturalizing epistemology allows for an almost exact analogue of the virtue ethics I have just been discussing.

The dispute in the recent epistemological literature between internalists/anti-naturalists and externalists/naturalists largely centers around terms like "justified" and "warranted" which, as we have seen, have aspects favorable to both sides of the

---

[8] Cf. Ernest Sosa, "The Raft and the Pyramid: Coherence versus Foundations in the Theory of Knowledge," in *Midwest Studies in Philosophy* V, esp. p. 23.

dispute. This can lead one to reject all evaluative epistemic terms and move into pure psychology-biology, etc. But, as we saw with ethics, a selective elimination may be possible in which one rejects the terms which underlie and are the source of recent disputes in favor of other evaluative terms that give rise to no similar difficulties, but are less frequently used by epistemologists than the controversial terms "justified," "vindicated," "warranted," etc.

Instead of using the latter, why shouldn't we talk of cognitive mechanisms or strategies or habits that allow or cause *better or worse adaptation* to a creature's (or a person's or a species's) environment or talk of *better or worse cognitive functioning* (of functioning well or poorly)? Such notions/terms take in extra-subjective factors and are clearly relational and externalist; but unlike the terms that are presently the cause of so much epistemological controversy, these notions wear their relationality on their sleeve. Talk of functioning and of adaptation clearly has to do with more than what is inside the mind (or even the body, in most cases) of the individual whose functioning or adaptation is being evaluated as better or worse. And if internalism has no plausibility whatever in regard to such notions, then there is no reason to deny that luck or accident or the unforeseeable can play a role in their applicability. So if we are selectively eliminative in epistemology, we can undercut the problems of rational or epistemic luck analogously to the way in which virtue ethics can undercut the problems of moral luck.

Thus a naturalizing epistemology that seeks to get beyond the opposing positions in recent disputes about epistemological naturalizing need not go all the way to psychology and biology. Or, since much psychology would be willing to talk about cognitive dysfunction and much biology about maladaptiveness, perhaps I should say, rather, that leaving internalism or naturalizing reductionism for science does not, as one might suppose, force one to give up all epistemic or cognitive evaluation(s). Talk about how well and adaptively one's cognitive mechanisms are functioning seems noncommittal on the questions of justification and rationality that have been the focus of recent and traditional epistemological debate. And an epistemology that makes use of the former notions and avoids the latter is indisputably a version or example of naturalizing epistemology.[9] Since, by dint of its Spinozistic talk of better and worse or more and less excellent, the virtue ethics we have been talking about seems a very close analogue of the just-mentioned form of naturalizing epistemology, it may also now be clearer why I have spoken of such an approach to virtue ethics as naturalized or naturalizing. However, I would like at this point, and finally, to consider one further familiar aspect of the naturalizing tendency in epistemology. It too has an analogue in ethics, and in this case I think ethics, and in particular the virtue ethics we have been describing so sketchily, has a great deal to learn from its counterpart in epistemology.[10]

---

[9] Unless it brings in God's purposes as the basis for understanding "functioning well," etc. In "Positive Epistemic Status," *Philosophical Perspectives* 2 (1988): pp. 1–50, Alvin Plantinga makes this sort of notion central to his epistemological view without committing himself on the necessity of relying on theism. Plantinga also doesn't point out the analogy with Spinoza's ethics, and I should perhaps mention that non-egoistic naturalistic virtue ethics need have nothing to do with theism or Spinoza's pantheism.

[10] The just-sketched form of virtue ethics is described and defended at length in *From Morality to Virtue*.

4. Ethics in Mid-Voyage

In our discussion so far of the naturalizing tendency in epistemology and its ethical counterparts, we have not mentioned what is perhaps the historically most important and currently most familiar aspect of naturalizing epistemology. The idea that in philosophy as in science, we must proceed with our actual beliefs and doubts, rather than base our thinking on some isolated set of pure certainties arrived at through some methodological ideal of absolute indubitability, goes back at least to Peirce and is perhaps most forcefully and famously expressed in Neurath's image of sailors who must repair their ship in mid-voyage.[11] In "Epistemology Naturalized," Quine refers to the Neurath simile in describing what he clearly takes to be an essential element of epistemological naturalizing: the commitment to working what one has and already accepts in order to improve the latter and learn more about the world.[12] But although this methodological conservatism has been typical of inquiry in the natural sciences, it has been notably absent from Cartesian-influenced attempts to reconstruct all knowledge on the basis of idealized and absolute certainties. And according to Quine epistemology should change its stripes and, by adopting a similar attitude of methodological conservatism, become properly scientific and naturalistic.

Note, however, that it is hardly clear that methodologically conservative natural science must ipso facto commit itself to reducing or eliminating certain (ordinary) terms. In letting our critical and inventive faculties loose on the corpus of what we already accept, we needn't perhaps prejudge the issue of whether the progress to be made thereby must inevitably occur through the reduction/elimination of various terms/concepts. So Quine and Peirce and Neurath's sober ideal of epistemology done in mid-voyage seems both more fundamental than and at the same time logically independent of the aspects of naturalizing discussed in earlier sections of the present essay. As such, moreover, it has an analogue in ethics that we have so far left unmentioned. If, given the history of ethical theory, anything has a right to be considered the most fundamental task of ethics, surely it is the task of showing that justice pays—or, more generally, that morality and a concern to do well by other people can be justified. Typically, attempts to show the validity of morality in this fashion have centered around arguments intended to refute egoism, the attitude of pure or fundamental selfishness. And what seems interesting here in connection with the issue of naturalizing is the resemblance this traditional ethical enterprise bears to Cartesian epistemology.

The Cartesian/Kantian epistemologist starts with the subjective data or consciousness of a single individual in isolation and seeks by argument to bridge the putative gap between the subject and the world. Such epistemology starts with what it takes to be the indubitable or more certain and attempts to justify belief in what it takes to be initially less certain and more in need of epistemic/epistemological validation. As such it clearly falls under Quine's strictures, and even without committing

---

[11] See Otto Neurath, "Protokollsaetze," *Erkenntnis* 3, 1932, p. 206; and C. S. Peirce, "The Fixation of Belief," in J. Buchler, ed., *The Philosophical Writings of Peirce* (N. Y.: Dover, 1955).

[12] See Kornblith, ed., *Naturalizing Epistemology*, pp. 15–29.

ourselves here either to agreeing or to disagreeing with those strictures, we should at this point be able to recognize the possibility of a similar move in a methodologically naturalizing ethics.

Why should an ethics that is properly sure itself, that wishes to proceed as far as possible in the manner of natural or other science, treat the standpoint of self-concern or self-interest not only as more secure than concern for others, but as a theoretically necessary point of departure for any attempt to justify or vindicate the latter? Why does (basic) concern for others need this kind of justification? Why can't we say, rather, that (almost) everyone in recent ethics has rejected (basic) egoism, and that current ethical theory has a perfect right to assume the validity and ethical justification of concern for other people until and unless our accumulating ethical ideas and theories give us reason to reject this fundamental assumption? There were notable egoistic theories (e.g., Stoicism and Epicureanism) in the ancient world, but that need not and should not disturb our own long-standing and on-going assumption of the validity of (non-egoistic) concern for others, any more than the existence of epistemological skeptics in the ancient world and in some cases more recently is a sufficient reason to go in for Cartesian epistemology. If a proper naturalizing methodology undercuts any need in epistemology to vindicate our beliefs about the world and others on the basis of assumptions about the subject in isolation, then a similarly naturalistic attitude in and toward ethical thought and theory should allow us to accept the ethical validity of a fundamental concern for others without (successfully) attempting to show how concern for others can be based in sheer self-concern or self-interest.[13] Both epistemological Cartesianism and the traditional task of defending altruism to the egoist treat the individual or individualistic standpoint as more fundamental than and necessarily involved in the justification of some larger or more inclusive picture of things, and, again, even if we remain neutral or uncertain about the relevance of scientific methodological conservatism to these areas of philosophy, we can surely see that ethics contains a plausible analogue to the naturalizing epistemological attitude of a Peirce, or Quine, or Neurath. An ethics or an ethical theory that adopts for itself the same methodological attitude as these philosophers recommend for epistemology—though clearly they wouldn't have wanted to limit its application just to one area of philosophy—deserves to be called a naturalizing or naturalized ethics, and I think ethical theory therefore needs at this point to recognize the possibility of such an approach and consider its merits and demerits. And it may be worth our while to consider in particular whether some philosophers who accept the validity of basic concern for others have recently been too concerned about finding a way to refute egoism.

However, I also want to point out that a methodologically naturalizing approach in ethics is perfectly compatible (at least on the face of it) with the alterations in our ordinary ethical thinking that utilitarianism and Spinozistic virtue ethics urge on us for their respective theoretical reasons. As I mentioned earlier, utilitarians believe various elements in our common-sense moral thinking to be incoherent or without

---

[13] This point is, in effect, a naturalized version of Prichard's intuitionistic thesis that other-regarding moral claims present themselves as binding on us quite independently of any eudaimonistic assumptions we may or may not make. See his "Does Moral Philosophy Rest on a Mistake?" in *Moral Obligation* (Oxford, 1949).

adequate foundation, and it is largely on that basis that they propose some version of the principle of utility as the ultimate criterion of right and virtuous action. But the principle of utility retains the concern for others that is fundamental to commonsense morality; it merely gerrymanders it—in some ways shrinking, in others ways enlarging it—in the light of the difficulties and confusions it claims to find in our ordinary morality. This procedure seems in no way out of keeping with the ethical instantiation of methodological conservatism, and given the obvious connection between utilitarianism and the naturalizing tendency, this should come as no surprise. So utilitarianism in appropriate methodological fashion retains concern for others while rejecting other elements in ordinary moral thought, and a naturalizing methodological approach to ethics generally would then insist that utilitarianism has every reason to retain its commitment to a concern for other people and needn't feel any need to present a refutation of egoism.

By the same token, anyone nowadays who starts with the assumption—either theoretically or in daily living—that we should be concerned with other people and who decides, on the basis of their inherent difficulties, that we should abandon Kantian, common-sense, or utilitarian moral theory for an ethics of virtue, should favor an altruistic over an egoistically Spinozan ethics of virtue. We saw earlier that what distinguishes an ethics of virtue that seeks to handle the paradoxes of moral luck (and other theoretical problems that we have no space to mention here)[14] is the absence of those concepts of morality that give rise to the paradoxes. Such an ethics eliminates the notions of moral blameworthiness or moral goodness in favor of talk about what is better or worse, excellent or poor, admirable or criticizable in human conduct or motivation, and though it is true that Spinoza eliminates the former notions for the latter in a fundamentally egoistic manner, there is absolutely no reason, given methodological conservatism, why we should follow him in this respect.

An adherent of the naturalizing approach to ethics can therefore claim that we can and should formulate any virtue ethics we may wish to defend without assuming that we need to show how such an ethics can refute egoism. In other words, a virtue ethics that avoids (certain) specifically moral categories can fundamentally deplore attempts to harm or failures of concern for other people, and in the light of methodological conservatism has every right and reason to do so until and unless something turns up to cast substantive doubt on such non-egoistic terms of criticism.

Does that mean that we have no motive to show how other-regarding reasons/virtues can be derived from self-regarding (or non-other-regarding) reasons/virtues unless we reject naturalizing in ethics? Not at all.

To be sure, I have only analogized between naturalizing ethical and epistemological ideas and structures, rather than seeking to defend naturalizing across the board in any definitive way, and anyone who feels a pressing philosophical need to defend ethical concern for others might stand the present discussion on its head and reject ethical naturalism or naturalizing for its inability to comprehend the philosophical force of egoism. But, perhaps more significantly, even a naturalizer in ethics or elsewhere has reason to encourage attempts to argue from non-other-regarding virtues/reasons to other-regarding virtues/reasons or at least to welcome such an

---

[14] See the works referred to in footnote 2.

argument if one is ever successfully produced. The reason, however, has more to do with the metaphysical/reductionist naturalism mentioned earlier than with doubts about the appropriateness of methodological conservatism in science, epistemology, or even ethics.

If (all) other-regarding virtues/reasons can be derived from non-other-regarding virtues/reasons, then the latter can be reduced to the former and this opens up the possibility of an ethics of reasons or virtues that is fundamentally simpler and more systematically unified that an ethics that cannot effect such reductions. So a reduction of other-regarding values to egoistic or neutral coinage helps to achieve the scientific methodological desideratum of systematic unity in theory. There is thus reason even in a naturalistic or naturalizing ethics to applaud the reduction of the other-regarding to self-regarding terms, if such a thing ever turns out to be possible, but such an attitude is in no way incompatible with the naturalizing methodological belief that we can be and presently are justified in accepting certain other-regarding virtues and/or reasons without being able to produce such a reduction. Compare for example, Smart's version of central-state materialism. On his view we can reduce the mental to the physical or neurophysiological without having to presuppose, as clearly Smart does not, that our beliefs about mental states and processes are made more secure or stand in need of justification by such a unifying philosophical/scientific reduction. A similar view can be taken of the relation between ethical concern for others and egoism or self-interest.

If what we have been saying above is correct, there have been naturalizing tendencies in ethics—e.g., utilitarianism—for a long time now.[15] But they have not been conscious of themselves in relation to the wider spectrum of naturalizing possibilities explored in this paper. It will be interesting to see how ethics can accommodate itself to the broader picture.

---

[15] Some recent naturalizing trends in ethics that I have not mentioned here include: the use of ethical claims as (best) explanations of historical phenomena by Nicholas Sturgeon and others; attempts by Georges Rey, Daniel Dennett and others to reduce moral-psychological notions like weakness of will and free will to computational/naturalistic categories; and, of course, continuing attempts to give naturalistic *analyses* of ethical terms.

I would like to thank Michael Devitt for extremely helpful comments on the present paper.

19

Nietzsche and Virtue Ethics

In recent years virtue ethics has been undergoing a remarkable revival, and Aristotle has been the principal focus and model of attempts to formulate a contemporary virtue ethics that can hold its own against utilitarianism, Kantian ethics, and contract theory. But other historical names are also associated with virtue ethics and Nietzsche's is among them.

However, there is a fairly well-known difficulty with treating Nietzsche as a virtue ethicist. I am referring not to the fact of Nietzsche's general elusiveness and lack of systematicness, but to his reputation for being a perfectionist, that is, a consequentialist who thinks our main duty is to bring about or promote power in individuals and also ideal individuals or supermen. This greatly oversimplifies a certain approach or set of approaches to Nietzsche interpretation, but I hope this audience of experts will forgive my lack of Nietzsche scholarship. Perhaps they will be able to state more accurately and appropriately what I have said and shall say about Nietzsche's relation to virtue ethics. I certainly hope so, but let me return to the task at hand.

As I said, Nietzsche is commonly thought of as a perfectionistic consequentialist, as an ethicist who thinks we should promote the good, but who has a distinctive and controversial view of what that good is. However, Nietzsche's affinity with virtue ethics also seems very obvious, and one wonders then whether Nietzsche's perfectionism is compatible with his being a virtue ethicist or whether, instead, there is simply a deep tension in his ethical thinking. And though I again am getting out of my depth, it seems to me that there really is a tension here. Much of what Nietzsche says points toward perfectionism, but a great deal seems consonant with a virtue–ethical approach that looks inward rather than to results for a criterion of ethical excellence and a criterion of ethical deficiency.

Thus on the very first page of *The Antichrist* Nietzsche says that good is whatever enhances or promotes the will to power, the (pleasurable) sense of power, and power itself. But he then goes on to say that evil or bad is whatever comes from weakness. This latter claim, if followed through consistently, represents a kind of virtue ethics, a rather radical kind at that, but, of course, the former seems perfectionistic. So it is difficult to categorize Nietzsche as an ethicist, and I don't want to claim that he really is a virtue ethicist, that his seeming perfectionism is an illusion. However, it would be interesting, perhaps, more fully to characterize the virtue-ethical side of Nietzsche's thought, the side embodied in the idea that it makes the greatest ethical difference whether one acts from weakness or from strength or power; and that is what I would like to do in the remainder of this paper. If we think of ethics in this way, we are engaged, as I said, in a very radical form of virtue ethics, so let me first say something about this issue and then try to fit what I am saying to Nietzsche's own thought as it strikes someone who is clearly not a Nietzsche scholar.

If we treat as the sole criterion of ethical admirability or deplorability whether one's actions (or even large-scale institutions) come from strength or from weakness, we are committed to what I call "agent based" virtue ethics. Such ethics treats all ethical characterizations of actions as derivable from fundamental and independent aretaic characterizations of the inner states–in particular the motives or character–of the agents who perform them, and a good example of such agent-basing would be a moral view that regards benevolence, or universal benevolence, as fundamentally admirable–as admirable in a way that requires no further backing or justification–and that then treats the moral goodness or permissibility of actions as entirely dependent on whether they reflect sufficient benevolence on the part of the agent. I have recently been working on and testing the implications of a theory of this particular sort (the result is about to appear in a long-overdue issue of *Midwest Studies in Philosophy*). But most relevant here is the fact that the virtue-ethical side of Nietzsche also seems to be agent-based.

That is, Nietzsche seems to be saying that weakness is ethically deplorable in and of itself and without reference to any further test or justification. And when he writes in this mode, he seems to be saying that actions and other things are to be evaluated in terms of whether they reflect, exhibit or express either inner weakness or inner strength. But in what sense, then, is such virtue ethics radical as a form of virtue ethics?

The answer, I think, is that agent-basing makes the moral or ethical quality of actions more completely depend on the excellence or deficiency of the agent's inner states than anything we find, say, in Aristotle. When Aristotle says that the virtuous individual is the measure of rightness or nobility in actions, he certainly seems to be saying something that might be interpreted as agent-based. But he also says that the virtuous individual perceives or sees what is right or noble to do in any given situation, and the perceptual metaphor is best interpreted, I think, as telling us that actions or acts have a somewhat agent-independent moral status. An act isn't right or noble simply because it is performed by a certain kind of agent, but rather an agent counts as virtuous only if and because s/he reliably sees and enacts what is morally called for in various situations. Moreover, if it is objected that Aristotle's view is teleological and treats virtue and right action as a matter, most fundamentally, of how things relate to independently characterized human happiness or eudaimonia, then, once again, ethical excellence or virtue is not the ground floor of ethical evaluation and we have something other than an agent-based form of virtue ethics. (I am inclined, moreover, to think that such a teleological interpretation is inadequate, but that is a story for another occasion.)

So agent-basing places greater and more fundamental emphasis on the inner states or character of agents than anything we are likely to find in Aristotle. Or, for that matter, most other virtue ethicists. For reasons I can't go into here, Plato, Spinoza, Hutcheson, Kant, Abelard, Augustine, Leslie Stephen, Hume, and Schopenhauer all offer varying forms of resistance to interpretation as agent-basers; and so too, given his perfectionistic tendencies, does Nietzsche. But still if–if–we see Nietzsche as saying that all goodness and badness is a matter, ultimately, of the motivational sources of a given action or practice or institution, he is an agent-baser and in rather select (if that is the word) company. For the only clear-cut historical example of agent-based virtue ethics that I know of is James Martineau in *Types of Ethical Theory*.

Martineau's ethics of motives is widely regarded as inadequate, but the most famous reasons that have been given for dismissing Martineau, those offered by Sidgwick in *The Methods of Ethics*, actually point toward and support an agent-based virtue ethics of the kind I alluded to above, one that makes universal benevolence the basis of all moral evaluation. There is certainly, again, no time to say much about this here, but an ethics that treats acts as right or wrong as depending on whether they come from motives sufficiently close to universal or impartial benevolence is not a form of utilitarianism, but rather, as one might say, a virtue ethics that turns utilitarianism outside in. (Of course, it might immediately strike one that such an ethics contravenes "ought" implies "can," but that worry would in fact be misplaced. Even if my motivation is irrecusably malevolent, a free-will compatibilist can say that I have it in my power to avoid an action that, to the best of my knowledge, would hurt people, and such a refraining would not, then, exhibit or reflect or come from my malevolence. It would be morally permissible.)

Agent-basing is a possible and possibly promising approach to ethics, and I would like now briefly to explore what might be said in favor of a virtue ethics that based its evaluations in inner weakness and strength. It all depends, of course, on one's views of inner strength and weakness. For Nietzsche, presumably, those who give to others out of guilt or conscience or pity are acting from weakness and condemnable as such. But Nietzsche also holds and frequently says that it is possible to give to others out of an overflowing sense of superabundance, and this would represent a form of strength, rather than weakness. To that extent, Nietzsche offers a justification for (occasional acts of) altruism, and I use this term deliberately. When one gives out of superabundance, one isn't giving now in order to receive later and thereby enhance one's well-being. One gives out of a sense of well-being, but not necessarily in order to promote that well-being, so the kinds of actions Nietzsche here recommends or praises are altruistic, given the usual philosophical understanding of the term. To be sure, Nietzsche also thinks his view is somewhere beyond the egoism-altruism debate or distinction, but let me simplify.

Now Nietzsche focuses on certain important kinds of inner strength and weakness, but, arguably, there are other kinds he doesn't mention. So if one feels that a plausible total ethics simply couldn't be based in Nietzsche's idea of strength, still there may be other forms and ideals of strength which combined with what Nietzsche has to say about inner strength might yield up a viable and even plausible form of agent-based virtue ethics. One might wonder, for example, whether the kind of strength Nietzsche talks about could allow for or justify a democratic or even an orderly society and whether, therefore, his views can yield any sort of plausible social ethic. Of course, the assumption that we need to justify social institutions and even perhaps speak of social justice seems very un-Nietzschean. But most of us aren't fully Nietzschean, however sympathetic we may be to much of what he says, so I think it is worth asking whether one could expand on Nietzsche's ideas about strength in the direction of a more sociable or society-friendly form of virtue ethics.

I have been encouraged to attempt such an expansion myself through a consideration of certain ideas about self-sufficiency which, though not actually to be found in Nietzsche, have a certain resonance with what he says. Clearly, the individual who overflows to others out of strength acts from a sense of sufficiency or self-sufficiency that we would intuitively think of as strong rather than weak. But consider, then, what we think of people who are content to depend on the labor of others rather than themselves working. Such people include both so-called welfare chiselers and, at the other end of the spectrum, the idle rich. Willing parasitism constitutes a lack of self-sufficiency—as Hegel arguably showed us in his discussion of master and slave. And if we say that a truly strong individual must in every way be self-sufficient, we might have the basis for a social ethic and also for altruism beyond what was supported, in Nietzschean terms, above. If someone with inner strength is unwilling to be a parasite, then such a person will want to repay what society gives him or her and do useful work. Once again, this motive is altruistic. It aims to repay others or society for what has been done or is being done for one, and though this may come from a feeling of being well-off, it doesn't rest or doesn't have to rest on a desire to promote one's future happiness. And perhaps society could cohere and perpetuate itself on the basis of a motive such as this.

For a long time I believed that a notion of inner strength that incorporated Nietzschean and other elements might offer us, in very un-Nietzschean fashion, a justification for social morality and norms, in particular, of social and legal justice. (I defended such a view in an article entitled "Virtue Ethics and Democratic Values" that appeared in the *Journal of Social Philosophy*.) But I now have two sorts of doubts about this sort of approach, and I would like to conclude my remarks by spelling these out.

To begin with, I wonder about the idea that altruism has to be justified in terms of strength in order to be ethically attractive. What if, in Humean fashion, we simply have fellow-feeling and are on that basis inclined to act sympathetically and helpfully toward other people? Such giving seems morally attractive, or at least not unattractive. There need be no turning inward of aggression in such giving, yet it also doesn't come from strength in Nietzsche's sense. Nietzsche, with his idealization of living and being alone, would presumably consider such fellow-feeling base, the stuff herds are made of. But would we agree? I don't think I would, and in that case it seems to me that society can and perhaps should be based on human fellow-feeling in ways that a Nietzschean virtue ethics of power or strength cannot accommodate or take advantage of.

Secondly, and this relates to my first doubt, it would seem that an ethic that treated self-sufficient strength as the touchstone of ethical evaluation would have to consider it admirable for people to be psychologically independent of one another. Certainly, the Stoics held that virtue required one not to depend or count too much on other people, and there is obviously a strong element of this in Nietzsche's thought as well. But I just don't buy it. I don't think there is anything particularly attractive or even admirable in a godlike emotional detachment from others, and if we think that way, then the idea of self-sufficiency cannot be accepted as a universally valid human ideal nor form the basis of a total ethics. If love for others expresses or exhibits weakness or a lack of self-sufficiency, we still, most of us, don't want to criticize or depreciate such love, and that unwillingness will make us most unlikely to embrace the sort of agent-based virtue ethics one finds inconsistently and partially embodied in Nietzsche's philosophy.

20

Caring Versus the Philosophers

I

I am sure that everyone attending these meetings knows about the justice/caring debate. Carol Gilligan's distinction between two ways of approaching morality and Nel Noddings's subsequent systematic discussion of a "feminine" ethic of caring have had an enormous influence on psychological and educational theory over the past decade or so, but until more recently, the impact on philosophy and on philosophical discussions of ethics has been much less. I remember my own original reaction or lack of it to the new ideas. I thought the idea that men and women think differently about moral issues was absolutely fascinating and very possibly correct, but I didn't see how Gilligan's and Noddings's views could affect the ethical theorist's efforts to come up with a comprehensive view of morality. If anything, it seemed that the duality of human moral thinking threatened us with a kind of relativism, one that left men and women talking past one another and gave them no basis for thinking critically and constructively *together*. That idea was certainly daunting, if not frightening, to the aims of ethical theory, so, as I just indicated, I preferred to leave the justice/caring issue to one side and do ethical theory as I always had.

I think very differently now, and so too, I believe, do a great number of other philosophers. Many ethicists now think that caring has an important role in the moral life, one not much noticed before Gilligan and Noddings wrote, and so, even those philosophers who pursue supposedly masculine thinking about justice and rights of autonomy often argue that such thinking needs to be supplemented or complemented by a consideration of the role and moral significance of caring and its attendant ideas of responsibility for and connection to other people. Still other philosophers have placed an even greater emphasis on the moral ideal of caring. Rather than say that independent ideals of caring and justice both have an important role to play in the moral life, these philosophers–and I count myself among them–have attempted to show that caring can be the basis for all of morality, so that whatever validity ideals of justice have can be subsumed under the notion of caring and grounded from within that notion.

But from the standpoint of the original caring ethicists, such an attempt to make caring do all the work of ethics may seem extreme and implausible. Both Noddings and Gilligan have wanted to limit the terrain of caring and to allow for a somewhat independent role for justice, rights, and autonomy, and from their perspective philosophical ethicists who try to make caring cover the whole of the moral life may seem to have got the bit between their teeth; or, to switch the metaphor, such philosophers seem to have gone from the frying pan of indifference to caring to the fire of a caring monomania.

The original insight about the specific role and importance of caring may thus seem to have been lost in the philosopher's eagerness to find a single neat theory of morality.

But even when philosophers give justice an independent weight alongside caring, their efforts to integrate these two factors within a total theory of ethics may seem, to those advocating the importance of caring, to distort the caring ethic. When the philosopher asks the caring ethicist how caring fits together with justice, her or his desire for a total or systematic view of morality stands revealed as such, and I have heard caring ethicists say that such a desire violates the very spirit of such an ethics. So I would like to begin by considering this issue and attempting to show that the questions philosophy asks and the aims it exhibits need not be regarded as incompatible with the ethic of caring. Thereafter, I would like to consider some distinctively philosophical arguments and questions that seem initially to threaten the caring ethic, but that turn out actually to help us toward a better understanding of the significance of caring.

II

One objection that caring ethicists sometimes have to philosophical ethics concerns issues of sensitivity and particularity. Caring as Noddings and others have described it involves being focussed on, absorbed in, another person or other persons, and this, they have argued, involves a sensitive concern with the particularity of another person's needs. By contrast, standard monolithic ethical codes and theories can seem to offer a single criterion for all moral decisions and, in doing so, to shunt aside subtle differences in the particularity of situations and persons. The Kantian Categorical Imperative, Bentham and Mill's Principle of Utility, and the simple sets of prima facie rules offered by intuitionists like W. D. Ross have all been criticized in terms like these, and, interestingly enough, the Kantians, for example, have taken the criticism sufficiently to heart so that many of them now advocate a caring-like sensitivity to nuanced need and circumstance within the moral requirement, derived from the Categorical Imperative, to promote the happiness of other people. But, in addition, the Utilitarian can claim that seeking the greatest happiness of the greatest number precisely involves being sensitive to people's differing needs and to the opportunities and obstacles inherent in differing social situations, and the intuitionist can argue– indeed they have argued–that any finite set of rules needs to be supplemented or enhanced by a nuanced sense or intuition of the situationally varying relative weights of those rules. So to a first approximation, familiar moral theories needn't be or needn't at any rate remain the blunt instruments that a caring ethic would have to reject out of hand.

And the same point can be made about attempts to extend the idea of caring so that it covers all of morality. Noddings has said that caring is essentially about relations with people with whom one is or will be personally involved. How one should act toward people one doesn't know, distant people who are, say, sick or starving, is or has been for her a question outside the purview of caring, but in recent years Virginia Held and I have advocated the idea that there are two different kinds of caring.[1] There is intense personal caring toward people one *knows*, but there also can be a general humanitarian caring or concern about people one only knows *about* (as part of a group), and a morally decent person, we have argued, will combine in some fashion these two kinds of caring or concern (together with self-concern, but let us leave that aside, to simplify matters).

Now philosophers who advocate a combination of personal with humanitarian caring will want to say how those different modes of caring are combined in a single moral view and/or in a single moral individual. But the criticism that such combined caring is somehow too blunt an instrument to give us a realistic picture of the moral life seems largely beside the point. If there is nothing blunt or insensitive in the original caring ethicists' idea that morality contains elements of both caring and justice, it will be blunt or insensitive to say that morality consists in two kinds of caring, only if there is something insensitive or insufficiently nuanced in the idea that *humanitarian caring can do the work that justice does in more traditional approaches to morality*. Well, perhaps there is. But I have elsewhere argued that the caring ethicist can cover the essential ideas of justice through the idea of humanitarian concern for others,[2] and I don't want to repeat those arguments here, because I think the fundamental objection to what philosophy is doing here relates to a different issue, the issue of integration or system-building.

Whether the moral life involves justice and caring or simply two kinds of caring, I think the caring ethicist will object to the idea of *combining* two such elements within a single theory or view. Good, moral, just and caring people don't operate with or use some total theory in which considerations of justice and of caring are mentioned and somehow integrated. Rather, they go about their lives, sometimes dealing with issues of justice, sometimes being involved in caring relationships– alternatively, sometimes acting from humanitarian concerns and sometimes acting

---

[1] Noddings made the point about the limitations of caring in a talk given to the Society of Women in Philosophy in 1988. See also Virginia Held, *Feminist Morality*, Chicago, 1993, and my "Agent-Based Virtue Ethics," *Midwest Studies in Philosophy*, 1995, and "Caring in the Balance," in J. Haber and M. Halfon, eds., *Norms and Values: Essays on the Work of Virginia Held* (Rowman and Littlefield, 1998).

[2] See "The Justice of Caring," *Social Philosophy and Policy*, 1998.

out of concern for the perceived needs of people they know. And there is no more integration than *that*.

For the philosopher to suggest otherwise is really, it seems, to distort the moral life and indeed, furthermore, to do so in the name of a factitious unity or integration that actually *gets in the way* of morality. For consider someone who operates constantly with some overarching theory or principle that tells him or her how much weight to put, and when to put weight, on concern for those s/he knows and loves and how much weight to put, and when to put weight, on general humanitarian goals. Such preoccupation with a principle, it can be argued, will actually interfere with one's concern for other people, and, to borrow a famous example from Bernard Williams, the husband, forced to choose between saving his drowning wife and saving a stranger, who uses a moral principle to determine whether it is all right or obligatory to save his wife can be seen as having an insufficient or distorted love for his wife. (Such a husband is said by Williams to have "one thought too many.") In her original book on *Caring*, Noddings made a similar point, and the eighteenth-century moral sentimentalist Francis Hutcheson also argued that someone with a genuine benevolent concern for the well-being of others would be concerned directly with people's well-being rather than being concered with whether s/he was acting rightly or admirably according to some principle or rule. (The similarity between Hutcheson and Noddings shouldn't be surprising, given that caring and benevolence are both sentiments and that, therefore, Noddings is, at least within limits, a kind of modern-day moral sentimentalist.)

In a recent essay in a Festschrift for Virginia Held, Noddings has substantially qualified her insistence that the moral life not be mediated by rules and rule following, but I think her original impulse in *Caring* was in fact more correct.[3] If we really are concerned with the well-being of others, we are focussed on them and their well-being, not on questions about our own moral status and that of our actions relative to certain moral rules or standards, but this is a complex and controversial notion, and I won't try to defend it further here. For the moment, let me just use it to see whether the criticism of philosophical/ethical theorizing mentioned above can really undermine the kind of systematic approach philosophers love and want the caring ethicist to emulate.

According to a morality of caring (or benevolence, a la Hutcheson), a good person isn't attentive to and guided by moral rules, principles, or standards but has a direct or unmediated concern for (other) people's well-being. But that doesn't mean there can't be such a thing as a valid morality of caring, it only means that that morality can be used to judge the moral quality of people's actions without our having to insist that those who are judged should themselves have to think in explicitly moral terms. When a person seeks the well-being, say, of his children, and does so without being concerned about the moral character of his own actions relative to certain rules, a caring ethic can say that that person acts morally well and even praiseworthily, but it may also insist that if the person had been concerned with moral standards and with whether his actions were conformable to them, he and his actions would be *less* morally worthy.

---

[3] See "Feminist Morality and Social Policy," in Haber and Halfon, eds., *op. cit.*

The caring ethic thus represents a standard or criterion of right or admirable action and motivation that the moral individual isn't supposed to apply to herself. To that extent, such an ethic insists on a kind of split (Michael Stocker calls it a schizophrenia, but that seems a bit tendentious) between what guides good people and how we evaluate that goodness. The people themselves, according to the ethic of caring, are not to guide themselves by the principle that it is right to act caringly, wrong not to; rather, they are to be directly concerned with people's well-being. But that principle can still represent a valid moral standard against which their conduct and motivation can be measured by those who would wish to do so.

So the caring ethic can tell us when behavior and attitudes are praiseworthy or bad, but it also tells us that the morally best attitude doesn't involve a concern as such with being moral or conforming to the ethic of caring. And perhaps a near analogue in our ordinary thought and action can be found in the morality of self-defense, for we think one can be justified in killing when that is necessary to saving one's own life, but we would consider it weird and in any event unnecessary if the person who defended himself, say, against someone coming at him with a meat cleaver had to clear his self-defense with his conscience, before acting. What is precisely permissible, when someone is coming at one with a meat cleaver, is that one act to save one's own life *without worrying whether one is acting rightly or whether one is in general morally permitted to act in self-defense*. There may be no time for such thoughts, but the self-defense will still be justified, and so the principle that self-defense is permissible is not one we expect to guide those whose actions are deemed permissible according to that very principle.

I think an overall morality of caring has this same feature, and that it is an attractive feature, and though there are a host of objections to such a view that I haven't had and won't have time to consider, let's see how it bears on the issue of integrated philosophical accounts of morality. An account that spoke of some sort of balance between caring and justice or between two kinds of caring would indeed be flawed if it had to function as an action guide for moral agents. For the guide would get in the way of genuine caring, interposing a fairly complex principle between the moral agent and those s/he cares about. But according to what I have just been suggesting, an integrated or systematic account of morality needn't function as an action-guide, but may simply represent a general criterion or standard for the external or post-hoc judging of actions and motives. Those who elaborate a non-simplistic theory of when actions are right, wrong, or praiseworthy needn't be supposing that good people should or can guide themselves or govern their lives by such a theory, and so this objection to philosophical integration or sytematicness may not have much force.

But can we really coherently suppose that two kinds of caring, say, can be balanced within an individual without the individual making use of a principle that recommends or requires such balance. If the theory says that the best person balances concern for those s/he knows well (considered as a group or class) with humanitarian concern for (the class of) people generally, doesn't the best person have to pay attention to that very principle, that very standard, in order to insure that s/he actually does balance those concerns? I think not.

Consider someone who loves her own two children equally. There may be a balance between the concern she feels for the one child and that which she feels for the other, but that doesn't mean that she has to guide her behavior toward them via the consideration that she ought to be equally concern with each of them. The concerns may simply *be* (roughly) equal, and in that case her interest, attention, and efforts regarding the two children will naturally flow in a balanced or non-lopsided way in their direction. And something similar can be said about the overarching structure of an ethic of caring.

For an ethic of caring to cover all of morality, it needs to accommodate the concern we feel for those we know and love but also the humanitarian concern that a good person will feel toward people generally. And in a morally good individual there will be some sort of balance between these concerns. More, much more, needs to be said about what such balance, which is not supposed to be exact equality, amounts to, and I have written elsewhere at considerable length about this issue. But for present purposes, it may be enough to point out that a unified morality of caring that advocates a balance between two kinds of caring needn't assume that individuals who exemplify such a balance will do so out of a conscientious concern to do what they ought to do according to an ethic of caring. A moral theory of caring may say, rather, that the moral individual will feel concern for (the class of) those near and dear to her and feel concern for (the class of) human beings generally and that neither of these concerns will dwarf the other. It will hold that a person's actions are wrong if they don't exemplify such a balance and right if they do, but that doesn't mean that a caring individual will deliberately try to act (or feel) in a balanced fashion or act that way out of a sense of obligation or duty. The correct moral-philosophical view of caring, whatever it turns out to be, needn't seek to impose itself on caring individuals and needn't, therefore, interfere with the particularity and sensitivity of concern for others that mark what is most attractive, and indeed compelling, about the ideal of caring.

Of course, advocating an ideal of balanced caring raises important issues of moral education. How does one get, persuade, educate people to care about others in the way specified as ideal by the theory? But this is a problem obviously too for the simpler or smaller ethic of caring that focuses mainly on our relations with people we know or are intimate with. Caring for others is not something one can inculcate simply by telling or even persuading people that they *ought* to care, so attention needs to be paid to the processes whereby people come to care about people they know, and, relative to the morally more systematic view of caring I have sketched or alluded to here, more, much more, clearly needs to be said about the ways people can develop balanced or non-lopsided concern as between those they are intimate with and humanity as such or generally. But there is no time to say that more here. Rather, I would like to discuss some other ways in which philosophy and its concerns may seem to clash with the ethic of caring.

III

As I mentioned earlier, some advocates of caring hold that caring doesn't cover the whole of morality and believe that beyond the sphere of our most intimate relationships and most especially in the area of politics, independent ideals of justice define what is morally appropriate. But I want now to mention some reasons for thinking that considerations of caring may not even cover our relations with intimates in a morally adequate way. Caring relationships rest on an attitude or motive of caring on the part of at least some individual participants (a newborn baby doesn't care about her mother in the way her mother cares about her), but what does a felt attitude of caring imply for actions taken on behalf of those we care about? If we deeply, genuinely care, then we shall not just wish certain people well, we shall also try to help them when they need our help and we will be moved by a general practical concern to promote their happiness. But what about situations in which we have to *choose between* people we care about? In the hypothetical case (and philosophers love hypothetical examples) where I have to choose between rescuing one person I love or care about and rescuing six other people I love or care about, most people and even most philosophers would agree that I do best to rescue the six.

However, in another kind of hypothetical case, we would hesitate or refuse to do what saves the most lives. For if, to save, say, six lives, we would have to kill one person we love or care about, few if any of us would seriously consider doing so. There is a difference between letting one person die when that is necessary to saving six others, and actually killing someone as a means to saving six others, and this difference defines the moral position philosophers call deontology. Deontology is the view, roughly, that it is morally wrong to destroy or harm innocent people as a means of preventing some greater number of people from suffering death or harm. In effect, deontology distinguishes commissions from omissions and claims that the end *doesn't* always justify the means, and most of us accept deontology in a deep way: we think it wrong to take one innocent life as a means of saving more than one life and would be reluctant and more than reluctant to do so.

But the philosophical justification of deontology is another matter, and the question of justification here threatens the ethic of caring in a most serious way. If one loves or cares about the members of one's family, one presumably wants what is best for them, but in that case, how can such caring preclude, say, killing one family member when that is the only way one can save the lives of the rest of the family? If, as individuals, we would refuse to kill in such a case, surely it is some intuitive deontological rule or principle that is influencing us, for how could the sheer emotion/feeling of love by itself preclude our doing what seems best overall for our family? And in that case, caring by itself doesn't encapuslate all the moral distinctions we need to make in talking about how we as individuals should act toward those we care about. Even on the individual and private level, the morality of caring apparently needs to be supplemented by other considerations, and if that is so, then the sigificance of caring is considerably less, I think, than its defenders have imagined.

But I believe that caring is actually in a better position than these philosophical criticisms suggest. Caring arguably has its own resources for disallowing killing as a means to saving (a greater number of) lives: rather than have to borrow from independently grounded moral rules or principles, a refusal to kill can develop from within caring as a motive. If one really cares about or loves people, then that feeling in an of itself can, I believe, generate a hesitation and refusal to kill someone one loves or cares about, even when that is a necessaary means to prevent the death of more people one loves or cares about. And one way to get clearer on this is to examine a motive or attitude diametrically opposed to love and caring, namely hatred.

Imagine an uncle who for some reason hates his three nephews. All three want to go to medical school, and (given that their parents are dead and other relatives unavailable) all three are living with a friendly neighbor, but hoping to get the money for medical school from their uncle. The uncle has reason to believe that the neighbor is willing to help the boys through medical school, but won't save money to that end, if he believes the uncle is willing to do so. So the uncle figures that if he helps the oldest of the boys, the neighbor will spend his extra money elsewhere and won't have anything to spare for the other two when, at spaced intervals, they are ready for medical school. If, then, the uncle doesn't help the first nephew, the other two will be helped, but if he does help him, he can prevent the other two from being helped. Still, there is something galling to him about this second option; the idea of doing something that will make his first nephew *grateful* to him simply sticks in his craw, and so it is hatred that leads him to deny the first nephew help and thus do something that on the whole is *less* bad for those he hates.

But if a negative emotion can understandably lead someone to produce results that are overall less bad, then why shouldn't positive feelings like caring or love lead someone to do what produces results that are on the whole less *good*? And the point of bringing in a negative emotion like hatred is that someone who acts from hatred is far less open to the suspicion that they are basing their actions on independent moral considerations than is someone who acts from love. When someone who loves another refuses to kill that person as a means to saving the lives of a number of others she loves, it can be philosophically suspected that that refusal is less a matter of love itself and more a matter of the fact that someone who loves will also wish to fulfill her independently given (deontological) moral obligations toward those she loves. (This very view can be found in Rawls's *A Theory of Justice*.)[4] But there is presumably no such thing as the morality or deontology of hatred or antipathy, so when the uncle acts as I am assuming he does, what he does comes from and is understandable in terms of his motives/feelings (on their own). However, once we see that negative emotions can yield a refusal to bring about overall worst results, what good reason to we have to deny the opposite possibility to positive attitudes like love and caring? We have no reason not to say, then, that an attitude of caring can in and of itself generate a refusal to kill someone one cares about even as a means to saving a plurality of others one cares about. (What I am saying applies not only to the concern we have for those near and dear to us, but to humanitarian caring as well, but the arguments must be left to another occasion.) Caring needn't borrow from an independent deontology, but can provide its own kind of basis for intuitive deontological thought and action.

IV

Thus we see that the ethic of caring is in a position to defend its own adequacy and importance against certain philosophical criticisms, but I would like now, and by

---

[4] Harvard, 1971, pp. 485–90.

way of a rather lengthy conclusion, to discuss another philosophical worry that can be directed at what defenders of caring have said about the nature of their own view. In particular, I have in mind the contention, to be found in Noddings work and that of many others, that such an ethic bases a certain kind of moral value in the value of certain *relationships*. According to this view, if it is from a moral standpoint better to care than not to care about (certain) people, that fact reflects and is grounded in the value of caring relationships, and those who make this claim draw attention to the relative neglect of such relationships in previous "masculine" moral philosophy.

Certainly, relationships of love and (both civic and personal) friendship have been relatively neglected during the course of modern moral philosophy, and the value of such relationships is not in dispute. But I think there are philosophical reasons for denying these relationships the foundational role that most caring ethicists have ascribed to them, though these considerations do not so much undermine caring and its importance as indicate that the foundations of caring morality should be seen in a different light.

What caring ethicists like Noddings have claimed is that caring about particular individuals is morally obligatory and admirable bcause it is necessary to important human goods that are realizable only in close relationships. But if parental caring, e.g., is obligatory and admirable *because* it is essential to the good(s) of family life, why is a child not just as obligated to take things from her parents and accounted admirable for doing so? More starkly, if the beauty and value of the bond between mother and infant is the basis for our high regard for maternal concern or caring, why isn't the infant's openness to and need for her mother's love just as praiseworthy? And it seems implausible to say such a thing. Rather, there is a difference in admirability or moral value here, and that is because there seems to be some sort of fundamental difference in moral admirability *between caring and being cared for*.

Similarly, the devotion of a tutor to a retarded child can seem very admirable, even if it might be *better* if their relationship were not needed. Again, the admirability of such caring seems not to be grounded in the desirability of the relationship, but rather to be a function of the kind of attitude caring (for or about a person) is.

In a nutshell, then, I am saying that it makes more sense to base an ethic of caring on the intrinsic moral value or admirability of the/a caring attitude or motive than on the desirability or value (for participants or in general) of caring relationships. The latter, more familiar mode of explanation ends up being unable to distinguish caring from being cared for in a principled way, and this typically philosophical consideration should lead us, I think, to regard the morality of caring as more immediately based in the value of caring motivation. Indeed, the very phrases "ethic of caring" and "morality of caring" suggest the primacy of motivation within such a view, but caring ethicists have in fact ignored this possibility or resisted it when it has been presented to them. And one can understand some of the reasons why. To deny that the morality of caring takes off from the value of certain relationships might seem to put the value of such relationsips in question and risk returning to a kind of moral philosophy where that value is underrated. And Noddings in particular also seems to hold that if we put primary value on a certain attitude, we have no explanation of the moral failure involved when someone cares for another person but that person never receives the benefit of knowing that s/he is cared for. Let us consider these reasons in reverse order.

The idea that there is a moral failure when the benefits of caring are not received or acknowledged by the person cared for is somewhat ambiguous. It might just mean that the *moral goals* of caring are somewhat frustrated if the person cared for doesn't know s/he is cared for or that if the cared-for person receives benefits and refuses or fails to acknowledge them, then that person is to some extent morally criticizable. With these assumptions I find it easy to agree. However, Noddings also appears to think that the moral virtue or admirabaility of the caring individual at least partly depends on whether the cared-for individual knows about or acknowledges the benefits they receive (or that the caring person is attempting to provide for them), and this is something I find somewhat objectionable. For it treats the moral value of caring as dependent on the accidental or unpredictable consequences of such caring, as dependent, to use Kant's phrase, on "step-motherly nature".

It seems more attractive, instead, to hold that when someone has done everything possible and reasonable on behalf of another person, the partial failure of their efforts doesn't detract from the admirablility and praiseworthiness of those efforts, of their actions. A caring person does her homework when she tries to help another person, she responds to the full particularity of the other, and she is absorbed in her effort to help that other. But if through uncontrollable and unpredictable circumstances those efforts to help fail, it seems intuitive to suppose that her efforts are just as morally good and praiseworthy as if she had been entirely successful. This Noddings has denied (and some fellow caring ethicists have already criticized that denial on grounds similar to those I am advancing here).[5] But if we place our most fundamental value on caring as an attitude or motive of individuals, then we can avoid this undesirable consequence and say that unsuccessful efforts to help or care for another can be as admirable as more successful efforts because of the admirable motive that underlies and actuates them.

This involves treating the ethic of caring as a kind of virtue ethics, as based in a certain personal virtue. But that virtue is one that reaches out toward the other and in a psychological sense–or by way of intentionality–involves connection with other people (of a kind one typically doesn't find in so-called masculine moral philosophies). It is just that the connection forged or sought isn't the source of moral value and that the personal attitude that reaches out to the other and seeks to create connection is. Understood as a pure virtue ethic, the ethic of caring is still very much on the side of connection with others rather than founding morality on our separateness from and autonomous rights as against others in the manner of the "masculine" moral philosophy of Kant and the contractarians. But the position I am defending has the advantage over previous understandings of the foundations of caring that it at least allows us to answer the philosophical criticism mentioned above and coherently hold that caring is morally better and more praiseworthy than being cared for.

However, there is also the worry that by locating moral value primarily in an attitude or motive rather than a relationship, we risk underestimating the value of loving and caring relationships. Here we need a distinction. What has an explanation

[5] See, e. g., Debra Shogan, *Care and Moral Motivation*, Toronto, 1988, p. 57.

and isn't primary within the field of explanation isn't necessarily for that reason less important within human life. Facts about biology help to explain the significance of marriage (rather than vice versa), but marriage may play a more significant and important role in our lives than the facts of biology do. And by the same token, the fact that, unlike relations of enmity and indifference, relationships that involve caring involve something we admire may help to explain why such relationships are so desirable, but that doesn't mean that the relationships are somehow less important than the motives/attitudes that help to make their value possible. All this needs to be worked out, and in other work I have myself been trying to do just that. But I would urge you to consider the possibility that friendship and love and other relationships involving caring are indeed enormously valuable; but that, for the philosophical reasons mentioned earlier, the ethic of caring cannot or shouldn't attempt to ground itself in such value.

However, if, instead and as I have suggested, we ground it in the moral value of a certain kind of motive, we should nonetheless remain clear that the dictates of that motive, what it will prompt us to do, depends very much on the interpersonal and social context in which that motive occurs. What friends we have and what interests and projects and expectations *they* have all help to determine the possibilities and (therefore) the tasks of caring.[6] The caring individual must be responsive and responsible to the particularities, nuances, and complexities of a larger interpersonal and social context, but as we have just seen, that needn't mean that the context, rather than caring itself, is the primary explanatory moral value within a plausible and promising ethic of caring.

---

[6] This point is well made by Marilyn Friedman in "Feminism, Autonomy, and Emotion," in Haber and Halfon, eds., *op. cit.*

21

Global Caring, Global Justice

I am very pleased to be at today's session on Global Justice. It gives me a chance to show, or show more fully, how some of the recent work I have done on care ethics extends to issues of international or global justice and, at the same time, to relate what I have to say to what others have been saying in this area. My recent book *The Ethics of Care and Empathy* was, basically, an argument for thinking of care ethics as covering the entire field of normative ethics, both personal and political.[1] I'd like to say something now by way of summarizing the discussion and conclusions of that book, enough, I hope, to make what I was saying there interesting to you and interesting, in particular, as a potential alternative to recent ways of thinking about international moral issues.

Obviously, care ethics is relatively new to the field of international politics and justice. But even those care ethicists who have dealt with such issues have typically felt that care ethics couldn't deal with such issues entirely on its own. Some, like Virginia Held, maintain that care ethics needs to supplement its resources with considerations and arguments derived from or at home in traditional justice ethics (I will assume that everyone here knows what I am talking about), if it is going to be able to treat issues of international or global morality.[2] Others, like Daniel Engster, make use of non-care-ethical foundations—in his case imported from Alan Gewirth's Kantian

---

[1] See my *The Ethics of Care and Empathy* (Routledge: New York, 2007).

[2] Virginia Held, "The Ethics of Care" in David Copp, ed., *The Oxford Handbook of Ethical Theory* (New York: Oxford University Press, 2006), pp. 548 f.

natural-rights approach—in order to ground a moral standard of caring that should be adhered to internationally.[3] But I don't think either way of doing things is necessary *or even possible* for a genuine ethics of caring. I shall now say a little bit about why I think this is so, but afterwards, when I attempt to explain to you how the kind of systematically consistent care ethics I favor would approach international issues, I shall make frequent references to Engster and/or Held. Their work is recent and both of them make critical reference to previous work of my own; and I would like to show how what I say in *The Ethics of Care and Empathy* and shall be saying here serves to answer those criticisms.

Perhaps the chief purpose of the book just mentioned was to demonstrate that care ethics needs to be systematic if it wishes to be entirely consistent. Held, Annette Baier, Marilyn Friedman, and others have claimed that care ethics and the traditional ethics of justice are consistent with and complement one another and that it is possible and advisable to integrate them into a larger picture of moral or ethical phenomena.[4] And though, for quite a long time now, I have thought and worked toward showing that care ethics can and should cover the whole field of ethical phenomena in its own distinctive terms, it was only recently that I saw what I take to be a powerful objection, in care-ethical terms, to trying to integrate care ethics with justice ethics. The belief that one can and should integrate the two approaches represents a kind of compromise with (or sop to?) traditional justice ethics a la Rawls and Ronald Dworkin, but I now think there is a decisive reason for care ethics not to make it. And that reason is the fact, as I argue at least in the recent book, that the ethics of care is inconsistent with the kind of Kantian liberalism that constitutes, at least for us in the present day, the paradigm case of justice ethics. Let me say briefly why I think this is so, but in order best to do this, I have to first say something about the central analytic tool of *The Ethics of Care and Empathy*, the notion of empathy itself.

Although the term "empathy" didn't exist till the early twentieth century and there is still some confusion, at least in academic circles, about how to distinguish empathy from sympathy, most ordinary English speakers do distinguish empathy from sympathy in a fairly uniform way. If we have to choose which of "I feel your pain" and "I am sorry you are in such pain and wish there was something I could do for you" expresses empathy and which of them refers to sympathy, most of us would unhesitatingly apply the term "empathy" to the first, Bill-Clintonesque utterance, and "sympathy" to the second. Empathy involves a kind of contagion or infusion (as Hume put it, using the only word he had, "sympathy") of feeling from one person to another, but as the relatively extensive recent and non-so-recent literature of developmental psychology indicates, there are two kinds of empathy, the projective kind that involves putting oneself deliberately into the shoes or mind of another, and the less

---

[3] Daniel Engster, *The Heart of Justice: Care Ethics and Political Theory* (New York: Oxford University Press, 2007).

[4] Held, *op. cit.*; Annette Baier, "The Need for More than Justice" in Virginia Held, ed., *Justice and Care: Essential Readings in Feminist Ethics* (Boulder, CO: Westview Press, 1995): esp. p. 57; and Marilyn Friedman, *What Are Friends For? Feminist Perspectives on Personal Relationships and Moral Theory*, (Ithaca, N.Y.: Cornell University Press, 1993): Chap. 5.

voluntary kind of associative empathy that psychologist Martin Hoffman and others have described and done so many studies of.[5]

I think associative empathy can be especially useful to care ethics. Nel Noddings in *Caring* spoke, not of empathy, but of "engrossment" in or with those one cares about because she thought caring involves a more open and receptive attitude than one finds in the notion of projecting oneself into or onto others, which many dictionaries stress as a feature of empathy.[6] But ordinary usage now indicates that "empathy" can also describe the non-deliberate communication or contagion of feeling from one person to another, and I want to say that this sort of receptive empathy is central to genuine caring.

Now both Noddings and, especially, Carol Gilligan sought to contrast moral ideals of caring about, connection to, and/or responsibility for others with a kind of thinking (which they sometimes characterized as typically masculine) that emphasizes the autonomy and rights of the individual and the just application of legal/moral principles or rules.[7] This latter is what I, following others, call justice thinking and find exemplified—perfectly—in modern-day Kantian liberalism. But consider the contrast drawn here between emphasizing our connection to and responsibility for others and emphasizing autonomy from and rights against others, an idea that highlights our ethical separateness from other people. Surely we should expect, should have expected, that these two seemingly opposed, seemingly *antithetical*, ways of approaching moral issues would at least sometimes yield conflicting moral judgments about particular cases or whole classes of cases. And that is what I finally realized and what, more than any other factor, led me to write up my ideas about caring and empathy in the form of a book.

What occurred to me was that there was one area at least (though in fact I believe there are others) where care ethics and Kantian liberalism yield mutually inconsistent moral judgments, the area of free speech. Liberals like Dworkin, Nagel, Scanlon, and others argue that hate speech should be protected or allowed because of the ethical importance of our autonomy as free rational beings.[8] With regard to cases or examples like Skokie, Illinois, where neo-Nazis wanted to hold a march and give anti-semitic speeches *because* there were so many Holocaust survivors living there, they want to say that the march or such a march should be allowed, not just on constitutional, but also on basic moral grounds. (Scanlon makes explicit reference to Skokie.) The right of free speech exists and should be honored, even if the exercise of that free speech is potentially offensive or hurtful to others.

But care ethics emphasizes, not our rights against or autonomy from others, but our connection to and responsibility for others, and a care ethics that is empathically

---

[5] Martin Hoffman, *Empathy and Moral Development: Implications for Caring and Justice* (Cambridge: Cambridge University Press, 2000).

[6] Nel Noddings, *Caring: A Feminine Approach to Ethics and Moral Education* (Berkeley: University of California Press, 1984).

[7] Carol Gilligan, *In a Different Voice: Psychological Theory and Women's Development* (Cambridge, MA: Harvard University Press, 1982).

[8] For references to these and like-minded thinkers, see Susan Brison, "The Autonomy Defense of Free Speech," *Ethics* 108, 1998, pp. 312–39. Brison offers trenchant criticisms of "autonomy defenses" of (the right to) free speech My own work has been greatly influenced by hers.

sensitive to the effects of hate speech on, say, Holocaust survivors, will realize that such speech is not only likely to offend and hurt those survivors, but has the potential to retraumatize (many of) them and thus seriously harm and damage them (beyond any damage they sustained during the Holocaust itself). This kind of potential harm is something which, interestingly, but also disappointingly, Kantian liberals never seem to acknowledge in regard to hate speech; but surely a care ethicist who is sensitive to such considerations and thinks in terms of our responsibility for others' welfare more than our rights against other people, will want to say that hate speech shouldn't be approved or allowed in Skokie-type cases. Of course, it is a real intellectual and practical challenge to say how such cases differ from cases where speech is merely offensive and to devise means for distinguishing such cases via legal institutions. But assuming that that can, in principle, be accomplished or worked toward, the incompatibility of care ethics and liberalism should now be apparent; and that has interesting implications for care ethics.

If care ethics is in its own terms inconsistent with liberal views about rights, justice, and morality, then it must either retreat before those views or attempt what it has often been reluctant to attempt: namely, to offer its own distinctive account not only of individual morality, but of the terrain of political and legal morality as well. It needs to come up with its own way of understanding autonomy, social justice, and rights, and over the years some care ethicists have been willing to move in this direction. Sally Ruddick's *Maternal Thinking* certainly didn't shy from the political and had a great deal to say about issues of international politics in particular. And in recent years Nel Noddings has started to take on questions of social justice. My recent book also did this, but sought to analytically nail down its account of political morality more than Ruddick did or Noddings has done, and its emphasis on empathy also allowed it to be more systematic about individual and political ethics than I believe anything else in the care-ethical vein has been.

And if, at this point, the listener is wondering how my recent work in care ethics relates to the work in virtue ethics I have done previously, let me just briefly say this: the kind of sentimentalist virtue ethics I have advocated might have different ethical foundations from those advocated by some care ethicists (I am thinking here mainly of Virginia Held, but also of Nel Noddings), but I have found that once one sees the significance of and starts working the notion of empathy, the issue of foundations seems less important and can at least temporarily be left aside. I am still inclined to believe in virtue ethics, but I think an ethics of care based in empathy can be developed without takes sides on the issue of the value or validity of virtue ethics. And that is what I sought to do in *The Ethics of Care and Empathy*. But now it is time to apply some of the ideas of that book and what I have been saying to you here, to issues of international or global caring and/or justice.

Talk of global caring and justice or of global just-about-anything is somewhat ambiguous. One can either mean to be talking of what we owe in the way of justice or caring to people outside our own country, and the contrast then would be between justice and caring within the borders of a given country and *international* issues of justice and caring concerning either individuals or countries. Or one can mean to be talking about how justice and caring would and should occur in a world governed by a single global government, and the contrast in that case would be between the way caring and justice work or fail to work within the present national/international framework and how well they would or could work under conditions of world government. Because this latter issue is so large and complex, I prefer not to engage it fully here. I will say a little more about it at the end of this talk, but before one says anything or much about global governance, one needs to be clearer, much clearer, about how caring and justice would, could, or should work internationally within the present "system" of nation-states. And in order to accomplish some of that, I first need to say something about how an ethics of care that stresses empathy conceives of the justice *within* or *of* a given state or society.

That is a topic I treated at some length in *The Ethics of Care and Empathy* (the book also spoke, briefly, about international justice, but that is precisely what the present occasion allows me to do more fully). The book modeled its treatment of social justice on what it had to say about individual morality, so I guess I need to begin by saying some more about the obligations of individuals. *The Ethics of Care and Empathy*—henceforward ECE—made considerable use of the recent psychology literature on moral development and relied heavily on Martin Hoffman's book *Empathy and Moral Development*, which, among other things, summarizes much of that literature and what it has to say, in particular, about the role of empathy in moral development. Many studies over recent decades support the idea that empathy is necessary to and powers human altruism and our use of moral rules or principles, and in ECE I also argued that our intuitive views about moral obligation largely correspond to what we know about our empathic tendencies.

For example, we tend empathically to respond more to pain we are witnessing than to pain we merely know about, and in fact we also think it morally worse not to respond to perceived pain than not to respond to pain known only by description. I also argue, in a separate chapter, that our ideas about deontology can be viewed in a similar way: that we are in fact more empathically sensitive to causing than to allowing harm or death—and some recent neuro-psychological studies in fact bear out what here seemed to me, at least, to be independently plausible. So I think and have argued that empathy offers us a way to frame a general criterion of right and wrong, that an act is wrong, in particular, if it exhibits, expresses, or reflects less than fully developed empathic concern for others.

However, as Hoffman points out, human empathy develops as we mature, and, even if we start out having empathy only for individuals in our family or immediately around us, teenagers end up having empathy for larger *groups* of disadvantaged or oppressed peoples. Empathy for those we don't personally know is more than possible, and Hoffman suggests a mechanism whereby such empathy can develop or be developed. He calls the mechanism inductive discipline or, simply, induction, and it occurs most rudimentarily when a parent whose child has hurt, say, his little sister calmly but firmly makes the first child aware of the pain or damage he has caused. Given our "natural" capacity for empathy, such induction makes the injuring child feel empathically bad about what he has done. But Hoffman also points out that similar mechanisms can work to make us more sensitive to and concerned about the harm that we or others have caused some whole (distant or local) group; he in particular stresses how these reactions can be influenced by literature or television or by the presence, say, of exchange students from a country we or others have attacked, oppressed, or damaged in some other way. (This also works for natural disasters.)

Our capacity for empathic concern for people we don't know is crucial to any account of social justice that appeals to empathy and caring. ECE argued that laws, institutions, legislatures, governments, and constitutional conventions can exhibit the same lack of empathic concern for compatriots that is often expressed in the actions of individual agents; and when they do that, they count, on our theory, as unjust. One of the illustrations I gave of how such an approach can criticize the injustice of social institutions or laws concerned religious freedom(s) and relied on a feature of empathy I haven't yet emphasized. Empathy for another person requires us to see or think of things from that person's point of view, and if we are genuinely, empathically, concerned with the welfare of another, we won't, therefore, ride roughshod over their desires, aspirations, fears, and opinions when we try to help them, make them better off.

Thus it is often said—Thomas Nagel says it in *Equality and Partiality*, but many others have said this as well—that we need rationally grounded independent rights of religious freedom because the sheer desire to help others won't prevent well-intentioned individuals from passing or issuing unjust laws that deny people religious freedom and doing so for the sake of their souls' salvation.[9] This sort of thing was often claimed about and by the Spanish Inquisition, but in fact the Inquisitors (and most of the rest of the Spanish in those days) didn't see or attempt to see religious matters from the point of view of those, like Jews, they were torturing, killing, or forcing to recant their views or to convert. Their persecutions in most cases amounted to total intolerance and to little less than *hatred* (for those denying the divinity of Jesus or the God they loved and worshipped). As John Locke deftly put it, the "dry eyes" of the Inquisitors and others who persecuted people for their souls' sake show that they weren't all that concerned about the well-being of those being tortured and/or denied religious freedom. The fact is that religious intolerance and persecution aren't humanly compatible with empathic concern for others, and so ECE could and did argue that we don't need the kinds of independently grounded rights to religious liberties liberals think we need to appeal to in order, morally, to rule out religious persecution and intolerance as unjust. Such persecution and intolerance can be seen to be unjust in sentimental, purely care-ethical terms, once the moral importance and significance of empathy is recognized. ECE framed these issues in national terms, spoke of the injustice, *within a given state*, of one, more powerful group denying religious freedom to another. But nowadays issues of religious intolerance loom large, very large, on the international scene and are immediately relevant to the topic of international justice. I won't talk here of Islam's possible intolerance toward the West and its religions, but only of how people and governments in the West need to view and treat Islam if what they say and do vis-à-vis Islamic countries or individuals is to meet care-ethical standards of justice. To the extent Western policies and actions manifest a lack of empathy toward countries and individuals, people have a great deal to answer for in terms of justice.

---

[9] New York: Oxford University Press, 1991, pp. 154–68.

Now of course one can say that the West has been provoked and that vital interests are being threatened by Islam or certain groups or individuals who claim to speak in its name. And one of the things ECE stressed was the way natural self-interest or self-concern gradually yields some *but hardly most* of its force to gradually developing and inculcated (or induced) empathic concern for other people and groups. So there are limits to how much empathy is likely to "demand" in the way of good treatment of those who threaten one, though let us not forget the extent to which present threats have themselves been provoked or evoked by the policies and actions of Western countries toward countries or groups in the Middle East. Still, there is no doubt in my mind that people in the West tend to be intolerant of people and groups in the Middle East, tend *not* to see things from their point of view and to act accordingly. All this, I think, is or leads to (international kinds of) injustice.

In his book *The Heart of Justice*, however, Daniel Engster (p. 22) accuses me of putting too much emphasis on motives in my previous work, and that charge might also be made about what I have been saying here. Let's consider that. After all, and as Engster indicates, it is sometimes counterproductive to accuse other people of bad motives when we are trying, otherwise, to work together or to resolve some issue, and doesn't an ethics of care that puts so much emphasis on empathy and therefore motivation risk being morally unhelpful? Yes, I think it does risk that, but one might also say that, even if too much reference to motives isn't helpful, someone's motives can nonetheless be relevant to the moral character of their actions. Not everything that is true need be spoken of or harped upon, and since someone motivated by empathic concern for others may see that speaking of motives will make certain sorts of agreement and (therefore) certain sorts of benefit impossible, they will have reason to stay silent on the subject of motives. But that doesn't mean that they think motives are irrelevant to and don't play a major part in determining the moral status of an action or actions.

In fact, moreover, reference to motives may sometimes be more helpful than we have just been assuming. After all, if someone questions his or her own motives, that can actually lead toward greater tolerance and easier agreements. But also we spoke above of the way Inquisitors sought to justify what they were doing by claiming to have benevolent motives. This illustrates the relevance of motivation to moral evaluation, but it also indicates a way that reference to motives might sometimes be helpful. If people claim to have good motives for doing what one thinks is wrong or terrible or, in fact, badly motivated, one may have reason to question those people's motives and try to get them or others to see those motives in a different light. This often won't be possible, but sometimes it might really be helpful. In any event, since the Inquisitors themselves tried to justify their actions by reference to considerations of motivation, it is fair game and seems entirely appropriate to respond to them in similar terms; and certainly the interests of moral truth may well be best served by questioning the Inquisitors' self-serving and rationalizing self-attribution of altruistic motivation. And this is precisely what an ethics of empathic caring asks us to do.

Interestingly, Engster accuses my previous virtue-ethical approach to caring (in the book *Morals from Motives*) as being difficult to apply, but notes that I do make an effort to apply the theory I defended there to cases like religious tolerance (see his page 22). He seems to think this shows that I am moving toward his kind of approach to care and away from an emphasis on motivation, but I think it shows nothing of the sort. The actions of individuals and groups can reflect and can frequently be seen to reflect certain motives, and what I argued above is that we have every reason to believe that the Inquisitors in Spain were not motivated by empathic concern for those they persecuted and tried, forcibly, to convert or make recant. But on the sort of view I am defending here (and it is in essentials not very different from what I said in my earlier book), this means that it is unjust and wrong to deny various religious freedoms, and in the end my theory isn't all that difficult to apply. I believe Engster thinks otherwise because he fails to see the causal and evidential connections that exist between actions, laws, and institutions and facts of individual and group psychology.

But let me now move to another area of social and international justice. In ECE I also took up questions of economic or distributive justice from the standpoint of care ethics, and once again considerations concerning empathy were central to the argument. The discussion took in economic justice within a given state or society and also, though to a lesser extent, questions of international economic justice, and let me review briefly what was said before I expand on what I think an ethics of care can say about international issues. I mentioned above that I think (and the recent psychology literature on moral development supports the idea) that human empathy is capable of substantial concern for fellow citizens one isn't personally acquainted with, and such concern is possible not only in individuals, but in legislatures and other governmental bodies. Given these assumptions (and facts about marginal utility), ECE argued that genuine empathic concern for others will lead governments to provide a safety net for the economically disadvantaged and institute some degree of progressive taxation. But these conclusions don't particularly distinguish empathy-oriented care ethics from utilitarianism or Rawlsian liberalism, and I went on to show that such care ethics also has some implications about economic justice that are more plausible than what either utilitarianism or Rawls allows us to conclude.

Briefly, utilitarian justice prefers a marginally larger improvement for people who are well off over a marginally smaller improvement for those who are very badly off, and Rawls's views make no distinction between cases where those who are relatively worst-off are very badly off in some sort of absolute terms and cases where the worst-off are actually doing quite well. But as a number of philosophers have pointed out in recent years, absolute badness of condition or state of well-being makes a moral difference to us. Compassion, for example, is much more concerned with helping those who are very badly off than with helping, even to some greater extent, those who are already well off, and, as I said, utilitarianism and Rawls don't provide for this kind of moral thinking. By contrast, an empathy-based ethics of care can offer a general theoretical account of why (what we can call) absolutely positionality at the low end can and does make such a moral difference to us. Empathy is much more sensitive to what seems absolutely bad in someone's situation or condition than it is to the mere or sheer lack of certain advantages on the part of someone who is already fairly well off. And a compassionate, empathically sensitive legislative body, government, or society will, therefore, through its laws, institutions, or practices, show special concern for anyone who is in absolutely bad straits and for any group of such people.

But, as I mentioned in ECE, all of this translates into the way a government or person will treat or deal with governments or people abroad. And living, as most of the hearers of this talk are, in a rich nation or country, we will be more obligated to take care of or help those in other countries who are in dire or awful circumstances than to do (even more) good for non-compatriots who are not in such circumstances. As I mentioned earlier, Daniel Engster has said that my views about caring and justice lack practical application or implications, and, once again, what I said a moment ago about compassion for absolute bad-offness already indicates that this isn't so. In fact, a moral view based on empathic caring yields many of the same conclusions about international (obligations of) justice that Engster himself defends—and what he says is very rich, complex, and interesting—in his book.

For example, Engster emphasizes the need to be "attentive, responsive, and respectful" to those one is attempting to help in less developed countries (p. 31 and *passim*), and he makes it clear that he thinks such an attitude has to be assumed if we are to draw the kinds of morally compelling conclusions about whom and how and when to help that he wishes to draw. If we aren't attentive and responsive to the point of view of those we seek to help, our efforts may be misdirected or counterproductive, and certainly, and as he mentions, the recent history of international aid efforts—whether directed at famine relief or at long-term development—offers many examples of unsuccessful efforts to help. But all of this is readily put in the terms I have been using here. Engster avoids using the notion of empathy, but empathy as we have discussed it clearly makes one be or constitutes one's being "attentive, responsive, and respectful" to those one is seeking to help. (One might wonder about respectfulness here, but it is precisely *not* respectful to ride roughshod over other people's aspirations or point of view when trying to help them; ECE in fact offers a general theory of respect in terms of empathic caring.) So the ways in which and the attitudes with which Engster recommends that we help those in dire straits reach at least a moderately decent level of well-being, are pretty much the same as those I would defend in the name of empathy. The care-ethical approach I am recommending does have attractive or plausible practical implications or applications, and that is because, once again, there are connections among attitudes, desires, and beliefs within individuals and in relation to the actions, institutions, or laws that they individually or in groups initiate and/or maintain.

I don't propose to go into details here, but one could, like Engster, do that at considerable length, though I think the audience probably has an idea at this point about some of the directions—I hope they seem plausible—in which such a detailed discussion would go. And I should also add that in skipping over details in this way, I am also not specifically engaging with—though I have certainly been influenced by—the vast recent literature on international aid and justice. Some recent authors have said insightful and informative things about how not to give foreign aid, e.g., about how certain ways of doing so unfairly disadvantage women or don't properly reckon with facts "on the ground" in the countries one is trying to assist. I have been implicitly drawing on this literature and will continue to do so in what follows, but time limitations don't allow me to be as specific about this as I would otherwise wish to be.[10]

However, because of our previous intellectual interaction, it *is* useful for me here to specifically mention various features of Engster's recent book, and at this point I would like to mention another common feature of his discussion and my own. Virginia Held has said that a virtue-ethical theory, like mine in *Morals from Motives*, that emphasizes caring as a character trait more than as a feature of relationships is in danger of allowing care to be unjustly or wrongly imposed on others for their own good. But Engster points out that if we require caring to be attentive, responsive, and respectful, caring isn't like to be paternalistic—far from it. And it seems to me that this point can also be made about an ethics of care that stresses empathy with the point of view of others. Of course, in some cases we approve of paternalism—as when we insist that a small child should see the dentist some time even though s/he loudly and perhaps even violently opposes ever making such a visit. However, an ethics of care that emphasizes empathy restricts the need for paternalistic interventions, and that is in keeping with what Held advocates for care ethics and what most of us think is morally valid. (In ECE I argued that there are some cases where it is difficult to know whether one should be paternalistic, but in a new book *Moral Sentimentalism*, forthcoming from OUP, I take a more definite stand about those cases.) But let me say further that, even though the term "empathy" wasn't much used in the book *Morals from Motives* that Held was referring to, I in fact said enough in that book about responsiveness to others' viewpoints to make Held's caveats and worries about virtue-ethical care ethics' possible paternalistic tendencies seem at least somewhat overstated. As I pointed out in that book, someone who ignores the viewpoint of others in trying to help them can be accused of not genuinely caring about them even without one's having to (explicitly) bring in empathy.

I want now to consider another aspect of at least potential disagreement between Engster and myself, one that he himself calls attention to in his book. Engster holds that care or caring entails or requires good results for people, and he constrasts this more consequentialistic conception of what care involves with what he characterizes, in my work, as a greater emphasis on intentions than on results (Engster, p. 182). There is certainly some truth to this, but I believe and would like now to show you why the more purely consequentialistic treatment of care or caring is morally less attractive or plausible than an ethics of care that makes much of motives and intentions. Certainly, the road to hell is or could be paved with good intentions. We all have to agree about that. But I think one can emphasize intentions/motives over actual consequences without in any way repudiating—and while in fact actually supporting and helping to make sense of—that old adage.

---

[10] On the way aid can unfairly disadvantage women, see, e.g., Jill Steans, *Gender and International Relations* (New Brunswick, N.J.: 1998), Ch. 6; and Eva Feder Kittay (with Bruce Jennings and Angela Wasunna), "Dependency, Difference, and the Global Ethics of Long-term Care," *Journal of Political Philosophy* 13, 2005, pp. 443–69. For discussion of some of the careless and irresponsible ways in which agencies, organizations, and/or governments have dispensed food aid, see, e.g., Alex De Waal, *Famine Crimes: Politics and the Disaster Relief Industry in Africa* (Bloomington, IN: Indiana Press, 1997).

The road to hell is paved with good intentions because someone can intend to do good, but fail to act when the decisive moment arrives or else act, but fail to follow through on their original intentions when obstacles arise and/or more effort is required than they had originally anticipated. But an ethics of care can take these facts into moral account. If someone genuinely cares about, is genuinely concerned to promote, the well-being of another or others, then they try to learn relevant facts that are relevant to their ability to help and they don't give up if and when their initial efforts are unsuccessful. If they give up too easily or don't bother learning facts that are relevant to the success of their efforts, that already, criterially, shows that they don't fully or genuinely care about doing the good they say they want to do. So a caring person has to be very concerned about results and pursuing (within certain limits) all necessary means to such results. And the field of international justice offers us fairly clear-cut examples of these conceptual/ethical facts.

As I just mentioned, there is a large and growing literature now concerning the ways in which foreign aid—either as humanitarian famine relief efforts or as long-term developmental assistance—has gone and therefore can go awry. The government of a country to which food has been sent can confiscate that food from those who need it and use it for nefarious political purposes: e.g., to crush resistance to its tyrannical rule.[11] The developmental assistance can turn out and often, in recent decades, has turned out to be ineffective, because of local factors that weren't taken into account by those offering the assistance. But, morally speaking, there are at least two different types of cases here. If the facts or factors that led to a failure to substantially help were known in advance or could, with reasonable efforts, been learned about in advance, then the point made above applies, and we can criticize those offering help in moral terms because they have (already) shown themselves to be less than genuinely or fully concerned to promote the good they say they want, and perhaps at least *intend*, to promote. To that extent, and for such cases, an ethics of care that makes much of motivation can take consequences into moral account, and that is because the intentions and motives it emphasizes *are themselves focused on and directed toward the producing of good results.*

The more difficult or interesting case, as far as I am concerned, is that in which the agency or government that seeks to provide international assistance couldn't really have anticipated the difficulties they end up encountering in trying to do some good. Can their efforts in that case be morally criticized because the good consequences being sought didn't actually materialize? That is what Engster seems to suggest, but my view is that this gives too much moral importance to actual consequences. Intuitively, I think that most of us wouldn't blame or even morally criticize a government or agency that ran into unanticipatable factors in its efforts, say, to provide famine relief or developmental assistance and that at least initially, therefore, was unable to produce good results and even perhaps produced unfortunate ones. As far as I am concerned, however, the really interesting question concerns what a government or agency *does at that point*. We now know that there are pitfalls that can be encountered in or for our efforts to provide international assistance, but the point about pitfalls is

---

[11] Compare Philip Gourevitch, *We Wish to Inform You that Tomorrow We Will be Killed with our Families: Stories from Rwanda*, NY: Farrar, Straus, and Giroux, 1998.

that at least initially they can't be anticipated. If a clever enemy thinks up the idea of digging deep pits and carefully concealing them, and no one has previously heard or thought of such a thing, then if we fall into one of those pits, we can't, at least the first time, be accused of imprudence or carelessness. But if we subsequently don't make efforts to avoid this happening again, if we aren't thereafter circumspect in traversing certain terrain or territory, then we *do* count as imprudent and careless of our own welfare. And I think this lesson clearly transposes to moral cases.

We often can't plausibly, and in moral terms, criticize those who initially fail to provide the help they want to provide; but we can criticize them, if they don't seek to learn from their mistakes and if they don't redouble their efforts to provide assistance. And that, again for the reasons mentioned earlier, is because genuine caring criterially involves following through on one's original good intentions if and when the going gets tough. Of course, there are limits on this. If it turns out that aid workers and/or medical personnel are likely to be killed if they go into a given country where there is hunger or epidemic disease, then even a genuinely strong concern to help others will likely yield to prudence and self-interest, and I believe that empathic concern for others is and should be seen in care-ethical terms as occurring against a persisting background of self-concern, self-concern that empathy can substantially attenuate, but can't be expected to obliterate. (Those who have less of such self-concern and who are willing, say, to take great risks with their lives in order to provide food for those who are starving may, from the standpoint of care ethics, be seen as going beyond the call of care-ethical duty, that is, as acting supererogatorily—and I have more to say about this in ECE.)

Engster also mentions the possibility that one should withhold aid from governments or people that need it, not because of the risks involved, but because of the proven irresponsibility (or worse) of a given government that has been given aid previously. And I not only agree with this, but suggested in my earlier book *Morals from Motives* that in such cases one expresses or evinces a morally acceptable "tough caring" that is analogous to what we familiarly call "tough love."[12] But I do disagree with Engster about the absolute importance of actual results to an ethics of care and don't believe that the way I approach things, and the focus I place on motivation, leads to unintuitive moral conclusions: quite to the contrary, I think the approach does justice to the somewhat complex and subtle understanding we most of us have about the connection between morality, motivation, and consequences.

I would like now to take up one final, major topic. ECE argued that an ethics of care that puts empathy front and center can plausibly address issues of economic justice and can explain why religious freedom and toleration (or, better, acceptance) are necessary to social or international justice, and these are issues I have been speaking about here. But ECE also attempted to show that democratic institutions and government are essential to social justice, and I am now going to place that discussion in a somewhat more international context.

When governments or rulers deny their compatriots the right to vote (or deny them civil rights or liberties that I am not going to discuss further today), they manifest less empathic concern for them that we humans are capable of. They are moved

---

[12] New York: Oxford University Press, 2001, p. 133 n.

more by greed, or a selfish desire to retain power or privilege, than by a concern for the good of (the people of) their country, and so the laws and institutions of such a country are morally criticizable and unjust according to a care ethics based in or on empathy. Or so, at least, I argued in ECE.

Now Engster's version of care ethics doesn't claim to be able to justify democratic institutions or government. He generates his views out of a Gewirthian argument that focuses on basic human needs, and democracy requires more than the fulfillment of those needs. Other forms of government seem, according to Engster, to be capable of reliably providing for such needs—and I don't necessarily disagree with him about that. But these limits of or on Engster's approach follow from the specific and narrow natural rights character of his defense of caring, and I not only think that the Gewirth-style argument is less forceful than Engster does (and people have been skeptical about Gewirth's own fundamental argument for our duties toward others for decades now); but I also think that if the ethics of care wants to treat of issues of social and international justice, it needn't borrow from the rationalist natural rights tradition that Gewirth inhabited. ECE tries to show that care ethics can derive and justify plausible moral conclusions in many areas without going outside its own sentimentalist resources. It doesn't need to supplement or complement its ideas with borrowings from traditional justice ethics, but can cover individual and political moral in its own terms. Those care ethicists and others who argue that traditional notions of autonomy of the kind liberals rely on should be reconfigured in terms of, or replaced by, a *relational* ideal of human autonomy are saying some of what I want to say here. Though I am far from sure that care ethics can in its own terms successfully or plausibly deal with all the topics that a moral philosophy needs to deal with, I think care ethicists ought to give their own approach a chance to do this. So at this point I think it is premature and quite possibly misguided to base care ethics in an alien or very disparate intellectual tradition like natural rights theory or Kantian rationalism, in the manner that Engster does. And if one relies more or entirely on what an ethics of care can say about empathy and empathically sensitive and developed caring (and I do talk much more about issues of moral development in ECE and in the forthcoming *Moral Sentimentalism*), then I think one obtains the additional intellectual/ethical benefit of being able to account for the moral importance of democracy, something that the narrow basis of Engster's argument doesn't allow him to do.

But given that we are today focusing on international justice, I want to consider a possible objection, or set of objections, to my view, defended in ECE and earlier here, that, on the human landscape at least, social justice requires that one not deny people the right to vote, not deny them democratic prerogatives and privileges if they seek them. I add this latter phrase because I don't want to talk about the case of preliterate societies where tradition rules and no one has ever pushed for democratic governance. We are to consider only modern-day large scale societies (*Gesellschaften* rather than *Gemeinschaften*). And I want in particular to talk about Singapore.

The leaders of Singapore and those impressed by the economic "miracle" that has occurred there in recent decades often claim that all the success and stability have been achieved not despite, but actually because of, the absence of popular, democratic rule. It has been said, for example, that in the United States the fact that politicians have to appeal to voters has led to the adoption of policies that disadvantage future generations and bode ill for long-term stability, whereas the leaders and bureaucrats of Singapore are free from such pressures, and also from the pressure of the sorts of business interests that distort electoral politics in the USA and work to the long-term disadvantage of the poorer members of society by promoting well-heeled "special interests." (Some of these points are made in a lovely recent book by Daniel Bell, where the discussion takes the form of a dialogue between a Singapore official and the author.)[13]

On the basis of such arguments, it is sometimes asserted that Singapore and other such places don't need democracy and that there are "Asian values" that differ from those in the West and that allow good and successful governance outside the democratic structures that Westerners so shrilly or arrogantly insist upon. However, as those who are somewhat skeptical of this questioning of democracy point out, it can certainly be wondered whether what non-democratic leaders say in defense of their forms of government isn't just a rationalization of their desire to have and hold onto power and privilege. (Bell wonders this in his book.) And this suspicion is exacerbated when one hears the leader in Bell's dialogue call the poor of Singapore "adult dogs." That doesn't sound like someone who accepts and adheres to a certain form of governance out of empathic and sympathetic concern for the present and future interests of *all* the people of his country, and I must say that I not only suspect, but also am strongly inclined to believe that the governance of Singapore (or other such polities) isn't based on substantial concern for all compatriots and is probably even incompatible with such concern.

As I just indicated, many leaders in Asia and those who defend what they do speak of "Asian values," and one thing that is often asserted is that Asians aren't insulted by not being allowed a vote, but rather willingly defer and listen to their betters. Deference is said to be part of Asian character, even if it isn't typical of people raised and educated in the West. But I don't think this helps support, in fact I think it gives us a basis for questioning Asian values and their ability to support or justify non-democratic Asian politics. After all, in the nineteenth century most women deferred to men in politics and other areas of life, and this deference, as we now know, resulted from the particular ways in which women were raised and educated. Most of the time they were told they were incapable of usefully participating in politics, and, as Carol Gilligan has so incisively pointed out, almost no one listened to women's voices. When they expressed a controversial or interesting opinion, it wasn't taken as seriously as when a boy or man said such a thing, and if, for example, they expressed a desire to become a doctor, they would be told that they really didn't want that; that what they really wanted was to be a nurse or even just to stay at home raising a family. This patriarchal response to women's or girls' incipient desires, opinions, and aspirations *leads* women to doubt themselves and their "voices" and to defer, while quite possibly feeling unsuspected anger beneath the surface, to what men say and do. Certainly, as I argued in ECE, such treatment represents a failure to empathize with what girls and women were at least originally thinking or hoping, and so a lack of *empathic* concern for their well-being that can be regarded as unjust treatment. (Also as showing a lack of respect.)

---

[13] *East Meets West* (Princeton: Princeton University Press, 2000).

But much of this critical analysis carries over to the case of Asian deference. If girls and women in America became more deferent and less independent in thought and action because of the way their point of view was disregarded or denigrated, wouldn't we imagine, to begin with, that similar things have happened to many Asian women and that their deference to and psychological/economic dependence on men is an artifact of patriarchy rather than a natural or inevitable feature of their character or personalities? But if sexist deference and dependency are produced in this fashion, even among Asian women, there is every reason to expect that the general political deference and dependency displayed by Asian women *and* men has a similar origin, and doesn't just come naturally. The idea of a deference or dependency gene distinguishing Asian from Western individuals does seem quite far-fetched, and what seems more plausible is to try to understand Asian political deference *on the model of earlier women's deference in the West*. If we do so, we will be inclined to think that Asians are indoctrinated about the advantages of their non-democratic political systems, that when the disadvantaged express, either as children or as adults, a desire to have more say in how things are run or managed, those desires, those aspirations are dismissed or made light of with responses like "we can't really believe you are so ungrateful for all we have done for you" or "you don't really want to worry about these matters, these are the sorts of questions best left to those who are used to dealing with them." Such responses in the context of people's political aspirations can just as effectively rob people of a sense of their own political voice as similar responses to women's aspirations and point of view ended up causing women to defer to patriarchal ideas and institutions, and to men generally.

I believe, therefore, that the arguments for democracy in Asia and elsewhere run parallel to those that support equal treatment for women. In both cases an ethics of care that focuses on empathy can help us to understand the injustice of (and the lack of respect manifested in) denying people the right to vote and denying women the right to equal participation in supposedly democratic institutions (and in the economic and cultural life of a given society). I would like now to conclude this talk by saying just a bit more about global justice as concerned with the possibility and potential advantages or superiority of global government.

Because of increasing globalization, many people are nowadays considering and debating the issue of whether we should try to move toward global government and the related issue of whether, even assuming that we can't from where we are successfully move in that direction, such global governance couldn't or wouldn't in principle be superior, in terms of economic efficiency or overall justice, to what we find in the world at present. Obviously, one worry that people have is that a global government that ran amok might terrorize everyone in the world more effectively than anything feasible under the current "system" of national governments. Global governance has the potential to create grave injustices beyond any we already find in the world; but still there are potential advantages in such governance that might be thought and have been said to outweigh, from the standpoint of justice, the potential disadvantages. To mention just the most obvious example, world hunger might be more effectively and fairly dealt with if the world were better *organized* and if we had a world government that had at least the modicum of concern for all citizens that democratic countries in the present world show toward *their* citizens.

I guess my own response to these issues is somewhat agnostic. But I don't think that that calls the sort of approach I have been taking to political and, more generally, moral issues into doubt. If one thinks, and perhaps one doesn't, but *if* one thinks that a care ethics that features empathy can usefully explain features of justice on the present-day national and international landscape, then one can reasonably hope that it will be useful in explaining or clarifying the issues that surround the question of the advisability, morally, of moving toward global government. If it is difficult to resolve that question at this point, if it seems too difficult to allow of an easy or definitive resolution that we can all accept, that may be because the issues involved are so complex and subject to so many gaps in our empirical/social scientific knowledge. But if we worry about the tyranny of a global government or aspire to such government because of the advantages it could bring for the elimination of world hunger and/or poverty, then I think the considerations that move us are considerations whose moral importance can be unpacked in the terms and via the kind of arguments that we have already seen an ethics of empathic care rely on. Such an ethics, like every other kind of ethics, clearly has its work cut out for it in the future.

22

Empathy and Objectivity

1. The Groundwork of Empathy

In this paper I want to explore the relevance of empathy to certain epistemological ideals. Although I have previously focused in a very large way on the nature and uses of empathy, that focus has always been on morality and moral theory, and I now believe that the phenomenon of empathy has an important role to play in helping us understand the epistemological ideal and intellectual virtue of objectivity. I would like to begin by reviewing some of the ideas about empathy I have relied on in previous work on morality, ideas that will be helpful to us when we come to consider the nature of intellectual objectivity largely in terms of empathy. (I know the latter idea may seem at this point strange, but I shall endeavor to make it seem much less strange in what follows).

In my *The Ethics of Care and Empathy* (Routledge, 2007), I reviewed some of the psychological literature on empathy for its bearing on moral issues. I was there

---

I am indebted to Harvey Siegel, Kristin Borgwald, and Daniel Hampikian for extremely helpful suggestions about this paper. I should also mention that some of the conclusions I shall be reaching are similar to conclusions Sandra Harding defends in *Whose Science? Whose Knowledge? Thinking from Women's Lives* (Ithaca: Cornell University Press, 1991). But we employ quite different arguments, and I emphasize empathy and its emotional aspects more specifically than she does. In any event, her work and mine here are perhaps best viewed as complementing one other. (For related, but somewhat less closely related, ideas, also see Alison Jaggar, "Love and Knowledge: Emotion in Feminist Epistemology," reprinted in A. Garry and M. Pearsall, eds., *Women, Knowledge, and Reality*, Boston: Unwin Hyman, 1989, pp. 129–55.)

exploring and defending a care-ethical approach to morality and to moral theorizing, and the moral development literature of recent decades argues that the development of empathy is necessary to becoming an altruistic, i.e., a caring person. But what is empathy?

Well, to begin with, it is worth noting that the term "empathy" didn't exist in English till the twentieth century, when it entered the language as a translation of the German word *Einfuehlung*. However, the *concept* of empathy seems to have existed much earlier, and Hume in *A Treatise of Human Nature* says important, groundbreaking things about what we would now call empathy. But he used the term "sympathy" to refer to it; and we nowadays talk (or chatter) a lot more about empathy than about sympathy, so perhaps I should at this point say something about the distinction between empathy and sympathy as we now understand these notions. In colloquial terms, we can perhaps do this most easily by considering the difference between (Bill Clinton's) feeling someone's pain and feeling *for* someone who is in pain. Any present-day adult speaker of English will recognize that "empathy" refers to the former phenomenon and "sympathy" to the latter. (Shades of J. L. Austin's discussion of our intuitive understanding of the difference between "by mistake" and "by accident.") Thus empathy involves having the feelings of another (involuntarily) aroused in ourselves, as when we see another person in pain. It is as if their pain invades us, and Hume speaks, in this connection, of the infusion of one person's feeling(s) into another person. However, we can also feel sorry for, bad for, the person who is in pain and positively wish them well. This amounts, as we say, to sympathy for them, and it can happen even if we aren't "feeling their pain."

The recent psychological literature contains many empirical studies of empathy and various discussions of the difference between empathy and sympathy (a small number of which run counter to what I have just been saying). But I would like to focus briefly on a couple of "results" from that literature that will help us to get our bearings on the potential relationship between empathy and intellectual/theoretical objectivity. First, most of the studies in that literature tend to support the "empathy-altruism hypothesis" according to which empathy is a crucial factor in the development of the kind of altruistic concern for (or caring about) others that lead us to help others who are in need or in distress.[1]

Second, psychologist Martin Hoffman, whose work has perhaps defined the psychology literature on empathy more than the work of any other individual, has argued that individual empathy develops through various stages, and that its connection with altruistic or moral motivations is more ambiguous or inchoate in the earlier stages of that development.[2] A very young child or even a newborn baby can feel distress and start crying at the distress and crying of another child within hearing distance, and this operates via a kind of mimicry and seems like a form of infusion or, as some like to say, "contagion." But as a child develops conceptual/linguistic skills, a richer history of personal experiences, and a fuller sense of the reality of others, a more

---

[1] On this literature and the "empathy-altruism hypothesis," see C. D. Batson, *The Altruism Question: Toward a Social-Psychological Answer*, Hillandale, NJ: Lawrence Erlbaum Associates, 1991.

[2] See his *Empathy and Moral Development: Implications for Caring and Justice*, Cambridge, UK: Cambridge University Press, 2000.

"mediated" form of empathy can be (involuntarily) aroused in response to situations or experiences that are not immediately present and are merely heard about, remembered, or read about. It also becomes possible for the (normal) child deliberately to adopt the point of view of other people and to see and feel things from their perspective. Although we sometimes speak of both these forms of later-developing empathy (and especially of the latter, *projective* type of empathy) as involving identification with the other, Hoffman and others insist that the identification isn't a total merging with or melting into the other: genuine and mature empathy doesn't deprive the empathic individual of her sense of being a different person from the person s/he empathizes with.

Third, Hoffman points out that as an individual's cognitive sophistication and general experience increase, they become capable of more and more impressive "feats" of empathy. Thus, at a certain point, empathy becomes capable of penetrating behind superficial appearances, and we may, for example, feel an acute empathic sadness on seeing a person we know to have terminal cancer boisterously enjoy himself in seeming or actual ignorance of his own fatal condition. In other words, we eventually learn to empathize not just with what someone is actually feeling, but with their (more objective) condition or situation. Similarly, adolescents become aware of the existence of disadvantaged groups or peoples, and empathy with the plight, say, of the homeless or the residents of Darfur becomes possible for them in a way that would not have been possible earlier in their lives.

Finally, Hoffman holds that the development of genuine caring about or for others requires the intervention of parents and others making use of what he calls "inductive discipline" (more simply "induction") to arouse or engage the child's capacity for empathy. Induction involves noticing when a/one's child has hurt others and then (non-angrily but firmly) making the child aware of the harm s/he has done—most notably by getting the child to imagine how it would feel to experience similar harm (or pain). Hoffman believes that if such training is applied consistently over time, the child will come to associate bad feelings (guilt) with situations in which the harm s/he can do is not yet done, an association that is functionally autonomous of parents' or others' actual intervention and constitutes or supports altruistic and, more generally, moral, motivation.

Now in *The Ethics of Care and Empathy* (ECE), I argued that empathic caring is all that we need in order to be moral individuals. I attempted to show, for example, that empathy is the (sentimental) basis for the deontological distinctions commonsense morality subscribes to, but I don't need to make the case for such larger conclusions in the present context. It will be enough if the reader is (already) convinced that empathy is an important factor in altruistic or caring motivation—however broad a role this latter can or should play in the overall moral life. What I want to do now is show how certain specific themes in ECE move us toward understanding objectivity as essentially an empathic phenomenon.

ECE contained a long discussion of what it is to respect the autonomy of other people. Although such respect is a crucial element in, and even basis for, Kantian morality, I argued that a care ethics that focuses on empathy can explain or explicate respect in its own sentimentalist terms. I pointed out earlier that empathy isn't supposed to require the merging of two souls or personalities. Someone who is overinvolved with another person may have difficulty in separating their own needs and desires from those of the other, and this may mean that they fail to respond empathically to what the other needs or wants. One familiar example of such overinvolvement can be found in the attitudes some parents have to their children. Some parents seek to live through (the successes of) their children and have a difficult time separating their own needs from those of their children. Such parents *ipso facto* have difficulty empathizing with the individual point of view—with the needs, wishes, ideas, fears, and aspirations—of their children. Thus, if the child says they want to do something different from what the parent has planned for them, the parent will often say, and believe, something like "you don't really want to do that."

This sort of parental overinvolvement has been labeled "substitute success syndrome" (henceforward "sss"). And it has been recognized that sss involves an inability to recognize or understand the individuality or wishes of one's own children or others. To that extent, furthermore, it also seems plausible to say, as I said in ECE, that sss parents *fail to respect their children*, since respect for individuals('autonomy) is naturally thought of as requiring respect for their wants, beliefs, fears, and whatever is individual or distinctive about them. I proposed the philosophical hypothesis that respect for individuals can in general be unpacked in terms of empathy and empathic concern for them, and in ECE this idea was tested in relation to a number of interesting ethical examples.

For example, arrogantly dismissive and intolerant attitudes toward other people's ways of life or religion clearly express both a lack of empathy toward them and what we would naturally say was a lack of respect for them. But the matter is complicated (in an intellectually fruitful way) by the fact that those who are arrogant and intolerant toward others typically hate and/or are angry with those others. Religious persecution has often been said (by those who ought to know better) to be based on a desire for the salvation and well-being of those being persecuted and even tortured; but as John Locke, in the *Second Essay on Government*, (wittily and wisely) points out, the "dry eyes" of the torturers and persecutors refute the notion that they are motivated by concern for people's well-being. And, as I said, it seems as if religious intolerance and worse are typically based on a kind of hatred or anger. This connects with what we are saying about empathy, because anger and hatred drive out empathy, make empathy with those one hates or is angry with either difficult or impossible.

The above has bearing on what we have to say about the connection between empathy and intellectual, critical, theoretical, or scientific objectivity. Since anger and hatred toward those one disagrees with intuitively seem incompatible with being objective about their opinions, it would seem that a degree of empathy incompatible with great anger and hatred is a necessary condition of being objective regarding the viewpoints or opinions of others, and that idea gets us part of the way toward the more general thesis of this essay: that objectivity with respect to ideas, facts, and/or arguments is basically and solely a matter of being empathic in certain (as yet here unspecified) ways. But let me not anticipate too much at this point. We have a lot more to consider and argue for before we can be in a position to maintain that general thesis, so let me continue.

SSS parenting tends to create children who doubt themselves and their own ideas and aspirations, children who, to that extent, are lacking in the kind of autonomy we think is desirable and even necessary to (an) adult (kind of) life. And, interestingly—or perhaps depressingly—enough, what sss parents do to their children (of either sex) is what, arguably, is done to little girls and women under patriarchy. As Carol Gilligan points out in *In a Different Voice*, patriarchy tends to deprecate women's and girls' opinions and aspirations.[3] If the nineteenth-century girl says she thinks it is unfair that she can't attend university, she may be told: "you can't really believe that (you're not the kind of ungrateful girl who thinks things like that); you know that your brother needs to go to university in order to have a profession, but that your place is in the home." Her viewpoint, her idea, her incipient belief in the unfairness of the system gets nipped in the bud through such statements, which are practically as likely to have come from a nineteenth-century mother as from a father. But in crushing the young girl's idea, the system also crushes her aspirations, as, for example, when the young girl who says she wants to become a doctor is told, not perhaps that she can't attend university (which might even no longer be true), but that she would *really* (wouldn't she?) rather be a nurse than be a doctor, which is such an unfeminine profession for a woman.

As Gilligan puts it, women and girls under patriarchy learn to distrust or dismiss their own voices; and they consequently lack the autonomy that men more typically have in such conditions. This too, and as we shall see better in what follows, bears on the issue of how objectivity and empathy connect. A person who doubts their every thought can no more be objective about evidence, arguments, or ideas than someone who is so filled with contempt, hatred, or arrogance toward those s/he is interacting with that they cannot pay serious attention to what those others are saying or arguing. But in order to demonstrate the crucial role empathy plays in (someone's) being objective, we need to discuss the question what sorts of entities or mental states can be the focus or subject of empathic reactions.

2. The Focus of Empathy

The kind of objectivity I want to talk about here is not the objectivity *of* matters of fact or things in the world, but objectivity in thinking and arguing *about* matters of fact and, also, of speculation.[4] We have seen that emotions like anger work against and/or undercut both empathy and objectivity, and I have said (though more needs to be and later will be said about this) that the unempathic way in which women and girls are treated under patriarchy (and in which sss parents treat their children) makes them incapable, to a large extent, of objective thinking. I want eventually to defend the idea that the idea of empathy is crucial to and, suitably supplemented, sufficient for the understanding of what it is to be intellectually or scientifically

---

[3] *In a Different Voice: Psychological Theory and Women's Development* (Cambridge, MA: Harvard University Press, 1982).

[4] We also sometimes speak of or question the objectivity *of some body of knowledge*, but that, again, isn't the same thing as talking about how objective someone is with respect to such a body of knowledge. I am assuming, by the way, that objective or rationally justified knowledge is possible in certain areas. Whether or not that is true, the assumption allows me more easily to make the distinctions I am interested in here.

objective about things. But this main thesis depends on a proper understanding of what one can be empathic with. I want to claim that an objective person, a person thinking objectively, will be empathic with the point of view of those, for example, whom she disagrees with (and may be engaged in discussions with). However, some readers may wonder whether it is really possible to empathize with a point of view or set of beliefs different from one's own. For them, the idea of empathy with hedonic, orectic, or emotional states or processes makes immediate sense, but they may be less sure about empathy with states or processes that are strictly intellectual and don't involve or necessarily involve any kind of feeling or conation. We need to address this issue.

As we saw earlier, Martin Hoffman thinks it is possible to empathize with a person's bad situation or condition even if the person is temporarily enjoying themselves or in a good mood—recall his description of empathy with the unwitting victim of terminal cancer. But it could be suggested that such empathy depends on empathizing with the feelings, desires, and misery one knows the person with the cancer will soon or eventually have or undergo and so is anchored in actual *future* hedonic, emotional, and/or orectic states. However, once one grants the possibility of the kind of case Hoffman talks about, it seems possible to imagine our feeling empathic sadness for someone who doesn't know they are about to die, when we also realize that they will *never* know or suffer "what hit them." One has to work a bit in order to construct such an example, but imagine, for instance, that we learn that somewhere right now a person is about to die painlessly from leaked gas in a way that that person doesn't anticipate and that we can do nothing to prevent. Presumably, we can feel empathy for such a person even though (we may know that) the person we are empathizing with will feel no relevant later pain, frustrated desire, or fearful emotion for us to empathize with. Hoffman says that empathy with someone independently of their present actual feelings is an empathic ability that develops as a child becomes more intellectually or cognitively capable, and perhaps this is also true of the sort of more extreme case I have just described. If so, then one can to a substantial extent empathize with someone's situation or condition independently of what they actually will ever feel (hedonically or emotionally) or desire.

But the person who thinks empathy needs to be anchored in such felt/orectic states might still want to claim that when, for example, we feel empathically sad in thinking about a person who is about to die from leaked gas, we are feeling empathy for the pain or emotion we imagine they *would* feel if they only knew what was about to happen to them (or if the gas only injured rather than killed them). And I don't know really how to argue against this last ditch refusal to allow (for) empathy with a person's or persons' objective condition or situation. I feel inclined to say that once one allows that there can be empathy with merely hypothetical or potential feelings, etc., empathy has become sufficiently sophisticated to also take on or take in non-hedonic, etc., situations or conditions *more directly*.[5]

---

[5] In "Empathy and Universalizability" (*Ethics* 105, 1995), John Deigh sees adult empathy as focusing on and sensitive both to general facts about human life and its vicissitudes and to instantiations of those facts in individual lives and circumstances. This seems to allow the focus of empathy to reach out to objective factors that aren't reducible to sheer feelings or hedonic/orectic states.

Now the issue or problem that arises for (the possibility of) intellectual empathy—by which I mean empathy with another person's state of belief or knowledge or their intellectual/scientific/cognitive "point of view"—is actually a bit different from the issue we have just been talking about. We have been speaking about the possibility of empathy in cases where the person we are empathizing with will have relevant feelings or desires only *later* or merely *would* have such feelings or desires in imaginable hypothetical circumstances. But the immediate issue for someone who doubts the possibility of intellectual empathy is whether there is enough affective/orectic/hedonic content to states of knowledge/belief or intellectual points of view to allow there to be empathy with such states or points of view. Nonetheless, what we said about the kinds of cases discussed earlier carries over to some extent to the purely intellectual cases. If (as the discussion at least tentatively concluded) we can relevantly empathize with someone independently of their actual present or future feelings, desires, etc., it would also seem possible to empathize with someone's present non-affective, non-hedonic, non-orectic intellectual/cognitive state or processes. And if someone says that the former kind of case depends on empathizing with possible or hypothetic affective, etc., reactions to a condition or situation, we can similarly say—and this is a new theme—that empathy with other people's cognitive states can work through empathy with the affective, etc., reactions that naturally go with such cognitive states. For example, if I accept a certain hypothesis, I may want to do experiments that test or support it and may feel displeasure when I hear that others right now maintain a contrary view. And one might say that our ability to empathize with states of cognition and purely intellectual points of view depends on such likely or hypothetical hedonic/affective/orectic reactions to what is in itself purely cognitive or intellectual.

In what immediately follows, however, I want to strengthen the case for empathy with what is intellectual or cognitive by pointing out how natural and easy it is to think of people as empathizing with this "side" of another person's life or psychology. And I shall go on to argue additionally that it may not, in fact, be possible (for humans) to hold intellectual positions independently of relevant affect, etc. All of this will help clear the way toward the view it is my main purpose to defend here, the view that intellectual objectivity can be explained in terms of empathy.

To begin on a personal note, the idea that objectivity might relate to empathy first began to take root in me when it occurred to me (one day) that I was empathizing with certain people's ignorance or lack of knowledge of the English language. Without thinking about it, I was adjusting my vocabulary in speaking to native Spanish speakers who didn't know a great deal of English. This seemed to me to involve, on my part, a process or state of empathic sensitivity, but it also seemed clear or likely that I wasn't empathizing with my interlocutors' affective states, etc. Of course, it is possible that native Spanish speakers in this country feel embarrassed and fearful speaking with a native English speaker and that I was empathizing with that rather than with their lack of knowledge of the English language. But I don't think this is what was happening. My experience in Miami tells me that native Spanish speakers don't fear conversation with speakers of English, because the lack of knowledge of English isn't much of a disadvantage here and because the city of Miami nowadays belongs at least as much to those who know Spanish as to those who know English.

These are facts that native Spanish speakers are as well aware of as I am, so I don't think my empathy with the lack of knowledge of English some of them demonstrate is a function of empathy with their negative feelings (or for that matter their positive feelings) about speaking with a native English speaker. Rather, I think what happens when I pretty much unconsciously adjust my speaking vocabulary to someone's lesser knowledge of English is exactly what I was first inclined to think it is, a state or process of empathy with and/or sensitivity to another person's cognitive state(s) or processes.

So apart from the arguments given earlier that started with issues about empathy with victims of cancer or poisonous gas, it seems to me commonsensical to suppose that I sometimes or often empathize with other people's cognitive states, and I am sure that I and others could find many other commonplace examples of this phenomenon.[6] And if we can empathize with cognitive states independently of other people's emotional/orectic/hedonic states or processes, then it should be possible to empathize with another person's intellectual point of view, assuming that such points of view are also independent of emotional, etc. states of processes, in other words, assuming that such points of view are purely or exclusively intellectual or theoretical. But a point of view is different from the kind of cognitive state I was registering when, at different times, I implicitly adjusted my spoken vocabulary to the linguistic knowledge or ignorance of a native Spanish speaker. Linguistic knowledge doesn't in any ordinary or obvious way involve making assumptions or claims about facts or values or anything else, but this is precisely what *is* involved when one adopts or has a certain point of view, A point of view involves making certain assumptions or claims in a way linguistic knowledge and ignorance both seem not to do, and yet many would say that just as linguistic knowledge doesn't have to involve any emotions, desires, or hedonic reactions, neither does an intellectual point of view and neither do particular intellectual/theoretical assumptions, doubts, or beliefs. But I have doubts about this.

Depending perhaps on what exactly one means by "involve," it seems to me possible, even likely, that the making of intellectual assumptions, the having of theoretical beliefs, and, more synoptically, the adoption or possession of an intellectual/scientific/philosophical viewpoint all do involve emotional, etc., states or reactions. By "involve" one might mean "logically involve," but I don't want to interpret what I have just said as a strictly logical or metaphysical thesis using that notion of involvement. Let's relax a bit and talk of what is (social-)psychologically involved when human beings adopt or possess an intellectual viewpoint or single intellectual belief. Is there, as we might put it, such a thing, really, as a purely intellectual viewpoint, belief, assumption, or doubt? I am inclined to some extent to think not. But to give my reasons I think I need at this point to bring in some interesting work that Michael Stocker has done in this area.

---

[6] The one place I know of where this phenomenon is mentioned is Frans de Waal's *Our Inner Ape*, NY: Riverhead Books, 2005, pp. 6f. But the example he gives is far from commonplace—in an effort to illustrate the great empathic capacities of bonobos, he describes a bonobo, Kanzi, who was on a given occasion empathically sensitive to his sister's (state of) ignorance of various facts and who tried to help her learn more.

In "Intellectual Desire, Emotion, and Action," Stocker discusses the ways in which our involvement in intellectual topics and/or disciplines calls upon and requires various emotions, desires, and even actions.[7] If, say, we are scientists, we will *want to know* the answer to certain questions, will in better or worse ways *investigate* certain issues, and will *want to know* how certain experiments we or others do come out. And our emotions or attitudes are also involved in pursuing science and other supposedly pure intellectual activities, since, when we have no sympathy with a certain area or line of scientific inquiry, we don't get involved in it and since, when we have *a great deal of* sympathy or respect for what is being said in a given discipline, we don't want, and don't summon the energy, to call its previous findings or present assumptions into question.

All this seems plausible to me, and for present purposes I just want to generalize and/or reconfigure it a bit. Stocker mostly focuses on good or bad intellectual traits like laziness or energy and how they bear on one's devotion to and pursuit of various intellectual/scientific disciplines, and he mentions the emotions involved in accepting a given intellectual position or belief only once or twice. The examples of sympathy and its absence mentioned above are in fact the only clear examples he gives of emotions tied to particular viewpoints or assumptions, but it is viewpoints or assumptions acquired or maintained in the doing of science (or the pursuit of other intellectual activities), rather than the (mere) fact of energetically or non-energetically, carefully or carelessly, doing science, that bears most directly on one's objectivity. A lack of energy, or of intelligence, or of ingenuity, or (perhaps even) of carefulness in the pursuit of a discipline doesn't call one's objectivity into question. Rather, objectivity depends on the way one arrives and defends various assumptions, beliefs, or whole points of view. And emotions and desires are certainly relevant here: both to the objectivity of one's beliefs, etc., and to one's actually acquiring or maintaining them. We need to consider the latter point first.

If a person accepts a certain point of view, then we say that the person favors that viewpoint over others. Now outside the area of supposedly pure intellect or science, favoring one thing or person over another involves a *feeling* or *attitude* of greater liking, and unless the defender of pure intellect wants to say that our use of similar language regarding scientific/intellectual viewpoints (sets of beliefs and assumptions) and regarding particular beliefs/assumptions is strictly metaphorical, the fact that we say that those who accept certain viewpoints or assumptions *favor* them indicates that there is no such thing as purely intellectual science or purely intellectual work in other disciplines either. But to take refuge in the charge of metaphoricalness seems to me at least to be question-begging. One says such a thing because one wants to maintain that there is such a thing as purely intellectual activity, and what seems more plausible, given the ways we naturally think and speak about these matters, is that both intellectual activities and non-intellectual ones involve emotions, attitudes, or feelings that are in effect unavoidable wherever and whenever human beings are involved in any sort of practical enterprise.

---

[7] In Amelie Rorty, ed., *Explaining Emotions* (Berkeley: University of California Press, 1980): pp. 323–38.

This idea has (at least) two important implications. It means that our worries, to the extent we have had them, about whether one can empathize with purely intellectual states of belief or processes of belief-formation are unnecessary because there are, in the human case at least, no such things. (Even total skepticism involves feelings or attitudes toward certain assumptions and the belief some people have in those assumptions.) And it also permits us, if we want, to think of empathy with states of belief or points of view as latching onto these things through or by means of the affective/orectic states that invariably accompany them. We don't *have* to make this claim, but we can or could, and given what we have been saying over the last few paragraphs, we are now in a position to explore and defend the idea that objectivity rests on empathy.

3. Objectivity Based in Empathy

As I mentioned earlier, intellectual objectivity isn't so much a matter of cognitive states generally, but, rather, of how one acquires and, I think, most particularly, of how one maintains certain beliefs. Knowing or not knowing English is certainly a cognitive distinction, but a person's objectivity doesn't at all depend on whether they know English or Spanish—it depends rather on how they maintain beliefs. There are, as I shall now argue, more or less empathic ways of maintaining beliefs, and *those distinctions*, I shall argue, are the ones that determine whether one is or is being objective with regard to a given intellectual or non-intellectual subject matter. (I hesitate to contrast intellectual subject matters with practical ones, given the naturalness of supposing, as Stocker and I here have in effect argued, that even intellectual subject matters involve us in practical, in the sense of action-oriented, questions and decisions.)

We already to some extent anticipated this idea when we earlier spoke of the ways in which anger with other people's beliefs or viewpoints (and with the other people) can undercut both empathy and objectivity regarding those beliefs or viewpoints. The Spanish Inquisitors obviously lacked both empathy and objectivity with respect to (the viewpoints or beliefs of) those they persecuted and tortured and tried to convert, and hatred and contempt for those who disagreed with them may have played a major role in producing or constituting that lack or empathy and objectivity. It is perhaps also worth noting that at the present historical juncture, the hatred Muslims feel toward the West (because of the situation of the Palestinians, because of American interference in Iranian political life decades ago, and for other reasons) and the hatred Westerners who are not Muslims feel toward Islam (because of 9/11, because of Muslim Holocaust denial, and for other reasons) make it nearly impossible for either side to be empathic with or objective about the other side's point of view. This fact, if it is one, is tragic.

However, there are examples of a lack or absence of objectivity that don't seem to involve emotions as strong as hatred or contempt, and these too, I think, can be understood in terms of issues of empathy or its absence. In the field of philosophy, for example, there can be disagreements and disputes where it seems (at least to outsiders) that neither side really understands or has tried to understand what the other side is saying (or the other's intellectual point of view). Such cases, I think, are naturally and plausibly regarded as involving a lack of empathy on both sides for the other side's point of view (alternatively, an empathic failure to see things from the other's side's point of view). For example, neither side may ever actually state the other side's views in an accurate way, a way that the other side would acknowledge as acceptable. And neither side may be *capable* of doing this, in part, presumably, because their strong or rigid commitment to their own point of view makes them not want to see things through the eyes or intellect of someone who totally disagrees with them. Doesn't it seem plausible to say that in such cases neither side is being (completely) objective about the issues that divide them? I assume that it *is* plausible to say this, and in that case we have another instance of how a failure or lack of empathy undercuts objectivity.

But notice what all this entails. Objectivity requires one to be able to empathize, and in various circumstances actually to empathize, with another person's intellectual point of view; and, given what I have been saying, seeing another person's position or argument from that person's point of view means empathically (i.e., through empathy) seeing it in something like the favorable light in which the other person sees it. And that, in turn, means having a certain kind of (possibly mild) favorable emotion toward it. So being intellectually/epistemically rational and objective really does require having certain emotions.

It is important to realize, moreover, that a theory that treats empathy as crucial to (and, as we shall see later, sufficient for) being objective, doesn't entail that objectivity will eventually lead to agreement. Just as a fully empathic mother may end up taking her protesting child to the dentist's (even while feeling bad about having to do so), so too, I think, may someone who has fully empathized with the point of view of those who disagree with her still end up disagreeing with them. This often *won't* happen because getting better acquainted with the point of view of those with whom one initially disagrees may lead one to modify one's position or at least, and this is really in a way the same thing, how one defends that position. But it seems plausible to suppose that it can be possible to empathize with a different point of view without essentially modifying one's own position; and that possibility means that objectivity, as I am conceiving and describing it, doesn't require or entail eventual agreement among all those who (continue to) think about or discuss a certain issue—a consequence of my position that seems to me to be very desirable.[8]

---

[8] Objectivity may require one to modify how one defends one's position in the face of criticisms and positive ideas deployed from a viewpoint inconsistent with one's own (let us assume that we are not talking about absolutely crazy ideas like the belief that the world is about to end). Now in the *Metaphysics of Morals (Doctrine of Virtue*, paragraph 39), Kant says that paying respect to another in conversation means understanding that there is some merit in their ideas. And if we accept this, it would seem that changing how one defends one's views involves acknowledging some sort of merit in another person's ideas and to that extent respecting them. But if objectivity in some sense requires respecting other people's ideas or beliefs, that doesn't in any way work against the idea that objectivity is based in empathy. In an intellectual context, I want to say, empathy with ideas or viewpoints *is* (a form of) respect, and ECE similarly argued that moral respect can be understood in terms of empathy with other people's desires and states of well-being.

The present discussion, finally, also suggests a parallel between what I said about justice in ECE and what can be said about justice in intellectual contexts. Being objective in empathic terms is tantamount

But in order to complete our basic picture of the relation between empathy and intellectual objectivity, we have to consider whether empathy is sufficient, not just required, for objectivity. It helps us here that it is plausible to claim that objectivity doesn't require eventual agreement, because empathy clearly isn't sufficient for eventual agreement. But the following kind of example might make one wonder whether empathy was in fact sufficient for objectivity. Imagine that someone is obtuse about accumulating or weighing scientific or other data and ends up with a totally (in intellectual terms) unjustified theory or set of beliefs. Such a person doesn't show or indicate any lack of empathy for anyone else's intellectual viewpoint and in fact may not have ever interacted with anyone else in the area where s/he makes her findings; yet the person has shown a great intellectual deficiency in coming to the views s/he now maintains.

But nothing we have said about this person indicates that their intellectual deficiency or failing is one of objectivity, rather, say, than one of deficient intelligence or imagination. We have to add that the person who comes to various conclusions doesn't care, for example, that others might or would find his methods or conclusions dubious, in order to make the accusation of non-objectivity stick; but once we do that we seem to be ascribing to the person a lack of empathy for the point(s) of view from which others might or would criticize him. He is insouciant or careless about what others may think, and this is a failure of empathy. But when and where someone *is* empathic with another viewpoint, s/he won't count as lacking objectivity with respect to that viewpoint, even if she is somewhat obtuse or unintelligent. Objectivity is not, I am assuming, the only element in being rational and thinking rationally, so when I say that a certain kind of empathy is sufficient for one's being objective, I am not saying it is sufficient for every other intellectual virtue or (thus) sufficient for full or complete intellectual/scientific rationality.[9]

Given our conclusions about the cases we have discussed, the presence or absence of intellectual, critical, or scientific objectivity seems, more generally, to be less a matter of how one actually acquires a given belief or viewpoint than of how one is prepared to defend one's views in the light of others' dissent from (or reluctance to accept) them. In that measure, being objective turns out to be more a *reactive* and

---

to doing intellectual justice to other people's points of view, and ECE argued that justice as a moral ideal governing societies internally and in relation to other societies is also a matter of appropriate forms of *empathic* concern among individuals or governments. Intellectual and moral respect, and intellectual and moral justice, center around our capacity, respectively, for intellectual empathy and for individual-welfare-oriented moral empathy.

[9] I am indebted to Seisuke Hayakawa on the subject of the distinction between objectivity and other aspects of rationality. For the opposed view that rationality and objectivity (in science) amount to pretty much the same thing, see Nicholas Rescher, *Objectivity: The Obligations of Impersonal Reason* (Notre Dame, IN: University of Notre Dame Press, 1997). But I think treating objectivity, being objective, as just one element in being rational comes closer to ordinary thought and usage. ("Objective" and "non-biased" seem closer to synonyms than "rational" and "non-biased" do.) I am also assuming that both objectivity and rationality come in degrees; and our theory allows for this. Finally, I should mention that although both intellectual rationality and intellectual objectivity are traditionally thought of as requiring emotional detachment vis-à-vis a given subject matter, the present paper argues for the contrary idea that rationality and objectivity depend on a *certain sort* of emotional *engagement*.

relational matter than one might have initially supposed.[10] The old adage "a word to the wise is sufficient" in effect characterizes wisdom in terms of its reactive tendencies, its reactions, to(ward) good advice, and though this may or may not be the whole of *wisdom*, I do want to maintain, and in the light of our discussion I don't think it is implausible to maintain, that intellectual/theoretical/critical/scientific objectivity *is* a matter of how one empathically reacts or would react to what others think and say.

But what about those who, because of the depredations of patriarchy or of sss parents, are so intellectually self-doubting and selfless that they can't properly weigh other people's opinions or their own? Well, I don't know what to say about the empathic capacities of such people. On the one hand, their selflessness might be thought to make them extremely empathic with, even to the point of always accepting, what other people think, and since this doesn't seem to be a way of being objective about either one's own beliefs or those of others, our account might at this point seem to be in a certain amount of trouble. However, as we saw Hoffman point out above, empathy isn't a kind of merging or melting into another, so the intellectually selfless might really seem to lack all empathy and objectivity as well.[11] This would make our theory seem to apply comfortably to such people (though we can't be comfortable with their intellectual or other fate). But there is a further point.

Whatever we say about the empathy or lack of empathy that intellectually selfless people have, it is clear (or it has to my mind been convincingly argued) that such selflessness is typically produced by a person's being raised by non-empathic sss parents or by a girl or woman's having been raised in a patriarchal environment (including a home) that frequently demonstrates a lack of empathy for girls' or women's desires, ideas, and aspirations. So even if we were to say that the intellectually selfless are (in an extreme and undesirable way) empathic with other people's points of view and yet deficient in intellectual objectivity, we could use the notion of empathy to offer a humanly sufficient condition of someone's being objective by saying that it is both necessary and sufficient for objectivity that one (be able to) empathize fully with other people's points of view and that one have been raised oneself in an empathic way that allows one to be confident, though not rigid or arrogant, about one's own beliefs and aspirations. Since empathy is central to both the (supposedly necessary) conditions just mentioned, we would have made good on the promise to offer an account of objectivity in terms of empathy. But if, for the reasons mentioned just above, the second conjunct of this equation turns out to be unnecessary, then

---

[10] Some important recent feminist literature argues against traditional (Kantian) views that see autonomy as something individuals contain in themselves and in favor of what it calls "relational autonomy"— autonomy seen as developing and existing in relation to other people. (See Ch. 4 of ECE for relevant citations and discussion.) The view of intellectual objectivity being developed here in like fashion sees objectivity in relation to (the views and arguments of possible or actual) others, so we can, if we want, speak of (the character trait of) relational objectivity, and the present account is aptly called *a relational theory of objectivity*. Notice too that the relational element comes in through the empathy that I am saying is necessary to being objective.

[11] In a forthcoming dissertation, Kristin Borgwald says that such people lack *epistemic personhood*, an idea that is modeled on and in some way parallels what people have said about moral personhood. If full empathy requires a full, non-merged *person* to do the empathizing, then Borgwald's idea supports the notion that the intellectually selfless aren't empathic with the viewpoint of others.

the first conjunct may be able to do the job of characterizing objectivity in terms of empathy and do so in a simpler or more unified way than the conjunctive account would allow.

4. Conclusion

I have sketched a theory of objectivity, of what is required for someone to count as being objective in some area or areas, in terms of empathy; and along the way I mentioned the problems that arise for us humans when we are incapable of being empathic with one another's viewpoints. The current state of opposition or enmity between Islam and the West (if that is a proper characterization of the present state of things in the world) is an unfortunate fact for humanity, or so at least I believe (others may disagree). That state prevents or works against intellectual empathy between the two sides, but it also prevents or works against empathic concern for the (non-intellectual) well-being of those on the other side. In other words, and assuming the present theory together with what I have argued in ECE, hatred and a lack of empathy make it difficult or impossible for people to be *intellectually/critically objective* about each other's viewpoints or beliefs, but also make it difficult or impossible to be *morally concerned* about the others' welfare or happiness. (By the same token, the presence of empathy also makes it possible to live in just and continuing peace with other people even though one doesn't agree with them about important matters.) Thus empathy is necessary to the fulfillment of both intellectual and moral ideals or objectives, and it therefore has an even larger human role to play than I thought when I wrote ECE and focused solely on the moral implications of (developing) empathy.[12]

The idea that empathy plays an important role in overcoming or preventing hatred and conflict between individuals or (very large) groups of individuals is familiar from the literature of psychology and of the specialized field of conflict resolution. And the related idea that empathy makes it easier to overcome disagreements and come to peaceable, constructive, or useful agreements is also a truism of that literature.[13]

---

[12] Objectivity probably shouldn't be regarded as an absolute human ideal, because there are times when we would rather see people be loving and act lovingly than be objective. In *Morals from Motives* (New York: Oxford University Press, 2001, Ch. 5), I argued—what seems very commonsensical—that a parent, say, who genuinely loves a child won't and can't, at least initially, be entirely objective about evidence that indicates the child has done something horrible or criminal. The parent will give them more benefit of the doubt than an objective observer knowing all the same facts would, and if one has to choose between full objectivity and love, love should sometimes win. (This means that the Enlightenment ideal of critical detachment/objectivity about all beliefs and ideas has at the very least to be qualified.) Note that in a situation where one isn't objective about the issue of what one's child has actually done, one isn't going to be empathic with the point of view of an objective observer who thinks one's child *has* done something criminal or horrible. In fact, one is likely to be angry with them. But *that's love*!

[13] For two examples of the discussion and defense of these ideas, see R. Lulofs and D. Cahn, *Conflict: From Theory to Action*, Boston: Allyn and Bacon, 2000, Chs. 11–12; and J. Zubek, D. Pruitt, R. Peirce, N. McGillicuddy, and H. Syna, "Disputant and Mediator Behaviors Affecting Short-Term Success in Mediation," *The Journal of Conflict Resolution* 36, 1992, pp. 546–72.

But unlike philosophy and philosophers, those who write and publish in these fields don't particularly focus on the issue of objectivity, so it is a distinctive feature of the present discussion that it ties empathy not merely to conflict resolution and to the overcoming of differences or disagreements, but to the philosophically and, as we have seen, humanly important notion of objectivity as well.

But note further that if empathy is a key ingredient in objectivity, it will sometimes be difficult to tell whether someone is being or has been objective in thinking about a given subject matter. Sometimes we can tell what someone is thinking or feeling, but at other times it is difficult or impossible to do so, and these differences and difficulties clearly carry over to empathy. Someone might seem to be taking in and seriously considering an intellectual opponent's viewpoint and ideas, but actually be deeply resistant to doing so, and so be either deceiving others or taken in himself about how objective he is being about some intellectual issue. And (as Harvey Siegel has pointed out to me) we can even more easily run into epistemological difficulties of this kind in cases of historical knowledge. When Lorentz, whose transformations allowed the difficulties in physics that eventually led to the special theory of relativity to be handled on an ad hoc basis, saw Einstein's theory, he rejected it and gave various arguments. But we (today) may never know whether he did so for good reasons that had force at the time or whether he was simply too resistant to changing his own ideas (and giving someone else credit for solving major problems) to give Einstein a fair or objective hearing.[14] In any event, the assumption that it can be difficult to know how objective someone is being or was in the past is no more implausible than similar assumptions about our knowledge that someone is morally good or has acted from good motives, and I bring up this point, not because it creates difficulties for the present approach that need somehow to be answered, but because it usefully places what we have been saying within a certain kind of epistemological context.

One final and (I think) important point. In recent years, there has been a lot of talk, speculation, and argument about the possibility that reason and emotion (or feeling) may be inextricably linked. People outside of philosophy (most famously, Anthony Damasio)[15] and philosophers as well have begun to take seriously the idea that reason may constitutively contain or involve emotion or feeling, but there has been a great deal of unclarity here about the exact meaning of this last thesis and about the data or facts that have been said to support it. However, the present essay, to the extent one accepts our previous conclusions, seems to offer a clear confirming

---

[14] Thomas Kuhn's *The Structure of Scientific Revolutions* (Chicago: University of Chicago Press, 1970/1962) stresses the ways in which scientists resist new theories that clash with ideas they have long held, and it has sometimes been said that Kuhn is (thereby) committed to a relativistic or irrationalist view of science. I won't get into the question whether this is the correct interpretation of Kuhn's ideas, but it is perhaps worth noting that if one believes there is or could be such a thing as scientific objectivity and rationality, then the widespread resistance to new ideas (as possibly with Lorentz) may only show that various motives prevent people from being as empathically objective about scientific matters as it is at least in principle possible to be. But one should be cautious about assuming that older scientists are typically less objective than younger ones. After all, even if the older scientists are resisting change, the younger ones may be so eager for change and for the glory of having brought it about that they end up treating the ideas of their elders unfairly in empathic terms.

[15] See, for example, his *Descartes' Error: emotion, reason, and the human brain*, Putnam, 1994.

instance of this general thesis. Intellectual objectivity is part of reason(ing) and (intellectual) rationality and to the extent it constitutively requires empathy with the (emotionally-charged) points of view of those who (may) disagree with one, reason and rationality also constitutively involve this kind of empathy. There may be other, even better, examples of the interpenetration of reason and emotion, but the one uncovered in the present paper illustrates it very clearly and solidly, and I take that to be one of the more interesting or significant implications of the present discussion considered as a whole.

23

In Place of Moral Reasoning

Moral reasoning is a topic that interests many philosophers, many ethicists. But I don't think that those with the interest have realized how tendentious that notion is, how entangled with particular notions of what (valid) morality is. The idea of moral reasoning sits well with rationalist approaches to ethics: with Kantianism and with Rossian intuitionism; and it sits well with the views many philosophers have about what common-sense moral thinking involves. But in the end, I think that common sense is less committed to the idea of moral reasoning, to its germaneness or centrality to the moral life, than many of us—including me for quite a long time—have thought. Unbeknownst to those who think common-sense moral thought gives great weight and importance to moral reasoning, rationalistic principle-based intuitionism and rationalistic Kantianism have infected their sense of what common-sense thinking is all about. I hope to show you that there is at least one alternative and ostensibly common-sense way of thinking about morality in which moral reasoning has a considerably smaller role. I believe moral sentimentalism can account for our ordinary thought about morality at least as well as rationalism does;[1] and yet if we

---

I am indebted throughout this essay to discussions with Jonathan Adler, Scott Gelfand, and John Horty.

[1] Rationalists tend to hold that it is irrational not to act morally, but in common-sense terms this actually isn't obvious. When someone doesn't care about his family, it is more obvious (to common ways of thinking) that he is heartless than that he is irrational. On this point, see my *The Ethics of Care and Empathy*, London: Routledge, 2007, Ch. 7. The book also attempts to show that an empathy-focused sentimentalist ethic of caring preserves and explains common-sense normative moral thinking at least as well as rationalist approaches do.

accept sentimentalism, we end up (as I am going to argue) with theoretical reason to think that moral reasoning has a less important role to play than those who talk about moral reasoning so much, think.

If, in particular, we accept sentimentalism as giving us the best account of *ordinary or common-sense morality*, then moral reasoning will definitely turn out to be much less important than philosophical discussions tend to assume. Most people who discuss moral reasoning think of it as involving reasoning from one or more fairly general or very general rules or principles to more specific moral conclusions: either more specific rules or concrete conclusions about what it is one's duty to do in one or another particular situation. But given that notion of what moral reasoning involves, it occurs less often than Kantians, Rossians, and defenders of the importance of moral reasoning think and is less necessary and central to an acceptable or praiseworthy moral life than they have believed.[2]

I want to begin by saying something about differing views of moral education. The Kantian/rationalist stress on good moral reasoning naturally goes with a certain view of how moral education takes place in favorable circumstances, a view according to which moral education is largely seen as teaching us to reason well. But there is an opposed sentimentalist conception of morality that says that the first view has moral education, and moral development more generally, all, or mostly, wrong; and this sentimentalist approach leads toward a rejection of the central importance of moral reasoning and toward placing greater importance on emotional sensitivity and on moral *understanding* as a phenomenon that includes both emotional and cognitive elements. In what follows I shall discuss these two views of moral education and the differing, opposed pictures of what good moral education leads to that they imply.[3] I favor the sentimentalist view of moral education myself, and shall be arguing that it offers a more realistic and attractive picture of how adults make moral decisions (decisions that are morally good or acceptable; I don't mean decisions about what is morally

---

[2] Aristotelian and other situationists don't (think we have to) subsume facts under moral rules or principles in order to come to moral decisions, and so although Aristotle talked about practical reasoning, his examples of such reasoning aren't cases where acts or less general principles are subsumed under moral principles, but are typically just practical situations where something like means-end reasoning occurs or needs to occur. (As we shall be seeing below, I allow ample scope to this kind of reasoning in moral contexts.) Since Aristotle doesn't think that general principles are used in coming to ethical/moral decisions, he doesn't think that any (to us) standard form of moral reasoning occurs in such contexts, and to that extent Aristotle doesn't place any more importance on moral reasoning than I do. But he does think (in a rationalistic fashion that is more than a little reminiscent of Kant) that self-conscious attention to situationally resultant moral facts—e.g., it would be ignoble for me to run away now—is frequently and ideally involved in ethical decision-making, whereas the sentimentalism espoused by Gilligan, Noddings, and myself holds that it is morally best not to be thinking explicit moral thoughts when one feels empathy-based compassion and decides to help another person. To that extent, sentimentalism moves further away from idealizing or emphasizing moral reasoning than Aristotle does. On the similarity between Kant and Aristotle, see Christine Korsgaard, "From Duty and for the Sake of the Noble: Kant and Aristotle on Morally Good Action" in S. Engstrom and J. Whiting, eds., *Aristotle, Kant, and the Stoics: Rethinking Happiness and Duty*, Cambridge: Cambridge University Press, 1998, pp. 203–36.

[3] I am assuming that the basic aim of moral education is promoting real moral development, but it may be politically easier to *sell* the idea of moral education if moral reasoning is stressed, since the latter can be defended as more readily integrated with the main school curriculum and as more in sync with its goal of promoting cognitive advance/growth. I am indebted on this point to Jonathan Adler.

good or acceptable) than one that stresses moral reasoning as the basis for such decisions.[4] Once we have laid out the opposing views on moral education and moral reasoning, we will be in a position to draw some interesting further conclusions.

1. Two Views of Moral Education

Those who believe in the importance or centrality of good moral reasoning to being a morally decent or good individual think—and why should they not?—that such reasoning has to be taught and that morally good dispositions have to be acquired at least in part through such teaching. (Personal insight, habituation or training, and other factors are also, plausibly, allowed a role.) Perhaps the most famous theory of how moral reasoning is taught and morality, as a good disposition, acquired comes from Jean Piaget via the work of Lawrence Kohlberg. Both Piaget and Kohlberg saw the teaching or learning of morality as occurring along Kantian lines and as essentially cognitive.[5] Kohlberg and Piaget conceived moral development, and the moral reasoning that they considered essential to it, as occurring through different stages, where each new stage reflects greater cognitive capacity on the part of the child or young adult. Moral development is regarded, as I said, as cognitive development, and in the final stage of such development, assuming someone gets that far, a person will think of morality in terms of very general and abstract principles like the Golden Rule or one or another version of Kant's Categorical Imperative.[6]

On Kohlberg's and Piaget's view the ability to use such abstract universal or general principles requires a *great deal* of cognitive development, more than, for example, is required at (what Kohlberg considers to be) the earlier stage in which a child simply wants to fit in with his or her group. That desire and ability represent what Kohlberg calls conventional morality, and conventional morality clearly requires fewer feats of cognitive abstraction and generalization/universalization than the supposed final stage where something like the Categorical Imperative is used. This seems true, and one can see how tempting it is or would be to use these facts as a basis for treating moral

---

[4] Moral reasoning can be used to justify decisions and actions ex post facto, but if that were the main use of such reasoning, it would (already) be less important than advocates of moral reasoning suppose. Moral reasoning is thought to be practically and morally useful—and the greatest and most obvious such use would be as a basis for making morally right decisions or choices—rather than as a way of assessing moral mistakes or misdeeds after the fact, when it is too late to avoid them.

[5] See in particular Lawrence Kohlberg, *Essays on Moral Development*: Vol. 1, *The Philosophy of Moral Development*; Vol. 2, *The Psychology of Moral Development*, NY: Harper and Row, 1981, 1984.

[6] Contemporary Kantians (e. g., Barbara Herman in *The Practice of Moral Judgment*, Cambridge: Harvard, 1993—and in more recent work) often don't think of moral development as centered around the inculcation or appreciation of very general moral principles to the extent that Kohlberg and Piaget do. They are often more concerned with the specification of our moral thought in particular circumstances. But they still think that some version or other of the CI is fundamental to (the background of) our moral thinking; and their ideas about how to approach particular decisions in particular circumstances place less stress on emotional sensitivity than care ethicists would. (Still, contemporary Kantians pay *more* attention to such sensitivity than earlier Kantians did. In the light of various criticisms brought by virtue ethicists, care ethicists, and others, they have to some extent moved closer to the views of their critics.) Again, I am indebted to Jonathan Adler.

development as a matter fundamentally of cognitive development. But in fact this approach, this scheme of things, doesn't say much about how the more or even the less abstract principles ever motivate anyone. This is an issue that Kohlberg never squarely faced, and he has come in for a good deal of criticism on that score.[7]

Kohlberg studied the reasoning of various groups of individuals of different ages and concluded from his studies/observations that there were three basic stages/levels in the development of moral reasoning and of morality: pre-conventional, conventional, and post-conventional. (Each of these was broken down into two parts, but the details needn't concern us here.) We have seen what Kohlberg says is conventional, namely, thinking (roughly) that one's group is the arbiter of what one (morally speaking) should do. And the use of the Kantian CI represents for Kohlberg the highest, post-conventional, stage of development.

However, the studies he had done to establish the nature and sequence of the stages had all been done on boys/men, and when the scheme of stages was eventually tested on girls/women, it was found that on average women advance less far through the stages than men do. The inevitable implication, then, was that women have less capacity for moral development than men do. But such a conclusion was subject to the objection that Kohlberg's scheme or picture of the stages of development might be distorted or unrepresentative precisely because it had been formed on the basis of studies solely of men. Women might not fit in with that picture, but that might simply show that they developed differently from men, through their own different set of stages. Thus nothing in Kohberg's methodology and the studies that had been done on boys/men and girls/women really justified saying that women were on average morally inferior *rather than simply different*.

The points I have just been making were all made—forcefully—by Carol Gilligan in her famous book *In A Different Voice*.[8] Gilligan had been associated with Kohlberg at Harvard, and her dissent from his methodology and the conclusions it seemed to yield led her to try to articulate the *difference* between men and women in a way that didn't presuppose or try to prove that either was *superior* to the other—hence the title of her book. The book had a seismic effect on discussions of moral development and has led to some highly important subsequent developments in the field of ethics.

Gilligan acknowledged that Kohlberg's original studies indicated that men tend to think in (what philosophers would call) Kantian terms about morality. She didn't herself focus on Kant, but her idea about men's typical way of dealing with moral questions was that they use abstract rules or principles to address them and in doing so invoke the ideal or value of individual autonomy. This means seeing moral issues in substantial measure in terms of the rights one individual has against others and seeing justice as a matter in large part of the honoring of such rights and as a freely-agreed-to or autonomously arrived-at set of principles for regulating those rights. What could be more Kantian?

---

[7] See, for example, Randall Curren's entry on "Moral Education" in L. Becker and C. Becker, eds. *The Encyclopedia of Ethics*, 2nd edition, NY: Routledge, 2001, p. 1129.

[8] *In a Different Voice: Psychological Theory and Women's Development*, Cambridge, MA: Harvard University Press, 1982.

But Gilligan saw women as being *anything but* Kantian in their approach to moral issues. Women don't approach such issues via general principles, but do so, rather, in terms of their direct connection with and concern about various other people. They emphasize and think in terms of how they are related *to* others, rather than in terms of their autonomy and separation *from* others, when they decide what to do, and that means that when they help other people, for example, they do because they are caringly focused on those others and concerned to do them good or help them, not because they necessarily have consulted a moral principle and used their knowledge of the circumstances of a given situation to argue for or reason toward a moral conclusion that follows from the principle and the "facts of the case." Gilligan eventually attenuated her claims about the correlation with gender, but not her claims about the difference between the two moral approaches. There is a difference between approaching moral problems via principles and reasoning a la Kohlberg and approaching them via one's direct concern about or for the welfare of someone who needs one's help, even though this difference is at best only imperfectly correlated with gender. (Gilligan later found in particular that many women think in terms of autonomy, principles, and justice, though not too many men approach moral problems in terms of direct caring as opposed to autonomy and principles.)

But what also essentially came out of Gilligan's approach were (at least) two major developments for moral or ethical theory. Gilligan briefly mentioned the idea of an ethic of care that would embody and articulate the approach to moral issues that is/was supposed to come more readily to women, and philosophers and others have in great numbers followed up on this. The ethics of care is now given space in encyclopedias and generally recognized as a major ethical approach, and as such an approach it says that being moral means caring about others and not necessarily using principles. This calls into question the importance of moral reasoning, but I don't think that anyone has taken that idea as far as I hope to do here. No one, to the best of my knowledge, has said that it follows or how it follows that moral reasoning is less important. *But it is!* And I shall say more about that here.

The other development has been slower in coming. It is the idea that if morality isn't paradigmatically based in highly abstract principles, then a picture of moral development that treats the arrival at abstract principles as the final and highest stage of morality is quite questionable and we *probably need a different picture* of how moral development occurs and moral education is best effected (at least in those who end up not thinking and reasoning in terms of abstract principles). Now Aristotle gives us a picture of moral development that doesn't require general principles but only sensitive moral responses to situational requirements, but this too involves more moral self-consciousness and explicitness than Gilligan and other care ethicists have thought desirable or necessary. And since Aristotle doesn't place much weight on the role of emotions/motives like compassion and sympathy in the moral life, his views on moral education and moral development more generally aren't going to help an ethics of care explain how such morally central emotions/motives are developed, learned, or taught.

In her book *Caring: A Feminine Approach to Ethics and Moral Education*, Nel Noddings, the first person to attempt fully to articulate an ethics of care, said that caring about others depends on "engrossment" with (the point of view of) those others, and she said a little bit about how engrossment takes place.[9] But it is clear that we need to say more than Noddings did about how moral education occurs. If the end point of moral development and moral education isn't universal abstract principles but something very different, though admirable and praiseworthy nonetheless, we need to say how admirable caring and compassion develop and are taught or learned. In effect, we need *at one and the same time to articulate better and better what ideal or moral caring involves and to say how such caring develops and can be taught: an equation with two unknowns that have to be determined simultaneously or by reference to one another*. This means that just as Kohlberg gave moral-psychological underpinnings to Kantian liberalism with his cognitive-developmentalist account of moral education, care ethics needs an account of its own of how the kind of morality it sees as valid can be taught or learned, its own account of moral education. In addition, it needs to say something about how (the idea of) moral reasoning fits or fails to fit in with (its account of) moral learning, education, and development. Till now care ethics hasn't been very mindful of these issues, and of the need to undergird itself with an account of moral education analogous to what Kohlberg and Piaget had provided for Rawls, Kant and recent ethical Kantianism. Noddings's idea of engrossment is really just a very small step here, but my view is and has been that if care ethics is to make progress in these areas, it has to pay more attention than it previously has to the recent psychological literature on empathy and moral development. Empathy is, I believe, the key to the kind of sentimental emotional/motivational development that treats direct (i.e., unmediated by principles) caring for others as the central feature of morality.

Now that psychological literature seems on the whole to tend toward the assumption that the development of empathy is crucial to altruism as care ethics understands it, that is, to genuine caring about (the welfare of) others. And by empathy here I mean the kind of feeling what others feel (I feel your pain) that occurs, as often is said, by a kind of contagion. There is also projective empathy that involves deliberately putting oneself in the shoes of another, but the kind I find most interesting and is most relevant to care ethics is an empathy that works not by voluntary choice but by a kind of psychological association. One sees the other writhing in pain and that pain (as Hume put it) "infuses" itself into the observer without the observer's making any deliberate choice that it should do so. This is what psychologist Martin Hoffman, who has studied and written more and to my mind better about empathy than any other recent writer (though Hume, using the term "sympathy" because the term empathy didn't then exist, was the first person to talk about empathy in an interesting way) has called mediated associative empathy: associative because not occurring via a deliberate choice and mediated because the character of empathy depends on one's degree of cognitive development. A child can't empathize with disadvantaged groups the way an adolescent can, in part because the adolescent has a clearer idea than any child is likely to have of what a group is *and of what it would be for a whole group to be oppressed by other people or to be suffering from a natural catastrophe*.

Empathy, then, is typified by contagion or what Hume calls infusion of emotion or feeling from one person to another. Sympathy, by contrast, and most people nowadays recognize the distinction this way, involves feeling bad about and sorry for

---

[9] Berkeley: University of California Press, 1984.

someone who is, say, in pain and wishing or wanting them to be better off. And of course acting on their behalf isn't *just* sympathy, though sympathy can lead to it; and we wouldn't call someone a genuinely caring person if they only *wished* people well and never were motivated to try to help them. So the question arises how developing or increasing empathy in a child can lead to a child's being or becoming a more caring person and thus, in the terms of care ethics, a morally better person. Empathy is a kind of mechanism whereby feeling is transmitted. But we also need a mechanism or at least a technique for developing that mechanism, for getting it to work, and Hoffman was the first person to suggest such a technique.[10]

According to Hoffman, caring is *induced* by appealing to and arousing our empathy. In particular, a parent teaches a child to become more caring by (firmly yet not menacingly) pointing out to the child how they have hurt, say, a younger sibling, on occasions where such a thing has happened. Hoffman holds and there are studies to show that such firm pointing out of the pain or harm they have caused a sibling arouses the child's naturally given capacity for empathy and eventually makes the child hesitate to harm or hurt others in advance of actually doing so. Hoffman says a good deal about how all this happens, but we needn't go into that here. And he terms this form of moral education inductive discipline or induction, which contrasts, as he points out, with two other methods of moral education or making children's behavior more acceptable that parents use. One is power assertion, which involves threatening the child if the child hurts a sibling: if you ever do this again I will do this and that to you, and because you have already done this, you will be spanked or have to go to your room. The other alternative technique is inculcating or trying to inculcate moral principles or rules by admonition and repetition: telling the child that such and such kind of action is wrong: e. g., it is wrong to hurt your little brother. This technique naturally goes with using principles and reasoning from (and toward) them.

And induction doesn't involve this. To tell a child that it has hurt another and in that verbal way to stimulate the child's empathic responsiveness and thereby make them more caring (I won't talk here about the details of care ethics: e. g., how much one is supposed to care for whom) doesn't involve them in reasoning from moral assumptions or principles. In fact, the notions of right and wrong don't come in at all. So induction is supposed to get us to become better, more caring people without making much use of what is ordinarily and within the Piagetian/Kohlbergian tradition thought of as moral reasoning. And if the technique of training or education doesn't involve the parent's use of principles, the child presumably isn't learning to use principles in moral contexts. So the fully developed moral adult—according to the view that says moral education works best via induction—is someone who doesn't typically reason from moral principles or assumptions in approaching moral problems, but, rather, is someone whose empathy is aroused when they notice that someone is in trouble and who is thereby moved to help people or a person without moral principles entering into it.

---

[10] See his *Empathy and Moral Development: Implications for Caring and Justice*, Cambridge: Cambridge University Press, 2000. In my *Morals from Motives* (NY: Oxford University Press, 2001, pp. 47f.), I independently advocated the same inductive technique for teaching or increasing empathy that Hoffman recommends. But this occurred long after Hoffman had started writing about induction and backing up his ideas with empirical studies.

This is reminiscent of what Hume said about the natural virtues, which, unlike what he calls artificial virtues, don't require specific moral thinking or exhortation. And Hume's clearest example is benevolence, which is close to the caring that care ethicists think likewise doesn't require attention to moral principles or facts.[11]

So care ethics advocates direct connection with and caring about others, and the technique of induction and the appeal in particular to empathy show how this sort of caring and connection can be developed and can actually occur. We can use the notion of empathy and the idea of inductive discipline (and the relevant literature of psychology) to give care ethics a theory of moral education that is every bit as fully developed as what Kohlberg offers Kantians and liberals. And I think the theory is arguably more plausible than Kohlberg's views because a technique like induction clearly engages our moral motivation in a way that, as I mentioned earlier, Kohlberg's ideas have a difficult time doing. Moreover, empathy and its development work along with or in the context of cognitive development: it isn't blind emotion that I am advocating as a basis for morality, but, rather, an emotion/motivation like empathic caring that, in light of increasing cognitive capacity, engages more and more sensitively with more and more perceived aspects of situations.

Note too that our developed empathic reactions needn't be confined to those we are in immediate contact with. Hoffman points out that in least partly as a result of cognitive maturation, typical teenagers are capable of great empathy for disadvantaged groups (most of) whose members they have never met. How sensitivity to such groups is developed or encouraged is an important issue I don't think I should take up here, but the point of indicating the possibility of such sensitivity is to answer those who might say that an empathic caring approach to morality is likely to be too narrow to account for and develop the full range of reactions most of us think are required by morality. Induction and empathy are never going to make us as concerned about distant others as about our own near and dear, but arguably morality tells us *to be* more concerned about our own near and dear, so I don't see a problem here for the kind of moral education I am advocating.

2. Moral Reasoning vs. Moral Understanding

We have seen that empathy and caring don't operate via moral reasoning, and the moral life according to care ethics isn't at its heart (sic) a matter of such reasoning.

---

[11] In "Persons, Character, and Morality" (in his book *Moral Luck*, Cambridge: Cambridge University Press, 1981), Bernard Williams mentions the example of a man who decides to save his drowning wife rather than a drowning stranger only after concluding or thinking that he is morally permitted, or obligated, to do so. Williams says that the man has "one thought too many," and indeed he has. So the idea that moral thinking and (therefore) moral reasoning aren't always relevant or appropriate to morally acceptable decision making (in contexts where helping is called for) antedates similar ideas among care ethicists. (I don't believe Hume ever made precisely this point.) But in the present paper I focus more on moral *reasoning* than Williams or care ethicists (much less Hume) do and also embed the rejection of models emphasizing such reasoning in a larger and more systematic account of moral education than one finds in care ethics or in other, sentimentalist sources. (Of course, care ethics itself is or can be more systematic than Williams ever was about the general demands of morality—ECE represents an attempt to be more systematic in this way than Williams or various care ethicists have been.)

It does allow for and require reasoning about means to ends and other matters, as we shall see in a second, but in its core it doesn't require reasoning, even though it does depend on cognition, knowledge, thinking, believing. When my empathic juices flow on seeing, say, an old man lying in a gutter on a street and needing help, my concern is aroused and I quickly decide to help; but I am thinking too, for example, about *how* to help—should I call 911 or ask the people around me to help or can I lift him out of the gutter on my own? And I make use of knowledge of my own strength to decide: e.g., I decide that I don't need to call 911 or ask others to help because I am strong enough to help the old man on my own. But this isn't moral reasoning, it is practical, means-end reasoning, and one's decision about *how* to help depends on it. However, the (original) *decision to help* is the basic *moral* decision, and it doesn't occur via or as a result of moral reasoning.

But if the process isn't one of reasoning, what is it? Well, I see the man in the gutter, see that he desperately needs help, feel empathy with his plight, with him, and out of concern for him decide (or form an intention) to help him. None of this is reasoning, but it does involve a certain kind of moral understanding of the situation that leads to decision and action; and it is worth dwelling on the word "understanding." We don't naturally speak of a reasoning heart or even of a thinking heart, but we do naturally speak of an *understanding* heart; and since empathic caring is a matter of the heart, it is appropriate to speak of the moral decision to help (before one has decided on means) as based on one's moral understanding of the situation. Remember that moral understanding doesn't mean that one uses moral claims or principles, only that it is an understanding that gets one to make morally good or acceptable decisions and that is part of being a moral person. Moral understanding, as I am conceiving it, isn't understanding *of* or *about* morality, but understanding that expresses how moral one is. So if care ethics is right, moral understanding, which is based largely on emotional/motivational development, can occur in the absence of moral reasoning and is centrally, crucially, important to the moral life.[12]

---

[12] Hoffman and I grant that moral principles, moral precepts, moral thinking, and moral reasoning can be useful and even sometimes necessary: most typically, perhaps, in cases where self-centered concerns tempt one to act wrongly and one needs to be explicitly reminded of where one's moral duty lies and in cases where the factors for and against a given decision are in near-balance and one's decision-making needs to slow down and take more account of itself and of the situation. But care ethics doesn't think such cases are actually the most central or important ones for the moral life, and it in any event holds that attention to moral principles, etc., is effective only if one has a commitment or allegiance to them that has accrued through the emotionally-engaged process of induction–or through other sentimental modes of learning that there is no time to discuss here, but that are considered in some detail in my forthcoming book *Moral Sentimentalism* (OUP).

Note too that I don't want to say that a Kantian couldn't be in favor of using induction to arouse and inculcate individual empathy/sensitivity; but induction won't be as central to a Kantian's view of moral education as induction is to an ethics that centers around caring. I also don't want to say that empathy is *active* in every case where we help others. We can get into habits of doing nice things for people and sometimes help them unthinkingly—as perhaps we sometimes do when we hold the door open for others. And, of course, there can be other major *motives* for helping—the belief, for example, that if one helps others, they will help you in return. Still, genuinely altruistic helping—helping based on genuine concern or caring about others—does, both in its origins and in order to continue for any length of time, require the operation of empathy.

3. Empathy and Logic

When inductive discipline occurs, the child is taught to recognize the harm she has done and to feel sorry about it. This process depends on the child's being normal enough to have the capacity for empathy and to have it aroused or engaged by her parent's calling her attention to the harm or pain she has caused. Eventually, the child hesitates to hurt others because she has become more sensitive to such pain or hurting and because she is (better) able to recognize the circumstances and actions on her own part that will most likely lead to such harm. But when I, as an adult walking on the street, see (e. g.) an older man lying down in, and struggling to get out of, the gutter, my heart will or can go out to him. I have an empathic reaction that leads me to want and decide to help.

As we have said, that decision depends on my background knowledge of my own capabilities as an adult (I know that I can pull him out of the gutter either on my own or with the help of others), and my decision about how to help the old man will also depend on background and circumstantial knowledge: e. g., knowledge that I am strong enough to help him out of the gutter on my own and without anyone's assisting me. Although, as Hoffman tells us and I mentioned earlier, empathy in adults is mediated through what the adult knows by way of facts and concepts, that doesn't mean that when, knowing what I do, I feel bad for the person in the gutter and decide to help, that decision involves a process of reasoning. I may have to reason about *how* to help, but the decision to help, I have said, comes out of the recognition of the straits of the individual (plus certain background knowledge) operating to arouse an empathic reaction in me and the consequent decision to help. There is no reasoning leading to *that basic moral decision*. So the most fundamental part or core of such moral decision-making doesn't involve reasoning; but rather moral understanding.[13]

Nor should the reader be misled by my repeated use of the term "moral" here. In all three of its instances the word *doesn't* indicate that one is thinking in explicitly moral terms. For the decision to help *needn't* involve the thought that that is the morally right thing to do or even that one *ought* in some more general sense to help.[14]

---

[13] Since that understanding and the decision that flows from it together involve the (active) use of some knowledge, we could say that they also involve (some) thinking. But it would then be important to distinguish thinking from reasoning, which doesn't, intuitively, seem to be occurring in cases like that of the old man in the gutter.

[14] I am saying, then, that when people decide to help others, they not only don't have to think in specifically moral terms (a point Williams, Noddings, and others make), but needn't base their decisions (and actions) on any thought or conclusion about what they—in some overarching practical sense that isn't specifically moral—should or have to do. Of course, this raises the issue of just when explicit moral or practical "ought" conclusions *are* relevant to our thinking and decision-making; for I certainly don't want to deny that they sometimes are. But the occasions when they are relevant and occur are, I suspect, those not-all-that-frequent occasions when moral or other decision-making has to *slow down and/or hesitate* because the factors for and against a given decision are more closely balanced than they are in the case of the old man in the gutter (as I have so far described it). Much more needs to be said about this topic, but that discussion is best left to another occasion. In any event, I should mention, finally, that the famous model of action offered by Donald Davidson in "Actions, Reasons, and Causes" (*Journal of Philosophy* LX, 1963, pp. 685–700) implicitly assumes that agents who act on desires and beliefs *don't have to draw conclusions about how they should or must act before they in fact act*.

Rather, and as I indicated earlier, the use of the term "moral" is supposed to indicate that the kind of understanding and the kind of decision-making process we are talking about help us in general to do the morally right thing and are therefore in an important part of being a morally decent or good person. (We can also say they are part of the moral life if, once again, we don't assume that the moral life has to always or even usually involve thinking explicitly about morality.)

But even when empathy is operating "normally," one wouldn't necessarily decide to help the person in the gutter or, at least, stick with that decision once it had been made. For if, at the same moment, one's life were threatened by some crazy or larcenous aggressor, the desire to protect oneself and preserve one's life would probably kick in strongly enough to make one attend to the threat rather than help the person in the gutter. That is both normal and morally acceptable, though if the threat goes away quickly and easily (because one is a master of karate), it would probably be wrong not to then help the old man out of the gutter. But the point is that until and unless the threat goes away quickly, one's empathy for the man is undercut or effectively countered by fear of death or injury and/or the desire for self-preservation. Motivations can clash in a person and one motive can overwhelm another, and this is what would typically happen to someone's empathy and their desire to help (right away), if they suddenly faced a life-threatening assault. But here, as in the case where there is no such countervailing motive, the process of decision making doesn't essentially depend on moral reasoning. One is permitted to defend oneself and not help the old man, but in a moment of self-defense thoughts about what morality permits one are likely to be quite far from one's mind.[15] What we have here is not, or not necessarily, one reasoning process being undercut by another within a larger total reasoning process; but one force or motive leading in one practical direction being overwhelmed by a force that moves one in a quite different direction.

However, within this non-rational or non-reasoning process, there are analogues to what happens when someone reasons in a complex fashion. Although it was long thought that the "logic" of ethics is some kind of modal logic (with a term like "permissible" meaning something like "morally possible"), people tend nowadays to recognize that moral reasoning has a structure that is more like what one finds in non-monotonic logics.[16] Non-monotonicity means, most importantly for our purposes here, that a conclusion that one was entitled to draw on the basis of certain premises or assumptions may be undercut *by adding further premises*. That is, after one accepts the new premises in addition to the old, one may no longer be entitled to draw a conclusion that, in the absence of those new premises, one was earlier entitled to draw.

---

[15] This is a point I make in "Morality Not a System of Imperatives" earlier in this volume. Note that my description of the case allows room for ex post facto moral reasoning arguing for the moral acceptability of defending (or having defended) oneself against attack rather than (immediately) helping the old man in the gutter. A principle like "it is morally acceptable, or permissible, not to help another person when one's life is threatened by an attacker and one needs to defend oneself" could be invoked to justify the relevant particular conclusion and the previous action itself.

[16] I believe the most important work here has been done by John Horty. See, e.g., his "Reasoning in Moral Conflicts," *Nous* 37, 2003, pp. 557–605.

Moral reasoning exemplifies this non-monotonic structure in important and familiar ways. If one has promised to return a book to someone, then one should or ought to return the book; but if one learns that returning the book will somehow do great damage to the person to whom one promised to return the book, then it would be a mistake to maintain that one should return the book; one can even, probably, conclude that one *shouldn't* return it. Now this process of revision can be seen as occurring within or to reasoning, and so moral reasoning of a highly familiar kind works in a non-monotonic way. And I don't at all want to deny that such reasoning and counter-reasoning can and often do occur. But part of the reason is that we tend to think more explicitly about morality and moral rules when deontology is at issue, which it certainly is when promising is the topic of interest. We shall see a bit later that even deontological considerations needn't issue in moral reasoning. But this kind of point is easier and clearer in regard to issues of beneficence, or helping, and that is why I have so far used such cases to illustrate the theses I have been defending here.

What I want to say now, though, is that in cases of beneficence, of helping, where empathy is aroused and moral reasoning needn't enter the picture, something analogous to the non-monotonicity of explicit moral thinking and reasoning can nonetheless occur. After all, as I said earlier, when fear for one's life or the desire for/instinct of self-preservation kicks in, it can undercut or outweigh the empathy that otherwise would lead or have led one to help the old man in the gutter and do so, if I may put it this way, just as effectively as explicitly reasoning that one shouldn't keep a promise because doing so will seriously harm the promisee can undercut or outweigh the reasoning that had previously led one to conclude that one should do what one had promised to do. (This is a bit artificial, but I think it can help illustrate the point I am trying to make.) In other words, just as certain arguments and forms of reasoning can undercut other arguments and forms of reasoning that occur within explicit moral thinking, so too can certain morally relevant forces or motives undercut others when explicit moral thinking isn't going on. We could say, then, that there is an analogue of logical non-monotonicity (regarding explicitly moral statements and forms of reasoning) within the sphere of morally-relevant (relevant because they have a tendency to lead to right action) motives and in the absence of explicit moral thought and moral reasoning. In other words, in this latter kind of case, the non-monotonicity (so to speak) is of emotional/motivational situational factors rather than of propositionally-expressible prima facie duties operating within a reasoning process.[17]

---

[17] I have avoided saying that when we reach a moral decision on the basis of our (emotional and other) understanding of a situation, we lack reasons for our decision or for what we do as a result. The notion of a reason is or can be very general and apply, for example, when it wouldn't be particularly irrational not to act on a certain reason: as I argued in *The Ethics of Care and Empathy*, a sentimentalist can hold that it isn't irrational not to care about one's children, but that someone who *does care* has (that as) a reason for doing things on their behalf. In that case, and given the empathic concern aroused, we assume, by seeing the old man in the gutter, one has a reason, an emotional/motivational reason, to help him, even if one doesn't want to say that a psychopath who didn't want to help would to that extent be irrational. Note too that a psychopath will not only lack the empathy that makes one want to help but be more likely (than a normally empathic person) not to notice the plight of the old man in the first place. On this point, see Lawrence Blum, *Friendship, Altruism, and Morality*, London: Routledge & Kegan Paul, 1980.

This seems interesting, and I have even wondered whether the idea of a non-monotonic *logic* might somehow be *extended* to cover morally relevant motivational factors that aren't expressed in statements/propositions or dependent on reasoning.[18] But I think it would be best to leave to others the issue of whether such an extension makes sense or would really be viable (or necessary). My main point here is and has been that there is enough structure in or within the motivations that lead to moral decisions in the absence of moral reasoning or explicit moral thought so that they needn't be regarded as too simple, unsubtle, or impoverished for our moral life, as we know it, to take root in. There are important areas of that life where moral reasoning is simply not as necessary or useful as those who have written in the past about moral reasoning have tended to assume.

But now I would like to explain why I think that even in the area of deontology and of justice, explicit moral reasoning is less necessary and less often useful than most people have thought. And let's begin with (social) justice. Justice is generally thought of as involving reasoning from and applying certain more or less abstract principles, rules, or laws, and those who believe that benevolence and concern to help others might operate without the use of such principles, will typically take the very opposite view of our thinking about justice and our acting justly. (After all, even a sentimentalist like Hume thought issues of justice involved artificial virtues requiring explicit moral thinking and exhortation.) However, I think even in the area of justice, the importance of reasoning and the use of abstract rules/principles of justice has been overestimated by liberals and Kantians (and by Hume).

It is often said, for example, that rationally-founded principles of justice are required to counter the possibly natural and benevolent tendency to restrict religious freedom and even persecute some religious groups for the good of, for the sake of, their souls. The liberal will hold, in other words, that it is because people have a right, founded on just and rational principles, to worship as they please that it is wrong and unjust to persecute, coerce, and torture those who one thinks are jeopardizing their souls and their prospects for the hereafter, by their apostasy, heterodoxy, or atheism/agnosticism. But, as I have argued at considerable length in my book *The Ethics of Care and Empathy*, care ethics can offer its own very different take on this issue. It can say that more empathy with the point of view of others would have prevented something like the Spanish Inquisition (when the persecutors lacked empathy because, so often, they actually hated or had antipathy and contempt toward those

---

Finally, let me just point out that if we reach moral decisions by a process other than moral reasoning, then such decisions can't really be seen as *conclusions*. But this sits well with the idea, mentioned earlier, that such decisions also needn't be embodied in or accompanied by statements like "I ought to help" or "helping is the thing for me to do."

[18] If we developed such a logic, we would probably need or want to make more of the distinction between undercutting and outweighing than I did in the text above. The danger of a child's drowning can outweigh, but doesn't undercut, a significant promise to be somewhere at a given time; but a person's releasing one from a promise (because the person no longer needs one's help) presumably undercuts (the force of) the original promise rather than outweighing it. This distinction has its analogue in the realm of motivational forces because, say, empathy with another can be outweighed by someone else's more serious difficulties, but can be undercut if it turns out that the person doesn't need help in the way one had originally supposed they would. I am indebted here to discussion with John Horty.

they persecuted). With greater empathy, there would have been no need to invoke or adhere to principles of justice in order not to end up with the persecution of certain minorities. But the empathy and empathic concern for others that are required for acting justly in such cases, and many, many others, arguably doesn't depend on, involve, or follow from moral reasoning. So in the area of justice, and assuming that a care ethics based in empathy is correct, moral reasoning is a lot less important than Kantians and liberals have thought, across a wide range of cases.

Of course, this still leaves deontology; but in the final essay in this volume I mention some reasons for thinking that the core of deontology, our greater aversion to causing harm and suffering than to (merely) allowing it, is based in the operations of empathy rather than in rationally justified rules or principles. In the light of that fuller discussion, it turns out that when we hesitate and then refuse to kill one to save five, our reactions and decision needn't be based, respectively, on (independent) moral principles and moral reasoning, but can come out of our empathic reactions and empathically-based concerns about other people (or animals) in the way that (as I have argued) decisions to help typically come about or occur. So both inside and outside deontology, moral reasoning may simply be less important than has typically been assumed.

24

Some Thoughts for the Future

When I first started thinking about philosophy, people interested in ethics did meta-ethics, and normative ethics was hardly visible as a discipline. But John Rawls changed all that, and because I was a graduate student at Harvard, I had the pleasure and useful opportunity to fall under his influence—even though I didn't actually begin to work in normative ethics till many years later.

In this short space I don't propose to offer any sort of account of what normative ethics is. I don't think I can define the notion, and I think some of the other contributors to this volume will have more considered views on that issue, views that I am confident will be expressed in some of the other essays here. However, I am fairly sure that most of the other contributors will think that normative ethics centrally involves ideas or theories about what is (morally) right or wrong. I believe they would also agree that questions about the good life and/or about what kinds of things/entities are good for their own sake are also part of normative ethics. But the kinds of answers that are currently given to questions of these kinds are enormously various. Normative ethics is a very rich and/or complex field at the moment and shows no signs of becoming less so in the future.

Also, there have been new developments over the past couple of decades, so that there is probably a greater variety of basic approaches to moral questions than there was not very long ago. This might be interpreted as indicating a lack of progress in the field, and I want to return to that question a bit later. But the greater variety I have in mind includes the recent revival of Aristotelian and other forms of virtue ethics and the development of what is called the "ethics of care" or "care ethics." I myself work or have worked in both virtue ethics and care ethics, and I would like to say something about how and why these new approaches emerged, before I turn to issues about the overall state of normative ethics and its prospects for the future.

The supposed failings of Kantian and utilitarian moral theory are often mentioned as the principal reason for favoring virtue ethics, which sees issues of right and wrong action as primarily depending on questions about the character or motivation of agents rather than on universal rules governing action or on the consequences of given (classes of) actions. And virtue ethicists have also claimed that (following Aristotle or Hume) they can offer a better picture of an individual's relations with his friends, family, or polity than anything to be found within the utilitarian or Kantian tradition. Interestingly enough, even though care ethics is most frequently not regarded as a form of virtue ethics, it makes rather similar criticisms of Kant and utilitarianism.

Now I don't think I have the space to discuss how valid those criticisms are and to consider, in particular, how Kantians and utilitarians would respond to them. (Not to mention the *advantages* they would respectively claim over virtue ethics and care ethics.) But I do want to say something about the origin and character of the ethics of care, since that is the kind of normative ethics I favor and since I think it is in fact unlikely that any of the other contributors to this volume will focus their attention on care ethics. I am also a believer in virtue ethics, but I don't think it is obvious that care ethics has to be inconsistent with virtue ethics, and in any event one of the other contributors to this volume, Rosalind Hursthouse, will undoubtedly have much to say about and in favor of virtue ethics.

Care ethics began in 1982 with the publication of Carol Gilligan's seminal work *In a Different Voice: Psychological Theory and Women's Development*. Gilligan argued that men and women tend to approach moral problems differently: men typically focus on issues of justice, rights, and autonomy and think in terms of the rational (and just) application of rules, laws, or principles to problem cases. Women more frequently (than men) deal with moral issues through the prism of their concern for others. Laws and rules are often less important for them than the connection they feel and have for other individuals as individuals.

Now the first thing that needs to be said about Gilligan's view is that it has, from the start, been very controversial. Anecdotally, or in terms of our own experience, there seems to be *something* to the distinction Gilligan made, but there is a vast literature questioning the empirical studies Gilligan and others have used to support the claim that men and women tend to think differently about moral issues. There is also an equally vast literature supporting Gilligan's original claims or at least qualified versions of them.

At the time Gilligan wrote her book, Freud, Piaget, and Lawrence Kohlberg had all fairly recently been saying that male thinking about morality is typically superior to that of women. But the studies her Harvard colleague Kohlberg had done on moral development had in fact been based solely on a sample of males. (This is also true of Piaget, who exercised an enormous influence on Kohlberg.) Kohlberg's theory said there were six stages of development, and when he applied it to females, it turned out that females typically advanced less far through those stages than men tend to do. This entailed or implied that men are on average morally superior to women, but Gilligan pointed out that, given his methodology, Kohlberg could or should only make the less strong claim that women's moral development *differs* from that of men. The importance she placed on that qualification or criticism is visible, moreover, in the title she chose for her book. Just because women don't on the whole follow the same stages of moral development that men do doesn't mean that they are morally inferior: they're just *different*.

And if women (to some extent) differ morally from men, it might well be worthwhile to understand, describe, and analyze what a distinctively female morality involves. The idea of an ethics of care is mentioned only briefly by Gilligan, but others have subsequently written a great deal about how an ethics of care should be articulated, and care ethics is now one of the major approaches to normative ethics. But the whole idea of such an ethics raises some enormous questions. How much territory, for example, is care ethics supposed to cover? Gilligan spoke initially of a contrast between thinking in terms of justice and thinking in terms of caring or connection, but if men think in terms of justice (and autonomy and rights) does that mean that an ethics of care has to leave that topic (those topics) aside?

This problem has been addressed by many care ethicists, and a variety of answers has been offered. Some have held that the ethics of care should confine itself to the non-political sphere and rely on standard "male" treatments and thinking for answers to questions about justice and rights (including rights of autonomy). On this view, roughly, care ethics and traditional male ethical thinking complement one another and can somehow be harmonized or integrated—even if women tend to think more or better about certain sorts of moral issues and men more or better about others. Other care ethicists have argued that women have or can develop their own distinctive way of understanding autonomy and even justice, and these ways, it has sometimes been said, are superior to what standard "male" moral theorizing has had to say about those topics. This is the way I *myself* have gone, though with one major proviso.

There is evidence that many women think in terms of traditional justice and autonomy, even if very, very few males approach morality in terms of caring (as Gilligan described it). So I don't think the difference between care ethics and traditional or standard thinking about justice, autonomy, and rights correlates very well with gender. Rather than think of care ethics as the ethics of women or as a female ethics, therefore, I think it best simply to see it as an alternative to certain forms of traditional thinking about justice, etc., most notably to the Kantian/liberal approach to these topics that is currently so dominant. (Gilligan herself is inclined to think of things in this way.) And in my present work I have been arguing that the liberal and care-ethical views of autonomy and justice are mutually inconsistent regarding whole classes of cases. Traditional and care-ethical thinking about these topics are, therefore, not harmonizable within some larger systematic morality, and if we are looking for a satisfying overall morality, we have to choose *between* liberalism, and the way it understands justice, rights, and autonomy, and what care ethics has to say about the whole range of moral topics. Let me explain why.

In what Joel Feinberg has usefully called "Skokie-type cases," liberalism argues that neo-Nazis' or others' rights of free expression trump the mental anguish and quite possibly even trauma that such speech would likely cause, say, in Holocaust survivors living near to where the neo-Nazis are proposing to demonstrate. Most feminists sharply disagree with this, and I think anyone holding an ethics of care would want to interpret autonomy in such a way that, in Skokie-type and other cases, it doesn't entail the broader or strong notion of our (rights of) autonomy that liberals subscribe to. Liberalism, in other words, defends the right to give expression to hate speech in Skokie-type cases, but an ethics of care would say that the fact that such hate speech is likely to cause anguish and trauma morally trumps the considerations that favor allowing such speech. We really do, therefore, have to choose between what liberalism tells us and what care ethics tells us, and the task, then, for the care ethicist, but also for the liberal, is to give some good or objective reason or argument for preferring their particular view of Skokie-type cases. If either side can do this, that will favor it as an comprehensive approach over the other, and I feel, therefore, that the issue of hate speech is both crucial to the prospects of care ethics and central to current normative ethical theory in a way that is not generally recognized.

The importance of these issues connects with the importance of Gilligan's findings and of the whole idea/challenge of an ethics of care, but, interestingly and (I would say) depressingly enough, contemporary liberals and Kantians (and, for that matter, utilitarians and Aristotelian virtue ethicists) don't take this whole nexus of thought and theory very seriously. Going by what you read in work done in those traditions, it is practically as if Gilligan had never written. Within "mainstream" normative ethics that contribution is very largely, and, I would say, very unfairly neglected in favor of business as usual.

I am not sure I know why this should be the case. Kuhn points out that adherents of an old paradigm invariably reject any new paradigm when it comes into view, even if the old paradigm is in crisis, is faced with troubling problems it has no idea how to solve or even deal with. And the current scene in normative ethics seems in any event different from what Kuhn describes as happening in science for a number of related reasons. Ethics isn't science, for one thing, and for another it is hardly clear that the ethics of care is going to eventually drive Kantian liberalism from the debating chamber. Because of the stress philosophy itself places on reason and rationality, rationalistic views have a certain natural appeal within the field of normative ethics, and Kantian liberalism is rationalism par excellence, while care ethics is deliberately and explicitly opposed to rationalism and sees itself as part of (and fulfilling?) the sentimentalist tradition of Hume and Hutcheson. I don't see the ethics of care taking over the field of normative ethics—but, then again, I don't see any one approach taking over the field. This is philosophy and philosophy doesn't develop, or progress, in the way science does, though there is no time to say anything more about this here.

In further disanalogy with what Kuhn says about periods of scientific revolution, the Kantian liberalism that currently predominates in normative ethics doesn't seem to be facing a crisis—though that appearance may be deceiving. What we are seeing now, within ethical rationalism, is an intensification, a heating up, if you will, of its commitment to a rationalistic understanding of ethical phenomena. When Thomas Nagel, in *The Possibility of Altruism*, first suggested that reason, rather than desire, can often motivate what we do, his arguments were intuitively forceful and constituted a real challenge to the widely accepted Humean desire-focused view of the explanation of action. But nowadays the rationalism has become much more extreme, and we have T. M. Scanlon, for example, arguing that the most basic ordinary human actions involve our being responsive to what appear to us to be reasons to do one thing rather than another. What is ordinarily thought of as (just) desire has become hyper-intellectualized into something entirely within the rational sphere. Scanlon acknowledges a major debt to Nagel, but what he and other rationalists working on issues of moral psychology have done is to remove the account of human action and motivation from anything related to empirical or scientific psychology and to treat the basic elements of action as entirely understandable in terms of distinctions of reason or rationality.

One also sees this tendency in rationalist accounts of feeling or emotion. Kant thought we should act from reason rather than from emotions or feelings like compassion or love, and these latter were not themselves seen as purely or even partly rational—which was a major part of Kant's rationalistic objection to their influence upon action. But I recently heard a paper by David Velleman in which he argued that far from being separate and distinct from the rational side of our natures, love is best understood (roughly) as the expression and embodiment of the value we place on the moral worth and dignity of other individuals as rational beings. This is another good example of the recent tendency, on the part of mainstream ethical rationalists, to see every element of human psychology in constitutively rational terms, and that is why I say rationalism is becoming more extreme.

Is this a crisis? Well, the rationalist obviously doesn't think so. From the rationalist side, the appearance, I'll bet, is that rationalism is going from strength to strength as it shows its ability to understand or account for more and more areas of the mind. But this period of intensifying rationalism also corresponds to a period in which rationalism has been increasingly challenged and criticized for overintellectualizing, overrationalizing human life and activity. The most philosophically famous example of such criticism is Bernard Williams's "one thought too many" objection to Kant's advocacy of universal conscientiousness. But Gilligan and the ethics of care clearly represent another—and rather more systematic—challenge to rationalism, and is it possible that the recent extremism of rationalism represents a frenetic reaction to the challenges and criticisms? Is it possible that the rationalists under fire prefer to increase speed rather than change course or turn back? If this were so, the reaction would be understandable. It's the kind of thing human beings often do—for example, in the sphere of international politics. But that doesn't mean that, either in normative ethics or in politics, it is a good idea to react in this way.

Right now the rationalists are largely ignoring (or desultorily swatting at) those, like care ethicists, who largely question their tradition. But the fault seems hardly to be all on the one side. Ethicists of care have ignored some of the most important questions of normative ethics: for example, the problem of how to justify deontological restrictions on the pursuit of good results and moral problems concerning legislation and constitutional design. And these are questions that rationalist Kantians and liberals work hard on and have interesting ideas about. So what we seem to have now, in fact, is two traditions ignoring each other or each other's issues. Since these two traditions correspond (very roughly, since many prominent Kantians and liberals are women) to the distinction Gilligan made between male and female approaches to moral issues, one might say that these recent historical developments are further evidence for the truth of what Gilligan was saying. But to that extent they may also justify a certain pessimism about the kind of progress that can or cannot be made in normative ethics. They certainly can make one wonder whether there is such and thing as a universally valid human morality or at least whether we are capable of knowing what it is. But in any event these are questions that ought to bother both liberal Kantian rationalists and care ethicists, and the former, at least, don't seem to *be* bothered.

This can, as I said, make one feel somewhat pessimistic. But the facts on the ground can also be seen as a call to action. Those, like myself, who think what Gilligan has said is important may want and try to see whether an ethics of care can deal with some of the issues that till now, or recently, have been the exclusive purview of Kantian liberals and utilitarians. (Aristotelian virtue ethicists have also tended to ignore the theoretical problems I have mentioned.) And by way of drawing this essay to a close, let me focus briefly on how I think the ethics of care might attempt to deal with the central normative issue of deontology.

Deontology is, roughly, the view that there is something wrong with certain kinds of actions—killing the innocent, theft, deceit—even apart from their (usual) bad consequences, and most normative ethical theories accept and/or seek to vindicate deontology because of the deep-seated intuitions most of us have that deontology has to be true. Rationalists either claim that deontology is intuitively valid and needs no (further) vindication or give elaborate philosophical arguments in defense of our deontological intuitions about particular cases. No appeal is (usually—Rawls is a notable exception) made to psychology or other sciences either in regard to this problem or in regard to other ethical issues.

But born out of the field of educational psychology as it is, the ethics of care has tended to see psychology as relevant to its claims. However, care ethicists have not yet seen the potential relevance of psychology to the question of deontology, and let me just say a bit here about how that might turn out to be possible. Care ethicists have said a great deal about the importance of caring, but less about how caring develops. But psychologists have done a great many studies of moral development in recent decades, and one thing that emerges from that literature is that genuine altruism—which is another name for caring—seems to depend and thrive on the development of empathy (roughly, feeling what some other person or, possibly, group feels). Psychologists have traced the course of empathic development within children and adolescents (idealistic empathic identification with disadvantaged or oppressed groups emerges during the teenage years), and the majority view, resulting from many empirical studies and much discussion, seems to be that empathy is a major force behind our concern for, or caring about, others.

The psychologists also note our tendency to feel more empathy and concern for our intimates than for total strangers and for those whose distress or pain we witness rather than for people we merely know *about*. These distinctions in fact correspond to moral distinctions we intuitively want to make. We think our obligations to intimates are greater than to strangers, and likewise (*pace* Peter Singer) someone who fails to respond to the pain or danger of a child drowning right in front of him or her seems to be acting worse than someone who fails to give money to Oxfam that would save some child in a distant part of the world. If the deontological distinction between killing and letting die, or, more generally, the distinction between doing and allowing is one that empathy is sensitive to, that might at least suggest a way in which an ethics of care could defend our deontological intuitions. And I think empathy is sensitive to that distinction in something like the way it is sensitive to what it perceives rather merely knows about. Our empathy tends to be more aroused and we tend to care more about a pain or suffering that we see, as opposed to pain or suffering we merely know about (great literature and vivid descriptions can blur this distinction). But we similarly react more strongly to pain or suffering we know we might inflict or cause than to suffering we might merely allow to happen. We *flinch* from the possibility of killing someone much more than from allowing someone to die, and this emotional reaction seems a form of (heightened) empathy. So perhaps that is why we morally care more about not killing than about not letting die and similarly for others of our deontological intuitions and commitments. This doesn't yet amount to an argument that explicitly justifies deontology, but it makes a strong gesture in that direction, and my recent *The Ethics of Care and Empathy* seeks to make the justification or argument stick.

For the moment, though, this example shows how care ethics might seek to answer some difficult normative ethical questions making use of the kind of empirical studies and claims that rationalism by and large avoids. This isn't *necessarily* an advantage for care ethics, since much of our ethical thought seems to be a priori valid (the analogy between ethics and mathematics goes back at least as far as Plato). But a priori vindications of deontology have, historically speaking, been notoriously unsuccessful. So both rationalist liberal Kantianism and sentimentalist care ethics have work to do. However, the normative ethical climate or situation might be somewhat better or healthier, if both sides paid more attention to one another.

Michael Slote,
University of Miami

Readings

Carol Gilligan, *In a Different Voice*, Harvard, 1982.
Rosalind Hursthouse, *On Virtue Ethics*, Oxford, 1999.
Thomas Nagel, *The Possibility of Altruism*, Oxford, 1970.
John Rawls, *A Theory of Justice*, Harvard, 1971.
Michael Slote, *The Ethics of Care and Empathy*, Routledge, 2007.
T. M. Scanlon, *What We Owe to Each Other*, Harvard, 1998.
David Velleman, "Love as a Moral Emotion," *Ethics* 109, 1999, pp. 338–74.
Bernard Williams, "Persons, Character and Morality" in his *Moral Luck*, Cambridge, 1981.

INDEX

Abelard, 257
Action-guidingness, 7, 138–49
Adams, R. M., 147 n., 167, 168 n., 170 n., 181 n.
Alston, W., 15, 20, 21 n., 27
Annis, D., 96 n.
Aristotle, 6, 7, 125 n., 131–33, 174–175, 187, 204, 218–20, 256–257, 304 n., 307, 317–318, 320, 322
Armstrong, D. M., 215 n.
Austin, J. L., 288
Ayer, A. J., 140 n.

Baier, A., 272
Baier, K., 140 n.
Batson, C. D., 288 n.
Bell, D., 284
Bennett, J., 89–90
Bentham, J., 8, 158–159, 167–79, 180–181, 225, 234
Berofsky, B., 83 n.
Blum. L., 314 n.
BonJour, L., 236
Brison, S., 273 n.
Butler, Bishop J., 192

Campbell, C. A., 112 n.
Care Ethics (Ethics of Care), 11–12, 260–70, 271–86, 303–16, 317–23
Cavell, S., 60 n.
Chellas, B., 130 n.
Cherniak, C., 235 n.
Chisholm, R., 115 n.
Cluster concepts/terms, 3, 16–17, 20–22, 27–28
Coburn, R., 75 n.
Commonsense morality/ethics, 9–10, 58, 67, 140, 156–57, 160, 165, 174–78, 181, 185–93
Conee, E., 235 n.
Curren, R., 306 n.
Cyert, R., 196 n.

Damasio, A., 301
Danto, A., 69 n.
Davidson, D., 55 n., 204–205, 230–31, 312 n.
Davies, M., 120 n., 129 n.
Deigh, J., 292 n.
Deontology, 12, 162, 164, 174, 205, 234, 266–67, 316, 322–23

De Waal, A., 280 n.
De Waal, F., 294 n.
Dworkin, G., 104 n.
Dworkin, R., 272–73

Earman, J., 82 n.
Edwards, P., 14 n., 27
Elster, J., 147 n.
Emotive/evaluative meaning, 4, 26, 33–36
Emotivism, 23, 29, 48
Empathy, 4, 214, 272–86, 287–302, 308–316, 322–23
Engels, F., 58, 60–66
Engster, D., 11, 271–72, 277–83
Epicureanism, 197, 207, 218, 252

Feinberg, J., 227, 319
Fenichel, O., 55 n.
Fine, K., 90
Finley, M. I., 132 n.
Firth, R., 50 n., 74 n., 236
Fitch, F., 128 n.
Foley, R., 129 n.
Foot, P., 7, 22–26, 29, 35, 69, 138–39, 142, 144–45, 189 n., 224
Frankfurt, H., 6, 103–118
Freud, S., 5, 55 n., 58, 60, 62–68, 70–74, 318
Fried, C., 194
Friedman, M., 270, 272 n.
Frink, H. W., 64 n.

Gallois, A., 119 n., 126 n.
Geach, P., 23 n.
Gewirth, A., 271, 283
Gilligan, C., 260–61, 273, 284, 291, 306–307, 318–23
Ginet, C., 115–30
Goldman, A., 241 n.,
Goodman, N., 6, 64 n., 76, 81, 83–84
Gourevitch, P., 281 n.
Green, T. H., 133 n.
Greenspan, P., 112 n., 233 n.
Grice, H. P., 4, 33–34, 96 n.

Habermas, J., 62 n.
Hacker, F., 60 n., 62 n.
Hambourger, R., 125 n.
Hampshire, S., 139–40, 148
Hardie, W. F. R., 114 n.

Harding, S., 287 n.
Hare, R. M., 23–25, 33, 36, 144, 183 n.
Harman, G., 99 n.
Harrison, R., 181 n.
Hegel, G. W. F., 61, 62 n. 258
Held, V., 11, 262–63, 271–74, 280
Hempel, C. G., 193, 240 n.
Herman, B., 305 n.
Hoffman, M., 273, 275, 288–89, 292, 309–312
Horty, J., 313 n.
Hospers, J., 20
Hughes, G. E., 117 n.
Hume, D., 150, 257–58, 288, 308–310, 315, 318, 320
Hursthouse, R., 323
Hutcheson, F., 7, 257, 263, 320
Hyperrationalism, 12

Jaggar, A., 287 n.
James, W., 21 n.

Kant, I. (Kantianism), 5, 9, 12, 59, 73–74, 138–40, 144, 149, 151, 176–77, 186 n., 192, 237, 239–40, 248, 251, 257, 261, 269, 271–74, 283, 289, 297 n., 299 n., 303–11, 315–23
Kaplan, A., 72 n.
Kittay, E., 280 n.
Kohlberg, L., 305–10, 318
Kornblith, H., 236 n., 241 n.
Korsgaard, C., 304 n.
Kripke, S., 5, 55, 120
Kroon, F., 235 n.
Kuhn, T., 301 n., 320

Lamb, J., 5, 115–30
Lecky, W. E. H., 67 n.
Lemmon, E. J., 59 n.
Levine, M., 64 n.
Lewis, C. I., 171 n.
Lewis, D., 76–77, 80 n., 82 n., 83 n., 86 n., 89–90, 92
Locke, D., 111 n., 113 n.
Locke, J., 27, 62, 90
Lulofs, R., 300 n.

Malcolm, N., 150, 153
Marcus, R., 157 n., 159, 224–25

Marcuse, H., 62 n.
Marx, K., 5, 58, 60–68, 70–74
McDowell, J., 131–36, 203 n.
Mill, J. S., 8, 52, 180, 261
Mondadori, R., 91
Money-Kyrle, R. E., 72
Moore, G. E., 140 n., 205
Moral dilemmas/cost, 8, 10, 156–66, 222–27, 235
Murdoch, I., 131–36

Nagel, T., 57 n., 236 n., 238, 273, 276, 320–21
Narveson, J., 138 n.
Neurath, O., 251–52
Neely, W., 6, 103–114
Nietzsche, F., 5, 10–11, 58, 60, 67–74, 105 n., 217, 255–59
Noddings, N., 7, 11, 260–63, 268–69, 273–74, 307–308, 312 n., 323
Nozick, R., 174 n.

Paradigm case argument, 22
Parfit, D., 164, 217 n., 234 n.
Pascal, B., 111 n.
Pears, D., 188, 230
Peirce, C. S., 251–52
Pettit, P., 164, 217 n., 234 n.
Piaget, J., 12, 305, 308–309, 318
Pitcher, G., 20 n.
Plantinga, A., 7, 150–55, 250 n.
Plato, 67, 69, 131, 187, 257, 323
Pollock, J., 82 n., 228 n., 232 n.
Pragmatism, 8
Prichard, H. A., 69 n., 252 n.
Principle of Sufficient Reason, 7, 152
Putnam, H., 240 n.

Rawls, J., 5, 9, 74, 137, 164, 184, 194, 209, 267, 272, 278, 308, 317, 322–23
Rescher, N., 298 n.
Roazen, P., 62 n.
Ross, J., 7, 152 n.
Ross, W. D., 223, 261, 303–304
Ruddick, S., 274
Ryan, C., 133 n.

Sabine, G. H., 62 n.
Saint Anselm, 150–51

Saint Augustine, 257
Saint Thomas Aquinas, 150, 152
Sandbach, F. H., 110 n.
Sartre, J.-P., 157 n.
Satisficing, 9, 158, 195–221, 227
Scanlon, T. M., 273, 320, 323
Scheffler, S., 160 n., 184 n., 192, 205 n., 236 n.
Schopenhauer, A., 257
Scriven, M., 41 n.
Segerberg, K., 130 n.
Sen, A., 168 n., 194–95, 202 n., 205 n., 217 n.
Shoemaker, S., 153
Shogun, D., 269 n.
Sidgwick, H., 8, 146 n., 168, 172 n., 179–80, 194, 209, 246 n., 257
Simmons, A. J., 120 n.
Simon, H., 9, 196, 198, 207
Singer, P., 322
Smart, J., 146 n., 183, 186, 254
Smiley, T., 121
Smith, A., 238 n.
Snyder, D. P., 130 n.
Sorabji, R., 125 n.
Sosa, E., 215 n., 249 n.
Spinoza, B., 67, 103–104, 107, 109–110, 246–53, 257
Stalnaker, 76–77, 90, 92
Steans, J., 280 n.
Stephen, L., 257
Stevenson, C., 13–14, 27, 140 n.
Stocker, M., 144–47, 264, 294–96
Stoicism, 109–111, 213, 218, 252, 259

Taylor, R., 115 n.

Unger, P., 6, 95, 101
Urmson, J. O., 98 n.
Utilitarianism, 7–10, 137, 146–47, 156–66, 167–79, 180–93, 194, 206, 233–46, 252–53, 262, 278, 318, 320, 322

Value Judgments, 2, 22, 23–38, 39–52, 138–49
Van Fraassen, B., 123 n., 157 n. 163 n.
Van Inwagen, 6, 115–30
Velleman, J. D., 321, 323

Virtue, 6–9, 131–37, 180–93, 194–221, 247
Virtue Ethics, 9–11, 237, 246–54, 255–59, 269, 274, 317, 320, 322

Wallace, J., 216n.
Watson, G., 6, 103–114
Wiggins, D., 6, 115–30

Williams, B., 5, 122n., 144n., 147n. 157n. 162–63, 187, 223n. 229, 263, 310n., 312n. 321, 323
Wisdom, J., 14n., 20n. 25, 27, 31, 215n.
Wittgenstein, L., 3, 20, 153–54

Zubek, J., 300n.